The Affirmative Action Hoax

New
Century
Books

The Affirmative Action Hoax:

Diversity, the Importance of Character, and Other Lies

Second Edition

ⳓ ℬ

Steven Farron

New Century Foundation

Other titles from New Century Books

Jared Taylor, Ed., *The Real American Dilemma: Race, Immigration, and the Future of America*, 1998

George McDaniel, Ed., *A Race Against Time: Racial Heresies for the 21st Century*, 2003

Jared Taylor, *Paved With Good Intentions: The Failure of Race Relations in Contemporary America*, 2004

Michael Levin, *Why Race Matters: Race Differences and What They Mean*, 2005

Carleton Putnam, *Race and Reason: A Yankee View*, 2006

Samuel T. Francis, *Essential Writings on Race*, 2007

Published monthly by New Century Foundation:
American Renaissance (www.amren.com)

Library of Congress Cataloging-in-Publication Data

Farron, Steven.
   The affirmative action hoax : diversity, the importance of character, and other lies / Steven Farron. — 2nd ed.
      p. cm.
   Includes bibliographical references.
   ISBN 978-0-9656383-8-8 (alk. paper)
1. Affirmative action programs in education—United States. 2. Discrimination in education—United States. 3. Discrimination in employment--United States. 4. Reverse discrimination—United States. I. Title.
   LC213.52.F37 2010
   379.2'60973—dc22   2010018809

To my darling wife Esther

Contents

Appendices

CR ဢ

The Author

Steven Farron received BA and PhD degrees from Columbia University. Until 2001, he was a professor of Classics at the University of the Witwatersrand in Johannesburg, South Africa. His specialty was ancient Greek and Latin epic poetry, on which he published over 20 articles and a book.

He resigned his academic position in order to devote his time to the study of the catastrophic results of trying to solve the perceived problem of the unequal success of ethnic, racial, and social groups: American affirmative action, the Holocaust, Armenian genocide, slaughter of the *kulaks* in the Soviet Union, and persecution of Chinese in Southeast Asia and of Indians in East Africa.

Acknowledgements

For years, Helen Savva, the reference librarian at the United States Government Public Affairs Office in Pretoria, South Africa, and Suzette Jansen van Rensberg of the University of the Witwatersrand Interlibrary Loans Office fulfilled my requests for articles and books with alacrity and efficiency.

It is also a pleasure for me to express my gratitude to my friend Robert Terdiman, who sent me many of the articles from the *New York Times* from which I quote; to my friend Eugene Valberg and my ex-students Ayal Rosenberg and John Wiblin, who offered helpful comments on some of the content of this book; and to Louis Andrews, who offered valuable observations and encouragement.

Last, but certainly not least, I thank my wife Esther for her enthusiasm, encouragement, and, more practically, proofreading.

Preface to the Second Edition

The re-issue of this book by the New Century Foundation offered me a chance to correct mistakes in the original edition, to reorganize it; and, most importantly, to add relevant information that became available after its original publication in 2005. These additions have made this second edition one-seventh longer than the first edition. I will advise readers who have the first edition that large-scale changes begin in Section C of Chapter 2.

I will post further additions and corrections on my website www. affirmativeactionhoax.com, which I will update every six months. That website also contains relevant documents that I have prepared, which can be downloaded.

Introduction

Affirmative action is the standard euphemism for that type of discrimination meant to solve the perceived problem of the unequal success of ethnic and/or racial groups. In some instances—for example, against Chinese in Southeast Asia, Indians in East Africa, and Jews in Germany between 1933 and 1939—its extent and purpose have been clearly stated. But in the United States, whose ethos is individualistic and democratic and where the victims are the majority, its extent has been hidden and its purpose justified by liberal-seeming excuses. That is why attacks on affirmative action, including this one, concentrate on exposing its extraordinary magnitude and the fraudulence of its justifications.

This book also resembles most other criticisms of affirmative action in that it concentrates mainly, although not completely, on universities. Universities have been at the center of the American affirmative-action debate for two reasons: First, academic ability and achievement can be clearly defined, measured, and, consequently, compared. Second, discrimination at universities is more disturbing than elsewhere, since American universities pride themselves on being bastions of liberalism.

However, this book differs from most criticisms of affirmative action in six ways.

First, it names the premise that is the basis of the vicious anti-white discrimination that has pervaded American society since the 1960s.

Second, it demonstrates that the non-academic admissions criteria— diversity, importance of character, etc.—that American universities use to defend anti-white affirmative action never had any purpose except to justify discrimination. No American university ever considered using any non-academic admissions criteria until the need arose to justify discrimination in favor of upper-class, private-school-educated Anglo-Saxons because they could not compete academically with the children of poor, non-English-speaking Jewish immigrants.

Third, it demonstrates that if racial discrimination cannot be eliminated, then by far the most efficient and fairest way to practice it is by explicit quotas.

Fourth, it avoids the gentlemanly self-restraint that inhibits most critics of affirmative action from labeling its defenses as the shameless frauds and deliberate lies that they are.

Fifth, it discusses not only affirmative action in university admissions but also the much more important but much less publicized practice of affirmative grading and graduation.

Sixth, it focuses attention on the damage that affirmative action does to its real victims—whites—instead of claiming that it harms its black and Hispanic recipients or that Asians suffer worse discrimination than whites. It shows that, on the contrary, the black and Hispanic recipients of affirmative action obtain an undiluted advantage and that Asians also benefit from affirmative action.

CR ЄꙨ

Chapter 1
The Beginning of Affirmative Action: Kennedy and King's Moral Crusade

Most opponents of anti-white discrimination think that it is a blatant distortion of the non-racialism that was espoused by the two icons of twentieth century American liberalism, President John Kennedy and the Reverend Martin Luther King. As proof, they quote three statements that Kennedy and King made in the early 1960s. One is Section 301 of President Kennedy's Executive Order Number 10,925 of March 8, 1961, which contained the first application by the federal government of the term *affirmative action* to race relations: "[A]ll government contracting agencies . . . will take affirmative action to ensure that applicants are employed, and that employees are treated during employment, without regard to their race, creed, color, or national origin."[1] The second is from Kennedy's civil

---

1. The first governmental use of *affirmative action* was in the National Labor Relations Act (NLRA) of 1935, which instructed the National Labor Relations Board to redress an unfair labor practice by ordering the offending party "to cease and desist from such [an] unfair labor practice, and to take such affirmative action, including reinstatement of employees with or without back pay, as will effectuate the policies of this Act." New York State's pioneering Fair Employment Practices Act of 1945 incorporated terminology from the NLRA, including (Section 297. 2, c) the obligation of the commission enforcing it to order an offender to "cease and desist from such unlawful discriminatory practice and to take such affirmative action, including . . . hiring, reinstatement, or upgrading of employees . . . as will effectuate the purposes of this article" (Graham 1990: 33-4, 487, note 27).

Affirmative action then entered civil rights discourse, sometimes with the meaning of rectifying statistical inequality. For example, in an article in the Fall 1954 issue of the *Cornell Law Quarterly* (pages 40-59), in which Elmer Carter described and praised the work of the commission that enforced New York's Fair Employment Practices Act, he stated (page 47), "[I]t may not be possible to satisfy all the purely legal requisites of proof

rights speech of June 11, 1963, "[R]ace has no place in American life or law." The third is from Martin Luther King's "I Have a Dream" speech of August 28, 1963: "I have a dream that my four little children will one day live in a nation where they will not be judged by the color of their skin, but by the content of their character."

Most opponents of affirmative action quote these statements in order to show that shortly after they were made, the racial views of American liberals mutated into the opposite of the non-racialism that Kennedy and King championed. However, they should look more carefully at Kennedy's speech of June 11, 1963:

> [I]t ought to be possible for American citizens of any color to register to vote. . . . The Negro baby born in America today . . . has about one-half as much chance of completing high school as a White baby born in the same place on the same day, one-third as much chance of completing college; one-third as much chance of becoming a professional man . . . one-seventh as much chance of earning $10,000 a year. . . . The heart of the question is whether all Americans are to be afforded equal rights and equal opportunities. . . . We face, therefore, a moral crisis. . . . [R]ace has no place in American life or law . . . [The federal government] has upheld that proposition in the conduct of its affairs, including the employment of federal personnel.

Kennedy thought that Negroes had as much a right to occupational and economic equality as to the vote, because occupational and economic inequality meant that Negroes were being denied "equal rights and equal opportunities," which was "a moral crisis." Based on the unexpressed premise that all races are equal in innate ability, he assumed that race would have no place in American life only when occupational and economic equality would be attained, because statistical inequality must mean racial discrimination.

In this speech, Kennedy boasted that the federal government had upheld the principle that "race has no place in American life or law" in "the employment of federal personnel." In his hagiographic biography of Kennedy,

---

of discrimination . . . although certain indicia [*sic*] may strongly suggest a discriminatory hiring policy: there may be a history of employment marked by an absence of members of complainant's ethnic, national or religious group." Carter provided (pages 50-51) the following example of what he called "affirmative action": in a banking and travel agency, "out of a total of upwards of 1,000 clerks there was not a single Negro . . . . The investigating commissioner informed . . . the agency that there appeared to be resistance to the employment of Negro girls even though the finding of no probable cause had been made."

which was published in May 1965, Arthur Schlesinger Jr., who was a close personal adviser to Kennedy, described (1965: 932-3) the zeal with which Kennedy pursued that ideal (italics added):

> He issued a strong executive order *against discrimination in federal employment* and [not "but"] made a special effort to seek Negroes for high federal jobs. . . . Requesting reports from all departments and agencies on Negro employment, especially at the higher grades, he was appalled at the result . . . [H]is Special Assistant for civil rights . . . impress[ed] on all parts of the federal government their duty to use their full powers in the cause of *equal opportunity*. The joke in Washington was that every department was sending posses out to recruit Negroes in order to avert the wrath of the White House. The number of Negroes holding jobs in the middle grades of the civil service increased 36.6 percent from June 1961 to June 1963; in the top grades, 88.2 percent.[2]

Indeed, Schlesinger observed (1965: 165) that Kennedy's fervor for this concept of non-discrimination was manifest in his first act as president. During the inaugural parade, "Noting that there were no Negroes in the Coast Guard contingent, he [Kennedy] demanded an immediate explanation and was shocked to discover that the Coast Guard Academy had no Negro students, a condition he ordered changed forthwith." Kennedy did not demand to know if the Coast Guard Academy was discriminating against Negro applicants, which was extremely improbable. He assumed that lack of Negroes was itself discrimination.

In another hagiographic biography of Kennedy by a close adviser that was published in 1965, Theodore Sorensen (1965: 473-4) also narrated Kennedy's demand that the Coast Guard Academy institute "special recruiting efforts" after he noticed "no dark faces in the honor guard of the Coast Guard" at his inauguration. Sorensen (1965: 473-4, 495-6) described this incident as the beginning of the "Presidential journey" that culminated in his speech of June 1963. "[T]he moving force of that address was the unequivocal commitment . . . 'to the proposition that race has no place in American life'." Kennedy's unequivocal commitment to the proposition that race has no place in American life began with his order that the Coast Guard Academy institute special recruiting of Negroes.

---

2. The number of black government employees in 1961 had already been increased by preferential hiring and promotion, since the Truman and Eisenhower administrations also regarded statistical underrepresentation as proof of discrimination (Skrentny 1996: 113-17; Blumrosen 1971: 271-2; Belz 1991: 15).

Consequently, the Kennedy administration enforced Executive Order Number 10,925 of March 8, 1961 ("[A]ll government contracting agencies . . . will take affirmative action to ensure that applicants are employed, and that employees are treated during employment, without regard to their race, creed, color, or national origin") with "a massive statistical analysis of racial hiring patterns of . . . companies . . . [in order] for Negroes to enjoy a respectable proportion of the nation's better jobs" (Skrentny 1996: 117-18; cf. Belz 1991: 18-19).

It is true that American governments have always tried to make their personnel reflect to some extent the ethnic, religious, and geographical distribution of their constituents. Schlesinger records (1965: 148) that in making upper level appointments, the Kennedy administration "was striving to make sure that all groups and regions were represented . . . . They cast their net especially for . . . westerners. After a time, to be a Harvard graduate, a member of the Cambridge academic complex or an Irish Catholic was almost a handicap, surmountable only by offsetting evidence of spectacular excellence."

However, there is a crucial difference between this traditional demographic hiring and the Kennedy administration's desperation to hire and promote as many Negroes as possible; and that difference is manifested in Schlesinger's descriptions. Enlightened people have always regarded traditional demographic hiring as an unfortunate concession to the irrational human tendency to think in terms of groups; and they have tried to reduce it to a minimum, especially through the use of qualifying examinations. Therefore, Schlesinger devoted only one paragraph to it and discussed it among the difficulties that the Kennedy administration faced. But he lovingly dwelt on the Kennedy administration's crusade to hire as many Negroes as possible. (I quote only a small part of his discussion.) The reason is that Schlesinger and Kennedy regarded the frantic hiring of Negroes as a moral crusade against racial discrimination.

Opponents of anti-white discrimination should also look more carefully at Martin Luther King's "I Have a Dream" speech. In that speech, King also said, "[T]he Negro lives on a lonely island of poverty in the midst of a vast ocean of material prosperity" and "We can never be satisfied as long as a Negro in Mississippi cannot vote and a Negro in New York believes he has nothing for which to vote."

At the time of this speech, Negroes were 14 percent of New York City's population, paid four percent of its taxes, but received half of its expenditures, along with massive preference in civil service hiring and promotion (Jacoby 1998: 83).

In fact, less than a month before his "I Have a Dream" speech, King called for "discrimination in reverse . . . a sort of national atonement for the sins of the past."[3] Moreover, King provided a precedent, and maybe the source, for the most famous passage in President Johnson's commencement address at Howard University on June 4, 1965, which is usually regarded as marking a radical break with the non-racialism of the original civil rights movement. In that speech, Johnson announced, "the next and more profound stage of the battle for civil rights . . . not just equality as a right and a theory but equality as a fact and equality as a result" and explained, "You do not take a person who for years has been hobbled by chains and liberate him, bring him up to the starting line of a race and then say, 'you are free to compete with all the others'." A year earlier, King wrote (1964: 134),

> Whenever the issue of compensatory or preferential treatment for the Negro is raised, some of our friends recoil in horror. The Negro should be granted equality, they agree; but he should ask nothing more. . . . [But] if a man is entered at the starting line in a race three hundred years after another man, the first would have to perform some impossible feat in order to catch up with his fellow runner.

What, then, was the meaning of King's constantly quoted "dream that my four little children will one day live in a nation where they will not be judged by the color of their skin, but by the content of their character"? If all groups of people are equal in ability, then if one group is less successful than another, the inevitable conclusion is that its members are not being judged by the content of their character. Their lack of success must be the result of discrimination.

This is well illustrated in the Moynihan Report (formally, *The Negro Family: The Case for National Action*), published by the U.S. Department of Labor in March 1965. In it Daniel Moynihan, who co-authored President Johnson's Howard University commencement address, made explicit (Chapter IV) the premise that has underlain all federal racial policies since President Kennedy's inauguration: "There is absolutely no question of any genetic differential: Intelligence potential is distributed among Negro infants in the same proportion and pattern as among Icelanders or Chinese or any other group." Moynihan stated this premise without any argument or proof, but he was unusual in stating it at all. Usually it is simply assumed, even though it has controlled American racial policy for half a century, is contrary to all empirical evidence, and *a priori* is so improbable as to border on impossible. Moynihan mentioned only whites and blacks in his study and attributed the socioeconomic gap between them to "three centuries of sometimes unimaginable mistreatment" (Introduction). But from the premise

---

3. "The Right to a Job." *Newsweek* (August 5, 1963): 51-52.

of the innate equality of all groups of people, he drew the inescapable conclusion (Chapter I; italics added), "*the distribution of success and failure within one group [should] be roughly comparable to that within other groups.*"

The Moynihan Report illustrates an extremely serious and bizarre anomaly of American affirmative action. It was (and to a large extent still is) defended as redress for centuries of persecution. But from its beginning, it was applied to blacks who were recent immigrants and to ethnic groups that never suffered institutionalized discrimination in the United States.

The 1924 immigration law favored Latin Americans over Europeans by exempting them from national-origin quotas. As a result, the Hispanic population of the United States increased from approximately 125,000 (0.16 percent of the population of the United States) in 1900 to six million in 1960.[4] In New York, as soon as Puerto Ricans began arriving in large numbers, in the 1940s, they received preference in civil service hiring and promotion and special attention in education and poverty programs. Elite universities began actively recruiting Hispanics in 1961 in response to President Kennedy's plea that they recruit more "minority" students (Oren 2000: 225). (They were actively recruiting blacks by 1950 and had been giving blacks preference in admissions long before that.[5]) Also beginning in the early 1960s, federal contractors and federal agencies had to demonstrate non-discrimination by reporting the number of Hispanics as well as blacks that they employed (Graham 1990: 62; 2002: 136-7).

With the passage of the Immigration and Naturalization Act in 1965, the number of non-blacks eligible for affirmative action exploded. Between 1965 (when the American black population was less than 20 million) and 2000, 35 million immigrants entered the United States, of whom 26 million, along with their descendants, are eligible for affirmative action (Graham 2002: 129-30, 179). That does not include the descendants of the Latin Americans who were admitted preferentially over Europeans before 1965 or Puerto Ricans, who are not subject to immigration restrictions.

Hispanics, who constitute most of the non-black affirmative action recipients, increased from 6 million in 1960 to 9 million in 1970 to 15 million in

---

4. Hispanics were not a category in American censuses until 1970. Until then, Americans of Latin American origin were classified by country of origin. The figure of 6 million Hispanics in 1960 is from Lynch 1989: 149. I extrapolate 125,000 Hispanics in 1900 from the fact that 100,000 ethnic Mexicans lived in the United States then, and Mexico was the source of nearly all Latin American immigration at the time (Graham 2002: 104). All other ethnic and racial statistics in this book are from U.S. censuses.

5. Synnott 1979: 207-8; Karabel 2005: 213; Oren 2000: 197-8; Wechsler 1977: 208, note 21.

1980 to 22 million in 1990 to 35 million in 2000 to 47 million in 2008. By 1990, less than half of Americans eligible for affirmative action were black, and the black proportion keeps declining (Eastland 1996: 150). Moreover, as I will discuss in Section B of Chapter 19, most of the black recipients of affirmative action are immigrants and their descendants.

For many years, most beneficiaries of affirmative action have belonged to the only groups of people in American history who have received massive preferences from the time of their arrival.

Many recipients of affirmative action are not even American citizens. An example is the Fanjul brothers, who came to the United States from Cuba in 1959, but have not become American citizens so as to avoid paying estate taxes. They are descendants of a five-generation sugar dynasty, which was begun on the basis of slave labor. In the 1990s, when their business assets were worth $500 million, their securities underwriting company qualified as a Hispanic-owned firm for risk-free underwriting profits on hundreds of millions of dollars in government (both federal and municipal) bonds (Graham 2002: 154-5).

Hugh Graham (2002: 130) pointed out, "Virtually all parties to the congressional debates over civil rights and immigration policy in the 1980s and 1990s studiously avoided the topic of affirmative action for immigrants;" and that has remained true until the present (2010). Graham then observed, "Yet civil rights enforcement officials, when asked whether wealthy immigrants [and their descendants] from Hong Kong or Argentina [nearly all of whom are white] were eligible for American affirmative action programs, [they] acknowledged that all persons of Asian or Hispanic national origin are eligible."

Because of the constant influx of immigrants who are eligible for affirmative action and the fact, which I discuss in Chapter 5, that all offspring of marriages between "minority" and European-origin parents are eligible for affirmative action, the Census Bureau projected in 2007 that by 2011, *most of the babies born in the United States will belong to groups that are eligible for affirmative action.*

As the proportion of recipients of affirmative action who were immigrants and their descendants exploded, the justification that it was recompense for past discrimination became untenable. Indeed, the belief that American Negroes could not compete with whites because of past discrimination was itself deduced from the premise of innate ethnic/racial equality, not induced from historical facts. In the 1990s, half of the ancestors of European-origin Americans had arrived in the United States during the previous century (Bohannan and Curtin 1995: 13). Most European immigrants since 1890 have come from southern and eastern Europe, which at that time had a literacy rate that was less than half the black American literacy rate.[6]

So, another excuse for racial discrimination was needed.

It was found. Diversity is the most insidious and pernicious of all defenses of discrimination. The other justifications assume that discrimination is a necessary evil, a temporary expedient that is needed to create a society in which race and ethnicity are irrelevant. Diversity assumes that discrimination is an unqualified good and that it should be perpetual.

CB BO

---

6. In 1900, 56 percent of American blacks over 14 years old were literate. At that time the literacy rate among Sicilians was 29 percent, among Poles (i.e., the Polish area of the Russian Empire), 26 percent; among Serbo-Croatians, 25 percent; among Romanians, less than 25 percent; among Portuguese, 22 percent. Even a quarter of a century later, only 20 percent of Albanians were literate. In 1950 only 15 percent of adults in the entire world were literate (Cipolla 1969: 19, 128; Sowell 1998: 170, 181-2; Tortella 1994: 11; http://nces.ed.gov./nadlits/naal92/trends.htm: 3).

ଔ ଛ

Chapter 2
Bakke: Diversity Replaces Redress

A. *Bakke*

Diversity made its debut in one of the most important Supreme Court decisions of all time: *Regents of the University of California v. Bakke* (1978), the first case in which the Supreme Court ruled that anti-white discrimination is legal. My summary is from the record of the Court's decision, to which I refer by paragraph numbers (#).

The medical school of the University of California at Davis reserved 16 percent of its annual openings for blacks, Asians, Mexican Americans, and Native Americans. Allan Bakke, a non-Hispanic white, applied in 1973 and 1974 and was rejected in both years. His undergraduate grade-point-average (GPA) in science courses was 3.44 (on a scale of 0 to 4); his scores on the four sections of the Medical College Admission Test (MCAT) were in the 96th, 94th, 97th, and 72nd percentiles (i.e., higher than 96 percent, 94 percent, 97 percent, and 72 percent of those who took the test). The specially admitted students who entered Davis Medical School in 1974 had an average GPA in their undergraduate science courses of 2.42 and averages of 34th, 30th, 37th, and 18th percentile on the four sections of the MCAT (#277). (In that year, 32 whites who had higher GPAs and MCAT scores than Bakke's were also rejected.) During the court hearings involving Davis Medical School's admissions procedure, its defenders never presented evidence that these minority students or any others did better in medical school than their academic record predicted or that they had any non-academic strengths that compensated for their academic deficiencies. Bakke sued the University of California for violating the prohibition in the Fourteenth Amendment of the United States Constitution against states "deny[ing] to any person . . . the equal protection of the laws;" a section of the California constitution; and Title VI (Section 601) of the federal Civil Rights Act of 1964: "No person in the United States shall, on the grounds of race, color, or national origin . . . be subjected to discrimination under any program or activity receiv-

ing federal financial assistance." The California Supreme Court ruled that
Davis' minority admissions program violated the Fourteenth Amendment.
The United States Supreme Court reversed that decision, although it in-
validated the quota for minorities at Davis Medical School and ordered it
to admit Bakke.

This confusing decision occurred because four of the nine Supreme Court
justices ruled (#412-16) that all racial discrimination was illegal, and four
ruled (#325) that "government may take race into account . . . to remedy
disadvantages cast on minorities by past racial prejudice." The latter four
argued (#370-1), "Davis clearly could conclude that the serious and persistent underrepresentation of minorities in medicine . . . is the result of . . .
deliberate, purposeful discrimination against minorities in education and in
society;" and (#365-7) "there is reasonable likelihood that, but for pervasive
racial discrimination," the minority applicants would have been so much
better qualified that Bakke "would have failed to qualify for admission even
in the absence of Davis' special admissions program." They also pointed out
(#376-7) that Davis could not use "poverty or family educational background
. . . as a substitute for race" because "while race is positively correlated with
differences in GPA and MCAT, economic disadvantage is not . . . [E]co-
nomically advantaged blacks score less well than do disadvantaged whites."
(Amazingly, they did not see that this fact nullified their argument.)

Like everyone who uses the past-discrimination excuse, they piously
expressed their hope for a non-racial future (#401) "in which the color of a
person's skin will not determine the opportunities available to him or her,"
and they assumed that this non-racial future will have arrived when all groups
are equally successful. Therefore (#407), "In order to get beyond racism,
we must first take account of race. There is no other way."

Since four justices ruled that Davis' minority admission program was
illegal and four ruled that it was legal, the decision was determined by the
ninth member of the Court, Justice Lewis Powell. He ruled that Davis had to
admit Bakke because (#289-90) "The guarantees of the Fourteenth Amendment . . . of equal protection cannot mean one thing when applied to one
individual and something else when applied to a person of another color."
He also pointed out obvious weaknesses in Davis' defenses of its minority
admissions policy. For example, Davis argued that more minority doctors
were necessary for "the delivery of health-care services to communities cur-
rently underserved." Powell observed (#310-11), "[T]here are more precise
and reliable ways to identify applicants who are genuinely interested in the
medical problems of minority communities than race." Powell also easily refuted Davis' most important justification for its minority admissions
policy, that if there had not been any racial discrimination, Bakke "would

have failed to qualify for admission" "because Negro applicants . . . would have made better scores." Powell pointed out (#296, note 36):

> Not one word in the record supports this conclusion, and the authors of the opinion offer no standard for courts in applying such a presumption of causation to other racial or ethnic classifications. This failure is a grave one, since it may be concluded on this record that each of the minority groups preferred by petitioner's [Davis'] special program is entitled to the benefit of the presumption [that they would now perform better academically had it not been for past discrimination].

Here Powell put his finger on a confusion that pervades the past-discrimination argument. Immediately after the four pro-discrimination justices said (#370-1), "Davis clearly could conclude that the serious and persistent underrepresentation of *minorities* [italics added] in medicine . . . is the result of . . . deliberate, purposeful discrimination against *minorities* [italics added] in education and in society;" they justified that assertion by pointing out (#371), "From the inception of our national life, *Negroes* [italics added] have been subjected to unique legal disabilities;" and they outlined (#371-2) the educational discrimination inflicted on Negroes under slavery and after it was abolished.

Powell pointed out (#295-7) not only that there was no evidence for the presumption that Negroes would now perform better academically if they had not suffered past discrimination; but, more seriously, the pro-discrimination justices, without realizing that they were dealing with a separate issue, assumed that the same presumption applied to the other minority groups in the Davis program. Powell also observed that this confusion is heightened by the fact that "the white 'majority' itself is composed of various minority groups, most of which can lay claim to a history of prior discrimination." So, "There is no principled basis for deciding which groups would merit" preference.

Incredibly, Powell also stated (#296, note 36), "race may be . . . a factor in an admissions program . . . the portion of the judgement [of the California Supreme Court] that would proscribe all consideration of race must be reversed."

Powell ruled that there is only one justification for racial preferences (#311-12): "the attainment of a diverse student body," which creates an "atmosphere of speculation, experiment and creation—so essential to the quality of higher education." However, in pursuing diversity, "individual rights may not be disregarded." Davis' "dual admissions program . . . infringes his [Bakke's] rights under the Fourteenth Amendment" (#314). The

Constitution forbids "preferring members of any one group for no reason other than race or ethnic origin" (#307). The diversity that is constitutional is not "simple ethnic diversity, in which a specified percentage of the student body is in effect guaranteed to be members of selected ethnic groups." It must be a "diversity that . . . encompasses a far broader array of qualifications and characteristics of which racial or ethnic origin is but a single . . . element" (#315). "This kind of program treats each applicant as an individual," so it does not violate the Fourteenth Amendment (#318).

Justice Powell's description of the value of diversity and the proper way that a diverse student body should be attained came straight from an *Amici Curiae* Brief that Harvard, Princeton, Columbia, Stanford, and the University of Pennsylvania submitted in support of the Davis program. For example, Powell quoted (#317, note 51) the president of Princeton: "While race is not in and of itself a consideration . . . in some situations race can be helpful information in enabling the admission officer to understand more fully what a particular candidate has accomplished—and against what odds." But his greatest praise was for the "illuminating example" of "the Harvard College program" (#316), and he took the unusual decision to reprint (#321-24) Harvard's description of its admissions policy:

> The [Admissions] Committee . . . seeks a wide variety of interests, talents, backgrounds and career goals . . . Fifteen or twenty years ago, however, diversity meant students from California . . . and farm boys . . . . The result was that very few ethnic or racial minorities attended Harvard College. In recent years Harvard College has expanded . . . diversity to . . . disadvantaged . . . racial and ethnic groups. . . . [T]he race of an applicant may tip the balance in his favor just as geographic origin or a life spent on a farm may tip the balance in other candidates' cases . . . . the [Admissions] Committee does not set target-quotas.

Typical of Justice Powell's blind faith in the honesty of the elite universities, whose self-descriptions controlled his decision, was his ruling (#318-19): A "court would not assume that a university, professing to employ a facially nondiscriminatory admissions policy, would operate it as a cover for the functional equivalent of a quota system. In short, good faith would be presumed."

However, while Justice Powell was citing Harvard's "illuminating example," the fraudulence of its description of its minority admissions program was obvious to anyone who knew anything about it. Since the late 1960s, its medical school had committed itself to graduating (not just admitting) a rigid quota of minority students, which was larger than the proportion of the minority students that Davis Medical School was admitting. Two years before the *Bakke* decision, Professor Bernard Davis of Harvard Medical School publicized the fact that to attain that quota, it was granting medical degrees to black students who were manifestly unqualified.[7] Two days after the *Bakke* decision, the *Washington Post* reported (Peterson 1978), "The percentage of blacks entering the freshman class at Harvard and Princeton . . . has varied by only a hair during the last five years."

Equally fraudulent were Princeton's explanation: "While race is not in and of itself a consideration . . . in some situations race can be helpful information in enabling the admission officer to understand more fully what a particular candidate has accomplished—and against what odds" and Harvard's description of minorities as "disadvantaged." In fact, American universities give preference in admission to blacks in the highest ten percent of the American population in socioeconomic status over better qualified whites in the lowest ten percent.[8] Even Harvard's claim that it had started giving preference to blacks in the last fifteen or twenty years was a lie. Elite universities were actively recruiting blacks by 1950; they were giving them preference in admissions well before that (Karabel 2005: 213; Synnott 1979: 207-8; Oren 2000: 197-8; Wechsler 1977: 208, note 21).

Nevertheless, Justice Powell invented a social virtue of tremendous importance. None of the other Supreme Court justices said a word about diversity in their *Bakke* decisions. However, in a later case, Powell's diversity argument was quoted to justify racial discrimination by Justice Stevens, the author of the argument of the four *Bakke* justices that all racial discrimination was illegal, and by Justice Brennan, author of the argument of the four *Bakke* justices that past anti-black discrimination justifies present anti-white discrimination.[9]

They were reflecting a radical change in American thought. Before Justice Powell's decision, advocates of anti-white discrimination rarely mentioned diversity; and when they did, it was usually a subsidiary justification (Wood 2003: 103-12). However, the past-discrimination excuse was seriously and obviously flawed even with regard to blacks. It became increasingly absurd as the beneficiaries of racial discrimination included more and more people whose ancestors had never experienced discrimination in the United States. Diversity not only justified discrimination in favor of all less suc-

---

7. I discuss Harvard Medical School's minority quotas and Professor Davis' disclosures in Section D of Chapter 9.

8. I discuss this and similar facts in Section A of Chapter 6.

9. *Metro Broadcasting, Inc. v. Federal Communications Commission* (1990), #567-8, 602, note 71; cf. *Wygant v. Jackson Board of Education* (1986), #315.

cessful groups, it did it with the argument that anti-white discrimination has no victims, since whites benefit from the enlightening experience that diversity provides. At first, advocates of anti-white discrimination did not realize what a handy justification Justice Powell's decision gave them; but once they did, they made diversity into the ultimate social virtue (Wood 2003: 113-14, 212-14).

Indeed, as far away as India, "the nine-judge Bench in *Indra Sawhney* (1993) endorsed his [Powell's] arguments in favor of diversity as a compelling state objective" in Indian universities (Nesiah 1997: 145).

B. Diversity Reaffirmed

On June 23, 2003, in cases involving the admissions policy of the University of Michigan's undergraduate and law schools, the Supreme Court reaffirmed Justice Powell's decision. It ruled that diversity is the only legitimate excuse for academic racial discrimination and that it must be attained by the means that Justice Powell mandated. In paragraph 47 of the case involving the Law School (*Barbara Grutter v. Lee Bollinger et al.*), the majority quoted Justice Powell in *Bakke* (#315): "[A] race-conscious admissions program cannot use a quota system—it cannot 'insulate each category of applicants . . . from competition with all other applicants'." In paragraph 49, the majority stated, "We are satisfied that the Law School's admissions program, like the Harvard plan described by Justice Powell, does not operate as a quota."

The reason they were satisfied was that they accepted another crucial part of Justice Powell's decision (*Grutter* #6): "The Court endorses Justice Powell's view . . . the Law School's . . . 'good faith' is 'presumed';" (#37) "The Law School's educational judgment . . . is one to which we defer." Consequently, they simply paraphrased (#14) the Law School's official statement of its admissions policy: "The policy makes clear . . . that even the highest possible score [on the Law School Admission Test (LSAT) and undergraduate grade-point-average (UGPA)] does not guarantee admission to the Law School. Nor does a low score automatically disqualify an applicant."

However, Michigan Law School's description of its admissions policy was as fraudulent as the descriptions that the elite universities provided in the *Bakke* case. In their dissent to the Supreme Court decision, Justices Rehnquist, Scalia, Kennedy, and Thomas pointed out (*Grutter* #76-7) that in 2000 it admitted every black applicant with an UGPA of 3.00 or higher and LSAT scores between 159-160. But it admitted only 22 percent of white and Asian applicants with an UGPA between 3.25 and 3.49 and a LSAT score of

164-66 (Wood 2003: 131). Barbara Grutter, the rejected white applicant who brought the lawsuit, had put herself through college by working nights and had obtained a 3.81 UGPA and a 161 LSAT score (Krauss 2003: 30).

In his dissent, Justice Kennedy also observed (#89) that during the years from 1995 to 1998, "[t]he percentage of enrolled minorities fluctuated only . . . from 13.5 percent to 13.8 percent." In their dissent, Justices Rehnquist, Scalia, Kennedy, and Thomas pointed out (#79) that according to the statistics that the Law School submitted, in four of the six years from 1995 through 2000, the percent of black applicants that the Law School admitted differed by 0.3 percent or less from the percent of applicants who were black, and the percent of Hispanics admitted differed by 0.5 percent or less from the percent who applied. The statistics they quote also show that in five of those six years, the percent of black applicants who were admitted differed by 1.2 percent or less from the percent of all applicants who were admitted. The dissenters drew the obvious conclusion (#81): "[A]dmission [is] based on the aspirational assumption that all applicants are equally qualified academically, and therefore that the proportion of each group admitted should be the same as the proportion of that group in the applicant pool."

Two more aspects of *Grutter* are noteworthy. First, the majority quoted with approval the argument of the Law School's administration that (#19-20) it needed enough black, Hispanic, and Native American students "to ensure that a critical mass of underrepresented minority students would be reached so as to realize the educational benefits of a diverse student body. . . . '[C]ritical mass' means a number that encourages underrepresented minority students to participate in the classroom and not feel isolated . . . or like spokespersons for their race." In their dissent, Justices Rehnquist, Kennedy, Scalia, and Thomas pointed out (#74-5):

> From 1995 through 2000, the Law School admitted between 1,130 and 1,310 students. Of those between 13 and 19 were Native American, between 91 and 108 were African-Americans, and between 47 and 56 were Hispanic. If the Law School is admitting between 91 and 108 African-Americans in order to achieve "critical mass," thereby preventing African-American students from feeling "isolated or like spokespersons for their race," one would think that a number of the same order of magnitude would be necessary for Hispanics and Native Americans.

Another noteworthy aspect of Grutter was the majority's statement (#63-4):

> It would be a sad day indeed, were America to become a quota ridden society, with each identifiable minority assigned proportional

representation in every desirable walk of life. But that is not the rationale for programs of preferential treatment; the acid test of their justification will be their efficacy in eliminating the need for any racial or ethnic preferences at all. . . . It has been 25 years since Justice Powell first approved the use of race . . . . Since that time, the number of minority applicants with high grades and test scores has indeed increased. We expect that 25 years from now, the use of racial preferences will no longer be necessary to further the interest approved today.

But 25 years earlier, the *amicus curiae* brief that the American Association of Law Schools submitted in the *Bakke* case stated (#27), "the premise of these special admissions programs is that, in time, they will disappear. They are essentially a transitional device to correct a time lag."

However, as I point out in Section F of Appendix III, in the past 20 years, racial differences have increased on all measures of academic ability and achievement (SAT, SAT-II (achievement tests), ACT, school grades).[10]

On the same day that the Supreme Court decided the *Grutter* case, it also decided the challenge that was brought against the University of Michigan's undergraduate College of Literature, Science and Arts (CLSA) at Ann Arbor (*Jennifer Gratz and Patrick Hamacher v. Lee Bollinger et al.*). In that case, the majority ruled that CLSA's admissions policy was unconstitutional because it did not follow the guidelines set down by Justice Powell in the *Bakke* decision.

The majority pointed out (#59-60) that the number of points that an applicant was assigned determined admission. Among the examples it mentioned was that an outstanding essay earned a maximum of 3 points; being the child of an alumnus, 4 points; personal achievement, leadership, or public service, a maximum of 5 points; and being black, Hispanic, or Native American, 20 points. (As will be discussed in Chapter 5, in American affirmative action, the categories "black," "Hispanic," and "Native American" include everyone who has a black, Latin American, or Native American ancestor.)

The majority did not mention much more glaring comparisons with the 20 points that were automatically given to every applicant with a black, Hispanic, or Native American ancestor. Twenty points was also the difference between a 4.0 (i.e., A) high school GPA and a 3.0 (B). Because of grade inflation (which I discuss in Chapter 9. C) in 2004, 88 percent of students

10. Justice O'Connor wrote the majority decision in *Grutter*. In 2009, in a chapter of a book (Featherman, et al.) that she co-authored with Stewart J. Schwab, she stated, "That 25-year expectation is, of course, far from binding on any justices who may be responsible for entertaining a challenge to an affirmative-action program in 2028."

who took the SAT had GPAs of 3.0 and over; the average SAT scores of students with a 3.0 GPA were 480 in Verbal and 486 in Math. Even more striking was that only 12 points were awarded for a *perfect score* on the SAT or the ACT, which is the standardized test that is preferred by many colleges in the Middle West.[11]

No consideration was given to socioeconomic background. The child of a white single mother who worked as a waitress or the child of non-English-speaking Bulgarian immigrants got 12 points for a perfect SAT or ACT score; a multimillionaire got 20 points for having a black, Latin American, or Native American ancestor.

However, the majority did not object to the size of the preference that CLSA gave for having a black, Hispanic, or Native American ancestor. It ruled (#46) that CLSA's admissions policy was unconstitutional because the manner in which these preferences were bestowed did not follow the manner that Justice Powell mandated in *Bakke*: "We find that the University's policy, which automatically distributes 20 points . . . to every single 'underrepresented minority' applicant solely because of race, is not narrowly tailored to achieve the interest of educational diversity."

C. Quotas Are Best

In a dissent, Justices Ginsburg and Souter pointed out (#106-107),

One can reasonably anticipate . . . that colleges and universities will seek to maintain their minority enrollment . . . whether or not they can do so in full candor . . . . If honesty is the best policy, surely Michigan's accurately described, fully disclosed College affirmative action program is preferable to achieving similar numbers through winks, nods, and disguises.

The majority justices answered (#55, note 22) that these objections "are remarkable . . . they suggest that universities—to whose academic judgement we are told in *Grutter v. Bollinger* . . . we should defer—will pursue their affirmative-action programs whether or not they violate the United States Constitution."

On August 28, 2003, two months after the *Gratz* decision, the University of Michigan announced that its CLSA would do exactly what Justices

11. Thernstrom 1999A: 40. In this book, I use the term "standardized test" to mean a test that is graded in a uniform manner for all test-takers and is designed by professional psychometricians, who create it on the basis of their knowledge of statistics and empirical evaluations of the effectiveness of similar tests.

Ginsburg and Souter predicted it would do. It announced that "it had devised a new, essay-driven undergraduate-admission process to replace the point-based system that the U.S. Supreme Court struck down." It would require applicants to submit three essays. In one of the essays, applicants must explain either what they will contribute to Michigan's "widely diverse educational community" or "describe an experience you've had where cultural diversity—or the lack thereof—has made a difference to you." "University officials said they plan to monitor enrollments carefully to make sure that minority representation on campus does not decline" (Schmidt 2003). Clearly, in order to keep minority representation at its pre-*Gratz* level, Michigan will have to practice exactly the same degree of racial and ethnic discrimination that it practiced under the point system. As the University of Michigan's president, James Duderstadt, promised in 1996, "We will continue to do this [discriminate against non-Hispanic whites] until the Supreme Court says we can't any more. . . . [Then] we'll try to find other ways to get the same result" (Lederman 1996).

Other universities that awarded points for minority applicants have also responded to the *Gratz* ruling by replacing open discrimination with discrimination based on essays, while guaranteeing that they will maintain their current level of minority enrollment (Schmidt 2003A).

The admissions office of Michigan's CLSA had to hire 51 new staff members to enable it to comply with the Supreme Court's order that it practice racial discrimination in a circuitous manner (Ewers 2004: 11). Every one of them must know that an applicant can hire a professional essay writer to write his application essays, or he can buy application essays from a wide variety that are available on the Web.

Indeed, the fact that Michigan's CLSA used an explicit point system even though it violated the *Bakke* decision showed that it knew that a simple, honest manner of obtaining the number of minority students it wanted was so superior to a complex, surreptitious manner that it was willing to violate the law in order to use it. As the dissenting justices in the *Grutter* decision showed, Michigan's law school also based its minority admissions policies on preset quotas; although unlike the CLSA, it lied about it. Michigan is typical. After the *Bakke* decision, many universities tried to use the cumbersome means of practicing discrimination that Justice Powell mandated, but they soon returned to the simpler and more efficient means they had used before it (Thernstrom 1997: 418; Eastland 1996: 69-72).

Professor Richard Sander of UCLA Law School, in an article in the *Stanford Law Review* (Sander 2004)—in which he introduced himself (page 370) as being white and having a "son [who] is biracial, part black, part white"—demonstrated (pages 404-5) the fraudulence of University of

Michigan Law School's claim in *Grutter* that it does not use a quota system for admissions. In fact, "In every respect we can quantify, the law school's admissions process seems more violative [*sic*] of O'Connor's standards than the college's." (Justice O'Connor wrote the majority decision in *Grutter*, including (#49), "We are satisfied that the Law School's admissions program, like the Harvard plan described by Justice Powell, does not operate as a quota"; and (#6), "The Court endorses Justice Powell's view . . . the Law School's . . . 'good faith' is 'presumed'.")

Sander recalled (page 379) that when law schools began massive affirmative action in admissions, in the 1960s, "no bones were made about the application of different standards to minority applicants." In the *amicus curiae* brief that the American Association of Law Schools (AALS) submitted in the *Bakke* case, it asked the Supreme Court to allow law schools to continue to practice open, honest racial discrimination. The brief observed (Sander 2004: 380-82) that LSAT scores and undergraduate grade-point-average were accurate predictors of success in law school. Furthermore (brief #13), "We know that the test [LSAT] is not racially biased. Five separate studies have indicated that the test does not underpredict the law school performance of blacks and Mexican-Americans." The brief (# 34) also pointed out that consideration of non-academic factors would not increase the number of minorities admitted because "there is no reason to suppose that such subjective factors are distributed on other than a random basis among applicants of different races." Consequently, since the credentials of only an insignificant number of minorities were comparable to those of whites, applying the same standards to all applicants, would "exclude virtually all minorities from the legal profession." The AALS Brief ended with an argument that is hard to read now without a feeling of painful irony: some people "have suggested that in the effort to achieve racial equality 'we cannot afford complete openness and frankness . . . .' It need hardly be said in response that a constitutional principle designed to be flouted should not be imposed on schools dedicated to teaching the role of law in our society."

That is exactly what the *Bakke* ruling did. Sander pointed out (pages 383-4), "The response of law schools—and indeed, of higher education in general—was to go underground. Racially separate tracks were draped with fig leaves of various shapes and sizes to conceal actual practices, which changed hardly at all." "A survey of law school admissions officers in the late 1980s found that only 1% of the respondents felt that *Bakke* had a 'significant' impact on policies'." In fact, racial discrimination became constantly more extreme, as the proportion of blacks among law-school students increased and the proportion of Hispanics increased even faster (Sander 2004: 386).

Sander used freedom-of-information requests to obtain the admissions records of law schools. Every one (pages 408-10) practiced a similar level and the same type of racial discrimination as Michigan Law School. "Blacks and whites are admitted at almost the same rates [at which they apply]."

> I have thus far been unable to find a single law school in the United States whose admissions process operates the way Justice O'Connor describes in Grutter. . . . "[S]oft" [i.e., non-academic] factors play a role only for those relatively few cases that are on the academic score boundary between "admit" and "reject."

Thus the *Bakke* decision, which the Supreme Court reaffirmed in 2003, imposed a culture of all-pervasive lying on American universities. Sander recalled (pages 407-8):

> When Boalt [Hall, Berkeley's law school] was cited by the Justice Department in 1992 for running formal, racially segregated admissions tracks, the common view I heard expressed was not shock at Boalt's practices, but contempt for the school's stupidity in doing it so brazenly. In the mid-1990s, over a small lunch that I attended with the dean of an elite law school . . . and the school's chief admissions officer, the discussion worked around to Bakke. The dean turned to the admissions chief and casually observed that the numbers of blacks admitted in recent years had been too nearly identical from year to year. For appearances' sake, the dean went on, it would be best to vary the numbers a bit more.[12]

The issue of numerical quotas has been at the center of the debate over affirmative action since it began. Champions of affirmative action invariably denounce quotas. Opponents of affirmative action constantly point out that if discrimination is to be practiced, explicit quotas are by far the fairest and most efficient means of implementing it. Explicit quotas enable a university or employer to use the most reliable selection criteria, which, as I will demonstrate repeatedly in this book, are nearly always intelligence tests. The university or employer can then set a different passing grade for each race or ethnic group in order to obtain the number it needs.[13]

---

12. To be completely precise, Justice Powell forced all American universities to tell the same lies as the lies that the elite universities told in the brief they submitted in the *Bakke* case.

13. Throughout this book I use the term "intelligence tests" to describe a wide variety of tests. In Appendix IV, I explain what I mean by *intelligence* and why scores on all types of intelligence tests correlate closely with each other.

In both the *Grutter* and *Gratz* decisions, the justices who delivered the majority decision constantly cited Justice Powell's outline of Harvard's description of its admissions policy in its brief in the *Bakke* case. In fact, in both *Grutter* and *Gratz*, Harvard's description of its admissions policy in the *Bakke* case was the only example that the majority justices adduced of the correct, non-quota way to practice racial discrimination.

So, let us now look at the genesis of what Justice Powell called the "illuminating example" of "the Harvard College program."

Cg 80

ରେ ଶ୍ଚ

Chapter 3
Quotas Are Best: The Origin of Diversity and Other Non-Academic Qualifications at American Universities

In America today, few customs are more familiar than the annual ritual in which our leading universities sort through tens of thousands of applications . . . . So familiar are the features of this process—the letters of recommendation, the personal interviews, the emphasis on extracurricular activities . . . the boost given to athletes and alumni children, and the heavy emphasis on highly subjective qualities such as "character," "personality," and "leadership"—that they have come to be taken for granted. Yet viewed from both a historical and a comparative perspective, the admission practices of America's top colleges and universities are exceedingly strange. Just try to explain to someone from abroad—from, say, France, Japan, Germany, or China—why the ability to run with a ball or where one's parents went to college is relevant to who will gain a place at our nation's most prestigious institutions of higher education, and you immediately realize how very peculiar our practices are . . . .

Like the most prestigious universities of other nations, Harvard, Yale, and Princeton . . . admitted students almost entirely on the basis of academic criteria for most of their long histories. But this changed in the 1920s . . . . By then, it had become clear that a system of se-lection focused solely on scholastic performance would lead to the admission of increasing numbers of Jewish students, most of them of eastern European background (Karabel 2005: 1).

A. Admissions before the Jewish Problem

Until the middle of the nineteenth century, a student who wanted to attend an American college made an appointment to meet the col-lege's president. Often, a few faculty members were also present. They decided whether to admit him by questioning him on his knowledge of ancient Greek, Latin, and mathematics.[14]

As the number of subjects required for college entrance increased, regional organizations of colleges and high schools and national organizations of academic disciplines tried, with varying success, to establish uniform, published college-entrance requirements in literature and languages (ancient and modern), periods of history, and fields of mathematics and science. Mastery of these subjects was determined either by the college's own examinations or by a certificate issued by the principal of a high school whose curriculum and teaching had been approved by that college. Both methods had obvious defects. Principals could be swayed by parents or local officials. But department chairmen, who set and marked college examinations, often chose idiosyncratic questions and/or marked them idiosyncratically. Examinations differed widely in difficulty and approach between colleges, between subjects in the same college, and between one year and another in the same subject at the same college (Wechsler 1977: 46-55, 99).

In 1899, the Association of the Colleges and Secondary Schools of the Middle States and Maryland decided to establish the College Entrance Examination Board (CEEB). Colleges everywhere in the United States could join it. Its purpose was to set examinations of uniform difficulty, based on mutually agreed requirements, and to ensure that they were marked according to clearly specified guidelines. Moreover, the CEEB examinations were administered throughout the country, thus opening member colleges to students from everywhere in the United States. The CEEB's first examinations were given in 1901. Membership grew rapidly, as colleges found that CEEB exams not only ensured uniformity but also yielded better students than their own exams or high school certification. CEEB exams yielded better students both because they assessed academic ability and achievement more accurately than previous admissions criteria, and also because they opened the possibility of attending an elite college to a broader social stratum of students. Harvard adopted CEEB exams, in addition to its own exams, for the class it admitted in 1905. Of the class that entered in 1908, unprecedented percentages were from public schools and were Catholic and Jewish: 45, 9, and 7 percent respectively. Yale adopted CEEB exams,

---

14. Wechsler 1977: 7. Many colleges also required knowledge of geography (Shudson 1972: 39).

We now know that ancient Greek, Latin, and mathematics are the most *g*-loaded academic subjects; that is, performance in them correlates more closely than performance in any other academic subjects with the most important factor that intelligence tests measure: what Charles Spearman called "General Intelligence." The SAT is also extremely highly *g*-loaded (Jackson and Rushton 2006: 481-2).

in addition to its own exams, in 1907; Princeton in 1910. In 1909, Yale's dean informed the faculty that students admitted by the CEEB exams did better work than those admitted by its own exams. In 1915-16, Harvard, Yale, and Princeton abandoned their own exams completely in favor of the CEEB exams. Some member colleges continued to consider high school records. For example, Harvard allowed applicants with good high school records to take exams only in designated core subjects.[15]

The purpose of all these changes and variations was to identify as accurately as possible those applicants who had mastered clear, published academic requirements. No one questioned that this was the only purpose of any admissions procedure (Wechsler 1977: 3-4).

Then a serious problem emerged.

B. The Jewish Problem

In 1877, only 226,000 Jews lived in the United States. That rose to 400,000 in 1888, 938,000 in 1897, 1,777,999 in 1907, and 3,389,000 in 1917. Shortly afterwards, immigration was restricted by legislation (Oren 2000: 349-50). In 1900, the average immigrant arrived with 15 dollars, the average Jewish immigrant with nine dollars. Twenty-six percent of Jewish immigrants were illiterate, compared with one percent of English and Scandinavian immigrants, three percent of Irish, and five percent of German immigrants. The population density, dirt, noise, and poverty of the immigrant Jewish neighborhoods had few, if any, parallels in the world (Silberman 1985: 49-50; Steinberg 1974: 84). Nearly half lived in New York City, where "In 1902 a survey found that only eight percent of the city's Jewish families . . . had private baths" (Chauncey 1994: 208, footnote). The largest American Jewish neighborhood, the Lower East Side of Manhattan, was

> a district of squalor whose stifling air was fouled . . . with the odor of rotting fish, meat, and vegetables sold on uncovered pushcarts, the immense amount of animal waste from horse-drawn wagons and trucks, dirty streets and the stench of a crowded humanity (Nuland 1997: 34).
>
> In 1910, 540,000 Jews lived in the 1.5 square-mile area of the Lower East Side. A 1908 survey . . . showed that 50 percent slept three or four to a room; nearly 25 percent, five or more to a room; only 25 percent, two to a room (Goren 1980: 581).

By 1919, the proportion of Jews at elite American colleges was several

---

15. Schudson 1972: 44-5; Wechsler 1977: 97-104, 112, 246; Karabel 2005: 44-5, 56-7, 230; Synnott 1979: 6.

times the proportion of Jews in the American population; for example, 20 percent at Brown and Harvard, nearly 25 percent at the University of Pennsylvania, and 40 percent at Columbia; and these proportions were rising rapidly.[16]

As I explain in Section E of Appendix III, when the average intelligence of groups of people differs, the difference between them becomes more and more pronounced at the extremes. Consequently, the problem of Jewish overrepresentation was compounded by Jewish hyper-overrepresentation among the best students. The 1918 meeting of the Association of New England College Deans was concerned largely with the Jewish problem. The deans of MIT, Brown, Bowdoin, and Tufts all expressed concern over the rapid rise in the number of their Jewish students. Dean Jones of Yale said, "A few years ago every single scholarship of any value was won by a Jew. I took it up with the Committee and said that we could not allow that to go on. We must put a ban on the Jews." Four years later, Jones observed that "despite the handicap of poverty and the necessity of working their way, the Jews make better average records than their Gentile fellows" (Synnott 1979: 17, 147; cf. 85, 98, 114, 141; Karabel 2005: 75).

The Jewish invasion constituted a culture shock. Until the early 1950s, over half of Harvard undergraduates were from private schools. Of Yale's undergraduates, over 75 percent were from private schools into the late 1940s, and over 60 percent into the middle 1950s. At Princeton, over 80 percent of undergraduates were from private schools until 1937; and over 75 percent until 1947 (Karabel 2005: 116, 119, 226, 237, 257, 266). By contrast, between 1911 and 1922, three-quarters of the fathers of the Jewish undergraduates at Yale were born in central or eastern Europe, as were 19 percent of the students themselves. Many spoke English with a Yiddish accent (Oren 2000: 50, 175, 199, 225, 358).

In 1922, the Yale Committee on Limitation of Numbers recommended diverting scholarships from poor to middle class and rich students because:

> There seems to be an inclination among alumni associations to choose as the recipient of the various Yale Alumni Scholarships the corner newsboy or the son of the janitor of their building or a boy similarly circumstanced . . . The recipients are in quite a number of cases of Jewish boys (Oren 2000: 57).

---

16. I take these figures from Sachar 1992: 327. If anything, they are underestimates. Another source (Karabel 2005: 577, note 68) states that the proportion of Jews at the University of Pennsylvania was 52 percent, which Penn managed to reduce to 14 percent in the 1920s.

In this chapter, when I mention a university, I am always referring to its undergraduate college, unless I state otherwise.

This increased the anti-Jewish discrimination that Yale had practiced in awarding scholarships since 1909 (Oren 2000: 57). But private colleges cost much less then than now, even adjusted for inflation: between $150 and $160 a year at Harvard, Yale, and Columbia in 1914; the equivalent of $3,300-3,500 in 2010 (Oren 2000: 375 note 18; Wechsler 1977: 152). Consequently, diverting scholarships from Jewish students did not solve the Jewish problem.

C. The First Response to the Problem: Columbia

The first college to consider a more direct solution was Columbia, which was located in New York City, where 45 percent of all American Jews lived in the early 20th century (Goren 1980: 581). In 1908, Columbia's president, Nicholas Murray Butler, appointed a committee to investigate why the number of applications from the Horace Mann School, an elite private school bordering on it, was declining. The committee consisted of members of Columbia's faculty and administration, but its chairman was Horace Mann's headmaster, Virgil Prettyman. It reported that parents of private school students thought that Columbia's "undergraduate body contained a preponderant element of students who have had few social advantages and that in consequence, there was little opportunity for making friendships of permanent value among them." The Prettyman Report concluded that Columbia was "neither receiving its share of students from the better families of the City nor even holding the sons of its own trustees, professors and alumni" (Wechsler 1977: 147-8).

> Prettyman's report, filed late in 1908, turned into a full-fledged indictment of much of Butler's work in the previous decade. "[The] University," he said, "has repeatedly shown its desire to accommodate the [public] High Schools . . . and has thereby established a Columbia sentiment in these schools . . . ." Butler stood guilty as charged (Wechsler 1977: 148).

Butler was guilty because he was the moving force behind the creation of the College Entrance Examination Board and was its chairman from 1901 to 1914. Of the first 973 students who took the first CEEB exams, 758 applied to Columbia and Barnard (Columbia's women's college). Moreover, from the first CEEB exams, in 1901, Columbia abandoned its own examinations and relied completely on CEEB exams, which evaluated applicants without regard to their background and made comparisons among them transparent (Wechsler 1977: 97-101; Schudson 1972: 45).

The Prettyman Report urged Columbia to consider why many students went to college:

> The conditions and environment in which youth is to pass into man-
> hood, the associations and friendships which may be formed within
> the student body, are popularly esteemed not less important factors
> in the value of college education than the academic training and
> knowledge that may be acquired (Wechsler 1977: 148-9).

College administrators and professors always knew that many students regarded the social aspects of college life as equally or more important than its academic aspects, but they had regarded that as a problem. In a much discussed book, Edwin Broome's *A Historical and Critical Discussion of College Admission Requirements* (Macmillan, 1902), one of the arguments that Broome advanced (pages 150-51) for the superiority of examinations over principals' certification was that the type of students admitted on the basis of examinations are more interested in the academic than the social aspects of college life.

The Prettyman Report marked a revolution. For the first time, a college was urged to consider the social interactions of its students in making admissions decisions.

The Prettyman Report observed that because of public opinion, "it is clearly impossible to draw racial or class distinctions between applicants for admission."[17] So, discrimination had to be practiced circuitously. Consequently, it recommended that Columbia should stop relying exclusively on examinations for admission. In order to be able to admit applicants "from the better New York families" over more intelligent applicants "who have had few social advantages," Columbia should consider high school grades (Wechsler 1977: 149). Grades have two advantages over standardized tests for practicing racial discrimination. They are not uniform, so they make it difficult to prove that discrimination exists; and, as I point out in Chapters 12 and 13, they are less accurate measures of academic ability and achievement. Therefore, they do not reflect the full difference between Jews and Gentiles, whites and blacks, and, in mathematics-based subjects, between North-East Asians (Japanese, Chinese, and Koreans) and whites.

The Prettyman Report also recommended that Columbia appoint a permanent administrator whose sole job would be to recruit students from private schools. Shortly after, Columbia established an Office of Undergradu-

---

17. Wechsler 1977: 149. Until the 1940s, *race* meant any group to which a person belonged by ancestry, without regard to physical appearance. The forms that were filled out by inductees into the British army during World War II had a question about race. For the large majority, the answer was English, Welsh, Scottish, or Irish.

ate Admissions, which "not only made possible greater leeway in evaluation of academic admissions criteria; it also permitted the future addition
of non-academic criteria that could be subjectively evaluated" (Wechsler
1977: 149-150).

Now even a small college like Middlebury has a full-time admissions
staff of 18 (Sowell 1993: 103-4). This, of course, is part of a hypertrophic
growth in university bureaucracy. In the early 1990s, Stanford employed
1,400 faculty members but an administrative staff of nearly 7,000, which is
more than the number of its students (Sacks and Thiel 1995: 201). In fact, it
is more than the number of administrators that British East India Company
needed in 1830 to govern most of India. Of academic bureaucrats, the admissions personnel are the most obviously unnecessary. As a dean of admissions
at Stanford pointed out, "If we only admitted students based on SAT scores,
I wouldn't have a job" (Sowell 1993: 126). He meant that as a joke. But if
universities had not adopted and maintained the goal of ethnic discrimination,
they would have continued to use clearly defined measurements of academic
achievement and ability as their sole admissions criterion and would, in fact,
not have needed to introduce permanent admissions personnel.

Columbia soon made use of its new admissions officer, Adam Jones.
The dean of Columbia College, Frederick Keppel, told Jones that he was
concerned with the presence of so many "uncultured Jews" at the college.
Jones' position gave him considerable latitude:

> Did a student from a good preparatory school just miss passing an
> exam or two? . . . Might he not emerge as a leader of other students,
> and ultimately an important member of the community? Jones' deci-
> sion to admit on condition students for whom the answer to these
> questions was "yes" . . . permitted him to alter the "mix" of the student
> body (Wechsler 1977: 151).

Keppel, Butler, and Jones considered two other revolutionary means
to attract more of what Keppel called "Gentile boys of a desirable type:"
taking the geographical origin of applicants into consideration, thereby
reducing the proportion of students from New York City, where American
Jews were concentrated, and setting a limit on the total number of students
it admitted. It is difficult today to understand how revolutionary these ideas
were. No college had ever considered them before. Colleges and graduate
and professional schools had always set the admissions requirements they
thought desirable and admitted all the applicants who fulfilled them. Dean
Keppel explained in 1913 that if Columbia pre-set the number of students
it would admit, "When the number of [academically] qualified applicants
began to exceed this level, the Admissions Office could choose among

them using criteria such as 'personal qualities'" (Wechsler 1977: 151-4). This inaugurated another basic affirmative action ploy: "It is true that we take race/ethnicity into consideration, but everyone we admit/hire/promote is qualified."

The necessity of considering non-academic criteria is clear from Keppel's observation, "By far the majority of Jewish students who do come to Columbia are desirable students in every way. . . . Their intellectual ability, and particularly their intellectual curiosity, are above the average, and the teachers are unanimous in saying that their presence in the classroom is distinctly desirable" (Wechsler 1977: 135).

Nevertheless, the inertia inherent in old institutions and fear of public opinion prevented Columbia from adopting these revolutionary changes until after World War I. However, discriminatory recruitment has always seemed less blatant than discriminatory admissions. In 1914 Columbia established a scholarship fund for graduates of private schools. This began its use of scholarships to attract Gentile, especially Protestant, applicants.[18] The scholarship fund and the discretion exercised by the dean of admissions slowed the growth of Jewish enrollment, but they did not stop it. By 1919, 40 percent of Columbia undergraduates were Jewish, and the proportion was rising (Sachar 1992: 327). Clearly radical steps had to be taken.

In December 1917, President Butler, in his Annual Report, advocated limiting undergraduate enrollment and a concomitant "*affirmative* [emphasis added] process of selection and not merely a negative process of exclusion." Students would be admitted on the basis of "their record, their personality and their promise;" academic requirements would exist "solely for the purpose of creating an eligible list." This was necessary since, "Endless thousands of ambitious men and women . . . [from public schools are] ready to meet any test of . . . scholarship." Butler also provided an excuse for this radical departure from past procedures, which advocates of academic affirmative action have used ever since. Those students whom Columbia rejected for non-academic reasons could attend less competitive colleges.[19]

Butler's most strikingly recognizable trick was describing this discrimination as affirmative, in favor of its beneficiaries, which makes it seem more acceptable than if it is described as negative, against its victims; even though both describe the same process. So, Adolf Hitler's justification for

18. Wechsler 1977: 153. In 1937, 88 percent of the recipients of Columbia scholarships were Protestants, and most of the rest were Catholics (Wechsler 1977: 164).

19. *Annual Report of the President and Treasurer to the Trustees with Accompanying Documents for the Year Ending June 1917* (pages 12-15). This report can be obtained from Columbia.

the Nuremberg Law of 1935, "For the Protection of German Blood and Honor," was, "This legislation is not anti-Jewish, but pro-German. The rights of Germans are thereby to be protected . . . Jews, who formed less than one percent of the population, monopolized the cultural leadership of the people and flooded the intellectual professions, such as law and medicine" (Baynes 1942: 732-3).

Admissions Director Jones then created the first application form ever used by an American college (Levine 1986: 141). It asked for types of information that no college had ever dreamed of requesting before. Applicants in 1919 were asked about their participation in school publications, musical organizations, athletics, debating, student government, and religious and patriotic activities. They also had to have an interview, arrange for three letters of recommendation and submit an essay on their plans for the future and why they wanted to attend college and Columbia in particular (Wechsler 1977: 156-7).

Columbia had to devise these complex procedures and requirements and establish a bureaucracy to administer them because, as the Prettyman Report observed, "it is clearly impossible to draw racial or class distinctions between applicants for admission." In fact, as with later quota-substitutes, Columbia's only superficially masked its purpose. Its revolutionary application form asked questions such as the applicant's religious affiliation; place of birth; father's name, occupation, and place of birth; and mother's "maiden name in full," and her place of birth (Broun and Britt 1931: 72). If Columbia could have established an explicit Jewish quota, it could have continued relying completely on the CEEB examinations, which it had found to be the best admission criterion, and set different cut-off marks for Jews and Gentiles. That would have yielded the best students, without requiring even a permanent admissions officer.

Admissions Director Jones was troubled by the patent fraudulence of the process he was implementing. In a memorandum to President Butler, he raised three obvious objections, which advocates of affirmative action have never been able to answer. First, "[M]any would hold that since intellectual training is after all the business of a university, other than intellectual qualities were not matters of primary interest to it." Second, academic ability can be reliably measured, but that is not true of character:

> If a college were devoting itself to training men for leadership, demanding public spirit and unselfish devotion to the common good . . . the promise of those other qualities should also [in addition to academic ability] be considered . . . [But] such qualities can rarely be detected with certainty . . . [T]o exclude those who showed no promise of them would undoubtedly result in sending away many

who might later go farthest.

Third, Columbia's experience showed that if anything measures desirable character traits, it is the measures of academic ability that it had been using (Wechsler 1977: 157-8). That insight has been confirmed. As I explain in Appendix IV, we now know that intelligence tests taken in childhood are excellent predictors of criminality, divorce, good parenting and other crucial social attributes; and a person's family and social background have little or no correlation with these attributes, except through the intelligence that he or she inherits genetically from his parents.

Herbert Hawkes, who replaced Keppel as dean in 1918, made no attempt to answer Jones' objections. He simply said that no more than 20 percent of Columbia College students should be Jews because, "Every college should . . . admit as many divergent types of students as it can assimilate. . . . [F]or a college to consist entirely or mostly entirely of newly arrived immigrants makes it impossible for them to gain the contacts that they need and should have."[20]

Dean Jones died in 1932. His successor, Frank Bowles, did not have his scruples about obtaining a student body that was drawn primarily from what he called "desirable upper middle class American stock."[21] In the first

---

20. Wechsler 1977: 163-4. Keppel later became president of the Carnegie Foundation, where he was instrumental in funding studies of black American history and sociology, including two of the most influential ever published: W. E. B. Du Bois' *Black Reconstruction in America* and Gunnar Myrdol's *An American Dilemma* (Lewis 2000: 362-4, 423, 448-52, 480-1).

21. Into the late 1950s, *American* had an ethnic meaning, Anglo-Saxon, in addition to its political-legal meaning, a citizen of the United States (e.g., Chapter 14 of *The Godfather*: Vito Corleone "worked in [*sic*] the railroad . . . [M]ost of the foremen were Irish and American and abused the [Italian] workmen in the foulest language.") I was born in 1943, and I can remember *American* being used ethnically.

The term *WASP* (White Anglo-Saxon Protestant) is more recent than most people realize. Its first attested use was by Andrew Hacker in 1957 in the *American Political Science Review* 51 (pages 1009-26). The first entry in the *Oxford English Dictionary* (*OED*) is from 1962. It was used as a neologism until 1965, when E. Digby Baltzell popularized it in *The Protestant Establishment: Aristocracy and Caste in America*. The introduction of the term *WASP* marked a revolution. Anglo-Saxons became merely another ethnic group.

I use the term *Anglo-Saxon* with its common American meaning: anyone of North-Western European origin who is a practicing or nominal Protestant.

class he admitted, he reduced the proportion of Jews to 17 percent (Wechsler 1977: 167-8).

Columbia pursued diversity consistently. In 1945, when its anti-Jewish discrimination came under attack, it disclosed that it also discriminated in favor of blacks over white Gentiles (Wechsler 1977: 208, note 21).

D. A National Solution Is Found: The Harvard College Program

Columbia showed that the Jewish problem could be solved. Other universities followed its example by adopting nebulous admissions criteria like character, leadership, and public spirit, along with the objectively definable criterion of regional diversity, since Jews were concentrated overwhelmingly in the Northeast, especially in New York.

These circuitous machinations avoided scandal. That changed suddenly on May 31, 1922, when the *Boston Post* reported that Harvard was considering explicitly reducing the proportion of its Jewish students to 15 percent. In the next few days, Harvard's plan became national news. Harvard's President, Abbot Lowell, argued that this policy would enable Harvard to retain its character as a "democratic, national university; drawing from all classes of the community and promoting a sympathetic understanding among them." He was proud of doing openly and honestly what others were doing covertly and deviously through the smokescreen of character, geography and the other subterfuges (Synnott 1979: 63-5, 74; Wechsler 1997: 161-2).

In an exchange of letters with a prominent Jewish alumnus on the front page of the *New York Times* of June 17, 1922 ("Lowell Tells Jews...") Lowell said, "The question is with us. We cannot solve it by forgetting or ignoring it . . . Some colleges appear to have met the question by indirect methods, which we do not want to adopt."

The front page of the *New York Times* of June 23 quoted from Lowell's commencement address ("Names Men to Study Sifting [Admissions] at Harvard"):

> We often speak of Americanization as if the American were a finished product. The American has been in the making ever since the first white men set foot upon our shores, and will continue to be in

In the 1890s, Finley Dunne had his immensely popular humorous character "Mr. Dooley" observe, "An Anglo-Saxon is a German that's forgotten who his grandparents were."

The practice, which began in California, of labeling all Americans of European origin *Anglos*, marks a further revolutionary change. Americans of European origin are becoming merely another ethnic group.

the making so long as streams of foreigners pour into our lands. Americanization . . . means . . . the blending together of many distinct elements. No one of the peoples that have come from Europe . . . is devoid of qualities which can enrich our common heritage . . . In the blending of these different groups our colleges, where young men of all kinds mingle . . . can render an indispensable service.

Diversity had come to the front page of the *New York Times*. In the following decades, it would quote many liberal, progressive justifications for discriminating against people because they are members of an ethnic or racial group that is more intelligent than other ethnic or racial groups.

However, these justifications did not silence public outrage. The American Federation of Labor and Boston's City Council passed resolutions condemning the proposed quota. The governor of Massachusetts appointed a legislative committee to determine whether it violated a state law; and a proposal was made in the state legislature to review the tax exemption of Harvard's property. So, Harvard was forced to abandon an open, honest quota and to adopt instead the admissions policy that Justice Powell in *Bakke* and the majority of Supreme Court justices in the University of Michigan cases of 2003 cited as "an illuminating example" of how racial discrimination should be practiced (Synnott 1979: 77; Rosenstock 1971: 103; Oren 2000: 51).

The Harvard Board of Overseers appointed a faculty committee to consider "principles and methods for the more effective sifting of candidates for admission to the university." In his opening statement, the chairman of the committee, Professor Charles Grandgent, pointed out:

> [A different] college entrance examination would not solve the problem. The Jew is a remarkable student. He is intelligent. The Jewish race as a whole is intelligent. It is astonishing the number of Jews from poor districts who enter Harvard and become remarkable students (Rosenstock 1971: 106-7).

In April 1923, the committee submitted its report, and the faculty approved it. It unequivocally repudiated quotas and urged that "Harvard College maintain its traditional policy of freedom from discrimination on grounds of race or religion." However, it also proposed a new goal: to create a "student body [that] will be properly representative of all groups in our national life" by "the building up of a new group of men from the West and South and, in general, from good high schools in towns and small cities." Since many of these students could not pass Harvard's entrance examination, the committee recommended that students in the top seventh of their graduating class be exempt from the entrance examination. The Harvard

Board of Overseers and faculty adopted these recommendations by overwhelming majorities. This plan was widely praised, even by Jewish leaders,
as a victory for non-racism.[22]

However, "It was not until the influx of Jewish students that Eastern colleges began to worry about achieving a 'regional balance'" (Steinberg 1974:
30). Even the report in the *Harvard Graduates' Magazine* of June 1923 ("The
University:" 531-4) by Henry Holmes, Dean of Harvard's Graduate School
of Education, observed that regional balance would mean, "the proportion
of Jewish students would be reduced."

"[T]his plan provides the germ for the Harvard College Admission
Program about which Justice Powell spoke approvingly in *University of
California v. Bakke*" (Pollak 1983: 119). It was also the only example of
the correct way to practice racial discrimination that the majority of the
Supreme Court cited in the University of Michigan cases, when it supported
Powell's ruling.

If public opinion had allowed elite universities to use explicit quotas,
their admissions procedure would have been fairer, easier to implement, and
would have yielded better students. All they would have had to do was use
academic criteria and set different cut-off levels for Jews and Gentiles.

As is typical of quota-substitutes, Harvard's only half-heartedly maintained the pretence of non-discrimination. It added the following questions
to its application forms: "What change, if any, has been made since birth in
your name or that of your father?" "Maiden name of mother," and "Birthplace
of father" (Synott 1979: 258).

A few days after the new admissions policy was adopted, Lowell wrote
to the president of Amherst College about Harvard's recent action on "the
race question:" "We have dealt with it . . . by compromise, which was the
only possible thing at the time." In 1925, he assured alumni who were wor-
ried about the number of Jews at Harvard that they "need not doubt that
the matter is thoroughly understood by the authorities here;" but he added,
"My [original] plan was crude, and its method . . . unwise" (Synnott 1979:
106).

However, geographical diversity only slowed the rise in Jewish enrollment. In autumn 1925, Harvard's dean's office classified 27.6 percent of the
new class as definitely Jewish and another 4.3 percent as possibly Jewish.
President Lowell decided that Harvard had to supplement geographical
diversity with consideration of applicants' character. In 1922 Lowell had
reduced the proportion of Jews receiving scholarships to their proportion
of undergraduates by adding character to academic ability as a scholarship

22. Synnott 1979: 92-3, 105-6, 193; Pollak 1983: 119; Steinberg 1974:
29; Oren 2000: 52.

requirement. He now wrote to the chairman of the committee considering admissions criteria that Harvard must pre-set a limit on the number it admits and choose among academically eligible applicants on the basis of character: "To prevent a dangerous increase in the proportion of Jews, I know at present only one way . . . a selection by a personal estimate of character . . . If there is no limit, it is impossible to reject a candidate who passes the admission examinations." In 1926, Harvard announced that it would limit the size of its freshman class to 1,000 and introduce requirements for character testimonials, a personal interview, and a photograph. An editorial in Harvard's student newspaper, the *Crimson*, approved of this policy with the argument that the number of "non-assimilable elements . . . should be reduced."[23]

Character accomplished its purpose. During the 1930s, the proportion of Jews at Harvard varied between 14 and 16 percent (five times the proportion of Jews in the American population), which nearly perfectly matched Lowell's original proposed quota of 15 percent (Karabel 2005: 173). In 1933, when James Conant succeeded Lowell as Harvard's president, Lowell told him, "I tried, as you know, to find an open, fair, and practical solution, but was howled down by the preference of most people to profess one principle and act upon another. Any educational institution that admits an unlimited number of Jews will soon have no one else" (Keller 2001: 49).

Under Conant, Harvard's admissions office divided applicants into five categories, in descending order of desirability. The first three consisted of applicants from private boarding schools; the fourth of Gentiles from public schools; the last of Jews (Hodgson 2000). Recruiters from Harvard and other Ivy League colleges also avoided public schools in order to discourage applications from Jews (Oren 2000: 414, note 29). As Harvard Provost Paul Buck explained in the 1945-46 *Harvard Alumni Bulletin* ("Balance in the College"), "95 percent of the applicants for Harvard from the large metropolitan high schools of New York and New Jersey are of one category—bright, precocious, intellectually overstimulated boys" (Keller 2001: 34). (These were the defects that the adoption of character as an admissions criterion was designed to weed out.)

Meanwhile at Yale, the proportion of Jews was also rising with alarming

---

23. Synnott 1979: 59, 107-10; Rosenstock 1971: 107. In a letter to philosophy professor William Hocking, Lowell acknowledged that Jews do not have worse "character" than Gentiles and that "character" is a ruse:

The summer hotel that is ruined by admitting Jews meets its fate, not because the Jews it admits are of bad character, but because they drive away the Gentiles . . . . A similar thing happened in the case of Columbia College; in all these cases it is not because Jews of bad character have come (Karabel 2005: 88).

momentum. In 1920 Yale created an Admissions Board. In January 1922, Yale's president, James Angell, asked Yale's administrators to investigate the growth of Jewish enrollment at Yale. In April, Yale's registrar informed Angell, the dean of Yale College, and Robert Corwin, the chairman of the Admissions Board, that the proportion of Jews in Yale's entering classes had risen from two percent in 1897, to 7.5 percent in 1917, to over 13 percent in 1921. In May, in response to a request for information from Corwin, the dean of freshmen reported that Jewish students averaged 11.3 points higher on an intelligence test than the class average of 50. However, "many of them are personally and socially unacceptable" (Oren 2000: 45-7, 354-5; Synnott 1979: 139-43). Three days later, Corwin submitted a "Memorandum on the Jewish Problem" to the Yale Corporation Committee on Educational Policy. In it, he proposed several means to prevent the proportion "of low class Jews" from exceeding ten percent of Yale College's students. The first was to pre-set the size of the entering class at "a point that would make selection [based on non-academic criteria] necessary and logical among those satisfying the scholastic requirements." As Corwin explained in a letter to President Angell:

> This proposal is based on the assumption . . . that there are several characteristics other than scholarship essential to success in college—manliness, uprightness, cleanliness, native refinement, etc., which are . . . lacking in a large proportion of . . . this race whose parents have but recently immigrated from eastern and southern Europe (Oren 2000: 48, 52-3).

In 1923, the Yale Corporation voted to limit the size of the freshman class to 850, since, as the Committee on Limitation of Numbers reported, "the fixing of a maximum number of Freshmen admitted seems a necessary basis for any restrictions which have to do with character rather than with scholarship." Thus, "Yale . . . turned against more than a century of admissions policies that were open to all scholastically qualified, college-age males." "[A]cademic achievement had stopped being of paramount importance in Yale admissions. A highly subjective evaluation of personality had also become crucial." "[D]iscrimination against Jews would be a cornerstone of Yale undergraduate admissions for the next four decades." During those four decades, Yale succeeded in restricting the proportion of its Jewish undergraduates to no more than twelve percent, just marginally more than Corwin's goal of ten percent (Oren 2000: 56, 58, 68, 196, 355-6; cf. 62, 186, 189, 213).

That required constant additions to Yale's defenses against Jewish invasion. In 1934, a question about the applicant's mother's birthplace was added to questions about his father's birthplace and his mother's maiden name. The admissions director wrote to Yale's president, "This knowledge will give us a more accurate check on the race of the applicant" (Oren 2000: 65; Synnott 1979: 155).

Before that, in 1925, Yale became the first college to institute preference in admissions for sons of alumni, as another means of keeping the number of Jews in check. Of the class that entered Yale in 1920, 13 percent were sons of alumni. That rose to 30 percent in 1931.[24] Here again, if Yale could have adopted an explicit Jewish quota, it could have selected applicants by only academic criteria and set higher requirements for Jews than for Gentiles. That would have yielded much better students and been fairer than giving huge preferences to applicants because their fathers attended Yale.

However, an explicit quota was out of the question. In 1929, Corwin wrote to a member of the Yale Corporation, the "racial problem is never wholly absent from the minds of the Board of Admissions . . . [But] Harvard ran into rough weather by attempting to justify her proposed action publicly before putting it into force. She is now, however, sawing wood and saying not a word." The next year, when only 8.2 percent of the entering class were Jews, the chairman of the Board of Admissions wrote to Yale's president, "I trust you will be favorably impressed with the figures . . . [T]he result . . . was attained without hue and cry" (Oren 2000: 62-3, 60). In his 1944-45 annual report to Yale's president, admissions director Edward Noyes pointed out, "[T]he Jewish problem continues to call for the utmost care and tact" (Oren 2000: 190).

Student opinion strongly supported these policies. The *Yale Daily*

---

24. Karabel 2005: 116-17, 206, 449. Concomitantly, the proportion of Yale undergraduates who were from private schools *increased* from 76 percent in 1920 to 81 percent in 1930 (Karabel 2005: 116).

Selective colleges also began regarding athletic ability as an admissions consideration for the first time in the 1920s (Karabel 2005: 616, note 217). Unlike geographical diversity, "character," and having an alumnus father, athletic ability was not directed against Jews. When other non-academic attributes became important considerations in college admissions, it seemed natural to include athletic ability, which, unlike the others, is a genuine ability.

(In 1923 and 1924, when Yale won the Eastern Collegiate League basketball title, its star players were Jews (Oren 200: 86). The only college basketball team that ever won both the National Invitation Tournament and the NCAA Tournament in the same year was the basketball team of the City College of New York in 1950, all five of whose starting players were Jews. During the 1920s and 1930s, 16 percent of the boxing champions in the eight weight divisions of the time were Jews (Bodner 1997: 2).)

News of March 29, 1926 praised Harvard's decision to consider character in admitting students and to require applicants to submit photographs of themselves. It urged that Yale "go them one better and require applicants to submit photographs of their fathers also." The next day it said, "Yale must institute . . . immigration laws more prohibitive than those of the United States government." Otherwise, "Yale will no longer be a heterogeneous group of average citizens, but will be essentially a brain plant."[25]

Other elite colleges adopted similar policies. In 1922, Princeton transferred admissions decisions from a faculty committee, which considered only academic qualifications, to a Committee on Admissions, which considered non-academic qualifications in order to "develop not mere scholars but leaders." In 1925, less than half as many Jewish students entered Princeton as in 1922 (Synnott 1979: 182, 190-92, 195). By 1934, Stanford reduced its Jewish enrollment to less than three percent by assigning a 40 percent weighting to character in admissions decisions (Synnott 1986: 264). The University of Chicago's stated policy was "to keep the percentage of Jews at the University the same as the percentage of Jews in the city," in order to "have a representative student body" (Wechsler 1977: 230).

In the *Dartmouth Alumni Magazine* of November 1931, Dean of Admissions E. G. Bill reported that more than 10 percent of the entering class indicated that they were Jewish. Another 14 percent indicated no religion, and most of them were probably Jews. This was a five-fold increase over the previous decade. Dartmouth's president, Ernest Hopkins, told Dean Bill, "to do something drastic." In the *Dartmouth Alumni Magazine* in 1932, Dean Bill reported, "Wielding an axe rather than a fine tool, the Jewish delegation, which was 75 last year, is back to normal." The number of Jewish freshmen at Dartmouth remained 37 or 38 for the rest of the 1930s. The axe that accomplished this feat consisted of decreasing financial aid to poor students and increasing the importance assigned to leadership, good manners, sense of "fair play," and being the son of a Dartmouth alumnus. By the end of the 1930s, Dartmouth was accepting nearly three-quarters of its Gentile applicants but only one-tenth of its Jewish applicants (Levine 1986: 151-4, 241, note 41).

In 1922, Hopkins had written, "It would be incompatible with all conceptions of democracy to assume that the privilege of higher education should be restricted to any class defined by accident of birth . . . but there is such a thing as an aristocracy of brains, to whom increasingly the opportunities of

25. Synnott 1979:159. Yale students were "average" in the way (discussed at length below) the children of black and Hispanic doctors, lawyers, and corporate executives, who get preference in admission over the children of white car-park attendants, are "disadvantaged."

higher education ought to be restricted;" and he had lambasted non-academic college activities as "side shows [that have] swallowed up the circus." In 1932, he wrote to Dean Bill about the process they were instituting to decrease Jewish enrollment, "I shrink from and abhor the whole necessity." But it was a necessity since "any college which is going to base admissions wholly on scholastic standing will find itself with an infinitesimal proportion of anything else than Jews eventually" (Levine 1986: 141, 156, 241-2, note 38).

Non-elite colleges throughout the United States also adopted non-academic criteria in order to limit their Jewish enrollment. These were the same as those used by elite colleges, with one exception. Whereas colleges in the Northeast introduced geographical diversity to decrease the proportion of their Jewish students; many state universities in the West and South accomplished the same goal by introducing, for the first time, higher fees and more stringent academic requirements for out-of-state applicants (Levine 1986: 157-8; Synnott 1986: 250-51).

E. Professional Schools

The proportion of American medical school students who were Jews rose from seven percent in 1908 to 16.4 percent in 1918 (Synnott 1986: 251). The proportion of Jewish applicants continued to increase after that, but medical schools saved themselves from Jewish inundation by introducing two non-academic criteria: diversity and character. "[T]he belief prevailed in America that the best doctor was someone of the same ethnic background as the patient." In 1934, the head of the National Council of Christians and Jews wrote to the dean of almost every American medical school asking about their admissions policies. "Many asserted that Jewish students were academically superior and personally inferior" (Oren 2000: 156-60).

Columbia Medical School reduced its Jewish enrollment from over 50 percent in 1919 to below 20 percent in 1924 (Wechsler 1977: 170). Its dean explained, "The racial and religious makeup in medicine ought to be kept fairly parallel with the population makeup" (Sachar 1992: 332). In 1940, the dean of Cornell Medical School, 40 percent of whose students had been Jews in 1918-22 (Synnott 1986: 253), wrote, "Cornell Medical School admits a class of eighty each fall . . . from about 1,200 applicants of whom 700 or more are Jews. We limit the number of Jews . . . to 10-15 percent" (Bloomgarden 1953: 32). The dean of Yale Medical School explained in 1934,

From 50 to 60 percent of the applicants . . . each year are Hebrews . . . . The number of Hebrews admitted . . . has never been more than 10 percent . . . The Yale University School of Medicine is national .

. . [and] must endeavor to maintain a balance [that is] representative of the population which is to be served (Oren 2000: 160).

In 1946, a survey of the application forms for 39 major American medical schools found that all asked for the applicant's religion (Dinnerstein 1994: 159). However, beginning with New York in 1945, states began to pass anti-discrimination laws. Medical schools responded with "numerous, subjective, and shifting criteria for admission." For example, in the early 1950s a Jewish applicant to Flower Hospital Medical School was three and a half times more likely to be rejected than a Gentile applicant with the same academic record. "[A] rejected Jewish applicant . . . wants to know why. . . . [H]e learns that his 'diction, voice, physical appearance, grooming' have all been weighed." Here again, an open quota would have been easier to administer, fairer, and yielded better students. Most medical school administrators must have known that, since studies had already found that the only criterion that predicts success as a medical student and as a doctor is past academic performance (Bloomgarden 1953: 29, 33-4).

Other professional schools adopted the same practices. The proportion of law school students who were Jews rose from 13 percent in 1908 to 22 percent in 1918. The proportion of Jewish applicants kept rising after that, but law schools managed to reduce the proportion of their students who were Jews to eleven percent by 1946 (Synnott 1986: 258-9). In 1928, the dean of Columbia Law School explained, "[I]t is highly desirable that a group of men selected to engage in the study of law, a subject which involves the interests of all classes of people and all sections of the country, should be fairly representative of the class and sectional interests which are involved" (Wechsler 1977: 171). Similarly, between 1935 and 1946, the proportion of Jews in engineering, dental, pharmacy, and veterinary schools declined by 24 percent, 35 percent, 45 percent, and 70 percent, respectively (Synnott 1986: 257-8).

F. The Barriers Breached: The SAT[26]

The tests that the College Entrance Examination Board began giving in 1901 consisted of essays on the subjects required for college entrance. In 1926, the College Board introduced the SAT, which consisted of multiple-

26. SAT used to stand for "Scholastic Aptitude Test," then "Scholastic Assessment Test." Now the College Board says, "SAT is not an initialism [*sic*]; it does not stand for anything." Until 2005, the SAT consisted of two tests; Verbal and Mathematical Reasoning. Beginning in 2005, a Writing section was added. At the same time, analogies were dropped from the Verbal section, and it was renamed Critical Reading.

choice answers to verbal and arithmetic problems. In 1928, the arithmetic problems were deleted, and it became completely a test of verbal reasoning. In 1930, a separate Math test was introduced. (The Math section was not given between 1936 to 1941.)

James Conant, who became president of Harvard in 1933, was an outspoken advocate of increasing equality of opportunity without regard to social background, even advocating confiscatory inheritance taxes in an article in the *Atlantic Monthly* (Karabel 2005: 151-2, 156-8). To implement this goal at Harvard College, he established the National Scholarship program to attract the most brilliant students to Harvard without regard to their ability to pay. It involved a then revolutionary method of scholarship aid to those selected: a "sliding scale," on which payment was adjusted to each student's need. The main criterion for selection was the SAT. The appeal of the SAT was that it democratized college admission even more than the older College Board essay tests, because it measures academic ability without regard to the quality of the school that the applicant had attended. Of the ten first National Scholarship students, who entered Harvard in 1934, five graduated *summa cum laude*, three *magna cum laude*, and two *cum laude*; eight were inducted into Phi Beta Kappa. Of the 34 who entered Harvard in 1938, the annual family income of 15 was below $2,500, and of nine, below $2,000. This does not mean that they were poor; at that time, the annual income of nearly 90 percent of American families was below $2,500. But they were much less rich than most other Harvard undergraduates, 60 percent of whom came from families with annual incomes over $5,000 (Karabel 2005: 140, 159, 177-8.) Throughout the United States, between 1937 and 1940, public school students accounted for over 60 percent of those who took the SAT, but just over a third of those who took the older College Board essay achievement examinations. In 1941, Harvard, Yale, and Princeton substituted the SAT for the older essay achievement tests for all applicants (Schudson 1972: 54).

Harvard's National Scholarships showed how accurately performance on the SAT predicts academic performance and how independent it is of family and social background and the quality of the high school attended. I will demonstrate the former repeatedly in the rest of this book. The latter fact became incontrovertible when SAT scores began to be reported by race/ ethnicity and parental education and income. As I show in Chapter 6, Section A, the children of wealthy, highly educated black parents, who attend upper-class suburban or private high schools, do worse than the children of poor, uneducated white and Asian parents, who attend slum schools. The same discovery was made elsewhere:

[T]he British have discovered its [the SAT's] potential value in elevating smart kids at poor schools. A study . . . shows that kids in state-run schools who did well on the SAT are falling through the cracks of the current British testing system, which rewards those who have mastered specific subjects [in private schools] ... Britain's education czar said he thinks SATs could be compulsory there in a few years.[27]

However, the National Scholarship program did not affect the rest of Harvard's admissions procedures under Conant's presidency, in which, as I describe above, graduates of socially elite boarding schools were the most prized applicants and Jews the least. In fact, Harvard's National Scholarships were not open to students from the Middle Atlantic states, where over 60 percent of American Jews lived (Karabel 2005: 176, 593, note 55).

Elite colleges could get away with their mumbo-jumbo about diversity, character, and leadership when they were merely breaches of fairness and rationality; but by the end of World War II, they seemed to threaten national defense. In 1945, when Dartmouth's president defended limitations on Jewish enrollment in a letter to a New York newspaper, the *New Republic* commented that the atom bomb showed that Americans could not "handicap ourselves by arbitrarily rejecting certain elements, no matter how high their intellectual capacities, on the basis of religion and . . . race" (Levine 1986: 158). Criticism of the un-academic emphasis of American education became an outcry in 1957, when the Soviet Union launched a space satellite before the United States (Oren 2000: 217-18; Karabel 2005: 262, 265).

Between 1955 and 1960, the number of students who took the SAT increased from 63,000 to 400,000. In addition, in 1960, 132,000 took the ACT, which was introduced in 1959 (Schudson 1972: 58). Also, in 1958, perhaps in response to the Soviet technological challenge, the College Board began, for the first time, to inform students of their SAT scores. Before that, the College Board informed only their high school and the colleges to which they applied. Now students and the general public could see for themselves how much preference colleges were according to ethnicity, "character," attending a socially elite preparatory school, etc. If the average SAT score of one ethnic group is 200 points lower than the average score of another ethnic group at the same college, it is not plausible that the members of the lower scoring group are so superior in "character" that it could account for

27. Cloud 2001. So far, the SAT has not been adopted in the United Kingdom. I doubt if it will, because of the black-white difference. In Chapter 18, Section B, I show that standardized tests also opened employment hiring and armed-forces promotion to a much broader social stratum than other means of selection.

that difference. That is why champions of racial discrimination, from the Prettyman Report of 1908 to the present, have advocated de-emphasizing or abandoning standardized tests.

Increased reliance on the SAT created a revolution at elite colleges. Herrnstein and Murray began the main section of *The Bell Curve* (1996: 29-30) by pointing out that between 1952 and 1960 a radical change occurred in the social background of Harvard's entering classes.

> Harvard's Freshman Register for 1952 shows a class looking very much as Harvard freshmen classes had always looked ... Christian young men . . . . A large proportion . . . came from a handful of America's most exclusive boarding schools; Phillips Exeter and Phillips Andover alone contributed almost 10 percent of the freshman class. . . . An applicant's chances of being admitted were close to 90 percent if his father had gone to Harvard.

However, in 1960, "Public school graduates now outnumbered private school graduates." The reason for this social revolution was, "The average Harvard freshman in 1952 would have placed in the bottom 10 percent [of SAT scores] of the incoming class by 1960." In 1952, the median SAT scores of Harvard freshmen were 583 in Verbal and 598 in Math (Karabel 2005: 247). In 1960, they were 678 in Verbal and 695 in Math.[28]

How large was the discrimination in favor of private-school Anglo-Saxons and against public-school Jews? In 1959, Richard King, Harvard's associate director of admissions, presented a report to Harvard's Special Committee on College Admission Policy. King ranked the average performance at Harvard of the graduates of 79 secondary schools that had sent four or more students to Harvard in three Harvard graduating classes in the 1950s. Not one Eastern boarding school was among the top 30 schools. Of the 15 schools that ranked the lowest, 13 were private schools. The other two were public schools in Boston to whose applicants Harvard had always given preference in admission. Of the twelve schools whose students had done the best at Harvard, eight were from New York City, where 35 percent of American Jews lived; two others were from nearby Nassau County, where

---

28. Herrnstein and Murray 1996: 30 (Herrnstein and Murray mistakenly say that these scores are averages, not medians.) As I explain in Section E of Appendix III, in 1995, the manner in which raw SAT scores (i.e., number of correct and incorrect answers) are converted into reported scores was changed in a way that increased reported scores. On post-1994 conversion scales, the median Math scores of the 1952 and 1960 freshmen would be approximately the same as they were. But the median Verbal score of the 1952 freshmen would be 653; the median Verbal score of the 1960 freshmen would be over 740.

6 percent of American Jews lived. At the other two—Central High School in Philadelphia and Wilson High School in Washington DC—most of the students were also Jews. In additions, King analyzed the occupations of the fathers of Harvard students who graduated *magna cum laude* and *summa cum laude* and those who flunked out or dropped out. Of the sons of store owners (mostly Jews), five times more graduated *magna* or *summa* than dropped out or flunked out. Of the sons of business executives (at that time, nearly all Anglo-Saxons), twice as many flunked or failed than graduated *magna or summa* (Karabel 2005: 269-70, 613, notes 142, 144).

Two facts must be kept in mind about King's study. First, it was about Harvard students in the 1950s, when ethnic discrimination was less intense than it had been previously. In the late 1940s, Harvard began to relax (but not abandon) its *de facto* quota on Jews. As a result, as early as 1952, a quarter of Harvard undergraduates were Jews (Karabel 2005: 246, 597, note 175). Second, Harvard had always practiced less anti-Jewish and anti-public school discrimination than Yale and Princeton (Karabel 2005: 204-6, 622, note 95).

Herrnstein and Murray's description of the difference between the students who entered Harvard in 1952 and 1960 could be misleading. A genuine revolution in academic ability occurred, but selection of the class that entered in 1960 was far from completely meritocratic. In 1963, 48 students at the Bronx High School of Science (at which the large majority of students were Jews) were National Merit semi-finalists, but only 32 at all six of most socially elite boarding schools, which were called collectively the "St. Grottlesex" schools (Groton, St. Mark's, St. Paul's, St. George's, Kent, and Middlesex). In Richard King's study, three of these schools (St. Mark's, St. Paul's, and Middlesex) were among the 16 schools whose graduates had the worst academic records at Harvard. Nevertheless, among those who applied during 1959, Harvard admitted only 8 of 34 applicants from the Bronx High School of Science, but it admitted 13 of 17 applicants from St. Mark's and 15 of 19 from Groton. Moreover, Harvard discriminated even more against applicants from other New York City public schools than against applicants from Bronx Science.[29]

29. Karabel 2005: 270, 275, 293, 613, note 142, 616, note 229.

In 1940, Harvard accepted 210 of the 213 applicants from the twelve most socially elite boarding schools; in 1950, it accepted 245 of the 278 applicants from these schools, and 46 of 48 from Groton, St. Mark's, and St. Paul's. However, in 1940, only 20 percent at Harvard's freshmen came from the twelve most socially elite boarding schools, compared with 33 percent at Princeton and 35 percent at Yale (Karabel 2005: 188-9, 205).

I entered Columbia College in 1960 in a class that illustrates what would

The revolution between the Harvard entering classes of 1952 and 1960 was only partial because the chairman of its Committee on Admissions from 1952 to 1960, Wilbur Bender, tried desperately to obstruct it. In 1952, Bender wrote to Harvard's president, "[T]he last thing we want to do . . . is to stimulate more applicants from New York City" (Keller 2001: 51). In a report on Harvard's admissions policies, Bender advocated giving "considerable weight in both recruiting and selection" to athletes, especially in "the great American game of football." This would counter Harvard's reputation of being full of "pansies" and "decadent esthetes [sic]." It was a serious problem that Harvard had a strong appeal to "intellectual, musical or esthetic [sic] individuals," among whom "there is a large percentage of Jewish boys." In a speech to Harvard's Board of Overseers in 1954, Bender expressed concern that the proportion of private school graduates in Harvard's entering class had fallen below 50 percent; a further decline would cause Harvard to "lose its social prestige" (Karabel 2005: 252-3, 258). Harvard could maintain its historic character, "provided we don't raise the present academic level too much and do maintain our relationship with the private schools" (Keller 2001: 295).

Bender's views are important because the first paragraph of Harvard's description of its admissions policies that it submitted in the *Bakke* case, and which Justice Powell thought important enough to quote *verbatim* in his decision, was a direct quote from a document that Bender wrote to oppose giving greater importance to academic ability in admissions decisions (Karabel 2005: 279-82). In its submissions in the *Bakke* case, Harvard did not include Bender's accusation that the proponents of making academic ability the sole criterion for undergraduate admissions favored "graduate school admission criteria and goals" (Karabel 2005: 284). Not even Bender considered the possibility that academic considerations should not be the crucial factor in admission to graduate and professional schools. But the *Bakke* case was about admission to a medical school. Most other legal challenges to academic affirmative action have also involved medical and

---

have happened at that time if highly selective colleges admitted students nearly completely on the SAT. From the time my class arrived, it was called "Dudley's Folly" because the dean of admissions, David Dudley, based his admissions decisions overwhelmingly on SAT scores. When that class graduated, it won more fellowships than the graduating class of any other American college, despite its small size (675 students). But it was 90 percent Jewish. Of course, Dudley was immediately fired. His replacement, Henry Coleman, announced that he would give more consideration to character, geographical distribution, high school grades, and attendance at private schools. He also vowed to intensify recruitment of "minority" students.

law schools; and, as I have shown and will show repeatedly, American professional schools have always based admission decisions overwhelmingly on quantifiable academic criteria; with the sole exception of ethnic/racial discrimination (first against Jews, then against whites).

G. Faculty

The Jewish experience in American universities is also relevant to another common defense of affirmative action: the need for minority students to have minority professors as role models. Jewish students excelled at American universities when Jewish faculty members were nearly nonexistent and many of the professors who taught them were openly hostile. When Cornell Classics Professor Harry Caplan, who was Jewish, died in 1980, a letter was found in his desk signed by every member of the Cornell Classics Department in 1919: We "urge you to get into secondary teaching . . . .We have seen so many well-equipped Jews fail to secure appointments . . . brilliant scholars of international reputation, and yet unable to obtain a college position" (*Cornell Alumni News* (July 9, 1981): 7). In 1931, when Yale was considering appointing the eminent philosopher Morris Cohen, Professor William Phelps reported to the faculty that he is "Jewish and no gentleman. We don't need him." Cohen was not hired (Oren 2000: 132). In late 1933, President Conant of Harvard wrote about the prospect of hiring Jewish scientists who had lost their academic positions in Nazi Germany: "I think a deluge of . . . men of the Jewish race in scientific positions . . . would do a lot of harm" (Keller 2001: 155). Letters of recommendation written in the 1930s for Oscar Handlin, Bert Loewenberg, and Daniel Boorstin, all of whom became world-renowned historians, included praises like, "has none of the offensive traits which people associate with his race;" "by temperament and spirit . . . measures up to the whitest Gentile I know;" and "is a Jew, though not the kind to which one takes exception." Peter Novick, who quotes these recommendations (1988: 172-3), provides many similar examples. The author of the first two was the distinguished Harvard historian Arthur Schlesinger (Senior).

In 1948, two senior positions in Harvard's Economics Department became vacant. The Economics Department knew that "[t]he distinction and reputation of the Department for many years to come is at stake." Among the candidates was Paul Samuelson, who the year before had won the John Bates Clark Medal, which is awarded every two years to the most brilliant American economist under the age of forty. The appointment committee recognized that Samuelson had "a better record than anyone near his age in any field." But it did not choose him, at least partially because he was Jewish

(Keller 2001: 81-2; cf. 88, 96-7; Skousen 2001: 231, 353, 355). Samuelson later founded macroeconomics and became the first American to win the Nobel Prize in Economics.

Even at New York University's Washington Square campus, where in the 1930s over 90 percent of the students were Jewish, only eight faculty members were Jews; and seven of those were assistants with no prospects of promotion (Feuer 1982: 455-6). At the City College of New York, whose student body was 85 percent Jewish, the Mathematics and Sociology departments had a policy into the late 1930s of never hiring a Jew (Sachar 1992: 331).

In 1946, Yale College hired its first Jewish full professor, Paul Weiss, in philosophy. The head of the Philosophy Department, Charles Hendel, wrote, "I have the very highest opinion of his intellectual qualities . . . of his teaching abilities . . . [he is] a really great scholar. . . . So I welcome . . . the experiment with Weiss." It was an experiment because, as Hendel pointed out in the same letter, "It is difficult for men who like Weiss have been brought out of the lowliest social conditions to know how to behave in a society of genuine equality where it is not necessary to assert oneself" (Oren 2000: 282-4). As late as 1967, Harvard Classicist Sterling Dow opposed giving Glenn Bowersock tenure in Classics because he (mistakenly) thought that Bowersock was Jewish (Keller 2001: 243).

Nevertheless, by 1970 Yale's faculty was 22 percent Jewish, Harvard's was a third Jewish, and Columbia's was over half Jewish.[30]

CB BD

---

30. Oren 2000: 362; Lipset and Riesman 1975: 307; Hook 1979: 49. Anti-Semitism in faculty hiring is discussed by Oren 2000: 120-45, 163-6, 269-71.

CR EO

Chapter 4
Quotas Are Best: History Repeats Itself

Since Thucydides' *History of the Peloponnesian War* (I. 22) in the fifth century BC, historians have claimed that the study of history illuminates the present because the constancy of human nature causes actions and reactions to recur in similar ways. As a contribution to testing that claim, I will outline how the public university systems of California, Florida, and Texas reacted to bans on explicit racial and ethnic discrimination.

The University of California was forced to end racial and ethnic discrimination first by a decision of its Board of Regents in 1995, then by a state referendum in 1996. In 2000, Governor Jeb Bush of Florida, in order to forestall a referendum, issued an executive order banning the use of race in admission to Florida's state universities. In 1996, the U.S. Court of Appeals for the Fifth Circuit prohibited the state universities of Texas from practicing discrimination. In *Cheryl J. Hopwood, et al. v. State of Texas, et al.*, it ruled that Supreme Court decisions since *Bakke* rendered *Bakke* no longer valid. In 1997, the Texas legislature reacted to this decision by passing a law (Texas House Bill 588) that guaranteed admission to Texas state universities to all students who graduate in the top 10 percent of a Texas high school. In 2003, the Supreme Court reaffirmed the *Bakke* decision. However, the Texas legislature has not repealed Texas House Bill 588. Of the students admitted in 2009 to the University of Texas at Austin, more than 85 percent were admitted under the ten-percent rule. In 2005, the University of Colorado adopted the same policy of admitting all students in the top 10 percent of their high school classes.

All these university systems reacted to bans on explicit discrimination in the way Chang-Lin Tien, the chancellor of Berkeley, said Berkeley would react. In 1995, he was asked what Berkeley would do about the impending prohibition of racial discrimination in admissions. Chiang-Lin answered, "We can come up with some tricks" (Lubman 1995). The quotations below summarize the tricks that the public universities or California, Florida, and Texas have used, and their results:

[At Berkeley's law school] the number of entering students from underrepresented minority groups has more than doubled, from 15 in 1997 to 35 in 1998. Officials attributed the increase to more flexible admissions policies that de-emphasize scores on standardized tests (Mangan 1998).

[The president of the University of California recommended] that the university system adopt a less quantitative, more "holistic" set of admissions criteria (Selingo and Brainard 2001).

The University of California . . . has admitted more minority students [19.1 percent of the total] than it did when it relied on race-based admissions policies [18.8 percent] (Fogg 2002).

The Texas legislature voted that the state university should admit the top 10 percent of the graduating class of every Texas high school eligible for the state university, a far more radical lowering of standards for eligibility than any university administrator would have proposed. Even more remarkably, the Regents of the University of California, who had earlier voted that race should not be taken into account in admissions decisions, have voted that the top four percent of every California high school should be eligible for admission to the state university system! (Glazer 1999)

Florida Governor Jeb Bush announced . . . that the state's 10 public colleges would stop using race as a factor in undergraduate and graduate admissions . . . Instead . . . the institutions would automatically admit the top 20 percent of the graduates of every high school in the state . . . . The Governor said that he wanted to move forward with the policy before the state could be forced . . . through a ballot referendum to eliminate affirmative action. . . . A recent poll showed that Florida voters would approve such a measure [eliminating affirmative action] 2 to 1 (Selingo 1999).

The first freshman class selected to Florida's state college system since Governor Jeb Bush put an end to race-based admissions has shown, instead of a decrease in minority enrollment, an increase of 12 percent (Bragg 2000).

Let us now look at what these changes mean in practice. In Texas, George Mitzner was graduated 67th in a class of 640 from Bellaire High School with a combined Verbal+Math SAT score of 1470 (in the upper one percent of test-takers) and a high school grade-point-average (GPA) of 4.49, which included many advanced placement courses. But he was not in the top ten percent of his class, so the undergraduate business school of the University of Texas (UT) rejected his application. Erica Brown graduated from Worthington High School with a 3.5 GPA, none of her courses were advanced placement, and her combined Verbal+Math SAT score was 830 (in the lowest 18 percent). But she was in the top ten percent of her class and so was accepted by UT. Most of the students who graduate in the top ten percent at Worthington High School have SAT scores in the 800s.[31]

Two black students in Miami, Florida offer another illustration of the absurdity of using class rank. Michael Joseph took courses in subjects such as cooking at Edison Senior High School.[32] His high school GPA was 4.0, which put him fourth out of 370 students, so he could easily get into any college that admits on the basis of class rank. Joseph's Verbal+Math SAT score was 1000; Edison's valedictorian's Verbal+Math SAT score was 1080; its salutatorian scored 1010. At Edison, as in 13 percent of Florida's high schools, a C+ (2.5) GPA is in the upper twenty percent of the class and so qualifies for admission to the University of Florida system. The other student is Leah Burton. She took five advanced placement tests, the lowest mark in her entire high school career was a B, in an honors calculus course, and her Verbal+Math SAT score was 1150. But she was only 213th in her class of 634 at Palmetto Senior High School. Consequently, she could not get into the University of Florida system, which has the lowest class-rank requirement (upper 20 percent) of any university system that uses this criterion.

The contrast with white students at Palmetto Senior High School is even more striking. For example, Louis Fernandez moved to Miami from Italy in his junior year and had a 1210 Verbal+Math SAT score, but was not in the upper twenty percent of his class.[33]

The SAT provides an unambiguous comparison of students everywhere, no matter what schools they attend or courses they take. High school grades are distorted by the courses students take, the type of schools they attend and many subjective factors that I will discuss in Chapter 12. But class rank is by far the most unreliable of all measures of academic performance. That is why these university systems adopted it.

The *Journal of Blacks in Higher Education*, whose purpose is to promote academic affirmative action, observed, "Let us suppose we are going to give

31. Nissimov 2000. I will remind the reader that until 2005, the SAT consisted of two tests; Verbal and Mathematical Reasoning. So the maximum possible score was 800+800=1600. The SAT scores reported in this chapter would have been considerably lower before the 1995 re-centering, which I discuss in Appendix III. E.

32. Fifty-seven percent of American high schools include all high school courses a student takes in his GPA (Camara, et al., 2003: 5).

33. Selingo 2000. In 2005, a College Board study found that only half of the blacks and Hispanics who rank in the top tenth of their class score over 600 on either section of the SAT; all [yes, all] the whites in the top 10 percent do (MacDonald 2007).

a prize for the worst idea of the past year . . . The prize might well go to the 'X Percent' plans for college admissions," since it penalizes students for taking difficult courses, and it promotes residential segregation by conferring tremendous benefits on blacks who attend completely or nearly completely black schools."[34]

The liberal *New Republic* of December 27, 1999 ("Admitting Error:" 9) pointed out a more serious result:

> The ten percent plan Texas adopted has vindicated the professors' fears. Minority enrollments at the Austin campus, the University of Texas' flagship, have been restored to something like their pre-affirmative-action level, but at the cost of dramatically lowering the academic qualifications of entering freshmen. To address the gaps in preparation, Austin has scrambled to provide special classes and teachers for pre-med students with SAT scores 200 points below the university average. This is a tragic waste of resources. Like the handful of other great public universities in America—Virginia, Berkeley, UCLA, and Michigan—[The University of Texas at] Austin distinguished itself as a research powerhouse, fueling the development of the largest high-tech corridor outside of Silicon Valley. . . . [It has now been] forced to redirect its resources toward remedial education, which it is ill-equipped to provide.

The University of California (UC) reacted to the ban on open racial and ethnic discrimination with two other changes in its criteria for admission to its undergraduate divisions, besides making every applicant in the top four percent of his high school class eligible: it put more emphasis on non-academic qualifications, and it assigned greater importance to SAT-II tests (in specific subjects) than to SAT-I (aptitude) tests. These two changes circumvented the ban on explicit racial and ethnic discrimination both for admission to all of UC's campuses and for admission to UC's most prestigious campuses, Berkeley and UCLA, which admit only those in the top of the pool of students admitted by UC.

Of the non-academic considerations that UC has adopted, the one that seems the most unobjectionable is whether an applicant has overcome adversity. Consequently, that is the new consideration to which UC has given by far the most publicity. However, UC does not determine adversity by family income. It has not used this obvious criterion for two reasons. First, family income can be clearly and easily measured. Second, as will be discussed, poor whites and Asians are much more academically able than poor (and

---

34. "Fixed Percentage College Admissions Plans Are a Fixed Formula for Racial Segregation." *JBHE* 18 (Summer 2000): 14-15.

even rich) blacks and Hispanics. "Latino legislative leader Marco Antonio Firebaugh, a force behind adoption of the new system, [explained] . . . 'We found that using poverty yields a lot of poor white and poor Asian kids.'" (Most of the poor white and Asian students with high academic achievement were Eastern European and Vietnamese immigrants (MacDonald 2007).) So, UC came up with a wide range of personal, family, and psychological obstacles that applicants could report. "In some cases university staffers . . . have coached minority students on how to identify and present their hardships" in the essays they send with their applications. "The advice outreach workers give isn't guesswork: Some of them do double duty as evaluators of applicants." This expensive (to the taxpayers) and cumbersome system for practicing racial and ethnic discrimination has fulfilled its purpose. In 2003, Berkeley admitted 374 applicants with Verbal+Math SAT scores below 1,000, almost all of them "students of color." It rejected 3,218 applicants with Verbal+Math SAT scores above 1,400 (MacDonald 2007). In 2001, the average combined Verbal+Math SAT score of Hispanics who were *admitted* to UCLA was 1168; the average of Asians and non-Hispanic whites who were *rejected* was 1174 and 1209, respectively. (The average of Asians and non-Hispanic whites who were accepted was 1344 and 1355.)[35]

The information and quotations in the paragraph above that are not from MacDonald are all from an article by Daniel Golden (2002). He began it with the following example:

Stanley Park felt as if the University of California, Los Angeles, had revamped its admissions criteria just for him. UCLA was looking for students who had overcome "life challenges," such as family illness, being raised by a single parent or being the first in the family to attend college. After Mr. Park's parents, Korean immigrants of modest means, divorced three years ago, he lived with his mother. When she developed breast cancer, he began tutoring children to help pay the rent. Despite his work commitment, he scored an impressive 1500 out of 1600 on his SAT . . . exam. UCLA and . . . Berkeley both rejected Mr. Park.

Blanca Martinez also grew up in a working-class immigrant family, and also helped support it when her mother had breast cancer. Her SAT score, though, was 390 points below Mr. Park's. Both Berkeley and UCLA admitted her.

---

35. In 1999, the University of California spent $250 million of the taxpayers' money on efforts to increase the number of minority applicants ("Affirmative Action in California: Passed." *Economist* (April 8, 2000): 53). It undoubtedly spends much more now.

I point out above that the average SAT score of whites who were rejected and accepted by UCLA in 2001 was higher than the average SAT score of Asians who were rejected and accepted. Golden nearly certainly could have found a white applicant whose rejection was even more blatantly unfair than Mr. Park's. The reason that he chose Mr. Park was probably that he shared the unwillingness of most critics of affirmative action, which I will discuss in Section D of Chapter 19, to acknowledge that its main victims are whites and thus their tendency to represent its victims as Asians.

In fact, Asians are major beneficiaries of UC's radical change in the relative importance it assigns to SAT-I (aptitude) tests and SAT-II tests (in specific subjects). In 2001, it began to require applicants to take three SAT-II tests and to assign twice as much weight to each of the three SAT-II tests as to each of the two SAT-I tests. Why? The UC administration must have known that, except for the situation discussed below, scores on achievement tests correlate very closely with scores on aptitude tests, including the SAT (Ceci, et al., 1998: 290; Hauser 1998: 229).

The reason that UC assigned so much more importance to SAT-IIs than to SAT-Is is that SAT-IIs provide two valuable aids to practice discrimination by stealth. First, they increase the complexity of admissions criteria and so make clear comparisons between accepted applicants and groups difficult. Second, all applicants who were raised speaking a foreign language easily obtain an extremely high score on the SAT-II test in that language, even though their knowledge of it is unrelated to their ability to learn a subject in an academic setting; and, consequently, is unrelated to their performance on aptitude tests. In 2001, the average score on the SAT-II Spanish test of students at Jefferson High School in California, whose student body is pre-dominantly Hispanic, was 715 (out of a possible 800). Their average score on the SAT-I Verbal test was 390; on the SAT-I Math test, 402. But since the SAT-II Spanish test now counts as much as both SAT-I tests combined, the number of seniors from Jefferson High School who were accepted by UC increased by more than 50 percent (Golden 2001).

For the same reason, in 2003, 74 percent of all students who took the SAT-II in Chinese, 64 percent of all students who took it in Korean, and 48 percent of all students who took it in Japanese got scores above 749. In the same year, only nine percent of the students who took the SAT-II in English Writing and seven percent who took it in English Literature got above 749.

SAT-II language tests cannot benefit blacks, so the University of California has simply continued the same type of pro-black discrimination that it practiced before it was made illegal. In the years between the prohibition of racial discrimination and 2002, every 100 SAT-I points increased an applicant's chance to be admitted by UCLA by 1.38 times, but being black made an applicant 3.6 times more likely to be admitted than a non-Hispanic white with the same SAT-I score and the same high school grades (Wood 2003A: 20-21); and pro-black (and pro-Hispanic) discrimination in admissions to UCLA has increased since then (Erlandson 2007).

Another means that universities have adopted to circumvent legal bans on discrimination is by expanding transfers from community colleges. In 1998, the citizens of Washington State voted in a referendum to end affirmative action. As a result, "Like campuses in California and Texas . . . the University of Washington is using college-transfer policies, in part, as a way around the ban" (Hebel 2000). As with most substitutes for open discrimination, this takes much more time and energy, yields worse students, and has harmful side effects.

> [A]dministrators say recruiting minority freshmen has consumed much more of their attention since the referendum was passed. . . . To make transferring easier, administrators at Washington this year changed how applicants' grade-point averages are calculated. For instance, if a community-college student has repeated a course, the university will now count only the second grade, not the average of both. . . . [T]he University of California and the state's community-college system agreed in 1997 to try to increase the number of transfers by 33 percent by 2005-6 (Hebel 2000).

Professional schools have also concocted a host of devices to practice racial and ethnic discrimination. Thanks to them, in 1997, the first year that racial discrimination was supposed to be banned at the University of California university system, UCLA's medical school admitted 10.4 percent of its black and Hispanic applicants, but only 3.0 percent of its white and Asian applicants; even though the average undergraduate grade-point-average (GPA) of its white-Asian applicants was 3.79 and their average score on the subtests of the Medical College Admission Test (MCAT) was 11.6, while the average GPA and MCAT score its black-Hispanic applicants were 3.42 and 9.8 (Wood 2003A: 21; www.lagriffedulion.f2s.com/prop209.htm).

In 2002, the entering class of the University of Washington Law School had only two fewer black, Hispanic, and Native American students than the entering class of 1998, when Washington's citizens voted to make discrimination illegal. The most prestigious public law school on the West Coast, Berkeley's, had *more* minority students in its entering class of 2002 than it had in 1996, the last year that discrimination was legal. Berkeley's law school admits on the basis of a numerical index that is derived from applicants' college grades and scores on the Law School Admission Test. In

2002, of its applicants with index scores between 235 and 239, it admitted five percent of the whites but 75 percent of the blacks (MacDonald 2007). The University of Michigan Law School (UMLS) admitted every black applicant with Law School Admission Test (LSAT) scores between 159-160 and an undergraduate GPA of 3.00 or higher. But it admitted only 22 percent of white and Asian applicants with a LSAT score of 164-66 and a GPA between 3.25 and 3.49 (*Grutter v. Bollinger* #76-7; Wood 2003: 131). Nevertheless, despite the ostensible ban on racial preferences in California, the difference in average LSAT scores between blacks and whites entering Berkeley's law school in 2002 was the same as the average racial differ-ence at UMLS. UCLA's law school admitted several black and Hispanic applicants who were rejected by UMLS (Golden 2003).

Conspicuously absent from the devices used to achieve these results is consideration of applicants' socioeconomic background. The first reaction of UCLA Law School to the ban on racial and ethnic discrimination was "a formula giving preference to students from families and communities with low incomes and limited education. . . . [But] [t]he main beneficiaries were working class and lower-middle class white and Asian students . . . . [B]lack enrollment fell to 10 from 19" (Golden 2003). Herma Hill Kay, the dean of Berkeley's law school, explained that considerations of socioeconomic background do not increase the number of eligible blacks because, "African Americans who apply to our law school are not disadvantaged. Their mothers and fathers are professionals with good family incomes" (*NR* 1998: 6).

California's state community colleges have also come up with tricks to circumvent the referendum by which California's citizens made racial discrimination illegal. For their nursing program, which supplies 70 per-cent of California's practical nurses, they have made all students with a high school average of C or above eligible. They then allot places among eligible candidates by lottery or by who applied first. Consequently, many of their students are no longer capable of being taught "the single-variable algebra problem required to calculate medication dosages" (e.g., If X=100 cubic centimeters of a medication, then how many cubic centimeters is 2X?) (Leovy 1999).

Texas, California, and Florida are part of a nationwide trend. The *Journal of Blacks in Higher Education* of Winter 2001/2002 reported that by the end of 2001,

> [A]t least 383 of the nation's 1,788 four-year colleges and universi-ties no longer require students to take either the SAT or ACT test. . . . Public university systems in Arkansas, Kansas, Maine, Louisiana, Oregon . . . no longer require students to submit standardized test scores. In addition, some of the nation's most prestigious small liberal

arts colleges . . . have dropped the SAT requirement.[36]

The *Journal of Blacks in Higher Education* of Winter 2005/2006 reported that 730 four-year colleges and universities no longer require either the SAT or ACT for admissions, up from about 100 in 1994.[37]

In July 1995, the Board of Regents of the University of California system banned racial discrimination in employment, as well as admissions; and that prohibition was reinforced in November 1996, when the voters of California passed the California Civil Rights Initiative (Proposition 209; now Article I, Section 31 of the California state constitution), which prohibited considering "race, sex, color, ethnicity or national origin as a criterion for either discrimination against, or granting preferential treatment to, any individual or group in the operation of the State's system of public employment, public education or public contracting." But these prohibitions have had as little effect on hiring as on admissions: "Affirmative-action officers in California say they do the same job they always have. Most search-committee leaders [who look for new faculty] say their tactics haven't changed either . . . 'We're doing what we were doing before, but we're not making a big deal of it'."[38]

Cʒ ঽ৲

---

36. "California and the SAT: What If?": 58-9.

37. "The Growing List of Colleges That Have Rejected the Use of the SAT:" 45-6.

38. Schneider 1998. For more information on how the University of California system is blatantly circumventing the legal ban on racial discrimination in admissions and faculty hiring, I strongly recommend MacDonald 2007.

ᘒ ᙍ

Chapter 5
Defining Minority and Race

[I]n immigration policy, the reforms of 1965, intended to purge national origin quotas but not to expand immigration or to change its character, produced instead a flood of new arrivals . . . . [T]he ancestry of most immigrants . . . entitled them to . . . priority over . . . . native-born Americans under affirmative action regulations. Congress in the 1960s never intended to create such a system. And it is doubtful that any Congress (or White House) today, in the twenty-first century, would build such a system anew and defend it before voters (Graham 2002: 8).

In the rest of this book, I use the word *minority* with its current American meaning: a group that is eligible for affirmative action. I also follow current American English usage by sometimes using *minority* as an adjective, as in "minority student."

Hispanics have overtaken blacks as the most numerous beneficiaries of affirmative action. However, affirmative action for blacks is more extreme and much more studied than for Hispanics and Native Americans. Therefore this book, like most discussions of affirmative action, concentrates on blacks. When only blacks are mentioned, the reader can assume that the practice under discussion nearly certainly applies to Hispanics and Native Americans in a more moderate form.

Most people have no idea of the slapdash nature of the process that led to current definitions of minorities. I describe it at length in Appendix I. In 1977, when the process was approaching completion, the federal Office of Management and Budget issued Statistical Policy Directive 15 ("Race and Ethnic Standards for Federal Statistics and Administrative Reporting"), which summed up racial/ethnic categorization at that time:

White—an individual, not of Hispanic origin, with origins in any of the original peoples of Europe, North America, or the Middle East [which includes North Africa], black—an individual, not of Hispanic origin, with origins in any of the black racial groups of Africa. Hispanic—a person of Mexican, Puerto Rican, Cuban, Central or South American, or other Spanish culture or origin, regardless of race. This does not include persons of Portuguese descent or persons from Central or South America who are not of Spanish origin or culture.

Asian or Pacific Islander—a person with origins in any of the original peoples of the Far East, Southeast Asia, the Indian Subcontinent, or the Pacific Islands. . . . American Indian or Alaskan Native—a person with origins in any of the original peoples of North America who maintains cultural identification through tribal affiliation or has community recognition as an American Indian or Alaskan native (Chou 1996: 52, 55).

The reader has probably noticed the careless style of this directive; for instance, the shift, for no discernible reason, from "an individual" to "a person." Even more striking is the directive's carelessness with regard to content, especially when defining Hispanic. The first sentence of the definition of Hispanic seems to include everyone from Spanish-speaking Latin America, "regardless of race." The next sentence, which states exceptions, is odd. "Persons . . . who are not of Spanish origin or culture" should, logically, include "persons of Portuguese descent." So, why are the latter mentioned separately? The most plausible explanation is that "persons of Portuguese descent" was meant to exclude Brazilians; and "persons . . . who are not of Spanish origin or culture" was meant to exclude the large Italian-origin and German-origin populations of Argentina and Uruguay. Whatever were the intentions of the definition of Hispanic, it did not explicitly mention Brazil. This was a serious omission. Brazil takes up half the area of South America and has a large non-white population. Several federal agencies solved this omission by adding non-white Brazilians to affirmative-action recipients; others added all Brazilians. So, in programs supervised by some federal agencies, white Argentineans of Spanish descent are eligible for affirmative action and increase the diversity of the organization they join. But that is not true of white Brazilians of Spanish descent or of white Argentineans of Portuguese descent. If a business or government agency hires or promotes too many whites of Brazilian origin (who are simply whites), it can restore its diversity by hiring and promoting whites of Cuban origin (who are Hispanics).[39]

39. At the present time (2010), on the federal level, the Office of Management and Budget still uses the definition of *Hispanic* that it used in 1977 (above), as does the Equal Employment Opportunity Commission and the Department of Labor's Office of Federal Contract Compliance Programs. The Department of Transport and the Small Business Administration define

The process by which state and municipal governments arrived at their definitions of minorities was even more haphazard and jerry-built. I leave it to the reader to research this subject, if he or she has the time and a strong stomach for nonsense.

On the federal level, the Small Business Administration (SBA) played an important role in defining and extending affirmative-action categories, as I discuss in Appendix I. In 1973, the SBA designated five groups as eligible for preferential treatment: "blacks, American Indians, Spanish-Americans, Asian-Americans and Puerto Ricans." Hugh Graham observed (2002: 216, note 16) that "the curious distinction between Spanish-American and Puerto Rican testifies to the imprecision and general sloppiness of the closed bureaucratic processes that produced official minority designations to govern affirmative action policy."

Graham also pointed out (2002: 140, cf. 141, 145) that the "closed bureaucratic policymaking" that created these categories, which have had such a profound effect on American life, "was largely devoid not only of public testimony, but even of public awareness that policy was being made. . . . Closed deliberations facilitated sheltered bargaining." For example, the 1970 census forms were already at the printers with instructions to classify the large majority of Americans of Latin American origin racially as white and ethnically by national origin (e.g., Mexican American), like Italian Americans, just as previous censuses had done. But President Nixon lost Texas in the 1968 election because he won only six percent of the Mexican American vote. Consequently he acceded to the demands of a Mexican American Affairs committee member to add a Hispanic category. Thus, Hispanics came into existence (Glazer 2002: 27; Chavez 2002: 95-6, 106). The first draft of the 1970 census, like previous censuses, classified Asian Indians as white, as did the draft of the Federal Interagency Committee on Education's categories for federal programs. In response to Indian lobbying, Asian Indians were reclassified as Asians in the final draft, and so attained minority status (Glazer 2002: 27; Wright 1994: 50).

In pre-affirmative action American racial classifications, white was a catch-all category for everyone whose race did not matter; that is, everyone who was not subject to institutionalized discrimination, which meant everyone who was not an American Negro, Oriental, or Native American. Sattareh Farmaian related in her autobiography (1992: 170-72) that when she was

---

Hispanic as "persons of Mexican, Puerto Rican, Cuban, Dominican, Central or South American, or others of Spanish or Portuguese culture or origin, regardless of race." This definition could include immigrants from Spain and Portugal. Other federal agencies include all Brazilian immigrants but explicitly exclude immigrants from Spain and Portugal.

a student at the University of Southern California in 1948, she married a student from India. Farmaian was Iranian and, therefore, indistinguishable in appearance from southern Europeans; but her husband was brown skinned. In 1945, California had enacted a law prohibiting marriage between whites and "Negroes, mulattoes, Mongolians [i.e., Chinese and Japanese] and Malays." The clerk at the Los Angeles City Hall had never seen an Asian Indian, so he refused to give them a marriage license. However, when her fiancé showed him his passport, which proved he was not a Negro or mulatto, the clerk gave them the license. His brown complexion was irrelevant.[40]

Even foreign Negroes were "white." In 1948, four black university students from the West Indies were refused service at a lunch counter in Washington, DC. But when they showed their British passports, the waitress apologized and explained that she had mistaken them for "niggers."[41]

Even more striking is Piri Thomas' account (1967/1997: 185-9) of his experiences in the South in the 1940s. Thomas was a Puerto Rican Negro, who was born and raised in New York. On a trip through the South, he sat down at a lunch counter in Mobile, Alabama and was told, "We don't serve nigras." He then went to Galveston, Texas, where he met a Mexican American. He told the Mexican he wanted to break the ultimate racial taboo by going to a white brothel, even though "my hair ain't good [i.e., kinky] and my nose is too flat and my skin is too dark." The Mexican told him, "If you do not speak a word of English, you may pass for Puerto Rican." When they entered the brothel, the manager welcomed the Mexican, but he assumed that Thomas was an American Negro. However, when Thomas pretended that he did not understand English, the manager had no objections to him either. The manager told the Mexican, "[W]e got all kinds of people coming in, all kinds of foreigners . . . from Columbia and Peru and Cuba, and that's all right, but we got to keep these damn niggers down." After Thomas had intercourse with the prostitute and was about to leave, he started talking to her in English. "I watched her smile fall off and a look of horror fill the empty space it left."

Current affirmative action racial categories are just as capricious. I have discussed the absurdities involved in defining Hispanic. Black in the United States means anyone with any traceable black ancestry. An extensive study has been done of adopted black, white, and mixed race black-white

---

40. The governor of California who signed the bill prohibiting interracial marriage was Earl Warren, who as Chief Justice of the United States Supreme Court (1953-69) started it on the path of anti-white discrimination.

41. *Segregation in Washington: A Report of the National Committee on Segregation in the Nation's Capital* (Chicago: National Committee on Segregation in the Nation's Capital, 1948): 6.

children who were raised from infancy by upper- and upper-middle-class white parents, who have an average of 16.9 years of formal education and an average IQ of 115 (in the upper 16 percent of the American population). When the children were 17-18 years old, on the measures of mental ability and academic achievement that were studied—IQ, vocabulary, reading comprehension, school grades—the difference between the black adopted children and white adopted children who were raised in the same families from infancy was the same as the difference between blacks and whites in the area of the United States in which they lived. The adopted children in the study who had one black and one white biological parent scored midway between the average of the white and black adoptees who were raised in the same family from infancy (Levin 1994; Lynn 1994). Moreover, the parents who adopted twelve of the interracial children mistakenly thought that both their parents were black. But their average IQ was the same as that of the other bi-racial children.[42]

The mothers of most adopted bi-racial children are unmarried. The children of black-white marriages are undoubtedly more intelligent, because in 2004, nine percent of blacks with a four-year college degree had non-black spouses, but only five percent of married black high school dropouts had non-black spouses.[43] Nearly certainly, their non-black spouses had similar levels of education.

The SAT does not have a mixed-race category. But the ACT, which is the standardized test that many colleges in the Middle West, Rocky Mountains, and Deep South prefer, used to have a mixed-race category, which it has

42. Scarr and Weinberg 1976: 732-3. Sandra Scarr and Richard Weinberg undertook this study to try to prove that social environment influences mental ability and achievement. They acknowledged that every other adoption study found absolutely no influence of the adopting family and social background on IQ, academic performance, or temperament (e.g., Scarr and Weinberg 1983: 264-6: Scarr and McCartney 1983: 429-32). However, they thought that they could find some social influence if they studied black children raised by white parents. The media kept reporting that Scarr and Weinberg found that black children raised by white upper- and upper-middle-class parents had the same IQ and academic record as white upper- and upper-middle-class children. However, all Scarr and Weinberg claimed was that they found some social influence on the black adopted children. They kept reporting that result (e.g., *Intelligence*, 16, 1992: 117-35) until 1994, when Michael Levin and Richard Lynn reanalyzed their data (*Intelligence* 19, 1: 13-27) and pointed out that it came to the conclusions I have outlined.

43. "Interracial Marriage on the Rise." *Journal of Blacks in Higher Education* (Summer 2005): 44-5.

discontinued. In 2004, the average ACT score of "multiracial" students (on a
1-36 scale) was 20.9, much closer to the average score of whites (21.8) and
Asians (21.9) than to the average score of blacks (17.1), Mexican Americans
(18.4), Native Americans (18.8), or "Puerto Ricans/Hispanics" (18.8). Since
the beneficiaries of affirmative action are the most intelligent members of
the eligible groups, a large (and growing) proportion of its "black" beneficiaries must be mostly white. I point out in Section B of Chapter 19 that of
the black undergraduates at Harvard in 2003, two-thirds were from either
immigrant or non-immigrant mixed-race families. Some are undoubtedly
indistinguishable in appearance from whites. During the 1990 census, 5.8
percent of the people who classified themselves as black were seen as
white by the census interviewer. (Wright 1994: 53) The proportion must be
considerably higher now. Of Hispanic beneficiaries of affirmative action, a
large proportion is completely of European origin.

In this book, I use "white" with the meaning that it usually has in the
United States: anyone who is not eligible for affirmative action. Therefore,
it does not include people who are classified as black and Native American
but are indistinguishable in appearance from people of European origin; and
it does not include Americans who are completely of European origin but
whose ancestors came from Spanish-speaking Latin America. I will use the
term "racial discrimination" as a synonym for affirmative action because
affirmative action is based on categories determined by ancestry, which,
consequently, are as immutable as if they were based on clearly perceptible
physical features.

Ancestry is crucial. For example, Dartmouth admitted a blond-haired,
blue-eyed applicant over much better qualified applicants because he had
a Native American ancestor (Sowell 1993: 159); and a business owner in
California qualified for a government contract that was open to only minority
business owners because one of his great-great grandparents was a Cherokee
Indian (Zelnick 1996: 301). Consequently, the number of Americans who
classify themselves as Native Americans increased from 509,000 in the 1960
census, to 1.96 million in the 1990 census, to 4.12 million in the 2000 census;
thus increasing by eight times the proportion of "Native Americans" that
every American institution, public and private, must employ at all levels,
loan money to, etc., in order to avoid being judged presumptively guilty
of discrimination against Native Americans. During the 1990 census, 70
percent of the people who classified themselves as Native American were
seen as white by the census interviewer. (Wright 1994: 53) The proportion
is undoubtedly higher now. However, since the 1970 census, it is a person's
self-classification that determines his racial category.[44]

44. For the same reasons, the number of Australians who classify

Much more important is that it is illegal for an employer to override or even to question a job applicant's self-identification as a member of a minority (i.e., affirmative-action) group based on the employer's visual observation.[45]

The Census Bureau modified the 2000 census to try to diminish the absurdities of American racial classifications. The 2000 census allowed respondents to indicate more than one racial identity. That applies to many Americans. Even in 1990, 40 percent more babies were born to parents who were a combination of Native American and non-Native American than to two Native American parents (Welch and Gruhl 1998:162). In the 2000 census, 32 percent of second-generation Hispanics and 57 percent of third-generation Hispanics were married to non-Hispanics; 34 percent of second-generation Asians and 54 percent of third-generation Asians were married to non-Asians (Rodriguez 2003: 96). By 2004, more than 12 percent of married blacks under the age of 30 had a non-black spouse.[46]

However, the Office of Management and Budget instructed all federal agencies to consider everyone who identifies himself on the 2000 census as a mixture of white and a "minority race" as a member of the minority race for the purposes of "civil rights monitoring and enforcement" (i.e., enforcing racial discrimination). For instance, 2.48 million respondents checked only the Native American box and another 1.64 million checked the Native American box and the box for another race. But all federal agencies will work on the premise that there are 4.12 million Native Americans in the United States. As Stephan Thernstrom observed (2002B: 35), "The United States is the only country in the world in which a white woman can give birth to a black baby but a black woman cannot give birth to a white baby."

Black ancestors are even more valuable than Native American ancestors. A much publicized example involved the Malone brothers. When Paul and Philip Malone were children in Boston, they used to hang out around fire stations and dream of becoming firemen. Their dream seemed to have been shattered when they failed the Massachusetts civil service examination for

themselves as Aborigines increased by 42 percent between 1981 and 1986 (Sowell 2004: 9).

45. Office of Federal Contract Compliance Programs; FAQ: "May an employer override an individual's self-identification of race, gender or ethnicity based on the employer's visual observation?" "No. OFCCP's policy is that deference should be given to an individual's self-identification and it should not be questioned or overridden by an employer based on the employer's visual observation."

46. "Interracial Marriage on the Rise." *Journal of Blacks in Higher Education* (Summer 2005): 44-5.

firemen by a wide margin. But two years later, they took the exam again, identified themselves as blacks, and passed with grades of 57 percent and 69 percent. (The passing grade for whites was 82 percent.) They were members of the Boston Fire Department for ten years, when the Fire Department Commissioner, who knew Philip Malone personally, saw their names on a list of blacks proposed for promotion to lieutenant and began an investigation into their racial identity. (Philip Malone had the highest score of any black on the lieutenant's exam, although his score was lower than the scores of 39 whites.) The Malones are fair complexioned. They claimed that they learned they were black after they took the first examination when their mother discovered a sepia photograph of her grandmother, whom she said was black. However, Judge Wilkins of the Massachusetts Supreme Court and the Massachusetts Department of Personnel Administration (DPA) rejected their claim, and they were fired. According to David Haley, the head of the DPA, the Malones' worst crime was against the two "minorities who would have been selected to serve as Boston firefighters . . . As a result of the action of these two individuals [the Malones] . . . those two individuals [the two minorities] will never have that opportunity."

In response to the Malone scandal, Mayor Flynn of Boston ordered an investigation into the racial claims of the employees of Boston's fire department, police department, and schools. In the fire department, the Hispanic claims of eleven firemen were investigated, two others who had claimed they were Hispanic resigned, and five were required "to prove that they are not white" (i.e., that they had a black ancestor). If they could prove that, then they would be qualified to be firemen and would add to the diversity of the fire department ("Color Them Black." *Time* (October 31, 1988): 19; Hernandez 1989, 1988).

Fraudulent claims of minority status must be at least as common in applications for university admissions as in applications for hiring and promotion. I have mentioned the huge preferences that the University of Michigan awards for having an ancestor who is black, Native American, or from Spanish-speaking Latin America. That is typical, as I will demonstrate at length. As I will also demonstrate, an applicant knows that minority identification will gain him even greater preferences in admission to graduate or professional school and throughout the rest of his life. How many politically correct university administrators are willing to question a student's racial identification, especially since a blue-eyed blond legitimately qualifies as a minority if he has an ancestor who is Native American, black, or Latin American?

All sorts of proofs of eligibility are required of applicants for social security disability, driver's licenses, etc., but only self-identification is required for the immense benefits conferred by minority status.

In an article in the *California Law Review* of 1994 (pages 1231-85), entitled "Administering Identity: The Determination of 'Race' in Race-Conscious Law," Christopher Ford outlined the blatant non-sense of the current American non-system of defining race and pointed out (1283) that the United States has "never confront[ed] head-on the dilemmas of [racial] categorization [because] . . . the U. S. has managed to pretend that such choices are not made." This avoidance is disastrous because (1232), "Race . . . is a cornerstone of modern jurisprudence." Ford, who supports affirmative action, analyzed how castes are defined in India and how races were defined in the American South and South Africa when they were ruled by whites. He concluded (1284-85):

> If we are serious about writing laws and regulations tying benefits to racial or ethnic categorization, it may no longer be possible to avoid taking a hard look at the process by which we define groups . . . . India, South Africa, and a handful of old Jim Crow [American South] jurisdictions confront[ed] the dilemmas of classification with relative honesty.

An honest attempt to confront the dilemmas of racial classification was made by Luther Wright Jr. in an article in the *Vanderbilt Law Review* of 1995.[47] He mentioned cases of "racial fraud," like the Malones, and pointed out (518), correctly, that since the beginning of government-enforced affirmative action, "society's failure to define race substantively is one of the most compelling legal problems facing the nation;" and (550) that especially "the Hispanic classification" "calls the entire racial classifications scheme into question."

Wright proposed (563) that all Americans be assigned to one of five racial categories. Four—African Americans, Asian Americans, European Americans, and Native Americans—would be determined by whether a majority of a person's ancestors are from sub-Saharan Africa, Asia east of Afghanistan, Europe, or the aboriginal peoples of North, Central, and South America. The fifth—Biracial Americans—would consist of both Americans whose ancestors are from two or more racial groups and Americans most of whose ancestors are from North Africa and the Middle East. (North Africans and Middle Easterners are now classified as white.) All people now classified as Hispanic would be assigned to one of these categories. Since the determining factor would be majority of ancestry, it would be irrelevant if the Malones had proved that their great-grandmother was black.

---

47. "Who's Black, Who's White, and Who Cares: Reconceptualizing the United States' Definition of Race and Racial Classifications:" 513-69.

In his concluding section, "Enforcing Racial Classifications under the Sociopolitical Approach" (566-8), Wright advocated entering a person's race on his birth certificate. "Those who falsely allege their race should be charged with racial fraud and subject to criminal penalties."

Wright's classifications need refinement. He pointed out (page 538) that his inclusion of Americans of North African and Middle Eastern origin in his Biracial category acknowledges the legitimacy of the "significant amount of litigation" that Americans from these regions have brought to be reclassified as non-white. However, most people who live between the Mediterranean and Pakistan, outside of the Arabian Peninsula, are physically indistinguishable from southern Europeans; as are at least half of North Africans west of Egypt. Indeed, for centuries some French geographers have labelled North Africa as *l'Afrique blanche* (white Africa). Moreover, Wright's Asian category contains several clearly distinguishable races: Orientals; brown Caucasians from India, Pakistan, and Bangladesh; and Austronesians (a racial category that includes Malays, Indonesians, and Filipinos).

His proposal that the race of every American must be officially recorded in his birth certificate and that "racial fraud" be a punishable crime may seem harsh. After all, it was not until October 1938 that the Nazi government of Germany stamped *J* for *Jude* (Jew) into German Jews' passports, and that was at the insistence of the Swiss government to enable it to keep out German Jewish refugees. However, if affirmative action and diversity are to be practiced, they would be manifestly fairer and more sensible if racial categories were clearly defined and legally enforced.

Wright's proposals would also bring practice into line with rhetoric. Upon taking office, President Clinton boasted that his administration would "look like America;" that is, it would reflect the racial makeup of the United States. He also urged the American legal, medical, and teaching professions to radically lower entrance standards in order to "look like America" (Selingo 1999A). Yet it took him 17 months before nominating a chairman of the Equal Employment Opportunity Commission, during which time the position was vacant, because he was looking for a suitable Puerto Rican (not just Hispanic) nominee.[48] A Puerto Rican can be a member of any race, and most highly

48. "Appointments Dithering." *Washington Post* (June 14, 1994): A20. This is an excellent illustration of the type of equal opportunity that the Equal Employment Opportunity Commission enforces. Similarly, the president of Florida Atlantic University described its policy of offering free tuition to every black it accepts, without regard to financial need, as "giving minorities an even chance" (Taylor 1992: 176). Internal Revenue Service Publication 557 explains that to be eligible for tax-exempt status, a school must not discriminate on the basis of race. It then says, "A policy of a school

successful Puerto Ricans are white. Luther Wright's classifications would force diversity supporters to act in accordance with their professed ideal: that people should be judged on the basis of physical appearance.[49]

I will remind the reader that in the *Bakke* decision (#407), Justice Blackmun defended affirmative action with the standard argument, "In order to get beyond racism, we must first take account of race. There is no other way."

CB EO

---

that favors racial minority groups with respect to admissions, facilities and programs, and financial assistance does not constitute discrimination on the basis of race when the purpose and effect of this policy is to promote . . . the school's non-discrimination policy."

49. When President George W. Bush began his first term, he appointed more minorities to cabinet and sub-cabinet positions than Clinton did. But only a quarter as many blacks and Hispanics voted for Bush as for Clinton. Consequently, his pool of potential minority appointees was much smaller. In his desperation, he appointed to his cabinet people whose highest previous offices had been executive of Orange County (Martinez) and school superintendent of Houston (Paige).

CR SO

Chapter 6
Admissions I: The Lie That Affirmative Action is Compensation for Poverty and Other Handicaps

A. The Irrelevance of Socioeconomic Background

Affirmative action is a bait-and switch game. Black professionals, corporate executives and business owners cite statistics of black unemployment, poverty, and underrepresentation in high-status occupations. In return they get still more privileges and preferences for themselves and their children. The blacks who constitute the statistics get nothing.

(Black columnist William Raspberry (1990))

Every study that has been done of the beneficiaries of academic affirmative action has found that the large majority are the children of middle- and upper-class, well educated parents.[50]

One of the most astonishing revelations of *The Bell Curve* was that a black whose parents are in the upper one-tenth of the American population

---

50. For example, *NR* 1998; Zelnick 1996: 186, 191-2. In the large sample of universities that Bowen and Bok studied in *The Shape of the River* (1998: 341), 64 percent of the blacks who matriculated in 1989 had at least one parent who was a college graduate. The proportion was undoubtedly higher at elite colleges and is much higher now.

As early as 1973, an article in the *Harvard Bulletin* conceded that between 75 and 80 percent of the blacks admitted to Harvard College in 1973 were not from disadvantaged backgrounds (Karabel 2005: 405). In 1981, 70 percent of the black undergraduates at Harvard came from professional or managerial families, and 80 percent attended a high school most of whose students were white. A report at Cornell in 1990 labelled "not intended for public consumption" disclosed that most of its minority students were suburbanites. (Sowell 1993: 282.)

in SES (socioeconomic status) is given preference in college admission over a white with a higher IQ whose parents are in the lowest tenth of the American population in SES. When a black from *the top half* of American SES and a white *from the bottom half* attend the same college, the white has an average IQ .58 standard deviation (SD) higher than the black. That is the difference between an average IQ and an IQ in the upper 30 percent of the American population. When a black and white student from the lower half of SES both attend the same college, the difference in average IQ between them is 1.17 of a SD. That is the difference between an average IQ and an IQ in the upper 13 percent of the population. That is how much superior in IQ a white applicant has to be to a black applicant from the same SES to be judged an equally desirable student.[51]

IQ is vitally important. Scores on intelligence tests correlate closely with SAT scores (Jensen 1985: 203), which in turn correlate closely with ACT scores (Hauser 1998: 229). Scores on intelligence tests also correlate closely with scores on standardized achievement tests (Ceci, et al., 1998: 290). Moreover, as Theodore Cross, the editor of the *Journal of Blacks in Higher Education* (the purpose of which is to promote affirmative action) observed, there is "a direct and strong correlation between grade-point-average and SAT scores."[52] In fact,

> [t]he *Psychological Abstracts* contains some 11,000 citations of studies on the relation of educational achievement to IQ. If there is any unquestioned fact in applied psychometrics, it is that IQ tests have a high degree of predictive validity for . . . scores on scholastic achievement tests, school and college grades, retention in grade, school dropout, number of years of schooling . . . probability of

51. Herrnstein and Murray 1996: 463-7, 782, note 27 (note 27 is on page 758 of the 1994 edition). SES was determined by parental educational level, income, and occupational status (1996: 597-8; 1994: 573-4).

In their analysis, Herrnstein and Murray use "minority" and "black" interchangeably. I assume that they are referring only to blacks. If their comparisons are between all minorities and whites, the advantages enjoyed by blacks are greater than the ones I mention, since other minorities—Hispanics and Native Americans—receive smaller preferences than blacks.

52. Cross 1994A: 53, note; also Cross 1994: 46, note. Races differ less on high school grades than on standardized aptitude and achievement tests. As will be discussed in Chapters 12 and 13, the cause is the inaccuracies inherent in grading. However, as I will also point out in Chapter 12, racial differences in grades are still enormous. Consequently, the smaller racial difference on grades than on standardized tests does not affect the present discussion.

receiving a bachelor's degree (Jensen 1998: 277).

The students in Herrnstein and Murray's sample attended college in the late 1970s and early 1980s (1996: 36, 49). Full-scale academic affirmative action began in the early 1960s. So, for decades, American colleges have been admitting the children of black corporate executives and doctors, who were raised in upper-class suburbs, in preference to the children of white single mothers who work as waitresses and the children of non-English-speaking European immigrants who have better academic records.

The objection will be raised that colleges also consider non-academic accomplishments in making admissions decisions. However, as Theodore Cross pointed out (1996: 67, note) in the *Journal of Blacks in Higher Education*, increased emphasis on non-academic accomplishments would not help blacks. In fact, the National Center for Education Statistics assessed the effect on the racial composition of leading colleges if they assigned more importance to extra-curricular activities and teachers' recommendations. It found that these considerations would *reduce* the proportion of blacks (Thernstrom 1997: 403).

In summary: For decades, American colleges faced with a choice between the child of a black professional who attended an elite private school and the child of a white unemployed coal miner, have admitted the black, even if the white has better SAT/ACT scores, grades, and extra-curricular achievements.

Black students also receive huge preferences in financial aid. Although black students do much worse academically than white students, in 2004, 76 percent of black undergraduates were receiving financial aid, but only 62 percent of white undergraduates.[53] In graduate school, 18 percent of the whites but only 8.7 percent of the blacks who earned doctorates in 2004 had supported themselves as teaching assistants.[54] Among graduates of American law schools in 2000, financial aid from their law school covered nearly three times more of the law-school expenses of blacks than of other races.[55]

Many of the blacks receiving these preferences are children of parents (and, by now, often grandparents) who themselves went through their whole

53. *Journal of Blacks in Higher Education* (Winter 2008/2009): 43; citing the U. S. Department of Education.

54. "Doctoral Degrees Awarded to African Americans Reach Another All-Time High."*JBHE* (Winter 2005/2006): 6-10.

55. Sander 2004: 477 and note 291. Financial aid paid for 14 percent of the expenses of the black law students. The next highest were Hispanics, 5 percent; even though the average parental income of Hispanic law students was considerably lower than that of black law students.

life receiving preferences.

These facts will undoubtedly surprise many readers since universities constantly argue that affirmative action is necessary to compensate for the poverty and poor schools from which their minority applicants come. For example, in an article in the *Los Angeles Times* of July 18, 1995,[56] Berkeley's Chancellor Chang-Lin Tien justified affirmative action with the argument, "[T]he contest between white suburban students and minority inner-city youths is inherently unfair." When Chancellor Chang-Lin wrote that, he must have known the following: During the debate that led up to the ban on affirmative action in California, its supporters constantly reiterated that applicants' socioeconomic background could be considered in admissions decisions. A study by Berkeley's admissions office found that preferences for applicants from poor families would not significantly increase the proportion of its black, Hispanic, and Native American students. In 1994-95, thirty percent of Berkeley's black freshman came from families with incomes over $70,000 a year, which was double the median income of white families at the time ($36,000) (Slater 1995: 59; Lubman 1995). In fact, three months before Chancellor Chang-lin wrote this article, he acknowledged that considering applicants' economic background would not significantly increase the number of minority students (Zelnick 1996: 186).

Every proposed and actual ban on racial affirmative action has explicitly and emphatically allowed socioeconomic affirmative action, to compensate applicants from poor, uneducated families. This option has never been taken because most of the beneficiaries would be whites and Asians.[57]

The reason is that intelligence is nearly completely genetically determined. That is usually obscured since the children of educated, wealthy parents have higher average IQs and better academic records than children of poor, uneducated parents. But that is because wealthier, better educated people are, on average, more intelligent than poorer, less well educated people and they transmit their genes to their children. By late adolescence, there is no correlation between the IQs, academic performance, or tempera-

---

56. "Perspective on Affirmative Action; A Tool for a Colorblind America:" B9.

57. Slater 1995; Bowen and Bok 1998: 47, 51. According to the Code of Federal Regulations, "Individuals who certify that they are members of the named groups (black, Hispanic, Native American, Asian-Pacific, Subcontinental-Asian) are to be considered socially and economically disadvantaged." So, in 1999, there were nineteen separate federal regulations to provide preferences for "disadvantaged [i.e., minority] bankers" (i.e., bank owners) (Chavez 1999). In normal discourse, "disadvantaged bankers" would be an oxymoron.

ment of adopted children and the parents who raised them from infancy or between two or more adopted children raised in the same family.[58]

Another factor that illustrates genetic determinism of intelligence is Galton's Law of Regression towards the Mean: If parents are abnormal for their gene pool in a genetically determined trait, their children tend to regress approximately half-way to the mean of their gene pool. SAT scores are an example. Between 1976 and 2002, the College Board made available on request the average SAT scores of test-takers of different racial groups at different levels of parents' combined income, the highest level of formal education that their parent with the most education had attained, and whether their first language was English.

The racial differences are striking. Until 2005, the SAT consisted of only two sections: Mathematical and Verbal Reasoning. The latter was renamed Critical Reading in 2005. In 2002, the average combined Verbal+Math SAT scores of whites and Asians neither of whose parents had more than a high school diploma were 985 and 995, respectively. The average combined SAT score of blacks at least one of whose parents had a post-graduate degree (MD, PhD, etc.) was 954. On the Math section, the average score of blacks at least one of whose parents had a post-graduate degree was 474; of whites neither of whose parents went beyond high school, 494; of Asians *neither of whose parents graduated from high school*, 517.

The average Verbal score of whites whose parents' income was less than $10,000 (the lowest category) was 483. The average Verbal score of blacks whose parents' income was between $80,000 and $100,000 was 470. The average Math score of blacks whose parents' income was $100,000 or more (the highest category) was 490. The average Math score of whites and Asians whose parents' income was less than $10,000 were 497 and 518.[59] Also in 2002, the average Verbal SAT score of whites whose first language was not English was 490. That is ten points higher than the average Verbal score of blacks at least one of whose parents had a post-graduate degree.

Until 2002, the College Board made the same information available for Mexican Americans, Puerto Ricans, and "Other Hispanics." In 2002, the average combined Verbal+Math SAT scores of Mexican Americans, Puerto

---

58. See Appendix IV of this book and Scarr and Weinberg 1983: 264-6: Scarr and McCartney 1983: 429-32; Harris 1998: 37, 411, note 261 (bibliography on page 394); Levin 1994; Lynn 1994.

59. In 2002, the U.S. Census Bureau classified a family of four with an income below $18,244 a year as poor.

The category *Asians* understates the performance of North-East Asians (from Japan, China, and Korea). Many of the "Asians" were from less intelligent ethnic groups.

Ricans, and Other Hispanics at least one of whose parents had a bachelor's degree were 985, 944 and 981 respectively. I will remind the reader that the average Verbal+Math SAT scores of whites and Asians neither of whose parents had more than a high school diploma were 985 and 995.[60]

After 2002, the College Board stopped making available this extremely valuable information about race and socioeconomic background. However, the *Journal of Blacks in Higher Education* (*JBHE*), whose purpose is to promote academic affirmative action, does occasionally publish comparisons between blacks' and whites' SAT scores at different levels of parental income (although not at levels of parental educational attainment). The racial gap increased after 2002. This is in accordance with fact, which I discuss in Appendix III. F, that for the past 20 years, the gap between blacks and whites has increased on all academic indicators.

In 2002, the average combined Verbal+Math SAT score of whites at the lowest level of parental income (less than $10,000) was 980, which was two points lower than the average Verbal+Math SAT score (982) of blacks in the highest income category (over $100,000). But *JBHE* of Autumn 2005 reported (page 90) that in 2005, the average Verbal+Math SAT score of whites with parental income below $10,000 a year was ten points *higher* than the average SAT score of blacks with parental income above $100,000 a year. (*JBHE* did not provide the actual scores.)

The lowest parental income category was then raised to under $20,000 a year, and the highest parental income category to over $200,000. In 2009, The average Verbal+Math SAT score of whites from families with incomes below $20,000 a year was 972, which was 117 points higher than the average of *all* blacks. It was also 12 points higher than blacks from families with incomes between $160,000 and $200,000 (*JBHE* (Autumn 2009): 85).

These racial differences exist despite the fact (which I discuss in Section E of Appendix III) that in 1995 the way SAT scores are reported was changed in order to decrease racial discrepancies.

They also prove that the SAT accomplishes the purpose for which it was designed: democratizing college admissions. They show that performance on the SAT is not affected by family, social background, or school attended.

Performance on academic achievement tests is closely correlated with performance on aptitude tests (Ceci, et al., 1998: 290; Hauser 1998: 229). By far the most important and best known academic achievement tests in

---

60. Camara, et al., (2003: 38-9) provide the average Verbal and Math SAT scores of blacks, Asians, whites, and Hispanics (all Hispanics considered together) whose parents have less than a bachelor's degree, have a bachelor's degree, and have more than a bachelor's degree, in several years from 1976 to 2002.

the United States are the federal government's National Assessment of Educational Progress (NAEP) tests, which are given to large representative samples of American pre-university students. It is well known that blacks do much worse than whites on these tests. For instance, in 1994, the average black twelfth grader could solve science problems as well as the average white sixth grader (Thernstrom 1997: 357). What is not well known is that *if only the children of Black and White college graduates are considered, the difference in their average performance is six percent* **greater** *than the difference between all Blacks and all Whites* (Thernstrom 2003: 126-7).

Discrepancies between races at the same socioeconomic status (SES) are even greater in college performance and on tests for admission to professional and graduate schools than in high school performance and on admission tests to college. An excellent source for this information is Linda Wightman's article "The Threat to Diversity in Legal Education,"[61] which she wrote in order to defend affirmative action. Wightman was Vice President for Testing, Operations, and Research of the Law School Admission Council. That position enabled her to compile a database of over 27,000 students who enrolled in American law schools in the fall of 1991, comprising 70 percent of those who enrolled that year in law schools that were accredited by the American Bar Association.

Wightman showed that in order to preserve diversity in legal education, massive racial discrimination must be maintained in admission to law schools, because preference to law school applicants from low SES backgrounds would not increase the number of minority students. To demonstrate that, Wightman (1997: 40-45) divided the students in her database into four SES categories. In the highest, "Both mothers and fathers of students in this group had graduate or professional training and held professional jobs." In the lowest, "Both mothers and fathers of students in this group tend to be blue-collar workers and are not college educated. Many have less than a high school education. In addition . . . family income . . . [w]as below average."

The most reliable units to compare sets of data are standard deviations (SDs). At the time of Wightman's article, the Law School Admission Test (LSAT) was graded on a scale from 1 to 48. Wightman did not supply the overall SD on the Law School Admission Test (LSAT) of the students in her database. Instead, she provided (page 42) the SD of each racial group in each SES category. The average SD of whites was 5.03 points. I have calculated that the SD of all the students in her database was roughly 5.10 points. One SD is a large amount. Each SAT test is graded on a 600-point scale (200-800). Among all students who took the SAT in 2004, the SD

61. *New York University Law Review* 72, 1 (1997): 1-53.

was 112 for Verbal and 114 for Math. That was larger than the difference between the average white and black scores (98 points difference in Verbal and 104 points in Math).

Among students who entered law school in the fall of 1991, the whites in the *lowest* SES category had an average LSAT score of 36.24; the blacks in the *highest* SES category had an average LSAT score of 30.62. So, *after four years of college*, the difference between blacks in the highest SES category and whites in the lowest SES category was more than one SD, and one SD is more than the difference in average SAT scores between all whites and blacks who took the SAT. The average LSAT score of all other minority law students in the *highest* SES category was also considerably lower than the average of whites in the *lowest* SES category. Puerto Ricans in the highest SES category had an average of 32.15; Native Americans, 34.70; Mexican Americans, 34.78; and "Hispanics," 34.95.

In Wightman's database, the undergraduate grade-point-average (UGPA) of all groups of minority law students in the highest SES category was also considerably lower than the average of whites in the lowest SES category. The average for whites in the *lowest* SES category was 3.29. In the *highest* SES category, the average UGPA of blacks was 2.87; Native Americans, 2.86; Puerto Ricans, 3.00; Mexican Americans, 3.08; and Hispanics, 3.16. Even Asian American law students in the highest SES category had a lower average UGPA (3.26) than whites in the lowest SES category (3.29). (On the LSAT, Asian American students in the *two highest* SES categories had slightly higher average scores than whites in the *lowest* SES category; but Asian Americans in the next to lowest SES category had a lower average score (35.60) than whites in the lowest category (36.24).)

After decades of attributing the racial gap in academic performance to poverty, the media have begun to acknowledge some of the facts mentioned above. On July 4, 1999, the *New York Times* had a front-page article entitled, "Reason Is Sought for Lag by Blacks in School Effort." It explained that *the* question is "why the academic achievement of black middle class and upper class students lags behind whites of comparable socioeconomic status." Among its examples was,

> In Evanston, a comfortable, attractive community just north of Chicago, Vanessa Woods . . . who runs a high school program to help minority students do better, keeps coming across black students . . . who have fallen behind . . . . "The first thing that came to my head is, 'Oh, they're poor' or 'Oh, they're in a single-parent home,'" said Ms. Woods, who is African-American. "To my surprise, the students were living in the better part of Evanston . . . with two-parent families who have college degrees. They have computers. They have per-

sonal tutors. And they're getting C's and D's" . . . [In] 1997-1998 .
. . nearly 25 percent of black students had failed at least one class,
compared with 4 percent of white students. Seven percent of black
students' grades were A's, compared with 25 percent for whites. In
1996, on a state achievement test, 49 percent of African-Americans
at the school were reading below grade level, compared with 9
percent of whites.

The *Washington Post* of October 23, 1998 had a front-page article entitled "A Good-School, Bad-Grade Mystery; Educators Striving to Close
Racial Gap in Affluent Ohio Suburb." It concerned Shaker Heights, Ohio,
a "gilded suburb" with "wide lawns, winding streets" and a "school system
[that] has a reputation for being one of the best in America. The vast majority of students, black and white, are at least from middle class families.
The schools spend nearly $10,000 a year to educate each child . . . nearly
50 percent above the national average." However:

> School officials have been observing a racial gap in school achieve-
> ment for decades. It has always been an alarming issue in this city,
> which is proud of its reputation as a national model of racial integra-
> tion, and officials have attacked it with a varied arsenal of programs.
> Tutors work with small groups of kindergarten students identified
> as needing help to enhance their language skills. Regular sessions
> are offered to help prepare for state proficiency tests. Art classes are
> designed for the expressed purpose of boosting students' self-esteem.
> . . . [A] high school counselor works with students who exhibit strong
> academic potential but have low grades.

In addition, "High achieving black students mentor struggling younger
ones. And after-school, weekend and summer academies are available." The
result? "In four recent high school graduating classes, blacks made up just 7
percent of the students in the top fifth of their class, while they constituted
90 percent of those in the bottom fifth." The *Post* article also reported that in
1996, the average Verbal and Math SAT scores of blacks in Shaker Heights
were 485 and 471; the average scores of all white Americans were 526 and
523. Nevertheless, "nearly 90 percent of the system's graduates, black and
white, go on to college."

I will add that in the 1999-2000 academic year, more than half of Shaker
Heights' white twelfth graders attained honors in Ohio's proficiency tests
in basic subjects, compared with four percent of its black twelfth graders,
which was no higher than the state-wide average for blacks (Thernstrom
2003: 122-3).

B. The Irrelevance of Cultural and Psychological Factors

> The social scientist is trained to think that he does not know all
> the answers. The social scientist is not trained to realize that he does
> not know all the questions (Cronbach 1975: 13).

John Ogbu devoted an entire book to examining the possible causes
of the disastrous academic performance of black students from wealthy,
educated families in Shaker Heights.

From the late 1970s until his death in 2003, Ogbu, a black professor of
Anthropology at the University of California at Berkeley, was one of the most
influential scholars of black academic under-achievement. By far his most
influential contribution to this subject was an article that he wrote in 1986
with Signithia Fordham entitled "Black Students' School Success: Coping
with the Burden of 'Acting White'" (*Urban Review* 18, 3: 176-206). They
argued (page 177) that black students "began to doubt their own intellectual
ability, began to define academic success as white people's prerogative, and
began to discourage their peers, perhaps unconsciously, from emulating
white people in academic striving, i.e., from 'acting white'."

Since then, the media have constantly repeated this "Fear-of-Acting-
White" explanation for black academic failure as if it were a proven fact,
even though study after study has found the opposite at every school level.
Black students who do well in school are more popular with their peers than
white students who do well; black and Hispanic parents value academic
achievement more highly than white parents and give their children more
help in school; black and Hispanic children do more homework than white
children; black students have a higher regard for their academic ability than
white children and have higher expectations than white children of future
academic success and the level of education they will complete.[62]

---

62. For example, Stevenson, Chen, Uttal 1990. Even Abigail and Stephan
Thernstrom, who argue that blacks' disastrous academic performance is
caused by their un-academic culture, conceded (2003: 143) that the federal
National Assessment of Educational Progress found that in all three grades
it studied—fourth, eighth, and twelfth—a higher proportion of black and
Hispanic than white students did an hour or more of homework a day. (It
also found that Asian students did much more homework than white, black,
or Hispanic students.) They cited two studies that found that white students
did more homework than black students. But in both, the difference was
small. In one, the white students did an average of 15 percent more homework than the black students. In the other (Cook and Ludwig 1998: 383-4),
68 percent of the white students and 65 percent of the black students did an
average of two or more hours a week of homework. However, the Thern-

In his book on black students at Shaker Heights, Ogbu (2003: 189) mentioned many studies that failed to support his "Fear-of-Acting-White" hypothesis and claimed that he never proposed this explanation, which the media and educational "experts" have constantly repeated since he suggested it in 1986. Ogbu wrote (2003: 189),

stroms acknowledged (2003: 296, note 51) that the reason for this difference was that the white students took more demanding courses, which required more homework.

The *Journal of Blacks in Higher Education* (*JBHE*) has provided valuable recent information on this subject. A survey conducted by the U.S. Department of Education in 2004 found that 47 percent of white American high school students say that grades are very important to them, and 52 percent say that the subjects they are taking are interesting and challenging. Among black high school students, 62 percent say that grades are very important to them, and 63 percent say that the subjects they are taking are interesting and challenging (*JBHE* (Spring 2005): 49).

The U.S. Department of Education also found that among the parents of American students from kindergarten through grade twelve, 36 percent of black parents but only 27 percent of white parents expect their children to gain a professional or graduate degree; 79 percent of black parents but only 76 percent of white parents attend scheduled teacher conferences; 46 percent of black parents but only 32 percent of white parents help their children with their homework three or more days a week; 49 percent of black parents but only 41 percent of white parents visited a library with their children. The same survey also found that among students in grades 6-12, 26 percent of blacks but only 13 percent of whites participated in college preparatory activities outside of school (*JBHE* (Summer 2005): 55).

The Census Bureau found that in 2006, 49 percent of white children between the ages of three and five were read to seven or more times a week, compared with 54 percent of black children (*JBHE* (Spring 2009): 49).

A study by the U. S. Department of Education found that in 2007, of parents of children in grades 1-12, 82 percent of white parents and 94 percent of black parents checked that their children had completed their homework (*JBHE* (Autumn 2008): 39).

In 2007, the U. S. Department of Education found that 45 percent of white parents and 55 percent of black parents of fifth-grade students report that their children do homework five or more times a week (*JBHE* (Winter 2008/2009): 43).

The U. S. Department of Education found that in 2007, of parents of children in grades 1-12, 14 percent of whites, but 26 percent of blacks helped their children with their homework (*JBHE* (Summer 2009): 61).

Other researchers and the media have misinterpreted the Fordham-Ogbu (1986) article to mean that the reason for the academic achievement gap is that Black students refuse to make good grades because making good grades is "acting White." . . . Fordham and Ogbu did not claim that rejecting certain White attitudes and behaviors was the main reason that Black students fail to make good grades.

Among the studies that Ogbu cited, the most extensive was by Philip Cook and Jens Ludwig (1998), which used the data from the U.S. Department of Education's National Education Longitudinal Study. They found that black high school students expect to complete more formal education than white high school students of similar socioeconomic backgrounds, and they miss slightly fewer days of school. Moreover (389-90), "Black honor society members are substantially more popular than their classmates . . . The social benefits of academic success are generally greater for blacks than for whites."

Ogbu himself reported that black students in Shaker Heights do much worse than whites from elementary school on (2003: 5). However (204-5), "the idea that school success made a black student less black was nonexistent at the elementary school. Elementary school students did not accuse their schoolmates who made good grades of giving up their black culture, dialect, or identity. Rather, they teased students who got poor grades." Ronald Ferguson's detailed analysis of Shaker Heights students in grades 7-12 (2001: 364) also found no evidence for "the view that black students' peer culture . . . is more oppositional to achievement than whites'."[63]

Ogbu also (2003: 219) found that at Shaker Heights, "Black parents expected their children to do well in school. Children at every grade level knew this;" and (38):

---

63. In October 2003, after Ogbu's book was published, Erin Horvat and Kristine Lewis published the results of yet another attempt to find whether anti-academic peer pressure impedes black academic performance ("Reassessing the 'Burden of Acting White'." *Sociology of Education* 76: 265-80). Like all the other researchers who have studied this subject, Horvat and Lewis could not find the slightest indication that peer pressure or any other aspect of black students' cultural environment hinders their academic performance in any way. Instead, like the other researchers, they found that for academically successful black high school seniors, "friendship groups within the larger black peer groups offered positive reinforcement for academic success;" and, "All the participants found support from their friends (from both good and poor students) for their academic success. They had strong peer groups who valued their academic success."

In our observation of more than 100 classroom lessons from elementary school through high school we did not record a single instance of cultural barriers preventing a student from learning the subject; that is, we observed no instance in which black students said that they were unable to master a lesson because they were being taught European American culture and values in European American pedagogy.

Ogbu also looked for evidence that teachers had lower academic expectations for black than for white students. He reported (2003: 125, 129), "We did not observe any such incident or record an actual complaint of such an incident at the elementary school. . . . [In high school,] we did not see differences in teachers' calling on black and white students during lessons."

This observation confirms a general finding. Contrary to an often repeated accusation, teachers' estimation of students' academic ability is not affected by their race or their parents' level of education and income (Glascoe 2001; Thernstrom 2003: 196).

However, it would be irrelevant even if teachers' estimation of students' academic ability were affected by their race or class, because teachers' opinions about their students' capability have no effect. The belief that teachers' expectations affect students is still widely believed and is even still taught in some sociology and education courses. It derives from an experiment conducted by Robert Rosenthal and Lenore Jacobson. In September 1964, teachers in an elementary school in San Francisco were given a list of students in their classes who supposedly had done extremely well on an IQ test, but in fact were chosen at random. The students were then given IQ tests in January and May of 1965 and in May of 1966. On the second test, they gained an average of 12.2 IQ points, but they made no gains on the other IQ tests. In their book *Pygmalion in the Classroom: Teacher Expectation and Pupils' Intellectual Development* (1968), Rosenthal and Jacobson concentrated on the gains on the second test. They mentioned in less than 500 words that a similar experiment in Massachusetts had the opposite result. The children whom the teachers were told were exceptionally intelligent did significantly worse than the other students.

The press published long descriptions of the gains on the second San Francisco test. For example, a front-page article in the *New York Times* of August 18, 1967 was entitled "Study Indicates Pupils Do Well When Teacher Is Told They Will." [64] These articles did not tell their readers about the conflicting evidence or that the IQs of the children in the study ranged from an absurd 0 to an equally absurd 200, which means that either the test

---

64. Other examples are, "Great Expectations" in the *New York Review of Books* of September 12, 1968 (31-3); and "What Can You Expect?" in the *New Yorker* of April 19, 1969 (169-77).

or its marking were totally unreliable (Mackintosh 1998: 158).

In the subsequent decades, many researchers have tried to replicate Rosenthal and Jacobson's results. Not one has succeeded (Spitz 1999). That is not surprising. In 1968, Robert Thorndike, one of the world's leading authorities on mental abilities, reviewed *Pygmalion in the Classroom* in the *American Educational Research Journal* (5: 708-11). He observed, "Alas, it is so defective technically that one can only regret that it got beyond the eyes of the original investigators!" Thorndike also predicted, "In spite of anything I can say, I am sure it [*Pygmalion*] will become a classic—widely referred to and rarely examined critically." He was, of course, right.

(A common misconception is that Rosenthal and Jacobson claimed that teachers gave higher grades to students whom they thought were more intelligent. However, neither they nor any other researcher has ever claimed to have found such a result.)

Another frequently repeated explanation of poor black academic achievement is low self-esteem. However, Bernadette Gray-Little (who is black) and Adam Hafdahl (2000) reviewed and meta-analyzed 72 studies of the self-esteem of black and white children, adolescents and young adults over several decades. The *Journal of Blacks in Higher Education* observed (Autumn 2000: 105) that their study "is the definitive statement on the subject" and accurately summarized its result as, "[B]lack teenagers not only have a very high level of self-esteem but their self-esteem is significantly higher than that of white teenagers." Moreover, "Black teens have had higher self-esteem than whites for some time."

For example, in 1991, a higher proportion of the students in Washington, DC's public schools answered "yes" to the statement "I am good in mathematics" than the students in any state. But Washington, DC's students did worse than students in any state on tests of mathematical achievement. North Dakota's students did the best on these tests, but the proportion of North Dakota's students who said they were good as mathematics was less than 40 percent as high as the proportion of students in Washington, DC (Cohen 1993). At that time, 96 percent of the students in Washington, DC's public schools were black or Hispanic; those in North Dakota were nearly all white. North Dakota was 38th among American states in the amount of money it spent annually per student in its public schools and 40th in teacher-student ratio. Washington, DC's public schools had a better teacher-student ratio and spent more per student than any state, well over twice as much as North Dakota (*World Almanac for the U.S.A.*).

The facts I have been discussing concern blacks in pre-university education. Black university students are no different. In Chapter 9, I show that most black and Hispanic *college graduates* cannot pass tests in English and

arithmetic that are set at a tenth grade level. In Chapter 14, I summarize
the comparisons between white and black college students that William
Bowen and Derek Bok presented in *The Shape of the River*, which they
wrote in order to defend affirmative action. All the 28 colleges that formed
Bowen and Bok's database are at least somewhat selective in their admissions requirements, and they include some of the most selective colleges
in the United States. Bowen and Bok documented (1988: 26-7, 77-8) not
only the huge difference in average SAT scores between the whites and
blacks at these colleges, but also the fact that racial differences in college
performance were even greater than on SAT scores. This is a manifestation
of the universal phenomenon, which I discuss in Section D of Appendix
III, for qualifying tests to overpredict the performance of members of lower
performing groups.

Camille Charles, et al., (2009), in a book that was also dedicated to
defending affirmative action, analyzed the conduct, attitudes, and expectations of the students in the same 28 American colleges that Bowen and Bok
studied. At the end of their sophomore year, the students in these colleges
were asked "how important" it was to their "friends and close acquaintances"
to do a list of activities. The answers for each ethnic group are below (page
78). All the numbers are percents:

	Whites	Asians	Hispanics	Blacks
Study Hard	70	68	72	74
Get Good Grades	75	76	79	86
Go to Grad./Prof. School	39	50	51	55
Be Willing to Party	44	36	41	36
Be Popular	35	31	31	31
Hang out with Friends	77	72	67	62

During their sophomore year, these students were also asked whether
they were involved in a list of activities.[65] The answers for each group (in

---

65. It is interesting and perhaps significant that it is whites who stand out
as by far the least academically focused group of college students. As was
pointed out, among pre-university students, whites do the least homework
and Asians the most (Thernstrom 2003: 143). Also, a higher proportion of
Asians than any other group takes SAT coaching courses (Appendix III. B).
The information I present in this chapter shows that dedication and commitment cannot explain the large differences in academic success between
whites and blacks and Hispanics. But it may explain some of the smaller

percents) are below (page 81):

	Whites	Asians	Hispanics	Blacks
Career Development Group (e.g., "future CPAs" for accounting majors):	8	13	11	18
Varsity Sports	11	5	6	13
Intramural Sports	31	22	24	15
Fraternity or Sorority	27	15	21	11

Nor did the disastrous academic performance of the black and Hispanic students whom Charles, et al., (2009) studied diminish in the least their estimation of their academic ability. When the students at these colleges were asked in their sophomore year, what was the highest degree that they expected to obtain, 31 percent of the blacks and 32 percent of the Hispanics said a PhD or the equivalent, but only 27 percent of the whites (Charles, et al., 2009: 43). (The percent of Asian who expected to get a PhD or the equivalent was 32.)

An even more striking illustration of the extremely high opinion that black college students have of their academic ability is provided by a report in the *Journal of Blacks in Higher Education*[66] of a survey conducted in 2004 by the Cooperative Intuitional Research Program of UCLA. It compared the academic qualifications and expectations of first-year students at all American colleges with those of first-year students at historically black colleges, whose enrollment is still over 80 percent black.[67] Among freshmen at all colleges, 47.5 percent had a high school average of A or A-. At black colleges, only 22.5 percent had a high school average of A or A-. Nevertheless, 24.5 percent of freshmen at black colleges planned to get a PhD degree and 5.8 percent planned to get a law degree. Among all American freshmen, the percents were 17.4 and 4.9. Of the freshmen at black colleges, 12.5 percent intended to get a medical degree. The article gave no information on the proportion of students at all colleges who intended to get a medical degree or on plans for other post-graduate degrees.

Many readers of this book have undoubtedly read or heard about another difference in academic success between whites and Asians.

66. "For College Freshmen, Race Is Becoming Less of an Issue" (Spring 2005): 29-32.

67. In 2003, the enrolment at historically black colleges was 82.6 percent black ("A Racial Breakdown of Enrollments at the Nation's Black Colleges." *Journal of Blacks in Higher Education* (Summer 2006): 27-8).

explanation that has been proposed for poor black academic performance: Claude Steele's theory of "stereotype threat." Steele argues that when members of a minority group know that their group does poorly on a test, that knowledge hinders their performance. Steele's first publication on this topic (Steele and Aronson 1995) reported the results of an experiment involving white and black college students who were given the same test. Some were told that it was an intelligence test and the others that it was merely a problem-solving task that the researchers developed. Although it was, in fact, the same test, the white-black difference was less among the second group than among the first. Steele has since replicated this finding several times. Television (e.g., *Frontline*), newsmagazines (e.g., *Newsweek*, *Forbes*), newspapers (e.g., *The Boston Globe*) and even most scientific journals and psychology textbooks reported that Steele and his colleagues found that eliminating stereotype threat reduced or ended the difference in SAT performance between whites and blacks. But neither Steele nor anyone else has ever made this claim. I mention above a universal phenomenon, which I discuss in Section D of Appendix III, for qualifying tests to overpredict the performance of members of lower performing groups. So, blacks do worse on tests taken in college than whites with the same SAT scores. What Steele claims to have found is that eliminating stereotype threat lessened or ended that overprediction. In other words, without stereotype threat, the difference between the average performance of white and black college students on these tests is *the same as the difference in their average SAT scores*.[68]

C. The Irrelevance of School Quality

The Washington, DC school system illustrates the nonsense of another commonly alleged handicap that minority students must overcome: defective schools.[69] In the late 1990s, the American city that spent the most money per student was Newark, New Jersey, whose students, nearly all of whom were black and Hispanic, did so terribly that the state government took control of its schools.[70]

However, the expenditure of every other school district in American history was eclipsed by the Kansas City, Missouri, School District (KSMSD) in the late 1980s and early 1990s. In 1985, slightly more than two-thirds

68. Sackett, et al., (2004) give many examples of the misrepresentation of Steele's work.

69. The Thernstroms demonstrated (2003: 152-8) the fraudulence of Jonathan Kozol's best-seller *Savage Inequalities*, which since its publication in 1991 has been the most cited source for this accusation.

70. "The Costs of Learning." *Economist* (February 15, 1997): 50.

of the students in the KSMSD were black and five percent were Hispanic. Even then, it was 17th of the 451 school districts in Missouri in the amount of money spent per student per year (Wolters 1996: 421). The next year, 1986, Judge Russell Clark ordered the KSMSD to radically improve its schools. He mandated the hiring of more teachers, more kindergarten time for children who scored in the lowest 45 percent of children on the Kindergarten Inventory of Development Skills, an expanded summer school, and tutoring before and after school. He also rejected a proposal to repair or refurbish its schools and ordered that they be completely rebuilt (Wolters 1996: 415-17). The result was air conditioned classrooms, a 2,000 square-foot planetarium, huge elementary-school animal rooms for use in zoo projects (Thernstrom 1997: 345-6), and,

> a twenty-five-acre farm and a twenty-five-acre wildlife area . . .
> a model U. N. General Assembly that was wired for simultane-
> ous translation in several languages . . . vivariums . . . radio and
> television studios with laboratories for editing and animation . . .
> movie-editing and screening rooms . . . a 3,500-square-foot dust-
> free diesel-mechanics room and a temperature-controlled art gallery
> (Wolters 1996: 417-18).
>
> An "agribusiness" high school has two greenhouses and labo-
> ratories galore. There is a business and technology high school, an
> engineering high school, and an "advanced-technology" high school,
> which boasts sixteen areas of specialisation . . . The range of courses
> and variety of teaching methods available is [sic] mind-boggling.
> Two elementary schools use Montessori methods. Eleven schools
> concentrate on international studies and teach foreign languages
> through "total immersion." Eight schools concentrate on maths and
> science, six on visual and performing arts, four on Latin.... The
> Central High School . . . [had] one computer for every three pupils
> [in 1993, when very few American high schools had any computers]
> . . . instruction in Ancient Greek language and literature . . . a $5 mil-
> lion swimming pool, six-lane indoor track, a weight-training room,
> a lavishly equipped gymnasium, and a fencing course taught by the
> former head coach of the Soviet Olympic fencing team.[71]

Judge Clark said he had "allowed the District planners to dream" and "provided the mechanism for [those] dreams to be realized" (Thernstrom 1997: 346). This mechanism was expensive. By early 1993, Judge Clark's mandated improvements cost $1.3 *billion more than the normal school budget*; that was an *extra* $36,111 for each of KSMSD's 36,000 students. In 1995, the Supreme Court finally terminated Judge Clark's control of the

---

71. "The Cash Street Kids." *Economist* (August 28, 1993): 43-5.

KSMSD.

What were the results? Between 1987 and 1993, the dropout rate in the KSMSD increased every year, from 42 to 60 percent, and scores on standardized mathematics and reading tests plummeted. The *Economist*, which provided detailed charts of the disastrous results of the KSMSD experiment, pointed out that,

> [A]lmost 200 econometric studies have come to the same conclusion [i.e., students' performance is unrelated to the quality of the school they attend]. But such studies are too boringly statistical to influence political opinion, as witness the recurrent cry for more spending on public schools. Kansas City is different . . . an experiment based on every educationalist's daydream—what if I could build my own school system, regardless of cost?—and coming up with uniformly negative conclusions.[72]

D. The Irrelevance of Evidence

> [F]or the past 30 years our political scene has been dominated by the [erroneous] view that any and all government spending is a waste of taxpayer dollars. Education, as one of the largest components of public spending, has inevitably suffered.
>
> (Nobel laureate economist Paul Krugman in an Op-Ed in the *New York Times* of October 9, 2009 (page A31) entitled "The Uneducated American")

By 1998, 277 studies had been done on the effect of class size on first-twelfth grade education. Of these, 72 percent found no effect, 15 percent found that smaller classes have a positive effect, and 13 percent found that smaller classes have a negative effect. Studies that claim to show that small classes improve learning have been highly publicized; follow-up studies in which these claims were not replicated have received little or no publicity (Shea 1998). However, neither the accumulated weight of evidence nor the Kansas City schools fiasco has had any effect.

Between 1945 and 2007, the amount of money that the United States spent on pre-university public education increased by *eight times, adjusted for inflation* (Coulson 2009). Between 1970 and 2002, the ratio of students to teachers in American public schools fell from 22 to 16 (Greene and Winters 2005: 50). In 2000, spending per pre-university public-school student was $9,200, triple the amount in 1960, adjusted for inflation, and more than in any other country. That increased to $10,800 in 2003 and $11,470 in 2004 (McCluskey and Schaeffer 2009). By 2007, spending per public-school

72. "The Cash Street Kids." *Economist* (August 28, 1993): 43-5.

student was more than 2.4 times more than it had been in 1970, adjusted for inflation. During that period, reading and math scores of 17 year-olds on the National Assessment of Educational Progress Test remained the same, and their science scores declined (Coulson 2009).

In 2007, New York State spent an average of $15,981 per public-school student. What did the taxpayers of New York get for their money? In their first math class at one the four-year colleges of the City University of New York (CUNY), only a third of the 200 students could convert a fraction into a decimal (Schectman and Monahan 2009). I will add that between 1969 and 1998 CUNY admitted every New York City high school graduate. However, since 1998, in order to attend its four-year colleges, a student must pass tests in reading, writing, and mathematics. Only a third of black students pass these tests.[73] It was among the students who passed these tests and chose to enrol in a math course that only a third could convert a fraction into a decimal.[74]

Even the numbers I quote for educational expenditure understate the amount spent by between 20 and 30 percent since they do not include the cost of property acquisition, construction, and renovation.[75]

Indeed, the *Economist* itself, whose description of the Kansas City School District fiasco I quote above, provides an excellent illustration of how impervious to evidence is the belief that increasing expenditure improves academic performance. It constantly publishes reports of the futility of increased educational expenditure, but it also constantly advocates increased educational expenditure as a substitute for affirmative action.[76]

---

73. "Tuition Increases and Tougher Standards for Admission Take a Severe Toll on Black Enrollments at CUNY's Elite Campuses." *Journal of Blacks in Higher Education* (Summer 2006): 40-41.

74. During the first half of the 20th century, enrollment at the City College of New York was overwhelmingly Jewish. As late as 1970, it had graduated more Nobel Prize winners (eight) than any other college in the United States.

75. Hess 2004. In 2007, Education Next and Harvard's Program on Education Policy and Governance conducted a survey that asked a sample of Americans how much they thought their school district spent on education per student. The median estimate was $2,000. The actual average amount in 2004-05 in the districts surveyed was $10,377 (Salam 2010).

76. For example, on April 4, 1996 ("Training and Jobs: What Works?:" 23-5), the *Economist* reported that huge government expenditures on job training in the USA, Britain, Australia, and Germany had accomplished nothing (e.g., "In the United States, the Department of Labor runs $5 billion-worth of elaborate training schemes directed at the disadvantaged. How much

Another excellent example of the irrelevance of evidence is the Chapter 1 (also called Title 1) school program, which was inaugurated in 1965 to provide extra resources to public schools with low-income students. Children in these schools receive intensive instruction in reading and mathematics in

do they help their clientele? 'Zero is not a bad number,' concludes James Heckman of the University of Chicago, who directed a government study of the Job Training Partnership Act, America's largest such programme."). On June 22, 1996 ("More Money, Less Aptitude:" 58) the *Economist* reported that between 1981 and 1995 New York State's public school expenditure per student per year increased from less than $4,000 to $9,300. It also reported that in 1981 the average SAT score of New York State public school students was seven points above the national average, but in 1995, their average SAT score was nineteen points below the national average. On February 15, 1997 ("The Costs of Learning:" 50), the *Economist* printed a chart that showed that spending on American education, adjusted for inflation, nearly doubled between 1970 and 1996, with no results. The title of the chart was "Down the Drain." On January 27, 2001 ("The Education President (Part 2):" 47), it reported, "America has spent $120 billion trying to raise the achievements of poor children since 1965 without any appreciable closing of the education gap." The *Economist* of March 29, 1997 ("World Education League: Who's Top?:" 21-5) observed that in the Third International Maths and Science Study (1996), there was a negative correlation between the academic performance of a country's students and its educational expenditure. The United States spent more than three times as much per student as South Korea and the Czech Republic. But American eighth-graders were 28th in math and 17th in science; while South Korean thirteen-year-olds were second in math and fourth in science, and Czech thirteen-year olds were second in science and sixth in math.

Nevertheless, the *Economist* also constantly blames poor minority academic performance on poor schools. For example, March 30, 1996: 51; August 30, 1997: 14 ("[T]he basic problem . . . lies in the appalling state of too many primary and elementary schools"); October 4, 1997: 63; April 8, 2000: 53 ("Removing it [affirmative action] clears the way for the real work of getting to grips with the causes of the underrepresentation of blacks and Hispanics in higher education . . . dreadful schools"); February 24, 2001: 58 ("Mr. Atkinson [head of the University of California system] is getting rid of SATs not because they are uninformative but because they are all too informative. . . . The right way to deal with it [the racial gap in SAT performance] is to work like fury to change California's schools.") April 5, 2003: 12 ("the real place where discrimination occurs: through woefully inadequate education for huge numbers of poor minority students.")

small classes, with extensive use of audio-visual equipment. From its inception, the federal Office of Education (now the Department of Education) has
conducted study after study of its effectiveness in a desperate attempt to find
some positive results. In the first decade of the program's existence alone,
these studies cost $52 million (approximately $240 million in 2010 dollars).
To the present day, no beneficial results have been detected (Thernstrom
2003: 214-20). In 1984, "the largest and most comprehensive evaluation
of the effectiveness of Title 1 ever undertaken" found that "by the time
students reached junior high school there was no evidence of sustained or
delayed effects of Title 1" (Carter 1984: 6-7). Nevertheless, spending on it
kept increasing. Edward Zigler and Susan Muenchow reported (1992: 239)
that in 1991 over $6 billion was spent, even though, "After pouring billions
of dollars into Chapter 1 for over two decades . . . participating students
do not exhibit meaningful improvements in achievement levels." At the
beginning of 2001, Secretary of Education Roderick Paige observed, "After
spending $125 billion dollars of Title 1 money over 25 years, we have virtu-
ally nothing to show for it" (Thernstrom 2003: 213). The 25 years in that
statement should be 36, "virtually" is a euphemism, and the $125 billion
did not include the $8.6 billion that was spent on Chapter 1/Title 1 in 2001.
In 2004, when Paige was still Secretary of Education, $12.3 billion of the
taxpayers' money was allocated to Title 1; in 2009, $14.5 billion.

CR EO

Chapter 7
The Media vs. Reality I: Raising Intelligence and Improving Academic Performance

The main reason that public policy is not affected by the unanimous evidence of the futility of attempts to raise intelligence and improve academic performance is that this evidence does not reach the public. On the contrary, while these attempts are in progress, the media constantly report that they are spectacularly successful. When their failure becomes apparent, that is not reported.

An excellent example is the Milwaukee Project, which was the most intensive experiment in early childhood cognitive stimulation that was ever undertaken, or could be undertaken. It was analyzed in detail in two series of articles; one in the journal *Developmental Review* 9, 1989, pages 234-300; the other in the journal *Intelligence* 15, 1991, pages 295-349. Among the contributors to both series of articles was Howard Garber, who was the director of the Milwaukee Project since 1981.

Twenty pregnant black women in Milwaukee with IQs of 75 and below and an average IQ of 67 (70 is the borderline of mental retardation) were chosen for the project. When their children were three months old, paraprofessionals started working with them and their mothers in their homes, seven hours a day, five days a week. The initial claims for the mothers were that their "aspirations for all their children have been distinctly elevated" and they had "enhanced self-concept and self-confidence, a more responsive and verbal approach to their children" (*Intelligence* 1991: 305, 343-4). The paraprofessionals began bringing the infants to a Stimulation Center between two weeks and two months after they started visiting their homes. By the age of six months, all the children were in the Stimulation Center from 9:00 a.m. to 4.00 p.m. every weekday, all year. Later, the time in the Stimulation Center was increased to eight hours every weekday, all year, and remained at that. At first, there was one teacher for each child. Later, the teacher-child ratio declined to one teacher for two children; it was never lower than one to three. Every type of intellectual stimulation imaginable was used. It took a pamphlet of 24 pages merely to list all of them. The director of the project boasted that "the childhood environments of John Stuart Mill and Sir Francis Galton would seem very deprived by comparison." At the age of four, the children began pre-reading and pre-math training. When they started school, at an average age of 6.5 years, they averaged in the top 24 percent of children their age on school readiness tests. As many as possible were placed in schools whose students had at least average scores on academic achievement tests (*Developmental Review* 1989: 244-5, 253, 270-71, 281).

What were the results? At the end of the first grade, their average score on a standardized mathematics test, which was chosen by the program's head, was in the lowest 35.5 percent of children their age. Teachers were asked to assess the reading ability of ten of the children. They assessed nine as below average. The children then attended a summer tutorial program in reading and mathematics. However, by the end of their second year in school, their reading and mathematics scores were in the lowest 31 percent and 26 percent, respectively, of children their age (*Intelligence* 1991: 342-3). By the time they were in the fourth grade, their average reading comprehension had fallen to the lowest 19 percent of children their age and their ability at arithmetic problem solving to the lowest 11 percent (*Developmental Review* 1989: 254-5).

However, in the first few years of the Milwaukee Project, newspapers, magazines, television, social science journals, and psychology textbooks constantly reported that it was an amazing success (Sommer 1983). They especially emphasized that the average IQ of the children in it had been raised by a miraculous 33 points. Below are examples from the two most highly regarded and influential newspapers in the United States (and maybe in the world) and from the most widely read newsmagazine in the world.

The *New York Times* told its readers, "The Milwaukee Project . . . *has proved* [italics added] that they [the average IQs of black slum children] can be raised more than 30 [IQ] test points higher than other children from the same environment." In a syndicated article that was printed in newspapers throughout the United States, the *Washington Post* reported that the Milwaukee Project "revealed not that mental deficiencies are passed on genetically, but that mentally retarded mothers tend to create an environment that is less conducive to mental development" (Herrnstein 1982: 71).

In 1971, President Nixon's Committee on Mental Retardation relied on the Milwaukee Project to conclude that the IQs of black slum children can be raised by an average of 33 points (Page 1986: 117). This conclusion was in turn reported by the media. *Time* relied on the Committee on Mental Retardation when it informed its twenty million readers that the 80 percent of mentally retarded people who do not have "clearly detectable physical flaws," are victims of "a socioeconomic disease."[77]

The media's reaction to the Milwaukee Project was typical. In 1978, a series of articles in the *Harvard Educational Review* (*HER*) (48, 2: 128-192), which analyzed in great detail the total failure of preschool programs to achieve any positive results, began by explaining (page 130), "The audience we have in mind for this critique are the general public, who we feel have been misled by popular-press interpretations of evaluation findings."

Among the total failures that the *HER* analyzed in 1978 was Head Start, which is by far the most extensive preschool program. From its inception in 1965 until 2010, the federal government spent $166 billion (unadjusted for inflation) of the taxpayers' money on Head Start. In 2009, the government spent $9.2 billion on Head Start, up from $6.8 billion in 2008. Edward Zigler (*emeritus* Sterling Professor of Psychology at Yale) was a member of the committee that planned and began it and was its leading administrator for a time. In 1992 he co-authored a book about Head Start with Susan Muenchow. They recalled (Zigler and Muenchow 1992: 13) the intellectual climate in the United States when the program began:

> *Reader's Digest* published . . . a blurb on the cover that read, "How to Raise Your Child's IQ by 20 Points." . . . *Life* did a cover story . . . which proclaimed the importance of putting a mobile over an infant's crib. The article cited the "finding" that infants lucky enough to have had mobiles scored higher on certain developmental tasks.

Zigler and Muenchow pointed out that all such claims are false and have to be false because (pages 12, 52, 83): "IQ [is] the most stable of all psychological measures;" "the most stable measure ever discovered . . . [is] IQ;" "cognitive development [is] the area most subject to innate capacity." They also pointed out that the public has no way of knowing that because of the press' ignorance and partiality. For example (page 51), "the *New York Times* reported that children [in Head Start] gained an IQ point per month."

In February 2010, the Department of Health and Human Services, which runs Head Start, published the result of a multi-year study. Out of 44 cognitive tests given to former Head-Start children at the end of the first grade, only two showed even marginally significant results. However, on each of the 44 tests, there is a one in ten chance of a false positive; that is a positive caused by random chance. Similarly, the non-cognitive tests found no

---

77. "Retardation: Hope and Frustration" (May 8, 1972): 37-39.

"socio-emotional" benefits from Head Start.[78]

The media's reporting of experimental school programs is no more accurate than their reporting of preschool programs. In 1975, Marva Collins opened a private elementary school in a slum of Chicago. She claimed that in her school, children who had been regarded as un-teachable read Tolstoy and Longfellow by the time they were six, and third graders read Dante, Emerson, and Dostoevsky. These claims were reported uncritically by the media. In 1979 her wondrous achievements were featured on the popular and highly regarded TV news program *60 Minutes*. In 1981, they were the subject of a television docudrama entitled "Welcome to Success: The Marva Collins Story." She was awarded 38 honorary degrees and gave lectures throughout the United States, for which she was paid $10,000 each. She attributed her success to treating all her students as gifted; constantly boosting their self-esteem; not allowing them to speak in incomplete sentences; and not wasting their time with recesses, gym, or standard elementary school texts with "cutesy pictures" and sentences like "See the ball, see the red ball."

Collins scrupulously avoided publishing the performance of her students on any tests. However, in 1982, *American Teacher* disclosed that half of her students failed the California Achievement Test (CAT) (Spitz 1986: 82). That is a disastrous performance. The CAT became popular in the late 1970s and 1980s because it is extremely easy. Often, most of the whites and some of the blacks who take it answer every question on it correctly. This makes it a poor measure of academic achievement, but it greatly reduces racial differences (Scott 1987: 209-12). It was also disclosed in 1982 that the degree that Collins said she had from Northwestern University did not exist and that her claim that she had not received government money was a lie (Adler and Foote 1982). Nevertheless, for another decade, American newspapers kept reporting as facts Collins' descriptions of her success and her explanations for it.[79]

However, eagerness to report phenomenal success in increasing intelligence has long predated concern with minority performance. For two centuries, books, newspapers, magazines, and, more recently, television, have constantly told the public of the Western World about methods that increase intelligence.

Herman Spitz (1986) examined many examples since the early nineteenth

---

78. "'Head Start': The $166 billion Fed Ed Failure" (online).

79. For example: "Marva Collins Still Expects Much, Gets Much." *St. Petersburg Times* (July 23, 1989): 6A; "Chicago Educator Pushes Common-Sense Approach." *St. Louis Post-Dispatch* (December 2, 1990): 5D; "Pioneering Educator Does Not Want Post in Clinton Cabinet." *Star Tribune* (Minneapolis) (October 22, 1992): 22A.

century. I will outline one (pages 158-69): the effect of glutamic acid on the IQ scores of people and on the laboratory performance of rats. I have chosen this example because it involved a method and results that are incomparably easier to define and quantify than the variables involved in most claims of cognitive improvement. Consequently, the measurement of these variables seems to be impervious to error or distortion. Between 1943 and the late 1950s, researchers at Columbia and other leading universities reported that administering glutamic acid to rats tripled the speed and increased the ac-curacy with which they learned to get through mazes and quadrupled the proportion of rats who were able to step on a series of floor patterns in a specified sequence. Much more significant was the constantly reported effect of glutamic acid on humans; for example, people with Down's Syndrome gained height and weight. The most often reported results were gains in IQ, sometimes of 25 percent.

> [T]he popular press was quick, as always, to catch the fever. Articles appeared in the *Ladies' Home Journal, Time, Hygeia, Reader's Di-gest, Science Newsletter*, and *Science Digest*. As one example, Bliven (1947) in the title of his article for the *New Republic* asked, "Can Brains be Stepped Up?" and gave an affirmative answer, based . . . on the "remarkable experiments" which were "carefully conducted over a period of years by Dr. Zimmerman and his colleagues" (Spitz, 1986: 161).

However, beginning in 1950, while the press kept informing the public about the miraculous effects of glutamic acid, more and more articles ap-peared in scientific journals that reported unsuccessful attempts to find any effect.

In their last article on glutamic acid, in 1959, its most enthusiastic advo-cates, Frederic Zimmerman and Bessie Burgemeister, conceded, "Contradic-tory findings over IQ-point change in the past have been due to overemphasis upon this narrow aspect of mentation rather than on observations of the total change in the individual patient." In fact, in the heyday of glutamic acid publicity, Zimmerman and Burgemeister constantly emphasized IQ gains. Indeed, one of their articles consisted nearly completely of tables of IQ gains (Spitz 1986: 167).

This is a typical denouement. The propagandists of massive improve-ments in intelligence are forced by the weight of cumulative evidence to withdraw their claims of measurable gains and to claim instead that their technique improves attributes that cannot be measured or verified. Then, they quietly abandon the technique.

I will conclude this discussion of unfounded media hype with three recent examples. During the middle and late 1990s the media of the world reported that listening to Mozart's music significantly increases IQ. This was based on one article of less than a page in length that claimed that listening to Mozart increased IQ *for ten to fifteen minutes*; and even that finding has not been replicated by subsequent researchers.[80]

Also during the middle and late 1990s, front-page articles in newspapers and newsmagazines reported that mental stimulation in infancy and early childhood has a dramatic effect on the physical development and functioning of human and animal brains. A cover story in *Time* ("Fertile Minds" (February 3, 1997): 48-56) reported,

> children who don't play much or are rarely touched develop brains 20 percent to 30 percent smaller than normal . . . Young rats reared in toy-strewn cages exhibit more complex behavior than rats confined to sterile, uninteresting boxes . . . [and] the brains of these rats contain as many as 25 percent more synapses per neuron.

Newsweek published an entire special issue (Spring/Summer 1997) with the title *Off to a Good Start: Why the First Three Years Are So Crucial to a Child's Development*. It informed its readers (page 7), "Every lullaby, every giggle and peek-a-boo, triggers a crackling along his [the child's] neural pathways, laying the groundwork for what could some day be a love of art or a talent for soccer or a gift for making and keeping friends." This issue went through several printings and sold about a million copies. Prompted by this type of reporting, American federal and state governments have spent billions of dollars on early childhood stimulation.

All neurobiologists know that this is nonsense. John Bruer, in his book *The Myth of the First Three Years* (New York: Free Press, 1999), documented the glowing media reports of the effects of early childhood stimulation, the huge private and public expenditures of effort and money on it, and the total lack of evidence to support it. For example (pages 202-5):

> The special *Newsweek* issue published some stunning PET [positron emission tomography] images of a normal child's brain beside an image of a severely neglected child's brain. These images were picked up and published by newspapers around the country. . . . I eventually learned that the *Newsweek* brain scans had come from

80. Chabris 1998: 37-8; Steele 1998. *Science* (January 30, 1998: 663; "Mozart for Georgia Newborns") reported that the state of Georgia intended to play CDs of Mozart to every baby born in Georgia. Governor Miller stated, "No one questions that listening to music at a very early age affects the spatial, temporal reasoning that underlies math and engineering and even chess."

Dr. Harry Chugani's laboratory . . . I contacted Dr. Chugani . . . in early 1998 to find out where the brain images had been published in the scientific literature so that I could read his study. He told me that they had not yet been published . . . At a May 22, 1999 scientific meeting . . . Chugani . . . told the meeting participants that subsequent statistical analysis of his data revealed no significant differences between the brains of the neglected children and the brains of children in his "normal" comparison group. . . . Unfortunately, it is unlikely that *Newsweek*, *The Boston Globe*, or . . . *Chicago Tribune* will ever report the final outcome of Chugani's . . . study.

The media's desperation to report educational success is so intense that newspapers, newsmagazines, and television (e.g., CNN, the *NewsHour with Jim Lehrer*) even gave uncritical support to conservatives' claim that allowing public school students to use vouchers to attend private schools (many of them Catholic) significantly improves their performance on academic tests. The beginning of an editorial in the Boston *Herald* of August 30, 2000 (page 26) was typical: "The facts are clear and persuasive: school vouchers work." The "facts" were conclusions that Harvard professor Paul Peterson drew from the most comprehensive study of the effect of vouchers ever undertaken. However, Professor Peterson's partner in the study, the research firm Mathematica, pointed out that all the gains in the study were in just one of the five grades studied, and in that grade only black children had improved. White and Hispanic children made no gains in any of the grades studied. Princeton economist Alan Krueger re-analyzed Peterson's data and found that Peterson had failed to count the test scores of 292 black children who should have been included. Once they were included, vouchers had no effect on any children in the study. David Myers, the lead researcher for Mathematica, reviewed Krueger's reanalysis and concluded, "the impact of vouchers is not statistically significant." Professor Peterson has declined to comment on Krueger's re-analysis.[81]

81. Winerip 2003. Conservatives (e.g., Thernstrom 2003: 43-63, 248) have also trumpeted the success of charter schools; that is, public schools that are not subject to the authority of school boards. However, the first national study of the effectiveness of charter schools found that only 25 percent of the children in charter schools got scores that were considered "proficient" on national tests of reading and math, compared with 30 percent in reading and 32 percent in math among children from similar socioeconomic backgrounds in ordinary public schools. These findings replicated the results of local and state studies (Schemo 2004). Another study compared the performance on state proficiency requirements of children in charter schools with those in ordinary public schools in five states that have made considerable invest-

A. The Media's Compromise with Reality

The evidence that intelligence is genetically determined has been incontrovertible for decades, but its accumulated weight has now become so great that it has begun to break through the media's resistance to reporting it. On September 2, 2003, the *Washington Post* published a front-page article entitled "Genes' Sway over IQ May Vary with Class." It informed the public of two facts that researchers have known for decades. One is, "[S]tudies have repeatedly found that people's genes—and not their environment— explain most of the difference in IQ among individuals;" "Genes do explain the vast majority of IQ differences among children in wealthier families." The article proceeded to explain that "wealthier" means "middle-class and wealthy." At last, the public has been informed that there was never a reason to invent bogus explanations—low self-esteem, peer pressure, teachers' attitudes, cultural bias—for the disastrous academic performance of middle- and upper-class black children. The other fact about which the *Washington Post* informed its readers is, "IQ . . . remains the best predictor today of social and economic success in U.S. society." So, there was never a reason to invent mysterious, non-verifiable explanations, like institutional racism, to explain why blacks from middle- and upper-class families are much less successful than whites and Asians.[82]

The *Washington Post* finally informed the public about these crucially important facts because it was reporting a new study, which, the article's author, Rick Weiss, claimed showed that "environmental factors—not genetic deficits—explain the IQ differences among poor minorities." Weiss assumed that his readers would not look at the actual report of the study that he claimed to be summarizing. In it (Turkheimer, et al., 2003), Eric Turkheimer and his colleagues, like all researchers in this field, considered the fact that it is the low IQ of parents that causes poverty, broken homes, and insensitive and brutal parental conduct. Children raised in such environments tend to have low IQs because they inherit their parents' IQs genetically. They wrote (page 627), "It would be naïve, however, to interpret SES [socioeconomic status] strictly as an environmental variable. Most variables traditionally thought of as markers of environmental quality also reflect genetic variability."

---

ments in charter schools: Texas, Colorado, Illinois, Massachusetts, and North Carolina. The study found, "[E]ven when allowances were made for race and poverty, the charter schools were still less likely to meet state standards than regular schools" (Dillon and Schemo 2004).

82. In Appendix IV, I document the extreme accuracy with which intelligence tests predict future income and occupational success.

In the *Washington Post* article, Weiss quoted Sandra Scarr, who he pointed out "did seminal work in behavior genetics." So, it is appropriate to quote what Scarr (1985: 504) wrote on this subject:

> [M]y colleagues and I looked at . . . maternal control of children rated from 15-minute observations of teaching situations, and . . . interviews with mothers about their methods of disciplining their children . . . At the positive end are reasoning, explaining and other verbal ways of dealing with young children. At the negative end is physical punishment. . . . Both positive control techniques . . . and positive discipline . . . significantly predict children's IQ . . . The inference usually drawn from this sort of result is that parents who do not manage children in positive ways could have more intelligent children if they did. . . . As the editor of a developmental journal, I receive many papers of this sort. . . . [However] when . . . the mother's . . . score on the Wechsler Adult Intelligence Scale (WAIS) [the most commonly used IQ test for adults] [is] put into the equation, the mother's IQ dominates the prediction of her child's IQ. . . . The only significant predictor of the child's IQ . . . is the mother's WAIS . . . . The implications of this result for improving children's intellectual functioning . . . are dismal.

In her presidential address to the Behavior Genetics Society in 1987, Scarr pointed out (Scarr 1987: 219-21, 223, 228) that,

> [The study of] genetic variability in behavior . . . inflamed public opinion from the 1960s to the early 1980s. Then the outcries stopped, with the exception of a few eccentrics, such as Leon Kamin, Richard Lewontin, Steven Jay Gould, and Stephen Rose, who have audiences among the lingering social radicals. [Anyone familiar with the media's coverage of this subject will recognize these as the "experts" who are always cited as if their views are authoritative.]
>
> My interest in the possibility of genetic behavioral differences began when, as an undergraduate, I was told that there are none.
>
> The lack of systematic environmental variability among adoptees led us to examine social-class effects. What difference does it make to be reared by a working-class or rural family, compared to a professional family? . . . We were amazed to conclude . . . that young adults do not resemble their family members on anything but genetic grounds.
>
> Today there is virtually no dispute among responsible scientists.

The *New York Times'* resolution to keep its readers ignorant of what geneticists and psychometricians have known for decades has also finally buckled under the cumulative weight of evidence. Like the *Washington Post*, it has begun to report some of this evidence. On November 20, 2002 (page A37), the *Times* had an article entitled "Gene Study Identifies 5 Main Human Populations." It reported:

> Scientists studying the DNA of 52 human groups from around the world have concluded that people belong to five principal groups corresponding to the major geographical regions of the world: Africa, Europe, Asia, Melanesia and the Americas. . . . These regions broadly correspond with popular notions of race, the researchers said . . . [S]elf-reported population ancestry likely provides a suitable proxy for genetic ancestry. In other words, someone saying he is of European ancestry will have genetic similarities with other Europeans. . . . [T]he findings essentially confirmed the popular concept of race.

On November 5, 2001 (page A15), the *Times* had an article entitled "Study Finds Link between Intelligence and Size of Some Areas of the Brain." It reported, "[T]he size of certain regions of the brain is under tight genetic control and the larger these regions are the higher is intelligence [as measured by IQ]." Magnetic resonance imaging of the human brains found that "the quantity of grey matter in the frontal lobes was under particularly tight genetic control." "The amount of grey matter is a measure of the number of brain cells. . . . The frontal lobes are involved in planning and risk assessment."

So, finally, the *Times* is informing its readers of facts that researchers have known for decades. In 2000, in the journal *Personality and Individual Differences*,[83] John W. Wickett, et al., observed (page 1096) that a correlation between brain size and IQ has been "consistently found throughout 100 years of research. Obviously, replication of this effect is no longer required." In the standard textbook *Handbook of Intelligence*, edited by Robert Sternberg and published by Cambridge University Press in 2000, Philip Vernon, et al., (pages 245-50) reviewed every study that had ever been conducted of the relation of human brain size with some measure of intelligence (various intelligence tests, university grades, etc.). These consisted of 54 independent samples, involving 56,793 subjects. Every correlation was positive. Vernon, et al., concluded, "[T]here is no question but that significant correlations exist."

More recently (Wade 2005), the *New York Times* reported explanations that have been advanced for the extraordinarily high average IQ of

---

83. "Relationship between Factors of Intelligence and Brain Volume:" 1095-1122

Ashkenazi (i.e., European-origin) Jews, which is the highest of any group of people in the world. The article assumed without question what experts in this field have long known: the hyper-intelligence of Ashkenazi Jews is genetically determined.[84]

84. Also, the *Economist* of June 4, 2005 (listed as June 2 on www.economist.com) ("The Evolution of Intelligence: Natural Genius?")

Deniers of genetic determinism of intelligence, like deniers of biological evolution and the Holocaust, support their position by citing a small number of "experts." Although some of these experts attained eminence in another, related field, all are amateurs in the field in question. They entered it in order to provide what seems like counter-evidence to the unanimous conclusions of genuine researchers. This counter-evidence cannot fool any serious student of these subjects, but that is not its purpose. It is designed to seem plausible to the general public.

Since its publication in 1981 (reissued in 1996), Stephen Jay Gould's *The Mismeasure of Man* has been the Bible of opponents to genetic determinism of intelligence. I have prepared a document in which I first quote reviews it received in newspapers and general-interest magazines, all of which praised it uncritically. Then I quote reviews in scholarly journals, all of which pointed out that it is a mosaic of blatant lies and misrepresentations. This document is available on www.affirmativeactionhoax.com.

One of the main arguments that Gould and other opponents of genetic determinism of intelligence use is that there are no pure races. But no one who studies this subject thinks that there are pure races or that there is any causal connection between race and intelligence. There is not even a causal connection between species and intelligence. The average intelligence of each species rises and falls depending on whether its more or less intelligent members have more or fewer children who live to maturity. The present relative intelligence of races is the result of the relative birth rates of their more and less intelligent members in the past. The same factor has caused endogamous ethnic groups (e.g., Jews) within these races to become more or less intelligent.

Animal breeding has always been based on this fact. For instance, in the mid-1940s a trainer of guide dogs for the blind named Clarence Pfaffenberger found that he could train only nine percent of the dogs that started his program to perform the complex and demanding tasks required of them. He developed a series of problem solving tests and bred the dogs that did well on them. By the end of the 1950s, he had bred dogs 90 percent of whom could be trained to guide the blind (Coren 1994: 191-3). W. T. Heron and his colleagues at the University of Minnesota created maze-bright and maze-dumb strains of rats in four generations.

CR SO

Chapter 8
Admissions II: The Lie That Affirmative Action is One of Many Non-Academic Factors

Another basic affirmative-action lie is that race is merely one of many non-academic admissions criteria. In *Bakke* (#315-17), Justice Powell ruled that the Davis Medical School program was unconstitutional because it was limited to "simple ethnic diversity;" whereas,

> the diversity that furthers a compelling state interest encompasses a far broader array of qualifications and characteristics . . . [T]he race of an applicant may tip the balance in his favor just as geographic origin or a life spent on a farm may tip the balance . . . [Race is considered but] without the factor of race being decisive when compared, for example . . . [with] exceptional personal talents, unique work or service experience, leadership potential . . . .

In his description of the proper practice of racial discrimination, Powell was quoting and paraphrasing Harvard's descriptions of its undergraduate admissions procedures. However, as I point out in Section D of Chapter 3, whatever importance universities assign to non-academic criteria in undergraduate admissions, no university has ever questioned that quantifiable academic qualifications should be the crucial factor (with the sole exception of race and ethnicity) in admission to graduate and professional schools (like Davis Medical School).

Even in undergraduate admissions, colleges have exaggerated the importance of non-academic considerations in order to use them as a smokescreen to obscure the one non-academic factor that really has been crucial: race: first in favor of Gentiles, then in favor of minorities. A study of a large representative sample of American men who graduated from high school in 1972 found that the average white's combined Verbal+Math SAT score was 1,011 and he went to a college with a median SAT score of 1,019 (Thernstrom 1997: 409-10). In 2003 a survey of college admissions officers found that less than 10 percent considered interviews, work experience, or extracurricular activities to be "of considerable importance" (Haigh 2004).

Colleges' admissions policies have always implicitly recognized the validity of the objections that Columbia Admissions Director Adam Jones raised when non-academic criteria were first considered, which I quoted in Section C of Chapter 3: the purpose of a university is intellectual training; and even if non-academic strengths should be considered, they cannot be reliably determined, whereas academic ability can be (Wechsler 1977: 157-8).

I will now provide illustrations of the unimportance non-racial non-academic factors compared to race.

Defenders of affirmative action nearly invariably raise the issue of preferential admission for legatees—children of alumni—on the assumption that they receive the same degree of preferences as minorities. Even the *Economist*, which is usually more careful with facts than most newsmagazines and which opposes affirmative action, made this assumption. An article in its January 10, 2004 issue (page 37) was entitled "The Curse of Nepotism: A Helping Hand for Those Who Need It Least." It began with a cartoon that showed a white legatee escorted by his wealthy, alumnus father into Harvard, while black and brown applicants wait in a line in the background. However, between 1983 and 1992, the average Verbal SAT score of legatees who were admitted to Harvard was only 13 points lower than the average of non-legatees.[85] The article mentioned preferences for legatees at two colleges besides Harvard: Notre Dame and the University of Virginia. I could find no information on Notre Dame. But in 1999, being a legatee increased an applicant's chance of admission to the University of Virginia by four times over other applicants with the same SAT scores and high school grades. In the same year, being black increased an applicant's chance of admission to the University of Virginia by 111 times (Lerner and Nagai 2000).

The magnitude of legacy preferences is exaggerated by the practice of comparing the percent of legatee and non-legatee applicants who are admitted to a college. But legatee applicants tend to have much better academic credentials. The difference in admission rates between legatees and non-legatees with the same records is much less than the overall difference in admission rates (Bowen and Bok 1998: 28).

The unimportance of other non-academic factors compared with race is best examined by looking at actual applicants. I will begin with the lead plaintiff in *Jennifer Gratz and Patrick Hamacher v. Lee Bollinger, et al.*, in which, in 2003, the Supreme Court upheld the legality of academic racial discrimination. Jennifer Gratz's high school grade-point-average (GPA) was

---

85. Herrnstein and Murray 1996: 780-81, note 21 (pages 756-7 of the 1994 edition).

3.79 on a 1-4 scale, which was twelfth in a graduating class of 299 students. Like many Midwestern students, she took the ACT instead of the SAT. Her ACT score was 25. Before 2005, there were only two SAT tests—Verbal and Math—and an ACT score of 25 was the equivalent of a combined Math+Verbal SAT score of 1160-90 (in the top 25 percent of test-takers). She was also student council vice president, a national Honor Society member, a competitive cheerleader, and a volunteer for many community projects. She had always wanted to attend the University of Michigan at Ann Arbor, but it rejected her (Swain 2002: 298). When the University of Michigan at Ann Arbor rejected her, it was admitting more than 90 percent of black, Hispanic, and Native American applicants with GPAs over 2.8 and SAT scores above 830 (in the lowest 18 percent of test-takers).[86] (The reader should always remember that the categories "black," "Hispanic," and "Native American" include everyone with an ancestor who was black, Native American, or from Spanish-speaking Latin America.)

I will now outline the qualifications of five applicants who were rejected from Wesleyan, along with other colleges. The first, Matthew Lerner, graduated from high school in 1998.

> His S.A.T. scores were 750 . . . on the verbal section, 700 . . . on mathematics [a combined Verbal+Math score of 1450 is in the top 2 percent of test-takers]; he took all advanced placement courses this year and received the highest possible mark, 5, on his advanced placement calculus test. He was president of his school's political action club, drum major in the . . . band, religious director of his synagogue's youth group and is a published poet. Mr. Lerner applied to Harvard, Brown, Wesleyan Universities and . . . the University of Massachusetts. He was accepted only by UMass (Bronner 1999).

A year later, Wesleyan put Tiffany Wang on its waiting list. Her SAT scores were 720 in Math and 750 in Verbal. The latter score was especially impressive since she learned English as a second language. Her parents moved to California from Taiwan only five years earlier and spoke Mandarin at home. In high school, she took six advanced-placement, college-level courses; and most of her marks were As. During all four years of high school, she was on its basketball and track teams and did community service. For two years, she worked for a human rights club that she founded and took part in a program organized by her church to pick up drunken revellers on Saturday nights. The Wesleyan admissions officer who read the essay she wrote with her application, wrote about it, "Nicely done . . . well written;"

---

86. Thernstrom 1999A: 40. The Wikipedia entry for "SAT" provides conversion scales for ACT and SAT scores and the percentiles of SAT scores.

and he summarized her guidance counsellor's evaluation as, "Independent spirit and original thinker. Conscientious, thoughtful, involved" (Steinberg 2002: 124-9). Two other factors were in her favor.

> First, she was from California, and Wesleyan was always trying to expand its geographical range. The prior year's class had, as always, been heavily dominated (67 percent) by students from the Northeast and mid-Atlantic states. . . . Also . . . checking the Asian-American box on an application . . . [gave] a candidate an advantage . . . . Thirty-five percent of the applicants to the prior year's class who had identified themselves as Asian American had been admitted, compared with 29 percent of the applicant pool as a whole [and much less than 29 percent of whites] (Steinberg 2002: 130-31).

Nevertheless, Wesleyan put her on its waiting list. Very few applicants on waiting lists are accepted (Fallows 2003: 113). Wang went to New York University (Steinberg 2002: 196, 278).

Recommendations from influential people also add little to an applicant's chance of admission, as is illustrated by two applicants whom Wesleyan rejected outright in the same year that it put Tiffany Wang on its waiting list. One was from California, had a strong high school record, a combined Verbal+Math SAT score of 1400; and the president of another university wrote to Wesleyan's president urging him to accept her. The other played three varsity sports in high school, was the captain of the lacrosse team, had a Verbal+Math SAT scores of 1200, and was highly recommended by "one of the most respected professors at Wesleyan" (Steinberg 2002: 178-9).

I will provide one more example:

> [In 2002, a] senior at a competitive public high school . . . applied to seven schools and got into none. . . . [S]he had a 4.1 weighted grade point average [i.e., above an A average] . . . took mostly honors or Advanced Placement courses, played the upright bass, played softball and field hockey and ran cross-country, and had reached the regional level in a science competition. Her combined SAT score was 1380. She is also related to a longtime faculty member at one of the schools to which she applied early. But none of these things gave any of the highly selective schools to which she applied—Bowdoin, Colby, Cornell, Dartmouth, MIT, Vasser, and Wesleyan—sufficient reason to accept her (Ganeshananthan 2003).

I have outlined the records of five students who were rejected by Wesleyan. The *Atlantic Monthly* of November 2003 (page 129) rated the admissions selectivity of the 50 most selective American colleges. Wesleyan was the 35th in difficulty of admissions. The last mentioned student was also rejected by Colby, which was not in the top 50.

Now, let us look at the advantage conferred by being black. I will begin with Harvard and Yale, which are among the five most selective American colleges, and Brown, which is among the top ten. The *New York Times* of February 28, 1993 (page A1) began an article entitled "Colleges Lure Black Students with Incentives" with this example:

> George Watson is a high school senior in great demand. More than 100 colleges have sent him unsolicited application material, filling two crates in his house . . . . One . . . promised him a $20,000 scholarship, although his parents own a successful business. Last week Harvard University wrote to say that it had waived its January 1 application deadline for Mr. Watson so he could still apply. Mr. Watson . . . has a "B" average and scored 690 out of 800 in math on the SAT.

Of the students who took the SAT in 1996, six percent had A+ high-school averages, 29 percent had A or A- averages, 49 percent had B averages, and only 16 percent had averages below B.[87] What made Watson the object of such a furious bidding war was his 690 in the SAT-Math. (Watson's Verbal score must have been much lower than his Math score since the *Times* did not mention it.) In 1993, over 50,000 whites scored over 700 on the Math or Verbal sections of the SAT and over 14,000 scored over 750 on Math (Cross 1994A: 54). For years, Harvard has received more than 500 applicants a year with a perfect 800 on *both* the Math and Verbal sections of the SAT and has rejected most of them (Fallows 2003: 110). In 2000, 3,000 valedictorians applied to Harvard, which admits 1,660 applicants a year (Keller 2001: 467).

The *Times* article mentioned another black student, with combined SAT Math and Verbal scores of 1000, who applied to Harvard, Yale, and Brown, as well as five other colleges. Not only did all eight accept him, but they refunded his application fee after he asked them to do so. Brown defines SAT-Verbal scores below 620 as "academic risks" (Jensen 1980: 483).

The *Times* article also reported that Harvard managed to get only 55 percent of the blacks it admitted, so it "surveyed the black students who had rejected it and found they had turned Harvard down 'overwhelmingly for financial reasons.' . . . Several black students told Harvard that they had received scholarships . . . at other colleges, even though they had family incomes of more than $150,000 a year." The *Harvard University*

---

87. 1996 is the earliest year for which information about high school grades is available on www.collegeboard.com.

Gazette (Gewertz 1992) mentioned the size of one of these scholarships. One of Harvard's competitors gave a black student $85,000 plus $10,000 traveling expenses *per year* to bribe him to enroll. Huge bribes are by no means restricted to elite private universities. The University of Oklahoma (i.e., the taxpayers of Oklahoma) sent a Hispanic student from Houston an unsolicited offer of $56,000 and guaranteed to provide a personal tutor (Kleiner 2001).

The *Times* article observed that as a result of the desperate bidding war to attract minority students, "there are growing concerns that black students from affluent families are . . . depriving needier students of [financial] help." The *Times* also pointed out the terrible irony involved. Many colleges stopped giving scholarships based on academic merit in order to devote their scholarship money to poor students. However, they are now giving scholarships many times bigger than they ever gave to students with extraordinary academic achievement or ability. The recipients of these scholarships are often rich, and their academic achievements and ability are incomparably lower than those of the other students at these colleges. Their only merit is a black or Latin American ancestor.[88] Moreover, many are children of parents who went through their entire lives receiving similar preferential treatment.

The *Boston Globe* also began an article on college admissions (McGrory 1995) with a specific black high school senior, Fred Abernathy, who has received more than 60 unsolicited college brochures and applications. When he received an acceptance letter from the University of Illinois' College of Engineering, "I was really proud of myself. My mother was really proud of me." That is certainly understandable. Like many state universities in the Middle West, the University of Illinois prefers the ACT to the SAT. The ACT is marked on a 1-36 scale. Most white applicants accepted by the University of Illinois College of Engineering have scores in the 30s, which is in the upper 3 percent of all test-takers. Fred Abernathy's score was 19, in the *lowest* 40 percent.

The *Globe* continued:

> MIT [is] the foremost engineering school in the country . . . nevertheless . . . MIT admissions officers annually [go] to 110 cities from coast to coast [to attract minority applicants] . . . For MIT and most other schools, the recruitment begins with the purchase of expensive lists from the Educational Testing Service . . . More than 1280 of the country's 1600 public and private four-year colleges and universities request minority-specific lists. . . . From there, admissions counselors

88. At some colleges, every black student is given a full scholarship. The same bidding war is repeated by graduate and professional schools (Taylor 1992: 173-7; Thernstrom 1990: 24).

and a network of hundreds and even thousands of alumni fan across the country . . . . At Tufts University . . . recruitment is starting as early as grammar and junior high school. . . . Despite all the minority recruiting, the millions of dollars spent and the thousands of hours expended . . . Tufts is just 4 percent black, MIT is 5.7 percent black . . . .[89]

[At the University of California's schools of medicine] *24 percent of the non-poor* affirmative-action candidates who applied were accepted compared with *6 percent of the poor* non-affirmative-action candidates [italics added]. . . . At Bates . . . the assistant dean of students estimates that of the 46 blacks on campus, only five or six come from an underprivileged, inner-city background.

Bates College has abandoned the SAT in order to increase the number of its minority students. Bates could have admitted as many minority students as it wanted with low SAT scores. The advantage of abandoning the SAT is that it makes invisible the massive preference given to blacks who were raised in upper-class suburbs over the children of non-English-speaking white and Asian immigrants who were raised in slums.

Recruitment of minority students has become even more frenzied since these articles were written. On October 25, 1999, the *New York Times* reported in an article entitled "Elite Colleges Step up Courting of Minorities" (page A1), "They are treated in a way that they were never treated before . . . . The students hail from fancy private schools like Hotchkiss and Spence and from public magnet schools . . . . Few are from low-performing inner-city public schools."

The *Boston Globe* article also described the support that colleges give their minority students, most of whom attended upper-middle and upper-class suburban high schools or elite private schools: "Increasingly, colleges and universities are classifying minority students as at risk the day they set foot on campus and offering an array of programs ranging from private tutoring to mentoring by faculty and upper classmen, to summer school."

C3 80

89. MIT's frantic search for minority applicants is typical. But MIT is not typical of highly selective colleges in that, except for racial discrimination, its admissions criteria are completely academic. It gives no preference to athletes, children of alumni, etc. (Karabel 2005: 673, note 72).

ल्ड ॐ

Chapter 9
Affirmative Grading and Graduation[90]

T
he American public has known about the existence of racial discrimination in university admissions for a long time; although, as will
be discussed, its extent has only recently been disclosed. However,
most Americans are not aware of the much more pernicious phenomenon
of massive discrimination in grading and graduation.

A. The Statistics

When evaluating the statistics below, the reader should keep in mind a
crucially important fact, which I discuss at length in Section D of Appendix
III. All tests of cognitive ability—whether IQ tests, or tests for admission to
college (SAT, ACT), or to medical school (MCAT), or law school (LSAT), or
for hiring or promotion in government or private employment—overpredict
by a large margin the performance of members of lower scoring groups
relative to members of higher scoring groups. So, if a black and white have
the same score, the white will, on average, do much better than the black in
the activity for which the test is used to predict performance.

At every occupational level, from laborer to professional; and at every
educational level, from high school graduate to PhD, the average IQ of
American blacks is more than a standard deviation (SD) below that of whites
at the same level, and usually much more. Hispanics are between them,
but closer to blacks than to whites. Here it should be explained that one
SD above average in IQ is at the 84th percentile. So, if the racial difference
at any level were only one SD, 84 percent of whites at that level would be
above the average black.

Even among holders of bachelor's degrees in fields in which the criteria
of grading are nearly completely objective—engineering, physical science,

---

90. The term "affirmative grading" has been used for a long time inside
the academic community, where it is taken for granted (e.g., Klitgaard 1985:
248, note 38).

and mathematics—the difference between the average black and white IQ is 1.1 SD. Differences among holders of bachelor's degrees in other subjects (e.g., social sciences, education, business) range from 1.4 to 1.6 SD. The average racial difference for advanced degrees is 1.6. (Two SDs above an average is at the 98th percentile.) This difference means that the average black American with a post-graduate degree has approximately the same IQ as the average white American with no more than a high school diploma. So, a white American who is intelligent enough to graduate from high school would be intelligent enough to get a post-graduate degree if he were black.[91]

Linda Gottfredson (1986: 398-406) analyzed these differences from another perspective. She assumed that an IQ of 114 is the minimum needed to be a competent engineer or doctor. The proportion of blacks who have an IQ of 114 or more is only one-twentieth (5 percent) the proportion of whites. But in 1980, the *per capita* ratio of black to white engineers was 25 percent and of doctors, 30 percent. That means that five times as many blacks were engineers and six times as many were doctors as the proportion of blacks with the minimum IQ necessary for competence in those professions. Gottfredson provided similar statistics for many occupations. In all of them, racial discrepancies are huge. I have chosen medicine because it is the occupation in which granting a degree to an incompetent is most clearly criminal, and engineering because it is the occupation in which grading and graduation criteria are the most objective.

Moreover, Gottfredson's choice of an IQ of 114 as the minimum for competence in medicine was too low. I will show in Section D of this chapter that scores on the Medical College Admission Test (MCAT) are extremely accurate predictors of performance in medical school and as a practicing doctor. Scores on the MCAT correlate closely with IQ scores. Since the end of World War II, the IQ equivalent of the average MCAT score of white medical students has remained remarkably stable at about 125, and nearly no white medical student has had an IQ below 115. But American medical schools admit blacks with MCAT scores for which the IQ equivalent is as low as 104 (Gordon 1988: 89-90, notes 7, 9 and 11). For comparison, the average IQ of whites with no more than a high school diploma is 105-6 (Herrnstein and Murray 1996: 151-2).

Let us now turn from deductive to empirical evidence of affirmative graduation. In 1992, the United States Department of Education commissioned an evaluation, called the National Adult Literacy Survey (NALS), of the proficiency of American adults in "Prose Literacy," "Document Literacy," and "Quantitative Literacy." A summary of the NALS and its results is

---

91. Herrnstein and Murray 1996: 319-20, 488, 502, 788, note 41 (note 41 is on page 764 of the 1994 edition).

available online.[92] It was conducted by more than 400 trained interviewers, some of whom were bilingual in English and Spanish, who visited nearly 27,000 households to select and interview American adults. The final sample of interviewees consisted of a nationally representative sample of 13,600 Americans aged 16 and older (pages 5-6). The results of each literacy subtest were reported in a scale from 0 to 500. The scores were then arranged in five levels: Level 1 (0 to 225), Level 2 (226 to 275), Level 3 (276 to 325), Level 4 (326 to 375), and Level 5 (376 to 500) (page 9).

Scores were closely correlated with occupational and financial success. For example, while adults in Level 1 on each scale reported working an average of only 18 to 19 weeks in the year prior to the survey, those in the three highest levels reported working between 34 and 44 weeks. Moreover, across the three scales, individuals in the lowest level reported median weekly earnings of $230 to $245, compared with about $350 for individuals who performed in Level 3 and $620 to $680 for those in Level 5.[93]

Below (from page 10) are examples of problems at different levels of skill:

Prose Literacy

210: Locate one piece of information in a sports article.

250: Locate two pieces of information in a sports article.

304: Read a news article and identify a sentence that provides an interpretation of a situation.

374: Compare two metaphors used in poem.

Document Literacy

151: Locate the expiration date on a driver's license.

232: Locate an intersection on a street map.

314: Use a bus schedule to determine the appropriate bus for a given set of conditions.

379: Use a table of information to determine a pattern in oil exports across years.

Quantitative Literacy

191: Total a bank deposit entry.

308: Using a calculator, determine the discount from an oil bill if paid within 10 days.

---

92. http://nces.ed.gov/pubs93/93275.pdf: *Adult Literacy in America: A First Look at the Findings of the National Adult Literacy Survey* (Published in 1993 by the U.S. Department of Education).

93. Pages xix-xx. Another interesting correlation was that on all three literacy scales between 55 and 58 percent of those on Level 1 who were eligible to vote said that they had voted in the past five years, compared with 80 percent at Level 4 and 90 percent at Level 5.

375: Calculate miles per gallon using information given on mileage record chart.

421: Using a calculator, determine the total cost of a carpet to cover a room.

Below (from page 36) are the average scores on the NALS for American whites (W), blacks (B), Hispanics (H), and Asian/Pacific Islanders (A/P) at different levels of completed education.[94] A blank means that the number of adults in that category was too small to provide a reliable average.

Prose Literacy	W	B	H	A/P
0-8 years of education	202	159	139	blank
High School Diploma	278	242	242	209
Some College	302	267	265	264
Two Year Degree	313	276	291	blank
Four Year Degree	328	288	282	271
Graduate Degree	341	298	312	301
Document Literacy	W	B	H	A/P
0-8 years	191	151	131	blank
High School Diploma	271	235	242	214
Some College	297	261	263	261
Two Years Degree	305	263	288	blank
Four Year Degree	320	279	285	275
Graduate Degree	320	285	306: 298	298
Quantitative Literacy	W	B	H	A/P
0-8 Years	195	140	128	blank
High School Diploma	297	232	240	237
Some College	304	258	265	273
Two Years Degree	313	267	286	blank
Four Year Degree	329	280	286	286
Graduate Degree	338	285	312	314

94. The Department of Education commissioned a similar study in 2003, called the National Assessment of Adult Literacy (NAAL). A great deal of information on it is available, but not the average scores of racial and ethnic groups at various levels of education. At least, neither I, nor the information service of the U.S. Public Affairs Office in South Africa, nor the research librarians of the University of the Witwatersrand in Johannesburg could find this information for the 2003 NAAL.

The reader should note that in Prose Literacy and Document Literacy, the average score of blacks with a post-graduate degree (298, 285) was significantly lower than the average score of whites (302, 297) who attended some college, but did not acquire even a two-year degree. In Quantitative Literacy, the average score of blacks *with a post-graduate degree* (285) was considerably lower than the average score of whites (297) *with no more than a high school diploma.*

Now let us compare the average score of blacks with the sample of problems at different scores that I provide above. The average score in Prose Literacy (298) of blacks *with a post-graduate degree* was lower than the level needed (304) to read a news article and identify a sentence that provides an interpretation of a situation. The average score in Document Literacy (285) of blacks *with a post-graduate degree* was much lower than the level needed (314) to use a bus schedule to determine the appropriate bus for a given set of conditions. The average score in Quantitative Literacy (285) of blacks *with a post-graduate degree* was much lower than the level needed (308) to use a calculator to determine the discount from an oil bill if paid within 10 days.

Another important indicator of affirmative graduation is performance on state examinations that determine whether prospective or current teachers are qualified. Numerous careful studies have found no significant positive correlation between students' performance and class size, educational expenditure, student motivation, post-high school educational intention, self-esteem, teachers' degrees or any other factor except one: teachers' scores on these competence examinations (Thernstrom 2003: 206, 217-18, 306, notes 55, 56; Ferguson 1991; Hanushek 1991).

In 1982-83 first-try pass rates on teacher competence tests in representative states were (D'Souza 1995: 306):

	Whites	Asians	Hispanics	Blacks
California	76 percent	50 percent	38 percent	26 percent
Texas	62 percent	47 percent	19 percent	10 percent
Florida	90 percent	63 percent	51 percent	35 percent
Arizona	73 percent	50 percent	42 percent	24 percent

Racial differences would be greater if the examinations would be reasonably difficult or the passing marks reasonably high. However, in order not to fail even more minorities, the passing requirements are set at ludicrous levels.[95] The most that is required is tenth grade, and often less, ability at reading, writing, and mathematics, even though some of the teachers are teaching the eleventh and twelfth grades. Albert Shanker, who was president of the United Federation of Teachers from 1964 to 1984 and of the American Federation of Teachers from 1974 to 1997, described the passing requirements "ridiculously low," serving only to screen out "illiterates" (Thernstrom 2003: 203).

A typical mathematics question on these tests is, "If the sum of two numbers is 18, which *cannot* be true of the numbers?" Five possible answers are supplied, the first of which is, "Their sum is 0." (This is not a typographical error.) A typical American history question is, "The growth of which of the following was LEAST stimulated by the growth of United States railroad lines during the nineteenth century?" The possible answers are: wheat production, insurance companies, steel production, iron mining, tobacco production. A typical natural history question is, "Which of the following changes on earth has taken place most recently?" The possible answers are: appearance of humans, development of the atmosphere, formation of the seas, formation of the first fossils, appearance of reptiles. A typical English question begins with the quotation, "They embrace. But they do not know the secret in the poet's heart." The question is why the second sentence is not a typical stage direction. The possible answers are: poets do not often appear in plays, plays are not often built around secrets, the direction does not summarize the plot, the direction does not list the names of all the characters, the direction cannot be acted out for the audience to see.[96]

These questions are from the National Teacher Examination (NTE), the most widely used of these tests. The California Basic Educational Skills Test (CBEST) was even easier. It was set at an *eighth*-to-tenth-grade level. Above,

95. Basinger 1999; Herrnstein and Murray 1996: 787, note 21 (763, note 21 of the 1994 edition). Stephan and Abigail Thernstrom (1997: 375) described the desperation of American school systems to hire more minority teachers. In 1990, the New York City Board of Education intensified its attempts to recruit more minority teachers and administrators. This is terribly difficult since "urban school systems around the country are fiercely competing." New York School Chancellor Joseph Fernandez admitted, "there is no hard evidence that pairing students with teachers of the same race or ethnic background will enhance their performance;" "the board is going ahead with the plan because it does not want to foster even the appearance of discrimination." So, to avoid the appearance of discrimination against minorities, it intensified real discrimination against whites (Berger 1990).

96. "The Test: Untrivial Pursuit." *Newsweek* (September 24, 1984): 68-70; Thernstrom 1997: 349.

I list the first-try pass rates on it for candidates of different racial groups, all of whom had or were completing a bachelor's degree, and many of whom had a master's degree. But since there is no limit to the number of times a candidate can take it, eventually over 80 percent pass the CBEST. [97]

Another common means, besides allowing constant retakes, that states use to ensure that illiteracy does not bar minorities from the teaching profession is to pass nearly everyone. For example, in 1984, Texas instituted a requirement that in order to retain their positions, all public school teachers had to pass a test on which a typical problem was picking from five choices the answer to the question, "If it takes 10 hours to go from point A to B at 50 miles per hour, how long will it take at 40 mph?" But only 23 percent of blacks and 34 percent of Hispanics, all of whom had bachelor's degrees and many of whom had master's degrees, passed it. So, Texas adopted a different test, which 97 percent for all test-takers passed. Consequently, 82 percent of blacks and 94 percent of Hispanics passed; although eight thousand teachers did not show up to take even the easier tests, presumably because they knew they could not pass it (Elliot 1988: 344; Phelps 105-6, 110).

Alabama came up with more complicated means to reach the same end. Daniel Alexander, the president of the board of education of Mobile, Alabama, began a crusade for qualifying tests for teachers when a parent brought him a note written by a teacher *with a master's degree*: "Scott is dropping in his studies he acts as if he don't Care. Scott want to pass in his assignment at all, he a had a poem to learn and he fell to do it." (This is an exact, letter-for-letter, copy of the note.) More shocking to Alexander than the note was that when he showed it to the superintendent of education, he was not surprised by it. The board of education refused to require veteran teachers to pass a competency test, but in 1979 it began requiring the NTE for new teachers. About half of applicants for teaching positions in Mobile passed it. In 1981, black students at Alabama State University sued the state over the discriminatory racial impact of the test. In 1985, Alabama agreed to create a new test on which the black failure rate would be no more than five percent higher than the white failure rate. No such test could be devised. Finally, in 1999, an agreement was reached between the Alabama Department of Education and the plaintiffs, which provided three alternatives. The first is a qualifying test whose passing score is set in consultation with a panel dominated by representatives of the plaintiffs. Applicants who fail to attain even that score can count their college grades equally with the test score. Applicants who cannot pass by even that means can gain certification by taking a remedial course, if they have a 2.5 grade average. These qualifications

97. "Court to Reconsider Claim that Teacher Skills Test is Biased." *Los Angeles Times* (March 29, 2000): B2.

would not disqualify the teacher who wrote the note that began Alexander's drive for certifying exams.[98]

Moreover, schools employ black and Hispanic teachers who have failed to meet even the pathetic requirements that they set (Thernstrom 2003: 192, 204).

It is also noteworthy that in 2004, 8.7 percent of all public elementary school teachers and 9.2 percent of public high school teachers in the United States were black, but 16.4 percent of principals were black. Since most principals are drawn from the ranks of teachers, the racial gap in competence must be considerably greater among principals than among teachers.[99]

As always, the fairest, easiest, and most efficient way to administer racial discrimination would be an explicit quota. Then, reasonably difficult tests could be used, and the passing score for whites could be set high enough to ensure that only competent white teachers are qualified. The desired proportion of Asians, Hispanics, and blacks would be obtained by using a lower passing score for each group.

The reader may have noticed that the examples of affirmative graduation that I have used are from the 1980s and 1990s. I was unable to find more recent examples. However, it is safe to assume that the white-black gap at every level of higher education has increased since then. The reason is that, as I point out in Section F of Appendix III, the white-black (and white-Hispanic) gap on all measures of academic ability and achievement has increased considerably since 1990. But during the same period, the ratio of blacks relative to whites in higher education has constantly increased. The *Journal of Blacks in Higher Education* of Autumn 2009 provides a graph (page 42) of the percent of blacks relative to whites at all levels of higher education from 1970 to Autumn 2009. In 1970, 57 percent as many blacks as whites were enrolled in higher education. That rose to 63 percent in 1980, 65 percent in 1990, 69 percent in 2000, and 75 percent in 2009. Even these statistics understate the relative increase of blacks relative to whites in higher education because until 1998 Hispanics were included among whites; after 1998, the ratio is between blacks and non-Hispanic whites. Between 1985 and 2004, the proportion of American bachelor's degrees given to blacks rose from 5.9 percent to 9.4 percent; the proportion of American master's degrees given to blacks rose from 5.0 percent to 9.1 percent; and the proportion of professional degrees given to blacks rose

---

98. Basinger 1999A; "Help! Teacher Can't Teach." *Time* (June 16, 1980): 58.

99. *Journal of Blacks in Higher Education* (Winter 2005/2006): 63; Thernstrom 1997: 374.

from 4.3 percent to 7.1 percent.[100] Between 1987 and 2007, the proportion of doctorates awarded to American citizens that went to blacks increased from 3.6 percent to 6.6 percent.[101]

In fact, the academic ability and achievement of all Americans at each level of completed higher education has declined considerably. The reason is that in the 25 years from 1983 to 2008, the number of Americans enrolled in higher education increased by more than a third (McCluskey and Schaeffer 2009); but the average intelligence of Americans did not increase. I pointed out above that in 1992 and 2003, the U.S. Department of Education conducted surveys of the proficiency of a representative sample of American adults in Prose Literacy, Document Literacy, and Quantitative Literacy. The Department of Education published the average scores of racial and ethnic groups at various levels of education only for the 1992 survey. So that is the only one I discussed.

However, the Department of Education did publish comparisons for all Americans between 1992 and 2003.[102] It divided the scores into Below Basic, Basic, Intermediate, and Proficient. The proportion of American adults in the highest category (Proficient) declined in both Prose and Document Literacy from 15 percent in 1992 to 13 percent in 2003. The proportion of American adults who were proficient in Quantitative Literacy remained the same at 13 percent. Consequently, the average scores of all American adults at all levels of completed higher education was considerably lower in 2003 than in 1992. In 1992, the average scores of all Americans with four-year college degrees and no higher degree were 325, 317, and 324 in Prose Literacy, Document Literacy, and Quantitative Literacy, respectively. In 2003 the average scores of all Americans with only four-year college degrees were 314, 303, and 323. In 1992, the average scores of all Americans with post-graduate degrees in the three types of literacy were 340, 328, and 336; in 2003, the average scores of all American with post-graduate degrees were 327, 311, and 332. The reader should notice that the decline was greater among those who received post-graduate degrees than among those who received only a four-year college degree. The reason is the number of the former increased more than the number of the latter.[103]

100. "The Solid Progress of African Americans in Degree Attainment." *Journal of Blacks in Higher Education* (Summer 2006): 54-9.

101. "Number of Blacks Earning Doctorates in 2007 Increases by 10 Percent." *Journal of Blacks in Higher Education* (Winter 2008/2009): 36.

102. http://nces.ed.gov/naal/kf_demographics.asp

103. http://nces.ed.gov/fastFacts/display.asp?id=69. The proportion of Americans who received a high school diploma also increased, but the increase was much less than for university degrees. Consequently, the decline

When I discussed the results of the 1992 survey, I pointed out the pathetically low level of the average scores of blacks with post-graduate degrees.
For the reasons stated above, their average performance must have declined
much more than the average performance of whites since 1992.

B. The Causes of Affirmative Grading and Graduation

One cause of affirmative grading and graduation is government compulsion. For example, the 2003 health education bill specified the proportion
of black and Hispanic nurses that nursing schools must *graduate* to receive
government financial support, without which few nursing schools could
survive.

Accreditation associations are another cause. Accreditation distinguishes
a real institution of learning from a diploma mill. Only accredited universities
and colleges are eligible for federal grants, and only students at accredited
institutions can receive federal financial aid. Accreditation is conferred by
six American accreditation associations, each for a different region of the
country. They have always considered factors like the proportion of faculty
members with PhDs, the number of books and articles they publish, the
number of books in the university's library, the equipment in its laboratories,
requirements for passing courses, etc.

In 1988 the Middle States and Western accreditation associations added
another criterion: racial diversity in faculty, curriculum, administration, and
students.[104] This requirement must be met by graduating, not just admitting,
a specified proportion of minority students. In 1990 alone, the Middle States
Association delayed the re-accreditation of fifteen colleges and universities
until they improved their diversity records. The most publicized case involved Bernard M. Baruch College of the City University of New York, one
of the largest undergraduate business schools in the United States, *only 36
percent of whose students were white.* In 1990, the Middle States Association

---

among American adults who received only a high school diploma was much
less than the decline among those who received university degrees. The
average score of American adults with only a high school diploma in Prose
Literacy declined between 1992 and 2003 from 268 to 262; in Document
Literacy, the average declined from 261 to 258. The average in Quantitative
Literacy rose from 267 to 269.

This is the reason why a state's economic growth is negatively correlated
with the amount of money it spends on its public universities (Vedder and
Denhardt 2007).

104. The following information is from Yates 1994: 49-55; Leatherman
1990, 1990A; Weiner 1990; and Taylor 1992: 177-8.

threatened not to renew its accreditation unless it submitted a plan to hire more minority faculty members and administrators and remedy the "attrition [i.e., dropout] rate" of its black and Hispanic students. More than 40 percent of Baruch's students were receiving federal financial aid, which they would have lost if Baruch's accreditation was not renewed. Shortly afterwards, one of Baruch's professors was awarded the Nobel Prize in Economics, but that was irrelevant to the Middle States Association.[105]

The accreditation associations cannot be accused of hypocrisy. They have practiced what they preach and thereby have ensured that the process is irreversible. The director of the Western Association boasted (Weiner 1990), "Last year [1989], more than 20 percent of our team members were people of color, and more than 30 percent were women. Almost 50 percent . . . were new to the accreditation process, including many white males who strongly support the commission's new standards." By now, a large majority of the employees of the Western and Middle States Associations, and probably of the others as well, must have been hired on the basis of their race, sex, and/or enthusiasm for diversity criteria. They have little or no experience in assessing academic criteria. Most probably have no interest in academic criteria.

Of course, both accreditation associations deny that they are enforcing discrimination. The director of Middle States explained (Leatherman 1990), "the issue . . . [is] equity and nondiscrimination for all students." The director of the Western Association warned (Weiner 1990), "'diversity' should not be [construed as] a code word for granting preferences to one group over another."

I have discussed the Middle States and Western accreditation associations because they have adopted explicit racial diversity criteria. But the four other accreditation associations employ racial diversity criteria informally. Professor Peter Wood of Boston University reported (2003: 243), "In 2001, I served on a New England Association . . . accreditation site team and found myself alone in refusing to apply a diversity standard to the college we were reviewing."

Law and medical schools are also subject to diversity standards in order to gain and maintain accreditation (Welch and Gruhl 1998: 80-81). I will

105. In 1983, Baruch's black and Hispanic students demanded their own racially segregated alumni association, with campus office space, secretarial help, etc. The Baruch administration refused. It was sued and agreed to accede and pay court costs. So, Baruch has two alumni associations, both funded by the college (i.e., the taxpayers of New York). One is for all alumni; the other is open to only black and Hispanic alumni. I will remind the reader that whites are a minority at Baruch (Taylor 1992: 236-7).

provide one example. The American Bar Association (ABA) accredits American law schools. In nearly all states, only graduates of ABA-accredited law schools can take the bar exam and thus be qualified to practice law. In 2000, an ABA re-accreditation inspection found that 93.5 percent of the first-year law students at George Mason University Law School (GMULS) were white. The ABA conceded that GMULS had made a "very active effort to recruit minorities," but that was insufficient because it was unwilling "to engage in any significant preferential affirmative action admissions program," which means lowering its admissions standards for minorities. With the gun of dis-accreditation at its head, GMULS lowered its admissions standards and admitted more minorities: 11 percent in 2001 and 16 percent in 2002. But that did not satisfy the ABA. In 2003, it summoned GMU's president and law school dean and threatened them personally with dis-accreditation. GMULS lowered its admissions standards further and managed to raise its minority admissions to 17 percent in 2003 and 19 percent in 2004. That was still not good enough! The ABA complained, "Of the 99 minority students in 2003, only 23 were African American; of the 111 minority students in 2004, the number of African Americans held at 23." What about the blacks it did admit? From 2003 to 2005, 45 percent had grade-point averages below 2.15, which GMULS defines as "academic failure." For non-blacks (including non-black minority students), the figure was 4 percent. GMULS officials point out that the ABA's own Standard 501(b) states, "a law school shall not admit applicants who do not appear capable of satisfying completely its educational program and being admitted to the bar." GMULS dean Daniel Polsby explained, "Adhering to this principle is the greatest obstacle to our efforts to increase the diversity of the George Mason student body."[106]

106. Guess 2008; Heriot 2008. I have not been able to find the details of GMULS's admissions requirements for minority students. Nearly certainly, the problem of black under-representation among them arose because GMULS set the same standards for all minority applicants. Hispanics are, on average, more intelligent than blacks, and Asians are much more intelligent. So they were the ones who benefitted most. (Asians were among the minorities for whom admissions requirements were lowered.)

In February 2006, the ABA's Council of the Section on Legal Education and Admissions to the Bar adopted Standard 211 (b), which states, "a law school shall demonstrate by concrete action a commitment to having a faculty and staff that are diverse with respect to gender, race, and ethnicity." "Interpretation 211-1" states, "the requirements of a constitutional provision or statute that purports to prohibit consideration of gender, race, ethnicity or national origin in admissions or employment is not a justification for a school's non-compliance with Standard 211." In other words, in those states

George Mason Law School's attempted resistance is unusual. In most cases, requirements of affirmative grading and graduation are not imposed on unwilling victims. In January 1999, the University of Pittsburgh proudly announced that if the average grades (not just graduation rates) of the black and Hispanic students in any of its faculties do not equal the average grades of its white students, the budget of that faculty would be cut. The spokesman of the American Council of Education praised the plan because, "It's clearly designed to put some teeth into campus efforts to increase educational *opportunities*" (Gose 1999; italics added).

Even without conscious intention, blacks receive much higher grades than whites for the same work. Kent Harber (1998) wrote a large number of essays that he filled with errors in grammar and content. He then asked 92 white college students to act as markers and gave each one essay, along with a brief description of its putative author, which indicated the "author's" race indirectly but clearly (e.g., member of the Black Student Union). The markers' average rating (on a 1-7 scale) for content of the essays they thought were written by blacks was 3.5, but 2.7 for the essays they thought were written by whites. Forty-six percent of the markers wrote comments on the essays they graded. The favorableness of the written comments (on a scale of +1 to –1) was *plus* .57 for the essays they thought were written by blacks but *minus* .4 for the essays they thought were written by whites. (The markers were told that the authors would get their essays back.) Some markers wrote on the essays that they thought were written by whites comments like "when I read college work this bad I just want to lay my head down on the table and cry." Such negative comments were never written on essays supposedly written by blacks. On the contrary, many markers wrote on essays they thought were written by blacks how much they enjoyed reading them and how much potential they showed.

Harber repeated the same experiment with 103 different markers. Their pattern of rating and comments was identical.

It is reasonable to assume that supervisors and employers also evaluate the same work more highly when it is done by blacks than when it is done by whites.

C. Grade Inflation

However, the whole issue of marking is becoming hypothetical. In 2003,

___

and municipalities that have prohibited racial discrimination, law schools must violate the law in order to gain ABA accreditation. The mission statement of the ABA says that one of its primary goals is to "promote respect for the law."

between 44 percent and 55 percent of the grades at the eight Ivy League colleges, MIT, Stanford, and the University of Chicago were an A (Hoover 2004). Consequently, B is a compensatory grade for poor work, and failing is nearly impossible. In 1993, a student used a fake transcript to get into Yale. He had a B average for two years at Yale, before his deception was discovered. That was higher than his average at the community college from which he transferred (Gose 1997).

It might be argued that the quality of students at elite colleges partially justifies such grades. But grade inflation pervades all American tertiary education. A study of 10,000 undergraduates at 150 colleges of varying sizes and academic standards found that the proportion of grades of A- and higher rose from 19 percent in 1976 to 26 percent in 1993 (Comarow 1998). Grade inflation has accelerated since then. A study (www.gradeinflation.com), which was based on data from 210 colleges with a combined enrollment of over two million students, found that the average grade-point-average rose from 2.93 in the 1991-92 academic year, to 2.99 in 1996-97, to 3.07 in 2001-02, to 3.11 in 2006-07. The last two are within the A range.

In 2004, the National Survey of Student Engagement, which covered 163,000 full-time freshmen and seniors at 472 four-year colleges, found that 40 percent of the students said that they receive mostly A's; another 41 percent said that they receive mostly B's. Yet, only 11 percent of the same students said that they spend more than 25 hours a week preparing for classes, which is the minimum that faculty members say is necessary to succeed at college. Forty-four percent spend 10 or fewer hours preparing.[107] In the "Your First College Year 2009" survey (available online), only 28 percent of freshmen said that they sent more than ten hours a week on studying/homework.

Although the most publicized effect of grade inflation has been a bizarre increase in the proportion of A's, the most important effect has been a dramatic decrease in the failure rate. Among the students at the 28 colleges and universities that William Bowen and Derek Bok studied in *The Shape of the River* (1998: 68-9), the proportion of students who graduated from the college they entered rose from 77 percent of those who entered in 1976 to 85 percent of those who entered in 1989. Bowen and Bok observed, "graduation rates . . . increased quite considerably within each SAT interval. The greatest progress [*sic*] occurred in the below-1000 SAT interval." The inevitable result was that "the black-white gap [in graduation rate] narrowed."

Among the students at the eleven colleges and universities that Bowen and Fredrick Vars studied (1998: 474-5), the difference between whites and

---

107. "Students Study Less Than Expected, Survey Finds." *Chronicle of Higher Education* (November 26, 2004): A1.

blacks in average class rank increased slightly between 1976 and 1989. However, grade inflation lessened the difference between the average college grades of whites and blacks by 17.5 percent. A decrease between two groups in average grades reduces the difference between them in graduation rates. Consequently, throughout the United States, the proportion of blacks who graduated from college within six years after they entered increased from 28 percent of black men and 34 percent of black women who entered in 1984, to 34 percent of black men and 44 percent of black women who entered in 1996.[108] It was, therefore, understandable that when, in 1995, Stanford's new president reinstated the possibility of failing courses, many black students regarded that as a direct attack on them (Townsend 1994-95: 110).

Grade inflation has also been rampant at high schools. The proportion of high school graduates who attended college rose greatly between 1968 and 2004. Nevertheless, the proportion of college freshmen who reported having had an A or A- average in high school increased from 17.6 percent in 1968 to 42.9 percent in 2000 to 47.5 percent in 2004.[109] In 1991, 28 percent of students who took the SAT had a cumulative high school average of A- and above (90-100 percent). That rose to 35 percent in 1996 and to 41 percent in 2004, when 6 percent had an *A+ (97-100 percent) average*, and 18 percent had an A (93-96 percent) average.[110] Of the students who took the SAT in 2005, the average grade-point-average was 3.3, which equals approximately a percent grade of 90 (Kobrin, et al., 2008: 5).

This rise in high school grades of students who take the SAT has occurred while the proportion of high school seniors who take the SAT rose from 40 percent in 1990, to 44 percent in 2000, to 49 percent in 2004. It has also occurred while the proportion of American high school seniors who do five or fewer hours of homework a week increased from 53 percent in 1987 to 65 percent in 2001 (Young 2002).

D. Examples

Many authors have provided examples of affirmative grading and graduation. I will outline two autobiographical accounts, from opposite extremes of the academic world. One is in "Making up the Grade: Notes from the

---

108. "The Nation's Colleges Show a Modest Improvement in African-American Graduation Rates, But a Huge Gap Still Remains." *Journal of Blacks in Higher Education* (Autumn 2003): 109-17.

109. Camara, et al., 2003: 1-3; *Journal of Blacks in Higher Education* (Spring 2005): 30.

110. This information was from www.collegeboard.com. It stopped providing this information after 2004.

Antiversity"[111] by "Robert Berman," a pseudonym for an adjunct lecturer at the City University of New York (CUNY). He introduced his narration by pointing out that it applies to his experiences in "the 'Remedial U' world," which encompasses nearly all two-year colleges and many four-year colleges.

He observed (page 39; the italics are Berman's; the bold letters are mine):

> Remedial U is geared toward controlling a maximum in public funds, in order to dispense jobs to its middle and upper-class allies, while offering bread and circuses to its poor and lower-middle-class clients—the students. . . . (In 1997-98, the City University of New York represents a $4.45 *billion* dollar jobs program.) . . . Full-time campus "welfare agency" (e.g., Minority Education Office, Economic Opportunity Program, and SEEK [Search for Education, Elevation, and Knowledge]) staffers speak of "caseloads," while **students . . . may practically dictate their own grades.** Welcome to the "antiversity."

Berman then pointed out (40-42) that at CUNY, "68 percent of incoming senior [i.e., four-year] college freshmen cannot pass eleventh-grade reading and tenth-grade math tests" and "80 to 90 percent of New York's public school teachers are CUNY graduates."

Berman (page 43) listed five types of pressure that he encountered to increase grades:

> 1. As a "white male," not giving black, Hispanic, and female students what they want will surely result in charges of "bias."
>
> 2. Pushing students to produce will result in unfavorable student evaluations and complaints to my superiors.
>
> 3. Every failing grade costs the school money, as more students drop out or flunk out.
>
> 4. As I am an untenured faculty member, my superiors will treat even specious criticisms with the utmost seriousness.
>
> 5. Since even my best students will be disadvantaged by their degrees vis-à-vis graduates of "selective" schools benefiting from grade inflation . . . it seems doubly unfair to grade them based purely on merit.

After the second type of pressure, Berman appended the following footnote: "In May 1997, a CUNY/Hunter College student told me, 'If students don't like a prof. they would take him out, by complaining about him to administrators, lying if necessary. The student also noted that most of her

---

111. *Academic Questions* (Spring 1998): 38-52.

professors were 'scared' of their students."

Berman then gave examples (46-8):

> [W]hen I taught at a state college in New Jersey, [e]ach remedial composition final was graded by two instructors. Each of the graders, over 90 percent of whom were white females, could give a maximum of six points, for a total of twelve; seven points were required to pass. In one class, two black men and two Puerto Rican females received "eights" and "nines" respectively, for essays that were worthy of only "sixes" and "sevens" . . . [T]he same graders failed one of my best students, a young white man, with a six. . . . The above students had twenty minutes to write their essays. As grading practices apparently still had not evolved sufficiently to produce the desired curve, my chairwoman retired the traditional twenty-minute time limit in favor of an entire 75-minute class period, dropping as well a New Jersey standardized examination of basic skills, which had tended to trip up weak students. . . . Despite the additional fifty-five minutes . . . the grading was even more lax than in the past. . . . The new procedure flew in the face of the hard-won knowledge that a student who could not write an intelligent essay in twenty minutes would not be able to cope with the mounting time and workload pressures of college-level classes.
>
> Responding to critics . . . CUNY officials are developing a uniform Academic Certification Examination (ACE) as a graduation requirement. However . . . developers spend much of their time perfecting fudging mechanisms. For instance, on reading comprehension sections, they train faculty "raters" to pass students who cannot write in English. . . .
>
> At the community college level, the two main strategies I have seen used to pass students are "justification" and institutionalized test fraud. . . . "Justification" [is] a rubber-stamp process whereby a full-time professor needed merely to request of her department chairwoman that most students who failed the New Jersey basic skills test be passed. . . . [Test fraud involves] instructors giv[ing] their students copies of the final to take home. Students arrive at the test armed with complete written or memorized essays, often written for hire, which they copy into their blue books, while the full-time faculty proctor reads a magazine.

I will add to Berman's narration that in 1999-2000, 35.5 percent of American undergraduates had taken a remedial course at college (PUPI 2002: 132); and the cost of teaching a remedial course, in staff, overhead, and support services, is greater than the cost of teaching an academic course

(Manno 1996: 78-9). These courses accomplish nothing.[112]

I said that the two autobiographical accounts of affirmative grading and graduation that I would discuss come from opposite extremes of the academic world. The second is the description by Professor Bernard Davis (1986: 168-91) of the practices that Harvard Medical School uses to grant medical degrees to manifestly unqualified minority students and the tricks it uses to hide this practice. As Professor Davis pointed out in the beginning of his disclosures,

> Since the consumer is particularly blind in purchasing medical care, and his vital interests are often at stake, those who are in a position to screen for aptitude and competence in medicine have a grave moral responsibility…. [T]he M.D. degree leads to an unlimited license to make life-and-death judgments.

Harvard Medical School is by far the best and most selective American medical school.[113] So, it can choose the best minority students. Professor Davis recalled (171-2) that in 1968, when it instituted the policy that at least 15 of its entering class of 75 be minorities, the supporters of this policy argued,

> [I]f we tried hard enough, we surely should be able to find fifteen satisfactory candidates. . . . The underlying assumption was that the terrible legacy of slavery obligated us to short-circuit for blacks the gradual path that had been followed by other groups . . . . It was argued that among minority students who lacked proper academic qualifications many would have potential that had been buried by

---

112. In 2007, a study was finally published that compared the post-remedial performance of undergraduates who took remedial courses with those at the same level of academic ability who did not take remedial courses. The study was financed by the U. S. government and conducted by Francisco (Paco) Martorell and Isaac McFarlin Jr. Its title is *The Effects of College Remediation on Academic and Labor Market Outcomes*. It can be obtained online. The students in the study attended public colleges in Texas, where all students must take a test that is part of the Texas Academic Skills Program. Martorell and McFarlin could find no evidence that students who took remedial reading or mathematics classes were more likely to obtain a college degree than comparable students who went straight into academic classes.

113. The *U.S. News and World Report*'s *Best Graduate Schools*' surveys have consistently ranked Harvard Medical School the best in the United States. In 2002, it accepted only 4.6 percent of its applicants, and most of its applicants are extremely good.

previous discrimination, and so they should be able to do well once they were afforded the opportunity. . . . [A]t the faculty meeting that voted in the quota I asked whether we would also plan to lower our standards for passing courses. The dean, Dr. Robert Ebert, replied that . . . he had no intention of letting that happen.

Since Harvard Medical School adopted this policy before the *Bakke* decision, no one mentioned diversity. Typically, "black" and "minority" were used interchangeably; and the children of white Latin American multimillionaires whose ancestors owned slaves were included among the beneficiaries of a program whose justification was to compensate for "the terrible legacy of slavery."

For many decades the undergraduate grade average and scores on all sections of the MCAT (Medical College Admission Test) of minority students who have been *accepted* by American medical schools has been much lower than the averages of whites who have been *rejected*. In 1975, five of the 15 minority students admitted by Harvard Medical School had average MCAT scores in the mid-400s, on a 200-800 scale (Foster 1976: 17). That was approximately 100 points (which was one standard deviation) lower than the average MCAT of whites who were *rejected* by *all* American medical schools.[114]

114. In 1975-76, at ten representative American medical schools, the average scores on each section of the MCAT (Verbal, Quantitative, General, and Science) for whites who were *rejected* from medical school were 533, 573, 523, and 552; the average scores of blacks who were *accepted* were 479, 515, 466, and 500. On none of the four parts did the average score of accepted blacks come within fifty points of the average score of rejected whites. (The average scores of Mexican Americans who were accepted were 508, 554, 493, and 542.) (Klitgaard 1985: 244, note 4.) Since 1991, MCAT has had four sections: Verbal Reasoning, Physical Sciences, Biological Sciences, and a Writing Sample. Each is graded on a 1-15 scale. The Writing Sample is usually not as important in admissions as the other three sections. In 1992, on the first three sections, the average scores of *accepted* blacks were 7.4, 6.9, and 7.2; the average scores of *rejected* whites were 8.0, 7.3, and 7.5 (Cross 1994: 49). In 1996, blacks who were accepted had an average composite MCAT score on all three sections of 23.5; whites who were rejected had an average of 25.2; whites who were accepted had an average of 30.2. (*Journal of Blacks in Higher Education* (Spring 1999): 23).
Since 1996, the average grade-point-average (GPA), on a 1-4 scale, in undergraduate science courses of blacks who were accepted by medical schools was 3.09; of whites who were rejected, 3.28; of whites who were accepted,

As always, scores on aptitude and achievement tests accurately predicted academic performance. Professor Davis continued (1986: 172-4):

> The dean's office [of the medical faculty] pressed the departments to provide repeated reexaminations to failing students, and inevitably these examinations became less demanding. Virtually every student eventually passed each course. . . . [I]f they required five years or more to complete the four-year program, they could then be certified as being just as qualified as those students who mastered the material more readily. . . . The administration took several steps to make the radical changes in academic standards less conspicuous. First, letter grades were replaced by a system of either pass or incomplete . . . and when a student replaced an "Incomplete" by "Pass," his record retained no evidence that he had had difficulties. This change . . . provided the dean with a convenient device: he could honestly state that the performance records of the minority graduates could not be distinguished from those of the other graduates.

Professor Robert Gordon, in his review of Professor Davis' book, observed (1988: 85, 91-2 notes 17, 19) that all the research conducted after Professor Davis' revelations, like all before it, has found not the slightest evidence of a "catch-up" by minorities admitted to universities or hired for jobs with lower scores on qualifying tests than whites. In activities as different as law school and repairing telephones, initial test scores accurately predict all measures of later competence. Gordon mentioned in particular the close correlation between scores on the MCAT and on the NBME (National Board of Medical Examiners) tests taken during and after medical school.

Here I must explain that the courses in the first two years of medical school are devoted to basic sciences relevant to medicine (anatomy, biochemistry, etc.). The courses in the third and fourth years involve specifically medical subjects (surgery, obstetrics/gynecology, pediatrics, etc.) Then, after a medical student has an MD degree, he works in a hospital as an intern. The NBME had three parts. Part I was taken at the end of the second year of medical school; Part II at the end of the fourth year; and Part III at the end of internship. When a student passes Part III, she can practice as a doctor. But to be a specialist, she must do several years of supervised training

---

3.58 (Cross and Slater 1997: 16). In evaluating these numbers, the reader should remember that blacks receive affirmative grading.

Steve Sailer (2009) provides valuable comparisons between the whites, blacks, Mexican Americans, and Asians who entered American medical schools in 2007 on the three sections of the MCAT and undergraduate GPA. I quote them in Section D of Chapter 19.

as a resident in the specialty of her choice. Then, in order to be "Board Certified" in that field, which is desirable, but not necessary, she must pass a certifying examination.

Between 1992 and 1994, the United States Medical Licensing Examination (USMLE) replaced the NBME. It also has three parts, called steps, taken in the same sequence as the parts of the NBME. (Steps I and II take two days. Step III takes one day.)

The 2001 *Interpretive Manual* of the American Association of Medical Colleges (pages 15-16) reported that MCAT scores correlate .67 and .64 with first- and second-year medical-school grades and .72 with scores on the NBME I/USMLE I; college grades correlate only .54, .58 and .48, respectively. (A correlation of 1 means that the results are identical; 0 means there is no relationship.) These are extremely high correlations. (As I explain in Section A of Appendix III, these correlations are even more significant than they seem to be to a person who is ignorant of statistics.) The MCAT is a more accurate predictor than college grades of grades in the last two years of medical school by an even wider margin than for grades in the first two years of medical school (Huff, et al., 1999; Veloski 2000).

However, as I show in Section D of Appendix III, intelligence-based qualifications significantly overpredict the performance of members of groups that do poorly on them. So, the difference between the average score of minorities and whites on the NBME, which measures what students learned in medical school, is much *greater* (by a quarter of a standard deviation (SD) on Part I and two-fifths of a SD on Part II) than the average racial difference in MCAT scores and college grades (Klitgaard 1985: 163, 246; cf. Huff, et al., 1999).

Scores on the NBME, in turn, correlate closely with scores on the certifying examinations that are taken in medical specialties at the end of residency. The first study of this correlation involved the American Board of Orthopedic Surgery examination and Part I of the NBME. The contents of these tests had little in common. The NBME I tested factual knowledge; whereas, specialty certifying exams are based on problems and applications (analyzing clinical vignettes, diagnosing and planning on the basis of information provided, etc.). Consequently, the researchers were so surprised by the close correlation they found that they repeated the study several times. Then the correlations between NBME Parts I and II and the certifying exams for dermatology and preventive medicine were studied. In all studies, NBME I and II were found to have remarkable predictive accuracy. For instance, 50 percent of the students who scored below 400 on Part I of the NBME (on a scale of 200-800) failed the National Board of Dermatology exam, but none of those who scored above 600 failed it (Case and Swanson 1993).

Most importantly, performance on certifying examinations predicts performance as doctors. A study was conducted of the medical knowledge and skill of 259 specialists in internal medicine after they had been practicing doctors for between five and ten years; 185 were certified by the American Board of Internal Medicine, 74 either did not take the certifying exam or failed it (Ramsay, et al., 1989). They were assessed by a written examination that had multiple choice questions and patient management problems and by questionnaires filled in by associates—other doctors who specialize in internal medicine, surgeons, hospital chiefs of staff, and head nurses. Not only did the certified doctors do much better on both parts of the examination, but among them there was "a high correlation" between their score on the examination and their scores on the certifying exam. No other factor—type of practice, type of patient, medical school attended, residency training program—correlated with their score on the test independently of performance on the certifying exam. (Higher scoring doctors had, in fact, attended better medical schools, but only because graduates of better medical schools had higher scores on the certification exam.)

As for assessment by associates, "certified physicians received significantly higher ratings in [the] four major categories rated by internal medicine colleagues, [the] two areas rated by surgical colleagues, [the] two areas rated by medical directors and [the] six areas rated by head nurses." Again, there was a "significant correlation" between colleagues' ratings of their medical ability and their scores on the certifying exam; and no other factors, besides their scores in the certifying exam, correlated with associates' assessment of their ability.

A study in Quebec of 614 doctors who had recently completed family-care residency and passed Quebec's family-care licensing and certification exam found that those who did better on these exams prescribed fewer inappropriate medicines, prescribed more disease-specific rather than symptom-relief medication, referred more patients to specialists, and recommended more diagnostic screening for possible diseases. The researchers pointed out that these facts are highly significant since *71 percent of newly licensed physicians prescribed potentially inappropriate medication to their elderly patients* (Tamblyn, et al., 1998). In fact, *inappropriate medication is either the fourth or sixth (when calculated with extreme caution) leading cause of death in the United States* (Lazarou, et al., 1998). (I will return to these facts in Section E, below.)

To sum up: MCAT scores are extremely accurate predictors of scores on the NBME examinations; which are extremely accurate predictors of scores on certifying examinations in medical specialties; which, in turn, are extremely accurate predictors of actual performance as doctors. I will

130   The Affirmative Action Hoax

add here that the same person's scores on the MCAT and the SAT correlate nearly as closely with each other as the score of the same person taking either test twice.[115]

Now that the reader understands the importance of the NBME examinations, I will return to Professor Davis' exposé. Professor Davis disclosed that Harvard Medical School not only changed its grading system so that every student would graduate with the same record. In addition (Davis 1986: 174):

> Another move more deliberately deprived the faculty of objective feedback on student performance. In the past the ranking of our students in the National Board Examinations [NBME] in each subject was presented each year in a faculty meeting, and any department that fell below third place in the country virtually apologized. Shortly after the new admissions program started the dean's office quietly dropped the annual report. . . . [T]he faculty . . . voted to establish some kind of cutoff by ruling that the requirement for our M.D. degree would include passing the National Board Examinations.... [T]his cutoff. . . . settled for a minimum national standard. Moreover, a student could repeat the examinations up to five times.

Elsewhere (page 169), Professor Davis pointed out that "this minimal national standard [passing the NBME] is an extraordinarily low one." It is indeed. The NBME was normed so that the average grade each year would be 500. The passing grades were 380 for Part I and 290 for Part II. However, a study that asked directors of residency programs to rate the medical knowledge, data gathering skills, and clinical judgment of 1,994 medical residents concluded, "If the passing standards for the NBME examinations [Parts I and II] are intended to identify those examinees who are likely to

---

115. Klitgaard 1985: 92. The same person's scores on the SAT and the Law School Admission Test (LSAT), taken for admission to law school, and the Graduate Record Exam, taken for admission to graduate school, also correlate nearly as closely with each other as the score of the same person taking any one of these tests twice (Klitgaard 1985: 92).

Webb, et al., 1997 is often cited as evidence that non-academic factors affect performance in medical school. In fact, the study's conclusion begins (179), "This study confirms the importance of academic predictors [MCAT and undergraduate grades] for medical school performance." It found no effect of non-academic factors (leadership, motivation, self-confidence, etc.) in one of the two medical schools it studied, and minor effects in the other. The reason this study is often cited is that it is the only study that has ever found any effect of non-academic factors.

demonstrate only a marginal knowledge base in clinical practice . . . scores below a passing level of 421 would best identify this group." On a scale of 1-4, in which a score of 2 and below could be regarded as incompetent, 48 percent (31 of 64) of residents who scored 381-400 on the NBME I were rated 2 and below (22 percent were 1.5 and below, the rest were between 1.51 and 2.0). Of the 99 who scored between 401 and 420, 24 (24 percent) were rated 2 and below (7 percent were 1.5 and below). By contrast, of the 92 residents who scored between 601 and 620, only 4 were rated 2 and below. "A similar pattern was found for the Part II examination" (Turner, et al., 1987: 576, 579).

The entire faculty of Harvard Medical School colluded in this terrible devaluation of its MD degree without a hint to anyone outside the faculty that any changes in requirements had been made. Professor Davis publicized these changes only after Dean Ebert of Harvard Medical School arranged for the Administrative Board to grant an MD degree to a black student who had failed the NBME Part I all five times he took it and thus did not meet even the pathetically low qualification on which the faculty had agreed. (The fact that such a student passed all his courses at Harvard Medical School is itself frighteningly significant.)

By having the Administrative Board grant a degree, Dean Ebert violated university statutes, which required that all diplomas be granted by a vote of the faculty. However, he still had to inform a faculty meeting that their minimum requirement had been waived. If there were any evidence that in general, or in this case, NBME scores do not have the significance that every study has shown they have, the dean of Harvard Medical School would have known about it. Instead, Dean Ebert resorted to two lies. He did not tell the faculty that the student had failed the NBME five times; and, although he had never taught the student, he "assured us that he was a fine student with an excellent record in his clinical work." Professor Davis (1986: 175) later "found that his evaluation was sharply contradicted by colleagues who had taught this student."

It was this incident that Professor Davis publicized. The result was that his office was picketed; he was denounced in Harvard Yard before a crowd of 400; some students demanded that he be prohibited from grading "students whom he already considers to be inferior;" and an assistant to Harvard's President Derek Bok described his remarks as "a defamation and a smear" (Foster 1976: 16-17).

Dean Ebert released the following statement to the press:

Both the faculty and administration are certain that all the students granted the M.D. degree are highly competent and will make excellent physicians. I know of no evidence to support the view that the students at the Harvard Medical School have diminished in quality in recent years. . . . [S]tandards are as high as they have ever been—perhaps higher. . . .

[T]he case [of the black student who failed the NBME] was unique. The student was awarded his M.D. degree only after exceptional proof of his clinical competence (Davis 1986: 180).

Dean Ebert offered no evidence to support these assertions. On the contrary, he "sent a memorandum to all heads of departments stating that 'all information with respect to students . . . is confidential and is not for public release'." The dean then "informed me [Professor Davis] that under the circumstances he could not proceed with his earlier plan to make me director of the Center for Human Genetics" (Davis 1986: 180-81).

Since Harvard Medical School, by far the most selective American medical school, granted an MD degree to a black student who failed the NMBE I five times, it is reasonable to assume that it is a common practice. If it is, it involved a large number of students. Among all students who took the NBME I for the first time in 1988, the average pass rates among women were 84 percent for whites, 79 percent for Asians, 56 percent for Hispanics, and 44 percent for blacks; the average pass rates among men were 90 percent for whites, 87 percent for Asians, 72 percent for Hispanics, and 54 percent for blacks (Dawson, et al., 1994).

These failure rates cannot be attributed to lack of effort on the part of American medical schools. For decades, they have had intensive programs to help their minority students. In the *Journal of the American Medical Association*, Dawson, et al., (1994: 678) described,

[p]rograms aimed at enhancing students' academic preparation before medical school and improving their performance while in medical school [including] . . . programs teaching students how to organize their time and develop good study skills . . . special tutoring . . . alternate curriculum approaches . . . [and] programs to help students prepare for the Part I [NBME] examination.

I will remind the reader that nearly all the students in these programs are from upper- or middle-class backgrounds; and some of them graduated from the best colleges in the world, which paid many of them huge bribes to induce them to attend.

Between 1992 and 1994, Parts I, II, and II of the NBME were replaced by Steps I, II, and III of the United States Medical Licensing Examination (USMLE). (Step II has two sections: Clinical Knowledge (CK) and Clinical Skills (CS).)

I pointed out that the passing marks on the NBME I and II were 380 and 290, respectively; but they should have been above 420 on both, because nearly half of medical residents who scored 381-400 and nearly a quarter of those who scored 400-420 on the NBME I were deficient in medical knowledge, data gathering skills, and clinical judgment (Turner, et al., 1987: 576, 579). But passing the USMLE is much easier than passing the NBME. I mentioned that of the students who took the NBME I for the first time in 1998, the pass rates for white men and women were 90 and 84 percent and for Asian men and women, 87 and 79 percent. In 2008, of *all* the students who were enrolled in or had graduated from American and Canadian medical schools and who took the USMLE, the first-try pass rates were 94 percent on Step I, 96 percent on Step II-CK, 97 percent on the Step II-CS, and 95 percent on Step III. I will repeat, that is for all students who took the USMLE for the first time in 2008, among whom the proportion of affirmative-action medical-school graduates increases every year.[116] These are the pass rates for those taking the USMLE tests for the first time. I got them from the USMLE website.[117] Before it lists the first-time pass rates, the USMLE website states for every USMLE test, "Because failing examinees generally retake" it, "*the ultimate passing rate across test administrations is expected to increase to approximately 99%* [italics added]." That is for *all* medical-school graduates.

I will conclude this section with four relevant facts. First, every survey that has asked patients whether they prefer doctors of their own race has found that nearly no minority patients prefer doctors of their own race. Second, the often reported claims that American blacks receive worse medical

---

116. Women are recipients of affirmative action in medical school admission, although not nearly to the extent as minorities. Of all students who graduated from medical school in 1994, 91 percent of men and 86 percent of women passed Step I of the USMLE on the first try (Case, et al., 1996: S91). I have not tried to obtain pass rates for men and women on the most recent USMLE exams because the overall pass rate is so high that the sex difference must be negligible. But the proportion of women among matriculants at medical schools increased from 31 percent in 1982-83 to 48 percent in 2007-08 (www.aamc.org/data/facts/charts1982to2007.pdf). So, it is reasonable to assume that their competence relative to men has declined. Harvard Medical School's Associate Dean of Admissions, Gerald Foster, justified setting lower admissions qualifications for women with the explanation, "Women seem to communicate better in an interview" and they "bring some life experiences and maturity that adds to a class" (Murray 1996: 17). He did not explain how these attributes contribute to diagnosing diseases, prescribing treatment, or performing surgery.

117. www.usmle.org/Scores_Transcripts/performance/2008/html

care than whites are demonstrably false (Satel 2000: 175-6, 181-2, 155-64 and *passim*; Taylor 1992: 59-61). Third, Harvard Medical School instituted its policy of graduating (not just admitting) large numbers of blatantly unqualified minority students in 1968. By now, the children and grandchildren of these affirmative-action graduates have received or are receiving massive preference in university admissions, financial aid, and graduation over the children of white bus drivers and of non-English-speaking European and Asian immigrants.

Fourth, the Autumn 2003 issue of the *Journal of Blacks in Higher Education* (pages 118-21) reported,

> [G]raduates of the predominantly black medical school[s] at Howard University and Meharry Medical College are the most likely to come up for disciplinary actions than [*sic*] graduates of all medical schools in the United States. In fact, Howard and Meharry graduates were disciplined more often than doctors who had come to practice in the U.S. after graduating from medical schools in such third world countries as India, Mexico, Turkey, and the Philippines. The startling finding of the study is that graduates of Howard and Meharry are 10 times more likely to come before disciplinary review boards than are graduates of the medical schools with the best records. . . . The disciplinary agencies in the study include state licensing boards, federal Medicare and Medicaid programs, the Food and Drug Administration, and the Drug Enforcement Administration. Unlike medical malpractice lawsuits, which can be filed by almost anyone regardless of the validity of the claim, these disciplinary actions by state and federal regulators are often linked to cases of gross medical incompetence, extreme ethical lapses, or criminal behavior.

E. How Many People Has Affirmative Graduation Murdered?[118]

It is a matter of serious concern that doctors who exhibit "gross medical incompetence, extreme ethical lapses, or criminal behavior" had obtained medical degrees. It is even more serious that these doctors were enabled to practice medicine by passing national qualifying tests.

The purpose of making the passing rate on these tests 99 percent must

118. I use the word *murder* advisedly for the huge death toll from inappropriate medication that I document in this section. Most of the grossly incompetent doctors who prescribe these medications may not be aware that they should not be practicing medicine. But the medical schools who graduate them and the medical boards that allow them to pass national qualifying tests must know that they are killing large numbers of people.

have been to ensure that most minorities would pass them. However, the result is that there is no way to screen out white and Asian incompetents. Similarly, when Professor Davis (1986: 172) described how Harvard Medical School changed its grading policy so that every student would graduate with the same record, he pointed out, "[T]his policy had an unintended by-product . . . lowered standards provided a cushion for nonminority students whose performance would not have met the medical school's earlier standards."[119]

Again, as always, explicit quotas would be incomparably better. Then, every year, the American Medical Association would announce in advance how many of each ethnic and racial group will graduate from medical school and how many will pass national certifying exams. Medical schools and national certifying boards could then set passing grades for each group accordingly. That way, the public would know that at least the whites and Asians who pass are competent to practice medicine.

I will now return to two facts that I mentioned earlier: 71 percent of newly licensed physicians prescribe potentially inappropriate medication to their elderly patients (Tamblyn, et al., 1998: 994); and inappropriate medication is either the fourth or sixth (when calculated with extreme caution) leading cause of death in the United States. In 1994, 1,547,000 patients were admitted to an American hospital because of serious effects of inappropriate medication; another 702,000 suffered from serious effects of inappropriate medication that was administered to them while they were in an American hospital. That adds up to 6.7 percent of all patients in American hospitals in 1994. If non-serious results of inappropriate medication are included, the total is 15.1 percent of all hospital patients (Lazarou, et al., 1998).

How many people did inappropriate medication kill in 1994? Probably, 63,000 of those to whom inappropriate medication was given while they were in a hospital; and 43,000 of those who entered a hospital because of inappropriate medication. That is a total of 106,000 deaths, which was 4.6 percent of deaths from all causes in the United States in 1994. Only heart disease (743,000 deaths), cancer (530,000), and stroke (150,000) killed more Americans in 1994. If an extremely conservative estimate is used, then inappropriate medication killed 76,000 Americans in 1994, making it the sixth leading cause of death (behind pulmonary diseases: 101,000; and

---

119. I will point out in Chapter 16 that the American legal profession has adopted the same policies. In order to enable most minority students whom American law schools admit to become lawyers, American law schools graduate nearly every student they admit; and passing the bar examination has been made so easy that in 2004, 97 percent of white law school graduates eventually passed it.

accidents: 91,000) (Lazarou, et al., 1998).

I leave it to the reader to try to estimate the personal and family suffering and the costs to the American economy from non-fatal inappropriate medication.

When Tamblyn, et al., (1998: 994) pointed out that 71 percent of newly licensed physicians prescribe potentially inappropriate medication to their elderly patients, they made the obvious comment that this fact "raises the question of whether the passing standard was high enough." I have documented how accurately qualifying tests at all levels predict competence to practice medicine. However, passing them has been made constantly easier, until now it is a mere formability.

I will point out that the statistics I cite above are from 1994. The frequency of inappropriate medication and its effects must have increased since then, with the increase in the number of minority doctors and the concomitant decline in the difficulty for all prospective doctors of medical school graduation and passing qualifying tests.

I will conclude this discussion by quoting from a report that the U. S. Commission on Civil Rights presented to congress and the president in 1999, in which it criticized American medical schools for practicing discrimination *against* minorities by their "persistent yet baffling denial of the social, economic, and historical realities depriving our medical profession of minority physicians."[120]

CB BO

---

120. U. S. Commission on Civil Rights, *The Role of Civil Rights Enforcement*, page 116.

Chapter 10
Police Forces and Other Non-Academic Parallels

I know of only one systematic investigation of the effects of blue-collar affirmative-action hiring. Eugene Silberberg (1985) studied differences in performance between blacks and non-blacks who were admitted to two craft unions in Seattle: the electricians' union and the plumbers-and-pipefitters' union. On every measure that Silberberg studied, non-blacks' performance was much better than blacks' performance. For example, in the latter union, the difference between non-blacks and blacks in average grades in apprenticeship school and on-the-job training were 1.3 and .8 of a standard deviation (SD); and the difference in number of "quits and discharges" (nearly all for tardiness or absence) and in non-response to job calls was .6 SD.

The rest of the non-academic parallels I will discuss concern police hiring and promotion because, as in medicine, incompetence in police work has calamitous results. Moreover, police work is one of the very few occupations in which plausible arguments can be advanced that hiring more minorities might increase occupational effectiveness, by increasing trust and cooperation with minority civilians.

In the early and middle 1970s, Washington, DC's police department was one of the best in the country. It solved over 90 percent of all homicides committed in its jurisdiction. Between 1970 and 1976, the crime rate in most of the United States rose, but in Washington, DC, it fell by nearly half. Beginning in 1980, to increase the proportion of black policemen, the admissions test was lowered to a level at which many of those who passed it (all of whom had high school diplomas) were functionally illiterate. Some were borderline mentally retarded. Instructors in the police academy started devoting their time to teaching remedial reading and writing. That accomplished nothing. So, students at the police academy were given answers to tests before they took them; or they were allowed to take them again and again until they passed. In addition, the final examination was abandoned in 1988 (Rowan 1998; Carlson 1993; Miller 2001).

The result was that in the 1990s only 34 percent of murders in Washington, DC were solved; and over twice as high a proportion of murder indictments were dismissed than in other large cities, many because prosecutors could not read or understand the arrest reports. Of suspects who were acquitted, 32 percent were later arrested for other crimes, including 125 murders. Undoubtedly, many more acquitted suspects went on to commit other crimes but were not arrested because of the incompetence of the police force. While the crime rate declined in the rest of the country, in DC, which has more police *per capita* than any other American city, between 1985 and 1996, robberies increased 50 percent, murders by 169 percent, and auto thefts by 490 percent. At the same time, DC police killed more people *per capita* than any other American police force. Worse still, in 1992, when a convicted felon was discovered to have a gun that was supposed to be in police storage, an investigation revealed that nearly 3,000 guns supposedly in police custody were missing. One police station chains its typewriters to desks to prevent police officers from stealing them. Between 1992 and 1994, more than 200 DC police officers were arrested for crimes. Since most crimes committed in DC are unsolved because of the incompetence of its police, the number of DC police-criminals must be much higher (Carlson 1993; Siegel 1997: 111, 114; Rowan 1995; Miller 2001).

When black activist Coleman Young became mayor of Detroit in 1974, he promised to make half of its police force black. The qualifying examination was made easier; and, "Applicants who had difficulty with the qualifying exams were allowed to take them repeatedly until they passed, or were given answers by an instructor." (These tricks are as routine in getting minorities through civil service and business training programs as through colleges and professional schools.) "The average recruit [all of whom were high school graduates] was reading at a fourth-grade level." Even these tricks could get only a handful of blacks promoted to sergeant and lieutenant; so blacks were allotted half the promotions, no matter what their test scores were. The results? "[I]n mid-1978 . . . [f]our inadequately trained young officers shot and killed themselves with their service revolvers. Five others killed or wounded civilians—in several cases because they didn't like the way someone talked back to them." In 1992, William Hart, Detroit's black police chief, was convicted of embezzling $2.6 million from the police force (Jacoby 1998: 324-5, 346-7). In early September 1998, *Newsweek* reported that in Detroit, "Since January more than 20 police officers have been charged with felonies ranging from assault and armed robbery to murder. At least 100 officers are currently under investigation for ties with the drug underworld."[121]

In Miami, in 1985, an investigation into police conduct followed the discovery of hundreds of pounds of cocaine that had been hidden by police officers who were working with smugglers. Many police-criminals were convicted. Almost 90 percent had been hired through affirmative action (Herrnstein and Murray 1996:496).

A systematic study of the nationwide effects of affirmative-action police hiring and promotion was finally published in 2000 (Lott 2000). In it, John Lott Jr. used the data collected in comprehensive surveys conducted by the U.S. Justice Department in 1987, 1990, and 1993 of all American law enforcement agencies with 100 or more officers. He used this data to study the effect of "consent decrees," by which the U.S. Department of Justice forces police departments to hire and promote more minority and women officers. "Every 10 years after a consent decree goes into effect increases the number of blacks by another 4.1 percentage points and minorities by 4.8 percentage points" (page 252).

Lott found, "[B]oth violent and property crime rates . . . were declining in cities before consent decrees were imposed and were rising thereafter" (245). After consent decrees (246), "Controlling for changing city-level demographics as well as the average weekly wage, unemployment, per capita police officers, [and] city population . . . violent crime rises by 1.9 percent and property crime by 2.1 percent for each additional year the consent decree is in effect."

> [A]n increase in the percentage of a police force that is black is consistently associated with significant increases in crime. . . . The effects are dramatic no matter how one examines these estimates. For example, increasing black officers' share by one percentage point increases property crime by 4 percent and . . . violent crime by 4.8 percent (249).

In just the years between 1987 and 1990, in the 189 cities for which numbers of the racial and sex categories that Lott studied were available, the decrease in the number of white male police officers by 6,912 (6 percent) increased the number of murders by 1,145; the increase in the number of black male officers by 950 (5 percent) increased the number of rapes by

---

121. Salholz and Zeman 1998. Police Chief Hart's conviction was typical. Black elected officials are 5.3 times more likely to commit crimes than white elected officials (Gordon 1997: 253); and blacks commit several times more white-collar crimes—embezzlement, fraud, forgery, counterfeiting, etc.— than their proportion of the American population (Wilson and Herrnstein 1985: 462; Thernstrom 1997: 264).

300 (263-4).

Moreover (254, Lott's italics), "the increase in crime from hiring black officers is *greatest* in communities with the most blacks."

Hiring additional Hispanics and Native Americans also increases crime rates, but not as much as hiring additional blacks (251-2).

Lott emphasizes that (245, 261) these data greatly understate the effect of affirmative action, since political pressure and/or fear of consent decrees have forced nearly all (in fact, probably all) American police departments to adjust their hiring and promotion requirements to decrease the importance they assign to tests of reasoning ability, or to make such tests much easier, or to eliminate them completely.

> According to a 1993 survey of 23 large police and sheriff depart-
> ments . . . the cognitive portion of police tests have been completely
> removed in three cases . . . the remaining 20 had reduced their em-
> phasis on cognitive skills, with all the respondents indicating "that
> the adverse impact [on blacks and Hispanics] was considered . . .
> ." Nassau County removed all cognitive tests except for a reading
> comprehension test, which . . . requires that applicants had to score
> only as well as the bottom 1 percent of current police officers.[122]

Consequently, comparing police departments that operate under consent decrees with those that do not is merely comparing two levels of affirmative action. A consent decree increases by only a moderate extent the degree of affirmative action that a police department has been using. If there were police departments whose requirements were determined by no other consideration than hiring and promoting the best policemen, a comparison between them and police departments operating under consent decrees would result in much greater differences than in Lott's data.

Lott also studied the effect of hiring more women police officers. As with minorities, police work is one of the very few occupations in which a plausible argument can be made that more women might increase occupational effectiveness, since a victim of rape or physical abuse by a male partner might find it easier to report her complaints to a women officer. Thus, women officers might increase convictions for these crimes, which would deter their occurrence. However, Lott found (255) that increasing the proportion of women on a police force does not increase its effectiveness

---

122. Page 241. This test was accepted by the Justice Department after it had rejected three previous tests that Nassau County had devised, at great expense, because they did not pass enough blacks and Hispanics. Two of the three tests were rejected by Ronald Reagan's Justice Department (Zelnick 1996: 109-11).

in combating these crimes. On the other hand, since women are physically weaker than men, (256-7) "Increasing the number of female officers by one percentage point appears to increase the number of assaults on police by 15%-19%." Moreover (260), since women officers are less confident of their ability to handle suspects with physical force, they use their guns much more frequently than male officers. "[A] one standard deviation increase in white females increases shootings [of civilians] by .87" (i.e., it nearly doubles the rate at which police shoot civilians). Also (267-70), increasing the propor- tion of female and/or minority officers increases the proportion of car and foot patrols that have two rather than one officer: "[E]ach one percentage point increase in the percent of police who are women increases the share of two-officer foot patrols by two percentage points." In the case of women officers, a male officer is necessary to compensate for her physical weakness; in the case of minorities, a white officer is necessary to compensate for the minority officer's incompetence. The necessity of requiring patrols of two officers, rather than one, decreases the coverage that the same number of police can provide to an area.

Nevertheless, although increasing the proportion of women under the duress of consent decrees raises crime rates, the increase is much less than the increase in crime rates caused by increasing the proportion of minorities (251-2, 255). The reason (241, footnote 8, 271) is that additional women are usually hired by lowering the physical requirements (number of push-ups, running speed, marksmanship) for women only, so that the same proportion of women can pass the physical requirements as men. However, (260-61, 263) the huge negative effect of hiring more minority (especially black) po- licemen comes not only from the incompetence of the additional policemen but also because intelligence requirements are lowered for all policemen: (249) "Changing tests to employ a greater percentage of blacks can make it more difficult to screen out lower-quality candidates generally, including whites . . . [T]he size of the change in black employment may thus proxy for changes in the level of standards used to hire employees in general."

So far, I have outlined only Lott's analysis of the effect of consent decrees on police hiring criteria, but Lott points out (260-61) that their effect on promotion criteria also increases crime rates. Whites perform much better than minorities on all sensible criteria that could be used for promotion tests of reasoning ability. Consequently, they are being abandoned. For example (242), "After spending $5.1 million to have consultants develop unbiased exams, only to have minorities fare poorly again, Chicago moved to a heavily weighted seniority system for promoting police officers." Of course, such a promotion system eliminates all incentives for lower ranking officers. Similarly, the Washington, DC Police Department now "has virtually no objective means by which to rate the efficiency of officers, or to tie their performance to promotions" (Rowan 1995; cf. Rowan 1998).

The most efficient and fairest way to practice discrimination in hiring and promoting policemen, as in all activities, would be through explicit quotas. Then, police departments could maintain sensible criteria for whites and lower the requirements for minorities to the level at which the desired proportion would be hired and promoted.[123]

CR ଥା

---

123. The Justice Department obviously knows consent decrees are harmful, since Lott found (246, footnote 16), "Republican presidential administrations tended to impose consent decrees on relatively Democratic states, whereas Democratic presidential administrations tended to impose consent decrees on relatively Republican states."

CR ∞

Chapter 11
The Media vs. Reality II: Resolute Igno-
rance

Since anti-white discrimination became institutionalized in the 1960s, public opinion polls have invariably found that the large majority of Americans oppose and resent it.[124] Yet, few Americans have any idea of its extent. Even with regard to universities, where anti-white discrimination has been most publicized, the public has been kept ignorant of its extent in admissions and, more seriously, of its existence in grading and graduation.

Social scientists and the media pride themselves on being the public's watchdogs, but they have resolutely determined to ignore one of the most contentious issues in American life. In 1987, William Beer began an article entitled "Resolute Ignorance: Social Science and Affirmative Action"[125] by observing:

In the debate over the effects of reverse discrimination . . . social scientists have been almost entirely mute. . . . [T]here has been no systematic inquiry into the effects of affirmative action on American society, neither its costs to the nation's economy nor its impact on our country's morale. In an age of program evaluation, when most other social experiments are studied to death, our profession has shown a resolute ignorance about an extraordinarily controversial policy that has been in place for over two decades.

Beer did not mention that those social scientists who do study the effects of affirmative action have been condemned, ostracized and fired.[126]

---

124. Swain 2002: 190-97; Kuran 1995: 139-43, 372, note 13; Schuck 2003: 170-71.

125. *Society* (May-June): 63-69; cf. Lynch 1989: 130-33.

126. Lynch 1989: 123-6, 135; Kuran 1995: 149. In his *Summa Theologica* (I-II, Q. 6, Art. 8), Saint Thomas Aquinas pointed out that two types of ignorance do not excuse wrong-doing. One type is not taking the trouble

It is truly amazing that no systematic study of such a clearly important subject as the effect of affirmative action on police efficiency was published until Lott's in 2000. Both his study and Silberberg's analysis of the effects of blue-collar affirmative action, which I also outline in Chapter 10, were published in economics, not sociology, journals. Silberberg felt obliged to begin his analysis by claiming that it was merely an illustration of a long-discussed theoretical economics problem. Lott received his PhD from UCLA when he was 26. In the next five years he published over 70 scholarly articles. But he did not receive a single offer of a tenure-track position at an American university, even though he sent his résumé to literally hundreds of universities. In 2001, he became a resident scholar at the American Enterprise Institute (Lee 2002: 26).

The media criticize "a political system that inhibits serious debate," "politics of irrelevance and avoidance," and "legislators [who are] afraid to debate . . . controversial issues."[127] But they usually mention affirmative action only when it is being challenged; and when they do discuss it, they usually treat it as redress for past discrimination, ignoring the embarrassing fact that most of its beneficiaries are descendants of people who have received preferential treatment from the time they entered the United States (Lynch 1989: 89, 95-104, 112-13, 148, 151). As far as I know, not one newspaper, newsmagazine or television program has acknowledged the existence of Lott's analysis of the effects of affirmative-action hiring and promotion on American police departments.

William McGowan (2001: 150-57, 78-81) provides many examples of the non-reporting of the effects of affirmative action on American police departments. I will outline four. The policy of the *Buffalo News*, of Buffalo, New York, is to print photographs of city employees who are arrested for crimes. But when five policemen, all of whom were black and had been hired through a controversial affirmative action program, were arrested for involvement in narcotics trafficking; the *Buffalo News* disregarded its policy and did not print their photographs, or give any indication of their race in its report.

In 1994, when twelve policemen in Harlem's Thirtieth Precinct were arrested for extorting more than $400,000 in cash and drugs from narcotics

to acquire the knowledge that a person should clearly have in a certain circumstance. The other type is the type of which the media and sociologists are guilty: deliberate ignorance (*ignorantia affectata*): "when a person wishes not to know, in order that he may have an excuse for wrong-doing or that he may not be withheld from it [doing what he suspects is wrong]."

127. "Serious Times, Trivial Politics." *New York Times* (March 25, 1990): D18.

dealers and protecting some dealers and harassing their rivals, the press adduced the scandal as evidence that the police should be more representative of New York's population. In fact, eight of the twelve officers were Hispanic; and many had scored abysmally on the police hiring exam, as had many of the sergeants who supervised them.

The media—NBC's *Dateline*, CBS' *60 Minutes*, etc.—offered explanations for the fact that between 1993 and 1996 more than 50 New Orleans policemen were indicted for serious felonies: robbery, rape, narcotics dealing, and four first-degree murders. They did not mention New Orleans' minority hiring program, which had raised the proportion of minorities on the police force to 45 percent.

After four New York City policemen shot West African immigrant Amadou Diallo, the *New York Times* ran an average of *3.5 stories on it per day for the next two months*, most treating it as an example of rampant racist police violence. Not one of those stories mentioned that in 1999 the New York Police Department had an average of 0.48 fatal shootings per 1,000 policemen, while the mostly black Washington, DC Police Department averaged 3.12 fatal shootings per 1,000 policemen.

Similarly, in the early 1980s, the three main American newsmagazines devoted cover stories to the scandalous performance of American teachers and prospective teachers on qualifying tests, thus recognizing that it was a vital national concern. However, their stories hid from their readers that the cause was affirmative-action university graduation.

Newsweek[128] did not mention race at all. *Time*'s article[129] quoted ungrammatical, barely intelligible sentences written by American teachers and documented their terrible performance on qualifying tests. It offered several explanations, one of which (page 55) came close to the true one: "In Oregon, a kindergarten teacher who had been given A's and B's at Portland State University was recently found to be functionally illiterate." At one point (58) it carelessly included a parenthesis that disclosed how that could happen. Pinellas County, Florida, "required teacher candidates to read at an advanced tenth-grade level and solve math problems at *an eighth-grade level*. Though all had their BA in hand, about one-third of the applicants (*25 percent of Whites, 79 percent of Blacks*) flunked Pinellas' test" (italics added).

U.S. News and World Report[130] printed a selection of questions from the National Teacher Examination to show how risibly easy they were. It constantly blamed the problem on inadequate funding, and its cover showed a white teacher wearing a dunce cap. But in two sentences in the last column

128. "The Test: Untrivial Pursuit" (September 24, 1984): 68-70.
129. "Help! Teacher Can't Teach" (June 16, 1980): 54-63.
130. "What's Wrong with our Teachers?" (March 14, 1983): 37-40.

of the last page it mentioned, "In Florida, 84 percent of all those who took the exam last October passed. However, only 37 percent of black students in education passed, which has raised concerns about worsening an already serious decline in the number of black teachers." Of course, it is exactly this concern that has prevented the use of legitimate qualifying tests.

These examples are typical. For instance, an article in April 1978 in *New Times* entitled "What's the Opposite of Education?" reported that New York City had hired hundreds of incompetent, even illiterate teachers. The article did not mention that most of the teachers were Spanish-speaking (Lynch 1989: 97).

The media were forced to start discussing academic affirmative action occasionally in the 1990s, when popular and judicial assaults on it made it impossible to ignore. I will provide examples later of the misinformation that they report about affirmative action in university admissions. Here, I will outline an example concerning an affirmative-action graduate. The *New York Times Magazine* of June 11, 1995 had a front-page, 9,000-word article entitled "Taking Affirmative Action Apart" by Nicholas Lemann. The only evidence that Lemann adduced in favor of affirmative action was Patrick Chavis, one of the blacks admitted to the medical school of the University of California at Davis in the program that Allan Bakke challenged in *Regents of the University of California v. Bakke.* Lemann described Chavis as an "obstetrician-gynecologist with an enormous practice comprising entirely poor people on Medicaid." Chavis then became the subject of glowing media coverage. In the Senate Labor and Human Relations Subcommittee, Senator Edward Kennedy cited him as the "perfect example" of the benefits of affirmative action; as did opponents of the California referendum to outlaw racial discrimination. However, on June 19, 1997, the Medical Board of California suspended Chavis' license to practice medicine because of his "inability to perform some of the most basic duties required of a physician," and Judge Samuel Reyes found him guilty of gross negligence and incompetence and ruled that letting him "continue to engage in medicine will endanger the public health, safety, and welfare."

The most egregious examples of his incompetence were in his lucrative liposuction practice. For instance, on May 11, 1996, Chavis' operation on a woman left her vomiting and urinating helplessly as, in the court's words, "blood gushed down her pants leg." Instead of putting her in a hospital, Chavis took her to his house, where he left her for nearly 40 hours. He then sent her home, where she continued to suffer from bleeding and severe pain. He did not answer her phone calls and did not examine her when she came to his office, on May 17. By the time she entered a hospital, she had a severe abdominal infection and had lost most of her blood. Miraculously, she survived. But another woman died after Chavis left her in his office for four and a half hours until his clinic floor was covered with her blood. A doctor who worked with Chavis recorded him replying to patients' screams of agony with, "Liar, liar, pants on fire." The media responded to these disclosures with nearly total silence (McGowan 2001: 1-5; Jacoby 1997).

The media's silence not only left in the public's mind what seemed like strong evidence in favor of affirmative action, but it also prevented the public from asking obvious and important questions: What sense does it make for a state university to use taxpayers' money to provide a medical education for someone like Chavis instead of the incomparably better qualified white and Asian applicants whom it rejects. More seriously, how did someone like Chavis obtain a medical degree, pass national medical qualifying tests, and get through intern and residence programs to be certified as a gynecologist?

The non-reporting of Chavis' gross misconduct and incompetence is in line with the media's practice of reporting, uncritically, studies that claim to show anti-minority discrimination in hiring, promoting, lending money, etc., and then not reporting the counter-evidence when these claims are invariably shown to be bogus.[131] This non-reporting is deliberate. The *Dictionary of Cautionary Words and Phrases* (1989), published by the University of Missouri's school of journalism, which is generally regarded as the second best journalism school in the United States, warns (under the term "Qualified Minorities"), "Do not use in stories about affirmative action unnecessary description that indicates minorities are generally unqualified." Incidentally, the most highly regarded American journalism school is Columbia's; and its dean is none other than Nicholas Lemann, the author of the article I outlined above about Patrick Chavis.

CƷ ℬↃ

---

131. D'Souza 1995: 276-81; Zelnick 1996: 321-33; Sowell 1995: 40-42; Thernstrom 1997: 446-9, 503-5; Taylor 1992: 55-9; McGowan 2001: 83-94.

CR SO

Chapter 12
Grades vs. Standardized Tests[132]

O f the students who took the SAT in 2004, the differences in average high school grade-point-average (HSGPA) between whites and
other racial categories were: blacks, .41; Puerto Ricans, .30; "Other
Hispanics," .23; Native Americans, .18; and Mexican Americans, .16. (The
average HSGPA of Asian Americans was .01 higher than the white average.) These differences are large, but not as large as the racial differences
in SAT scores. The most reliable units to compare sets of data are standard
deviations (SDs). Below are the differences, expressed in SDs, between the
white average and the average of each non-white racial group.[133]

	HSGPA	Verbal SAT	Math SAT
Blacks	-.65	-.88	-.91
Puerto Ricans	-.48	-.63	-.69
Other Hispanics	-.37	-.60	-.58
Native Americans	-.29	-.40	-.38

132. In this book, I use the term "standardized test" to mean a test that is
graded in a uniform manner for all test-takers and is designed by professional
psychometricians, who create it on the basis of their knowledge of statistics
and empirical evaluations of the effectiveness of similar tests.

133. The College Board Web site (www.collegeboard.com) provided the
average HSGPA and SAT scores of each race and the standard deviation (SD)
for the Verbal and Math SAT (112 and 114 points). It did not provide the
SD for HSGPA. So, I used the SD for HSGPA in 2002 (.63), from Camara,
et al., 2003: 35.

Of the students who took the SAT in 2004, only one percent were in the
lowest fifth of their high school graduating class; four percent were in the
next fifth; and the worst students had already dropped out of school. If all
adolescents took the SAT, racial differences would be much greater.

| Mexican Americans | -.23 | -.67 | -.64 |
| Asian Americans | +.02 | -.19 | +.40 |

In Section B of Chapter 9 I mentioned one cause of the greater racial differences on standardized tests than in HSGPA: the strong tendency of markers to give higher marks to essays (and presumably examinations also) that they think were written by blacks than to those they think were written by whites (Harber 1998). Another cause was revealed in a study by the U.S. Department of Education in 1994, which found that students in high-poverty schools who got A's in English had, on average, the same reading scores as students in more affluent schools who got C's or D's (Camara, et al., 2003: 3). Differences between courses are as great as differences between schools. Fifty-seven percent of American high schools include all high school courses a student takes in his HSGPA (Camara, et al., 2003: 5). Many more blacks and Hispanics take non-academic courses in high school than whites and Asians; and many more whites and Asians take honors courses than blacks and Hispanics (Thernstrom 1997: 402).

Several random factors also make HSGPA an inaccurate indication of academic ability and achievement. The large majority of teachers base the grades they assign not only on academic performance but also on effort, motivation, participation, and attendance (Phelps 2003: 278-9; Camara, et al., 2003: 4-5). Moreover, high schools differ in the range of grades they use and the courses they include in HSGPA. The highest grade at 39 percent of high schools is A+, at the others the highest grade is A; 53 percent use D- as the lowest passing grade, the others use a higher grade; 57 percent include all courses in computing HSGPA, 43 percent exclude some courses. Among the latter, different high schools exclude different courses from HSGPA (Camara, et al., 2003: 5).

These random distortions affect all ethnic groups, and a fundamental law of statistics is that random distortions that apply to several entities decrease the differences between them.

The same distortions, along with deliberate affirmative grading, also diminish ethnic and racial differences in college marking.

Leonard Ramist, et al., (1994: 2-10) studied the predictive accuracy of the SAT and HSGPA for 46,379 students in 7,786 courses at 45 colleges, which were representative of American colleges in the average SAT score of their students and their size. Ramist, et al., divided the students into three groups, in accordance with their SAT scores and HSGPAs. They found that the groups differed in the types of courses they took. For example, 12 percent of the highest academic group, 7 percent of the middle group, and 4 percent

of the lowest group took an advanced course in physical science or engineering.[134] They also found that the courses that the highest group favored
were the most stringently graded; that is, the average grades in them were
lower than would be expected from the average SAT scores and HSGPAs
of their students. The courses that the lowest group favored were the most
leniently graded. (The courses with the most lenient grading were physical
education, remedial English, technical/vocational, studio art/music/theater,
and military science.)[135] The proportion of each ethnic group in Ramist, et
al.'s sample (1994: 30) in the highest, middle, and lowest groups were:[136]

Asian Americans	39 percent	33 percent	28 percent
Whites	37 percent	34 percent	29 percent
Hispanics	20 percent	30 percent	50 percent
Native Americans	17 percent	28 percent	54 percent
Blacks	9 percent	23 percent	68 percent

134. Even in introductory courses, the difference in academic ability
between students is huge. For instance, in 1974 at the University of California at Riverside, the average Verbal and Math SAT scores of students in the
introductory physics course were 534 and 590; in the introductory sociology
course, they were 432 and 477 (Goldman and Slaughter 1976: 12).

135. Charles, et al., (2009) studied the academic performance of students
at 28 colleges, all of which were at least moderately selective in admissions,
and some of which were among the most selective in the United States. The
average GPA in courses that more than 150 students took were (page 35):
physical education, 3.65; music and dance, 3.64; education, 3.55; Asian-
Mideast studies, 3.54; theater/radio/television/film, 3.54; African-American
studies, 3.45; women's studies, 3.44; foreign language, 3.42; physics, 3.04;
science (unspecified), 3.04; economics, 3.00; accounting, 2.97; biology, 2.96;
mathematics and statistics, 2.94; chemistry, 2.91. (The high average GPA
in foreign language was caused by the large number of students (mainly
Spanish-speaking) who took courses in languages that were spoken in their
home. Of the students in Charles, et al.'s database, 3.3 percent of the Hispanics took a foreign language, but only 1.2 percent of the whites, .08 percent
of the Asians, and 1.0 percent of the blacks (page 44).)

Of the sophomores in Charles, et al.'s database, the percent of each ethnic
group that said they would major in sciences, mathematics, or engineering
were (page 44): whites, 23.1; Asians, 28.1; Hispanics, 16.6; blacks, 18.7.

136. Some of these percentages do not add up to 100 because they are
rounded off to the nearest whole number.

Colleges also differ by as much as high schools in the academic ability of their students and the types of courses that they include in their students' GPA. In 1952, when colleges differed much less in the academic ability of their students than they do now, of the more than 74,000 men who took the Selective Service College Qualification Test, 98 percent at some colleges passed and only 35 percent at other colleges (Jensen 1980: 333-4). Some colleges include in students' GPA all the courses they take, some only courses that count toward a degree. Some include all the grades a student receives in a course he repeated, some only the last grade he receives in a repeated course (Klitgaard 1985: 92).

Even in the same department at the same university, grading patterns differ widely. A study done in 1998 by the English Department of Princeton found that throughout their careers at Princeton some faculty members awarded A or A- to 35 percent of their students, others awarded A or A- to 87 percent of their students. In required courses for sophomores, in which students were assigned to sections solely by their time schedule, the proportion of A's awarded varied from 22 percent to 67 percent (Mitchell 1998).

One more type of distortion in grading must be discussed. Teachers at all levels, from first grade through graduate school, give higher marks to girls/women than to boys/men in subjects in which boys/men attain higher marks on achievement tests.[137] Teachers also overestimate the IQs of girls relative to boys. When Lewis Terman began his study of a large sample of children with IQs of 140 and over, he asked teachers to choose the three brightest children in their classes. He then gave them an IQ test. Of the children that the teachers chose, nearly twice as many of the girls than the

---

137. Caldwell and Hartnett 1967; Camara, et al., 2003: 13-14; Benbow 1988: 174, 190; Benbow 1992: 57-8.

Of students who took the SAT in 2004, 39 percent of those who had an A+ average in high school were boys, as were 38 percent of those who had an A average; but 58 percent of those who had high school averages of C and below were boys. Yet, the average Verbal and Math SAT scores of boys were 512 and 537; the average of girls were 504 and 501. Moreover, 6 percent of the boys who took the SAT in 2004 and 5 percent of the girls scored above 700 on the Verbal section; on the Math section, 9 percent of the boys and 4 percent of the girls scored above 700; and 3 percent of the boys but only 1 percent of the girls scored above 750 on Math.

In 1980, in the extensive High School and Beyond database, of tenth-grade students who were in the top 5 percent in IQ, 14 percent of the boys but 33 percent of the girls got mostly A's, even though 22 percent of the boys and only 20 percent of the girls did ten or more hours of homework a week (Roznowski, et al., 2000: 97-8).

boys had IQs below 140 (Jensen 1980: 627). The reason is that girls tend to be better behaved, more pleasant, neater, readier to follow instructions without questioning them, and better at routine aspects of subjects. For example, in mathematics, girls make fewer errors in arithmetic computation (addition, multiplication, etc.), but boys are better at solving problems that require mathematical reasoning.[138] This sex bias in grading has led to a spate of newspaper, magazine, and internet articles about "affirmative action for boys" in college admissions. The evidence is that women have higher HSGPAs than men at the same college. However, this sex difference does not exist on scores on aptitude and achievement tests. In 2009, on the ACT, which is more closely tied to high school subjects than the SAT, the average score of males was 21.3; of females, 20.9.

The distorting factors I have discussed do not affect standardized achievement tests. Therefore, their scores correlate more closely with scores on the SAT and IQ tests than grades do (Ceci, et al., 1998: 290; Hauser 1998: 229).

All the distortions I have discussed in grading diminish racial and ethnic differences. That is why champions of racial discrimination, from the Prettyman Report of 1908 to the present, have always advocated substituting grades for standardized tests.

Cₒ ᵇↄ

---

138. Benbow 1988: 170, 173, 198. As I explain in Appendix IV of this book, ability at arithmetic computation has little connection with mathematical reasoning ability or with general intelligence.

Kimball (1989) summarized the evidence for the sex difference in grades vs. standardized tests in mathematics and discussed several possible explanations. Her summary came out too early to include Benbow's two important articles that I cite.

CR ℘

Chapter 13
What Standardized Tests Predict

The predictive accuracy of the SAT for college performance is beyond dispute. As Winston Manning and Rex Jackson observed (1984: 196-7),

It is doubtful that any other kind of test or even any other body of test validation research approaches the number of studies in which college admissions test scores are related to future academic performance. The studies have been repeated thousands of times, and the results consistently support the conclusion that . . . the higher the test scores the more successful, on average, the students are in college and graduate study.

Manning and Jackson speak of college admissions tests as a single entity because the scores of the same person taking the SAT and ACT are nearly as closely correlated as the scores of that person taking either test on two occasions (Klitgaard 1985: 92).

In Chapters 14 and 15, I discuss at length William Bowen and Derek Bok's *The Shape of the River* (1998). It is by far the longest and most detailed defence ever written of affirmative action at universities, or indeed in any setting. Their database consisted of the records of all the students at 28 colleges with a wide range of academic standards. On pages 74-5, they provide a chart that shows the correlation between the Verbal+Math SAT scores of the white and black students in their database and where their cumulative four-year grade college average ranked in their graduating class. The correlation is strong and linear: for both whites and blacks, the higher the SAT score, the higher their four-year average ranked in their graduating class. Bowen and Bok observed,

[C]lass rank varies directly with SAT scores. Among both black and white students, those in the highest SAT interval had an appreciably higher average rank in class than did those who entered with lower SAT scores. . . . Moreover, the positive relationship between students'

SAT scores and their rank in class . . . remains after we control for gender, high school grades, socioeconomic status, school selectivity, and major, as well as for race.

Every study that has ever been conducted has come to the same conclusion. In 2001, Hezlett, et al., published a comprehensive meta-analysis of approximately 3,000 studies of the validity of the SAT, involving cumulatively more than a million students. They found that the SAT accurately predicts grades through all four years of college. The correlation between SAT scores and freshman (first-year college) grade-point average (FGPA) ranged from .44 to .62, when adjusted for restriction of range. If the reader sees any correlation quoted that is lower than that, he can be sure that it has not been corrected for restriction of range.[139] In 2005, a Writing section

---

139. Kobrin, et al., 2008: 1. A correlation of 1 means that the entities being compared identical.

Academically inept students do not take the SAT. Of the students who took it in 2005, only one percent were in the lowest fifth of their high school graduating class, and three percent were in the next fifth; and the worst students had already dropped out of school. Consequently, the adolescents who take the SAT do much better on it and in college than a random sample of eighteen-year-olds would. In other words, the range of SAT scores and college grades is more restricted than it would be if all adolescents took the SAT and attended college. So, an adjustment must be made for restriction of range. For this reason, the correlation between SAT scores and GPA is highest at colleges with open admission and lowest at MIT and Caltech.

Since only extremely academically able students go to graduate school, the average correlation between scores on the Graduate Record Examination (GRE), which is taken by applicants to graduate school, and grades in graduate school is only .30. Scores on the quantitative section of the GRE do not correlate at all with the GPA of graduate students in mathematics at Berkeley (Jensen 1993: 151-2). The reason is that their scores on the quantitative section of the GRE are all in the upper two percent *of applicants to graduate schools* (Jensen 1980: 332).

Robert Klitgaard (1985: 94, 235, note 24) illustrated how restriction of range reduces correlations by an analogy from American football. In 1982, the correlation between the order in which wide receivers were selected by professional football teams and their running speed was .35. That is a significant correlation, but it does not reflect the fact that running speed is the most important consideration in selecting wide receivers. The reason that the correlation is not higher is that scouts consider only wide receivers who run fast.

was added to the SAT. At the same time, analogies were removed from the Verbal section, and it was renamed Critical Reading. Kobrin, et al., (2008) conducted a study of the correlation between the new SAT and FGPA. The sample they used was 151,316 freshmen at 110 colleges and universities. They found that the correlation between new SAT and FGPA was .53.

Kobrin, et al., (2008) also found, as did previous researchers, that the SAT is a more accurate predictor of college performance for non-whites, and especially for blacks, than it is for whites. This means, as Ramist, et al., (1994: 31) pointed out, "by far the greatest benefit in using the SAT as a predictor . . . [is] for black students." Ramist, et al., based this conclusion on their study of 2,475 black students at 45 colleges that were representative of American colleges in the average SAT score of their students, and also on a previous study of black students at eleven mostly white and eleven mostly black colleges. In Ramsit, et al.'s study and in the study at in the eleven mostly black colleges, the correlation between blacks' SAT scores and their FGPA was .57. Other studies have found even higher correlations at predominantly black colleges (e.g., Jensen 1980: 484). In fact, "standardized tests predict the performance of African-American students enrolled in historically black colleges even more accurately than they do in the case of black students in predominantly white institutions" (Thernstrom 1997: 638, note 34). Earlier, "in the 1920s and 1930s . . . blacks, who were often among the leading critics of mental testing, nonetheless were well represented among those who used such tests themselves in black schools and colleges . . . since they proved useful in measuring the great variation in the achievement of individual black students" (Degler 1991: 199-200, footnote). As Stephan and Abigail Thernstrom observed (1997: 638, note 34), "It is particularly striking that these supposedly biased instruments, allegedly devised by whites to keep blacks down, work so well for African-American students at predominantly black institutions."

I explain in Section A of Appendix III that a correlation of .50 is much more significant than it seems to a person who is ignorant of statistics. In fact, a correlation higher than approximately .60 would be impossible because of the unreliability of college GPA as an indicator of academic achievement. In the previous chapter, I discuss many causes of the unreliability of college grading. One is that students with high SAT scores take courses that are more difficult and more stringently graded than the courses that students with low SAT scores take. For instance, a student with a high SAT score is more likely to take courses in mathematics, and a student with a low SAT score is more likely to take courses in education. If the former gets a B+ in a mathematics course and the latter an A- in an education course, that enters the statistics as a negative correlation between SAT and college GPA. But their SAT scores were accurate, since a B+ in mathematics requires more academic ability than an A- in education. This difference in courses also explains the often cited fact that high school GPA (HSGPA) correlates more closely with college GPA than do SAT scores. The reason is that the correlation between SAT and college GPA is low in subjects that require little academic ability, such as physical education, remedial reading and writing, technical/vocational subjects, and studio art/music/theater.[140] The College Board's *Counselor's Handbook for the SAT Program 1998-99* provides (page 46) correlations between SAT scores and freshman college grades in 25 subjects, from a sample of 48,039 students at 23 colleges, which were representative of American colleges in the average SAT scores of their students. In 16 of the 25 subjects, SAT correlated more closely with freshman grades than did HSGPA; in six subjects, the correlations were the same; in only three subjects, did HSGPA correlate more closely with freshman grades than did SAT. In Ramsit, et al.'s study (1994: 4), the lowest correlations between college course grade and SAT score were in physical education (.21), remedial English (.25), technical/vocational (.27), studio/art/theater (.32), and remedial reading (.33).

I have now explained why a correlation between SAT score and college GPA of much higher than .60 would be impossible. However, Ramsit, et al., (1994: 3) worked out the correlation after adjusting for difficulty of courses and stringency of grading. It was .75, which is extraordinarily high. I again refer the reader to Section A of Appendix III for the significance of these correlations.

I began this chapter with an observation by Winston and Manning that college admissions tests predict performance in graduate school as well as in college. Bowen and Bok also pointed out that for the students in their large, representative database, SAT scores were not only extremely accurate predictors or undergraduate performance, but also (1998: 106-7), "Among both white and black graduates . . . the percentage earning advanced degrees increases as SAT scores rise;" "the academic skills measured by SAT scores continue to play a substantial role in predicting which undergraduates go on to attain higher degrees even after we take account of . . . high school grades, socioeconomic status, and [undergraduate] school selectivity."

---

140. Ramist, et al., 1994: 4. In a note in the previous chapter, I quote the average GPAs in courses in Charles, et al.'s database of 28 colleges (2009; 35). I will repeat some here: physical education, 3.65; music and dance, 3.64; education, 3.55; theater/radio/television/film, 3.54; African-American studies, 3.45; women's studies, 3.44; physics, 3.04; economics, 3.00; accounting, 2.97; biology, 2.96; mathematics and statistics, 2.94; chemistry, 2.91.

Standardized tests used for admission to professional and graduate schools have also been studied extensively. In Section D of Chapter 9, in which I discuss Professor Davis' exposé of Harvard Medical School, I cite the evidence that MCAT scores predict performance in medical school much more accurately than college grades and how well the MCAT and subsequent standardized tests predict performance not only in medical school, but also in internship, residency, and most important of all, in actual medical practice.

The predictive accuracy of the Law School Admission Test (LSAT) was investigated in over 600 studies at 150 law schools between 1948 and 1975 alone (Schrader 1977). Among their findings is that the correlation between the average LSAT score of a law school's students and the percentage of its graduates who pass the bar exam on the first try is over .90 (Klein 2001-2002: 37-8). (The bar exam consists of essay and multiple choice questions. It tests what a student learns in law school. Passage is required in order to practice law.)

Linda Wightman compiled two unparallel databases when she was the head of Testing, Operations, and Research of the Law School Admission Council. One was of over 90,000 applicants to law schools in 1990-91. The other was of over 27,000 students who enrolled in law schools in the fall of 1991, comprising 70 percent of those who enrolled that year in law schools that were accredited by the American Bar Association. (Wightman is a passionate defender of affirmative-action admissions to law schools, as I will discuss in Chapter 16.)

She found (Wightman 1997: 32), "the LSAT is a substantially better predictor of first-year performance in law school than is the UGPA [undergraduate grade-point average]." More importantly (Wightman 1998: 37), the correlation between a student's LSAT score and passing the bar exam is nearly twice as high as the correlation between his UGPA and passing the bar exam. Wightman also found (1998: ix, cf. 59-69), "When a series of background variables . . . were examined, they showed no relationship to bar passage or failure. These variables included academic expectation of self, language spoken in the home, need to work for pay during undergraduate school, and financial responsibility during law school." "Socioeconomic background—as determined by parents' income, level of education, and occupation—had a small correlation with bar exam pass rates among Asians and Hispanics, but none among blacks and whites" (Wightman 1998: 35-6, 41, 58).

Moreover, just as the SAT is a more accurate predictor of the college performance of black than of white students, so the LSAT is a more accurate predictor of blacks' performance in law school than of whites' (Wightman

1997: 34).

Richard Sander is a professor at UCLA's law school. He adduced important evidence on this subject in an article in the *Stanford Law Review* (Sander 2004), in which he introduced himself (page 370) as being white and having a "son [who] is biracial, part black, part white." In his discussion, he refers to the "LSAT/UGPA index." This is the index on which law schools base their admissions decisions. It combines the applicant's LSAT score and undergraduate grade-point average (UGPA) to create a 1,000 point scale. Because LSAT is a better predictor of performance in law school and on the bar exam, it contributes 600 points to the index, and UGPA contributes 400.

Sander observed (page 419), "Defenders of affirmative action say that the credential gap has little substantive significance . . . [because] [p]redictive indices (like the LSAT/UGPA index ...) don't predict well . . . [and] American standardized tests are unfair to non-Anglos in general and blacks in particular." Sander pointed out (pages 420-21) that the evidence that is cited for these accusations is easily refuted. The low correlations that defenders of affirmative action cite between LSAT scores and first year grades in law schools are "intrinsically invalid" because they are for students at the same law school and consequently are greatly attenuated by a severe restriction of range (which I discuss above). What is significant is that "LSAT scores have . . . a correlation of .59 with overall [California bar] exam results (including the eight-hour essay exam and the eight-hour practice exam)." (In Appendix III. A, I point out how significant a correlation of this size is.) Moreover (Sander 2004: 421-3; italics added),

> In research I conducted in 1995 with . . . the aid of many law schools around the country, thousands of first-year law students completed questionnaires on their school experiences . . . . [T]he sample LSAT/ UGPA index was several times stronger at predicting first-semester grades than direct information on how much students said they were studying, participating in class, completing the reading, or attending study groups. . . . Correlations based on individual behavior almost always . . . [were] unimpressive . . . For example, consider blacks who took bar exams in the "Far West" region [California, Nevada, and Hawaii] . . . during the mid-1990s. *For those whose pre-law school academic index was 720 or higher (out of 1000), the first-time bar passage rate was 97%. For those whose academic index was 540 or lower, the first-time bar passage rate was 8%.*

Sander then (page 424) considered a common objection:

[A]verage black performance in the first year of law school does not exceed levels predicted by academic indicators. . . . One might respond that law school exams and bar exams simply perpetuate the unfairness of tests like the LSAT—they are timed and undoubtedly generate acute performance anxiety. But almost all first-year students take legal writing classes, which are graded on the basis of lengthy memos prepared over many weeks, and which give the student an opportunity to demonstrate skills entirely outside the range of typical law school exams. My analysis of first-semester grade data from several law schools shows a slightly larger black-white gap in legal writing classes than in overall first-semester grade averages.

The findings of the 1995 National Survey of Law Student Performance also showed the crucial importance of academic entrance qualifications for performance in law school. Sander outlined its results (page 453):

[F]irst-semester black law students reported spending as much time studying as did white students, but found themselves substantially less prepared for class. Seventy-one percent of white students said that they completed the assigned reading before "all or nearly all" of their classes, compared with 52% of black students.

Sander outlined (pages 435-6) the results of admitting blacks to law schools with radically lower qualifications than whites. In a sample that consists of 22,969 students who graduated from law school in the 1990s, the cumulative three-year law school GPA of 42.5 percent of black students was in the lowest ten percent of their law school graduating class; 60.5 percent were in the lowest fifth. Sander pointed out that even these statistics overstate black performance because a much higher proportion of blacks than whites do not complete law school. Also, in a comparison between only blacks and whites, excluding Hispanic law students, a considerably higher proportion of blacks would be in the lowest tenth and fifth of their graduating class.[141]

I will repeat here that the scores of the same person on the SAT or ACT

---

141. In Linda Wightman's study of over 27,000 students who enrolled in law schools in the fall of 1991, when the students were in their second year of law school they were asked, "How well did your first year experiences match your original expectations about law school?" Three specific questions were asked: students' perception of the "quality of instruction," "accessibility of faculty," and "supportiveness of the school environment." Respondents rated each on a scale of 1 to 5, with 5 being the highest rating. The average ratings of black and Hispanic students on the three questions were 3.31, 3.55, and 3.14. The average ratings of white students were 3.29, 3.53, and 3.16 (Sander 2006: 1811, footnote 146).

and the tests for admission to professional or graduate school—whether the LSAT (for law school), MCAT (for medical school), GMAT (for business school), or GRE (for graduate school)—are nearly as closely correlated with each other as are the scores of the same person taking on any one of these tests on two occasions (Klitgaard 1985: 92).

The SAT is also an extremely accurate predictor of "real world" academic achievement. A study was conducted of thirteen-year-old children who scored in the upper one percent for their age on the SAT-Math. Ten years later, those whose SAT-Math scores had been in the highest and lowest quarters of that elite group were compared on several criteria. The average college GPA in math and science courses of the men and women in the highest quarter were 3.4 and 3.5, respectively; the averages of those in the lowest quarter were 3.0 and 3.3. These differences are significant. However, because both groups were in the top one percent, restriction of range decreased the difference between them. But differences in "real-world" achievement were great even within this extremely select group. Of those in the highest quarter, 17 percent of the men and 10 percent of the women had written articles that were published in journals, and 10 percent of the men and 3 percent of the women had won awards in math or science. Of those in the bottom quarter, 6 percent of both the men and women had written published articles, and 2 percent of the men and 1 percent of the women had won awards.[142]

The predictive accuracy of the SAT is just as great for non-scholarly success. In Section A of Chapter 9, I mentioned that the scores of teachers on qualifying tests are the only factor that correlates with their students' performance. Scores on these tests correlate closely with their SAT scores (Ferguson 1991: 471-6, 482; Basinger 1999). A study of managers of mutual funds, an occupation that seems to require totally different abilities from teaching, found that "managers who attended colleges with higher average SAT scores earn much higher returns [on investments] than do managers from less selective institutions," even though managers who graduated from high-SAT colleges did not differ from other managers in the types of stocks they bought (large or small companies, high or low market price relative to book value, etc.) (Chevalier and Ellison 1996: Abstract, 15-16). Chevalier and Ellison did not try to determine whether the superior performance of mutual fund managers from high-SAT colleges was caused completely by their high SAT scores, or whether the quality of the college they attended added to their investment ability. However, we know that the reason that

---

142. Benbow 1992: 58. Typically, although the men published many more articles and won many more awards than the women, the average college GPA of the women in both groups was higher than that of the men (Benbow 1992: 58).

graduates of colleges with high average SAT scores earn more money than graduates of colleges with lower average SAT scores is their own SAT scores, not the quality of the college they attended. The average SAT score of the college a person attended has no effect on his future income independently of his own SAT score.[143]

I outlined the evidence for the accuracy with which the LSAT predicts grades in law school. The grades that students obtain in law school accurately predict their income as practicing lawyers. We know that from a detailed survey that the University of Michigan Law School conducted in 1997 and 1998 of alumni who had graduated from 1970 through 1996. Law school GPA was closely correlated with income. No other factor—undergraduate major, work in the private or public sector, race, sex—was anywhere nearly as closely correlated with income as law school GPA (Sander 2006: 1764, 1793-5).

I will provide one more illustration of the accuracy and importance of the SAT. The American Association for the Advancement of Science devoted much of the November 13, 1992 (pages 1067, 1176-1232) and November 12, 1993 (pages 971, 1089-1135) issues of its journal *Science* to the "problem" of the extremely low number of minority scientists and the desperate attempts by governments, schools, universities, businesses, and scientific societies to solve this problem. The attempted solutions that *Science* mentioned include colleges and graduate schools discarding normal qualifications for admission, scholarships, and hiring; and one-to-one tutoring and mentoring in elementary school, high school, college, and graduate school. Following are examples from only one page (1134) of the 1993 issue:

> The American Society for Microbiology offers a package of support to minority undergrads, including summer research stints, and a trip to the society's annual meeting. Society members visit minority institutions . . . [T]he American Chemical Society . . . targets high schoolers and even elementary school students with a diverse selection of research opportunities, educational programs, and grants to community organizations . . . [T]he Society of Neuroscience focuses on [minority] postdoctoral researchers and young professors, offering a package of support to about 30 young neuroscientists . . . In addition, nearly all [scientific] societies offer minority scholarships to undergraduate and graduate students.

> The same frantic efforts have been made in engineering:

> Organizations . . . scour the United States for minority students they

143. Dale and Krueger 2002. In Appendix IV, I discuss the predictive accuracy of intelligence tests for future income and occupational success.

think could succeed in engineering school, then provide them with full scholarships [and] paid summer internships . . . . Other young blacks . . . spend one or more summers in their high school years at one of the many intensive "bridge courses" sponsored by engineering schools and other universities. When they get to college, most . . . [take] enrichment and counseling programs through undergraduate school and, when possible, beyond (Jacoby 1999: 25).

The result? "In truth, if the extraordinary effort of the past 25 years has demonstrated anything, it is the limit of what politics and money—and affirmative action—can do to help black would-be scientists" (Jacoby 1999: 24). Similarly, *Science* of November 13, 1992 observed (page 1185; the amounts of money mentioned would be several times more in 2010 dollars):

Ford Madox Ford began his famous novel *The Good Soldier* with the words, "This is the saddest story I have ever heard." Were he alive today, he might apply that line to the history of America's two-decade-long effort to bring [non-Asian] color to the scientific and engineering work force. . . . [S]ays Luther Williams, assistant director for education . . . at the National Science Foundation (NSF), "This was an incredible waste of financial and human resources." . . . Universities, scientific societies, and industry rushed to join the effort [to increase the number of minority scientists and engineers]. Across the country, Fortune 500 companies appointed minority affairs vice presidents to find minority workers . . . . The professional societies formed . . . major programs . . . . Government itself became proactive: In the late 1960s, the NSF inaugurated a slew of programs . . . [that] averaged $100 million a year, or about $1.5 billion in the past 20 years, to increase the number of minorities in science. . . . [T]he National Institute of Health . . . [spent] $675 million.

In 2004, less than one percent of all blacks who received bachelor's degrees majored in the physical sciences; and only 0.6 percent in mathematics. Only 0.3 percent of blacks' master's degrees were in the physical sciences; and only 0.2 percent in mathematics. Blacks received only 13 of the more than 1,200 PhDs in physics, less than one percent of the PhDs in mathematics, and none of the 165 PhDs in astronomy.[144] The *Journal of Blacks in Higher Education* of Winter 2005/2006, when reviewing the near-nonexistence of blacks who got doctorates in natural science in 2004, pointed out, "The percentage of all black doctorates that were awarded in

144. "Why African-American College Students Avoid Science." *Journal of Blacks in Higher Education* (Summer 2006): 22.

the natural sciences has been declining in recent years."[145]

What does this have to do with the social utility and accuracy of the SAT? In its August 25, 1995 issue, *Science* devoted a mere five paragraphs, in an article entitled "No Hostile Environment Found For Minorities" (page 1047), to a study done by the National Science Foundation on "the role of ethnicity in choice of and persistence in science majors." The study involved 3,534 whites, 355 blacks, 582 Asian Americans, and 216 Hispanics at American colleges. *Science* reported:

> The researchers found that a larger fraction of blacks than whites expressed interest in science when they first got to college. But only 34 percent of the blacks who expressed interest ended up majoring in science, compared with 60 percent of the whites. Ethnicity did not stand up as a predictor for any of the disparity. Rather, the authors write, "it was the pre-admission variables describing developed ability—test scores and science grades." . . . Furthermore, none of the comments in questionnaires . . . "constitute[d] even a small indictment of these institutions as being inhospitable, much less racist" . . . . Math scores on the Scholastic Aptitude Test (SAT-M) are an excellent predictor of who will major in science . . . . And they found that, among students with SAT-M scores of 650 or more, all groups were equally likely to major in science . . . . The new report is a complement to the one produced last year in which the researchers . . . investigate[d] the theory that a "chilly climate" in academia freezes women out of science. But . . . they found that "if you take account of grades and test scores, then . . . [there is no] gender-based factor to explain."

The *Science* article also provided a graph with SAT-Math scores on the horizontal axis and probability of completing a major in science on the vertical axis. The explanation under the graph points out, "Probability of majoring in science goes up linearly with math scores in the Scholastic Aptitude Test."

CR BO

---

145. "Doctoral Degrees Awarded to African Americans Reach Another All-time High:" 6-11.

CR SO

Chapter 14
Admissions III: The Shape Of The River:
The Lie Exposed

The first thing that a man will do for his ideals is lie.
(Joseph Schumpeter, *History of Economic Analysis* (New York:
Oxford University Press, 1954): 43)

Hypocrisy is a tribute that vice pays to virtue.
   (La Rochefoucauld (1665))[146]

Among the Harvard officials who lied about Professor Davis' disclosures about Harvard Medical School was its president, Derek
Bok, who made the following public statement (Davis 1986: 181):
"I find no basis for any implication that minority students are less than fully
qualified for the M.D. degree in accordance with the normal standards of
the Harvard Medical School."

In 1998, Bok co-authored with William Bowen, former president of
Princeton, *The Shape of the River*, a book that has rightly been hailed as a
landmark in the saga of American affirmative action. As Bok and Bowen
observed (pages xxiv-xxv), it is the first systematic, empirical defense of
academic affirmative action ever written. I will outline the information they
provide on admissions and then discuss again universities' admissions policies in the light that it sheds on them.

On pages 26 and 27, Bowen and Bok reported the probability of admission in 1989 to five highly selective colleges in their database of blacks
and whites with Verbal+Math SAT scores at each 50-point interval. (Until
2005, the only SAT tests were Verbal and Math.) A black applicant with a
Verbal+Math SAT score between 1250 and 1299 had a 75 percent chance
of admission, while a white with a combined score over 1500 had only a
65 percent chance. A black with a Verbal+Math SAT score between 1100
and 1149 had nearly a 50 percent chance of admission; it was not until the

---

146. *Réflexions Morales* number 218: *L'hypocrisie est un hommage que
le vice rend à la vertu.*

1450-1499 range that a white had a 50 percent chance of admission.[147]

In Section G of Appendix III, I quote an attack on the SAT by Eugene Garcia, Dean of Berkeley's School of Education. I point out that it is full of blatant lies. Among them is that SAT scores replicate parental income. Garcia's hypothetical example is the daughter of a migrant worker with an SAT score 100 points lower than that of the graduate of a private school who attended an expensive SAT preparation course. Even Garcia could not attribute more than 100 SAT points to the most extreme difference in social background.

Bowen and Bok continued (page 27, footnote): "Nor are any of the conclusions stated here altered if we add high school grades as a second numerical criterion." But that is not true. Colleges give greater preference to blacks in high school grades than in SAT scores. Nearly all the colleges in Bowen and Bok's database had average Verbal+Math SAT scores above 1100 (page 40). Nationwide, at colleges whose students have an average Verbal+Math SAT score of at least 1100, the difference in high school grade-point-average (GPA) between blacks and whites is the equivalent of 400 Verbal+Math SAT points; and that does not take into consideration the fact that whites take much more difficult and advanced courses in high school than blacks.[148]

---

147. Wikipedia " SAT" provides the percentiles for SAT scores in 2006. These scores would now be higher because of the 1995 re-centering of reported scores, which I discuss in Appendix III. E.

148. Kane 1998: 432. The reason that colleges discriminate more on GPA than on SAT scores is nearly certainly because they know that racial comparisons are usually made on the basis of SAT scores.

Bowen and Bok's chart on page 41 is misleading. It shows that without affirmative action, 2.1 percent of the students at the most selective colleges in their database would be black, instead of the current 7.8 percent. However, as they explain in the footnote on that page, the chart is based solely on Verbal SAT scores, on which there is less racial difference than on Math. If the criterion were Math SAT scores, the proportion of blacks would be 1.6 percent.

Terrance Sandalow, who was the dean of the University of Michigan Law School from 1978 to 1987, pointed out in his review of *The Shape of the River* (1999: 1882-83) that even combined Math+Verbal SAT scores "nearly certainly overstate the representation of African-Americans in selective institutions if race-neutral admission policies were to be employed" because admissions criteria include high school grades and the nature of courses taken in high school. Their inclusion "makes it virtually certain that blacks would be admitted to selective institutions at a lower rate than they

Bowen and Bok do not mention any admissions criteria besides SAT scores and high school grades. They were right to include only these two criteria. In an intensive study that Bowen co-authored (Vars and Bowen 1998: 473) about the effect of various factors on college performance, he pointed out, "personal ratings do not predict college grades at all." Nevertheless, supporters of affirmative action have constantly asserted that non-academic strengths are valid admissions criteria and that blacks and other minorities excel in non-academic qualifications. *The Shape of the River* ends the possibility of using that argument. In a book of over 450 pages, packed with statistics and 147 tables and graphs, whose purpose is to defend affirmative action, Bowen and Bok do not mention a single non-academic qualification—leadership, creativity, social conscience; writing, musical, or athletic ability, etc.—that could compensate, even to a slight extent, for the huge differences in SAT scores and high school grades between blacks and whites admitted to the same colleges.

So, race—skin color, hair texture, etc.—pure and simple is worth 350 Verbal+Math SAT points, plus a greater difference in high school performance, to ensure a fifty percent chance of admission to an elite college. Indeed, having a remote ancestor who had black skin and kinky hair is worth that much. And 350 SAT points is greater than the difference between the average Verbal+Math SAT score at the college in Bowen and Bok's database of 28 colleges with the highest average SAT score (Princeton, 1450) and the college with the lowest average SAT score (Howard, 1105) (Massey, et al., 2007: 248).

The Shape of the River does not provide similar information for Hispanics. But an ancestor from Spanish-speaking Latin America is also worth a huge advantage in SAT scores and high school performance, even if that ancestor was a white multimillionaire.

Bowen and Bok's acknowledgement that race confers tremendous advantages in university admissions is a revolutionary departure from previous defenses of affirmative action. In his *Bakke* decision, Justice Powell quoted Princeton's description of its admissions policy as an example of the proper use of race (#317, note 51): "race is not in and of itself a consideration." The author of that description was Princeton's president, William Bowen, co-author of *The Shape of the River*.

Into the middle 1990s, American universities kept information on their minority students' qualifications secret, even from their own faculties and from the Office for Civil Rights of the Department of Education.[149] This enabled them to lie that they did not practice racial discrimination, or, as a

[Bowen and Bok] assume."

149. Chun and Zalokar 1992: 108; Sowell 1993: 145, 280.

fallback lie, that the discrimination they practiced was marginal.

The Bell Curve (1996: 451-8) began to expose this lie. Herrnstein and Murray got their statistics on racial differences in qualifications from a report that was available only to participating admissions offices. Not even social scientists had access to it. Then, individuals and organizations began using state freedom-of-information laws to force public universities to divulge the average and median SAT and ACT scores and high school grades of their white, black, Asian, and Hispanic students.[150]

I will now provide examples of the lies that universities told, beginning with the two most highly regarded American public universities, the University of California at Berkeley and the University of Michigan at Ann Arbor.

Berkeley's catalogue always stated, "[T]he University of California does not discriminate on the basis of race, color, national origin, sex, handicap or age in any of its policies" (D'Souza 1991: 57-8). In 1989, Berkeley adopted the report *Freshman Admissions at Berkeley: A Policy for the 1990s and Beyond*, which stated (page 31), "Berkeley will absolutely not tolerate quotas or ceilings on the admissions or enrollment of any racial, ethnic, religious or gender groups. Such quotas or ceilings are both immoral and illegal" (Sarich 1990-91: 74-5).

In view of these and similar published statements, it is amazing that Berkeley's administrators had the effrontery to denounce the referendum that forced them to end the racial discrimination that they had constantly and categorically denied existed.

The principal of a private high school in California gave an example of Berkeley's policy of non-discrimination with a description of two students who graduated from his school in 1987 (Bunzel 1988:128):

> Student A was ranked in the top third of his class, student B in the bottom third.
>
> Student A had College Board [i.e., Verbal+Math SAT] scores totaling 1290; student B's scores totaled 890.
>
> Student A had a record of good citizenship; student B was expelled last winter for breaking a series of major school rules.
>
> Student A was white; student B was black.
>
> Berkeley refused student A and accepted B. . . .
>
> [W]hat message about effort, ethical behavior, and the consequences of one's actions were conveyed?

---

150. Chavez 2002: 212. They are available at www.ceousa.org. For whites, blacks, and, in some cases, Asians, statistics are also now available in Cross 1994A, and Thernstrom 1997: 408.

This example is not a perversion of affirmative action. It is the degree of racial discrimination that is necessary for the student bodies of selective colleges to approximate the racial proportions of the American population.

In Chapter 4, I outlined the complex, devious means that the University of California system is now using in order to be able to continue to enroll students like B instead of A.

Let us hypothesize another white student, C, whose record was better than that of white student A, so that he was entitled to attend the same college as black student B. At more and more American colleges, the government, accreditation associations, and/or progressive administrations ensure that student B has as much a chance of graduating as C student (and better than white student A, who was less academically able than C). The same process is then repeated at graduate or professional school and throughout their lives.

Thus, student B becomes one of the black role models who are universally cited to justify affirmative action.

Berkeley's admissions director when it chose applicant B over A was Robert Shaw. In 1988, the University of Michigan hired him. But Shaw's genius at increasing minority admissions made him too valuable for any university to be able to hold on to him for long. In 1992, Yale hired him away from Michigan (Lynch 1997: 310).

Like Berkeley, the University of Michigan always proclaimed that it "is committed to policy of nondiscrimination and equal opportunity for all persons regardless of race, sex, color . . . national origin or ancestry in employment, educational programs and admissions." Its administration attributed the fact that its black dropout rate is nearly three times its white rate to "institutional racism" (Chait 1997). This is a university with over 100 diversity programs, aggressive outreach programs to minority students that begin when they are in elementary school, summer workshops for high school minority students, constant monitoring of minority students' progress, and rewards for departments on the basis of their diversity records. It is a university that gives nearly all its scholarships for graduate students and junior faculty members to minorities and had such a strict speech code with regard to what could be said about race that a district court declared it unconstitutional (Lynch 1997: 274-319; D'Souza 1991: 143-4). A typical University of Michigan program brought 30 minority students to the university for six weeks during the summer, where representatives from 30 business schools try to persuade them to enter doctoral programs in business. The university (i.e., Michigan taxpayers) paid all travel and living expenses and a $2,500 stipend to each student just for showing up (Taylor 1992: 174).

Until 1996, the University of Michigan protected its claim that institutional racism caused the high dropout rate of its black students by constantly denying that it gave minority applicants preference in admissions. "Whenever the occasional right-wing malcontent complained about minority admissions preferences, the administration would politely and patiently explain that the university did no such thing" (Chait 1997).

Then, Philosophy Professor Carl Cohen used the Michigan's Freedom of Information Act to force the university to disclose its admissions records. They revealed that it arranged its applicants on a grid, with high-school grade-point-average (GPA) forming the vertical axis and SAT or ACT scores forming the horizontal axis. In 1996, over 90 percent of blacks and Hispanics with GPAs over 2.8 (on a scale of 1 to 4) and SAT scores above 830 were admitted. Whites and Asians needed a 3.8 GPA and SAT scores above 1200 to have the same chance of admission (Thernstrom 1999A; Cohen 1996: 42). The result was that the median combined Math+Verbal SAT score of its white students was 230 points higher than the median of its black students and 130 points higher than the median of its Hispanic students. Of course, this was the reason for the racial differences in dropout rates. (Six years after admission, 66 percent of black students, 76 percent of Hispanic students, and 87 percent of white students had graduated (Lerner and Nagai 1998: 4-12).) Michigan's professional and graduate schools practiced even more extreme discrimination. For example, in 2000, Michigan's Law School admitted every black applicant with LSAT scores between 159-160 and an undergraduate GPA of 3.00 or higher (*Grutter v. Bollinger* #76-7). But it admitted only 22 percent of white and Asian applicants with a GPA between 3.25 and 3.49 and a LSAT score of 164-66.[151]

Moreover, minorities received 80 percent of Michigan's undergraduate and graduate merit (i.e., non-need) scholarships, even though their academic merit is much lower than whites' and Asians' (Lynch 1997: 288). An example was Michelle Williams, both of whose parents are doctors. She reported, "I got a full-tuition scholarship, and I didn't need it. I didn't even apply for it." Her mother is white, but her father is black. That was her "merit" (Schmidt 1998).

After Michigan's administration was forced to disclose its admissions records, it changed its story to, "We do not have a separate review of files, nor do we have a different standard for minority applicants." Jonathan

---

151. Wood 2003: 131. University of Michigan's President James Duderstadt attributed Professor Cohen's motive in forcing the publication of its admissions records to his desire to "play to . . . the Christian right movement." That is an extremely serious accusation in an American university. It is also an unlikely motive for a Jew who was the chairman of the Michigan branch of the American Civil Liberties Union (Lynch 1997: 310-11).

Chait (1997), who recorded this justification, observed in the liberal *New Republic*:

> You can see how this line worked in the past, when the university's practices remained secret. But now it just seems self-defeating. Instead of waging a philosophical defense of racial preferences, or coming clean, or at least thinking up a different lie, Michigan's administration is simply wrapping its old lie in a bizarre point of semantics.

In 1998, Michigan changed its admission procedure to the one that was the subject of the *Gratz v. Bollinger* Supreme Court decision. In it, the number of points that an applicant was assigned determined admission. Being black, Hispanic, or Native American (i.e., having an ancestor who was black, Native American, or from Spanish-speaking Latin America) automatically entitled an applicant to 20 points. By contrast, twelve points were awarded for a perfect SAT or ACT score.

Nevertheless, Michigan's legal defense of this procedure described the 20 points it automatically awarded to every applicant with a black, Hispanic, or Native American ancestor as "a slight edge."

The "slight edge" lie was also used at Berkeley. In April 1995, Herma Hill Kay, the dean of Berkeley's law school, was asked on the MacNeil-Lehrer *Newshour* why there is "a widespread perception that the minorities who are admitted with those special considerations are the result of standards being lowered," Dean Kay had the audacity to answer that this accusation certainly did not apply to her law school, where race enters into consideration only "when you have to choose between two equally qualified persons" (Thernstrom 1998: 36).

When Dean Kay said this, the University of California was still keeping the admissions records for its law and medical schools secret. It was forced to disclose them shortly afterwards. They revealed that Berkeley's law school accepted every Black applicant with an undergraduate GPA between 3.25 and 3.49 and Law School Admission Test (LSAT) scores between the 70th and 74.9th percentile and rejected every white and Asian in the same GPA and LSAT range (Cohen 1996: 42).

Dean Kay later explained that considerations of socioeconomic background would not increase the number of Blacks at Berkeley Law School because, "African Americans who apply to our law school are not disadvantaged. Their mothers and fathers are professionals with good family incomes" (*NR* 1998: 6). In Chapter 4, I quoted the boast of Berkeley's law school's administration that "more flexible admissions policies that de-emphasize scores on standardized tests" are enabling it to admit more minority students from upper-class families, after the citizens of California voted to prohibit the racial discrimination that it claimed did not exist.

Professor Samuel Issacharoff of the University of Texas (UT) School of Law used the same slight-edge lie to defend its affirmative action program. Professor Issacharoff led the UT School of Law's defense of its affirmative program in the 1996 case *Cheryl J. Hopwood, et al. v. State of Texas, et al.*, in which the U.S. Court of Appeals for the Fifth Circuit banned considerations of race in its jurisdiction (Texas, Louisiana, and Mississippi). Two years later, he wrote an article entitled "Can Affirmative Action Be Defended?" He stated (Issacharoff 1998: 672): "One of the first decisions made in defending UT was to be candid about what affirmative action meant." In pursuance of this policy of honesty, he discussed the lies that are often used to defend affirmative action. One (page 670) is the lie that was the basis of Justice Powell's justification of academic racial discrimination in the *Bakke* decision and which the Supreme Court reaffirmed in 2003 in its two University of Michigan decisions: "[L]ike most faculty members I was aware of the general goals-but-not-quotas mantra from *Bakke* and [I was] deeply suspicious of the intellectual coherence of Justice Powell's opinion." Professor Issacharoff pointed out (674-6) the Harvard plan that Justice Powell held up as a model involved a *de facto* numerical set-aside, as any policy to admit a significant number of minority students must (678):

> The problem with diversity as a justification for a challenged affirmative action program is that it is an almost incoherent concept to operationalize, unless diversity means a predetermined number of admittees from a desired group. . . . [A]t the University of Texas School of Law, somewhere between 3,000 and 5,000 applications are received each year. These have to be processed in essentially a one-month period . . . [T]here is simply no way . . . [to] evaluate each applicant against the entire pool to determine that applicant's contribution to diversity. Instead, selective institutions must approach the applicant pool with predetermined notions of what an appropriately [racially] balanced incoming class should look like.

Professor Issacharoff's main defense of affirmative action was that (690-91) "the magnitude of the preference should be a central issue." He constantly used the words "modest" and "mild" to describe a defensible affirmative action program. His example of such a program is that of the UT School of Law. He explained at the beginning of his article (670), "I will attempt to give an account of what it means to defend an affirmative action program as it is implemented in the real world. *Hopwood* remains the only case in which the mechanics of such a program have been taken to trial with an actual factual record." So, even though the Supreme Court's decisions concerning the University of Michigan nullified the *Hopwood* decision, it is still well worth looking at.

In it, the Court explained (*Hopwood v. Texas*, I. A and footnote 1) that UT School of Law, like most law schools, ranked applicants on an index that combines their LSAT score with their undergraduate GPA (UGPA). Because the LSAT is a better predictor than UGPA of law-school grades and performance on the bar exam, it contributed 60 percent to the index, and UGPA contributed 40 percent. UT School of Law also considered the difficulty of the applicant's major, the college he attended, and any trend in his grades. Every applicant was placed in one of three categories: "presumptive admit," nearly all of whom were admitted; "presumptive deny," nearly all of whom were rejected; and a middle "discretionary zone."

The Court illustrated (*Hopwood*, footnote 8) the degree of racial discrimination with the example of the four white plaintiffs who had brought the case because they were denied admission. Cheryl Hopwood, who had a UGPA of 3.8, needed an LSAT score in the top 32 percent of all LSAT-takers to avoid presumptive denial. But if she were Black, she would have needed an LSAT score in the top 80 percent. Douglas Carvell, with a UGPA of 3.28, needed an LSAT score in the top 17 percent, but in the top 63 percent if he were black. David Rodgers, with a UGPA of 3.13, needed an LSAT score in the top 12 percent, but in the top 56 percent if he were black. Kenneth Elliot, with a UGPA of 2.98, needed an LSAT score in the top 10 percent, but in the top 53 percent if he were black.

The Court also observed (*Hopwood*, II. A.2) that if UT School of Law was really interested in whether applicants overcame obstacles or provided a different perspective, it would have considered Cheryl Hopwood's background. She was 32 and was raising a severely mentally retarded child. By contrast, at no point during the trial did UT claim that its minority applicants were more economically disadvantaged than its white applicants.

These enormous preferences illustrate the tremendous difference in academic ability between minority and white *college graduates*, since (*Hopwood*, I.A) UT School of Law employed them for the purpose of "admitting a class consisting of ten percent Mexican Americans and five percent blacks, proportions roughly comparable to the percentages of these races graduating from Texas colleges."

The lawyers who defended the University of Texas pointed out that in the entire country only 88 black law-school applicants had LSAT scores higher than the median score of whites at UT Law School (Rosen 1994: 28). Yet, by then, many black law-school applicants were the children of parents who had received massive preferences in admission and graduation at leading

American colleges, graduate, and professional schools.

At the time of the *Hopwood* decision, the University of Texas Law School was twelfth among the fifteen highest ranked American law schools in the proportion of its students who were black (Cross 1994: 44, note). Consequently, the degree of racial discrimination it practiced was considerably less than that at most leading law schools.

The reader may have noticed that the institutions I have discussed practiced discrimination in the manner banned by the *Bakke* decision: deciding the proportion of each race they wanted and attaining it by setting different cut-off points on grades and standardized tests. They knew that this method is so superior in efficiency, fairness, and quality of students it yields to the method mandated by *Bakke* (and reaffirmed by the Supreme Court in 2003) that they were willing to violate the law in order to use it.

Professor Issacharoff of the UT School of Law defended its affirmative action program as being "modest" two years after the U.S. Court of Appeals for the Fifth Circuit used the facts I outlined above to illustrate the difference in entrance requirements for its white and black applicants. Professor Issacharoff also claimed (1988: 685) that the advantage of using only modest preferences was that it yielded "qualified minority students who can succeed at elite professional schools." However, during the *Hopwood* litigation, UT School of Law was forced to make public a confidential letter, in which its associate dean wrote that because of "radically different admissions standards," approximately 90 percent of UT's non-minority students passed the bar examination on the first try; but the figure for blacks was "consistently under 50 percent;" and, "Even more seriously, half of our minority graduates who fail the exam fail again upon retaking." The associate dean also wrote that because of UT's minority students, the proportion of its students who passed the bar examination was lower than at less prestigious Texas law schools, which "have few minority students." This was "an embarrassment that does real damage to our reputation" because UT School of Law could not explain that the reason was that it admitted minority students with radically lower qualifications (Thernstrom 1998A: 21, 24-5).

Universities know that they can count on the media to support their "slight edge" lie. A front-page article in the *Washington Post* (Pressley 1997) reported that the *Hopwood* decision ended UT's "policy that led to acceptance of minorities with *slightly* [italics added] lower test scores than those of white students." The author of this article could have easily acquired the transcript of the *Hopwood* decision, which is only 39 pages, and which I, living in South Africa, obtained by simply telephoning the local United States Government Public Affairs Office.

When the media can get away with it, they even claim that there are no differences in admissions requirements for whites and minorities. On March 21, 1996, the *Los Angeles Times* ran a 1,474-word front-page article entitled, "Probe Finds No Bias in Admissions at Berkeley: Polices Do Not Discriminate against Whites or Hurt Academic Quality." It began: "A seven-year federal investigation into admissions practices at UC Berkeley exonerates the university . . . of charges that it discriminated against white students applying for entrance." The only evidence that the *Los Angeles Times* adduced was, "high school grade-point-averages and Scholastic Assessment Test [SAT] scores rose across the board." An article the next day in the *New York Times* (Applebome 1996) also reported that this "seven-year investigation . . . found affirmative action at Berkeley did not discriminate against whites and that the academic quality of the student body increased as the campus became more diverse. Grades, test scores . . . rose." Even though both articles assumed that high school grades and SAT scores are synonymous with academic quality, neither published a single statistic about them. They could not. If they had, they would have disclosed the lie implicit in their report of an "across the board" improvement. Average high school grades and SAT scores rose because white and Asian averages rose. The averages of blacks and Hispanics fell. Similarly, a year earlier in reporting the uproar caused by the president of Rutgers University's statement that it was "hereditary genetic background" that caused low black SAT scores, not one mainstream newspaper mentioned that the difference in average black and white SAT scores at Rutgers was nearly 350 points (McGowan 2001:165, 161).

When the nondiscrimination and slight-edge lies have been exposed, universities have fallen back on another lie: that non-measurable attributes compensate for the huge racial discrepancies in all measurable qualifications.

In 1991, Timothy Maguire, a student at Georgetown University's law school, was hired to file student records. He surreptitiously copied statistics from a sample of white and black students' admissions records, which showed a huge racial difference in qualifications, and published them in the law school's student newspaper under the title "Admissions Apartheid." He described the university's reaction in an article in *Commentary* (Maguire 1992):

> "Admissions Apartheid" did call the attention of the Georgetown community to a major institutional problem which had previously been ignored. Not that efforts were not made to continue ignoring it. . . . [T]he dean of the school, Judith Areen, had a letter placed in every student's mail folder in which, among other things, she criticized the paper for printing "this misleading mix of opinion

and data" . . . Yet Dean Areen did not explain what was inaccurate. . . . Officials . . . ordered the confiscation of every copy on school grounds of the offending issue of the student paper. . . . Then there was Dean Areen's public claim that race was not a part of the school's admissions policy. . . .

[T]he director of admissions at the University of California Law School at Berkeley noted several years ago that, *nationwide,* "only five Blacks who took the LSAT had scores and GPA's that equaled [Berkeley's] average."[152]

I found it difficult to obtain legal representation in fighting the move to expel me. When two members of the faculty of the DC School of Law, Robert Catz and Thomas Mack, stepped forward to aid the organization managing my defense... its dean ordered Catz and Mack not to represent me.... But Catz and Mack held firm.

Maguire did not mention Dean Areen's claim that "median LSAT scores for a group tell nothing about what individuals can and will achieve" (Wilson 1991). This statement would be patently absurd even without the huge number of carefully conducted studies, some of which I discuss in Chapter 13, that have invariably found high correlations between LSAT scores and performance in law school and on the bar exam. The LSAT measures abilities like discerning the main points in a written passage, perceiving the difference between concepts that are similar and concepts that are identical, reasoning deductively, evaluating arguments, and writing clearly and cogently. That the score on such a test would be unrelated to performance in law school or as a practicing lawyer is so improbable as to border on impossible. Dean Areen made no attempt to substantiate her incredible claim. She knew that the media would support her.

In an editorial entitled "A Numbers Game at Georgetown Law" (April 4, 1991: A24) the *New York Times* complained that Maguire's disclosures

> will fuel the debate over affirmative action—and illustrate a common weakness among its critics. That weakness is an obsession with numbers.... Timothy Maguire . . . seems to have read only the files that yield grades, aptitude scores and racial designations. From this narrow perspective he reached the unremarkable conclusion that . . . blacks were less qualified.... [An accurate evaluation] would require an appreciation of the non-numerical information in those folders, including written assessments, college activities and the applicants' own statements. . . .

---

152. The italics are Maguire's. In 1998, the average LSAT scores of students at Berkeley Law School were twelfth in the United States (*Best Graduate Schools* (*U.S. News and World Report*, 2000 Edition): 35).

What's alarming about this episode is not what it says about
the people Georgetown admits, but what it says about some of the
people it produces. Mr. Maguire, now in his final year, wrote about
numbers with a false precision about their meaning ... [He] hasn't
a clue about the broad purpose of a great law school—to find, not
merely accept, suitable, distinctive and diverse young people and
train them for . . . legal service.

There it is. No American university has ever admitted blacks who are
less qualified than whites.

However, obvious questions impose themselves. Thirty-one years earlier
(May 14, 1960: A22), in an editorial entitled "Ivy League Admissions," the
New York Times pointed out, "[I]f admissions were determined on a strictly
objective basis—an average of entrance examination scores or the like—
[that] would ensure that the best minds are accepted and avoid any suspicion
of unfairness." The wisdom of this recommendation has been confirmed by
many subsequent studies, all of which found that non-measurable criteria
(letters of recommendation, biographical information, essays written by
students, interviews, etc.) add nothing significant to the predictive accuracy
of standardized tests and grades for university performance (Klitgaard
1985:108).

However, in its editorial about Maguire's disclosure, the *New York
Times* claimed, in effect, that it had come to know with enough certainty to
report as an irrefutable fact that the folder of every minority student who
has been admitted by every division of every American university with
lower grades and test scores than its non-minority students contains "non-
numerical information" that compensates for the enormous discrepancies
in all measurable qualifications.

The *Times* must have known that most white Americans share Maguire's
abysmal ignorance. Why didn't it publish just a little of the evidence that
would have shown that they are wrong?

Since the media were so remiss, why didn't Georgetown disclose some
of this evidence? If universities really used non-numerical criteria, they must
have checked their validity in the same way that the validity of numerical
criteria has been checked: by many extensive, carefully conducted studies of
their correlation with academic and professional success. By disclosing this
information, Georgetown would not only have vindicated itself, but, more
importantly, have struck a mighty blow against the suspicion that pervades
American society that blacks and Hispanics receive preferential treatment
in universities and employment. No institution was ever in a position to
perform a greater service for American minorities than Georgetown at that
time. If counter-evidence existed, Maguire's disclosure was a godsend. It

provided the opportunity to lay to rest once and for all the stigma of suspected unearned success that attaches itself to every successful black and Hispanic American. Instead, Georgetown reacted by requiring everyone who worked with admissions records to sign a statement swearing to keep all information secret (CHE 1991).

If counter-evidence to the "narrow perspective" of the opponents of affirmative action existed and the media and Georgetown, through inexplicable negligence, did not use it, why did no other university leap into the breach? After all, for decades American colleges, graduate, and professional schools have admitted minority applicants with vastly lower measurable qualifications than non-minority applicants. During that time, innumerable extensive studies have demonstrated without exception the predictive accuracy of grades, the SAT, LSAT, etc. Every criterion of success that anyone has ever thought to use has shown that whites and Asians at American universities are incomparably more qualified than blacks and Hispanics. Most of this information was made public, like Georgetown's, despite desperate attempts to hide it. By an incredible stroke of bad luck, in all these decades not a single piece of the pro-minority evidence, which the press and universities claim is in the folder of every minority student in every division of every American university, has ever come to light. But what is the purpose of keeping that pro-minority evidence hidden any longer? There is no danger that it is too subtle for the public to understand. The non-quantifiable qualifications of all these students must be spectacular to compensate for their grades and scores on standardized tests.

While the LSAT was marked on a scale from 200-800, Harvard Law School admitted minority applicants with LSAT scores below 500 (Foster 1976: 20). At the same time, a graduate of Harvard College who applied to Harvard Law School with a LSAT score of 720 and an undergraduate GPA of 3.6 had only a 40 percent chance of being admitted (Klitgaard 1985: 36). Among the white applicants whom Harvard Law School rejected was Kenneth Krohn, who graduated from MIT with Honors, had a PhD from Harvard in mathematics, a perfect 800 on the LSAT, and had jointly devised the Krohn-Rhodes theorem, which was a mainstay of modern algebraic theory in computer science (Foster 1976: 19). So, nearly every minority student who has attended every elite American undergraduate, graduate, or professional school since the 1960s must have had hyper-stupendous "non-numerical" strengths. Disclosing just five or six examples would go a long way to dispelling the suspicion of unearned success that hangs over every black and Hispanic professional in the United States.

When Harvard Law School rejected Kenneth Krohn and was accepting minority applicants with LSAT scores below 500, its director of admissions,

Patricia Lydon, stated that race was a minor and informal consideration: "Someone on the committee may note on an application something like, 'He's come a long way,' and that may help a little . . . [W]e also want diversity and in some cases diversity includes some kind of disadvantage, whether it be economic, cultural, racial, or some combination thereof." Harvard Law School's dean, Albert Sacks, stated, "We definitely do not have a two-track system" (Foster 1976: 19).

At Harvard Law School, as elsewhere, the lie that race is only one among many considerations in admissions was combined with the logically contradictory lie that race is not considered at all. Harvard Law boasted (and still does), "Harvard Law School has long been committed to a policy against discrimination based on sex, race, color, creed or national origin." It proves that by not having a question about race on its application form. However, the director of admissions explained, "Usually the applicant or one of the people writing his or her recommendation states the applicant's race. If we still are unsure, we call up the college where the applicant was an undergraduate" (Foster 1976: 19). But at that time, one black applicant, Stephen Carter, did not indicate his race; and, for reasons he explains below (Carter 1991: 15-16), Harvard Law School's admissions office assumed that he had to be white; and, so, did not check on his race and rejected him.

> As a senior at Stanford back in the mid-1970s, I applied to about half a dozen law schools. . . . Harvard [rejected me]. . . . Then, within days, two different Harvard officials and a professor contacted me by telephone to apologize. They were quite frank in their explanation for the "error." I was told by one official that the school had initially rejected me because "we assumed from your record that you were white" . . . Stephen Carter, the white male, was not good enough for the Harvard Law School; Stephen Carter, the black male, was not only good enough but rated agonized telephone calls urging him to attend. And Stephen Carter, color unknown, must have been white: How else could he have achieved what he did in college? [153]

In 1976, while the dean of Harvard Law School was guaranteeing that "We definitely do not have a two-track system," the dean of Harvard Medical School was lying about its practice of granting MD degrees to manifestly

---

153. Carter chose to go to Yale Law School, which is even more difficult to get into than Harvard Law School. Carter's father was a professor at Cornell and his friends in school were other children of Cornell professors. If he were the son of non-English-speaking Bulgarian immigrants and had grown up in a mostly black slum, neither Harvard nor Yale Law School would have admitted him because he would not have added to their diversity.

unqualified black students and was being supported unequivocally by the entire Harvard administration. Two years later, in *Regents of the University of California v. Bakke*, Justice Powell established the legal basis of anti-white discrimination by citing the "illuminating example" of "the Harvard . . . program," in which (#316) "the race of an applicant may tip the balance in his favor." Justice Powell also ruled (#318-19), that a court should "not assume that a university, professing to employ a facially nondiscriminatory admissions policy, would operate it as a cover for the functional equivalent of a quota system. In short, good faith would be presumed." In 2003, in its *Gratz* and *Grutter* decisions, the Supreme Court reaffirmed Justice Powell's decision, including (*Grutter* #6) his ruling that a university's good faith in its description of its policies should be presumed. In both decisions, the only specific example of the correct way to practice racial discrimination that the majority justices adduced was Harvard's description of its admissions policy in its Brief in the *Bakke* case.

Two decades after the *Bakke* decision, American colleges were still using the same lies. In the Spring 1996 issue of the *Journal of Blacks in Higher Education* (page 12) the presidents of Amherst and Williams, two of the three most highly regarded American small liberal arts colleges, stated categorically that they do not practice racial discrimination. The president of Amherst said,

> [The] implication that the Black students we accept are less qualified than the White students we reject is simple-minded, incorrect, and even racist. Perhaps some of that opinion is based on the ridiculous notion that "qualifications" and test scores are synonymous, which has never been true in college admissions.[154]

Amherst's black students must have had truly remarkable non-academic qualities to compensate for their test scores. In 1995, Amherst accepted 19 percent of all its applicants, but 51 percent of its black applicants. In 1990, it admitted less than half of its applicants who had Verbal SAT scores over 750; it also admitted 26 with Verbal scores below 400. (Amherst has 440 students in each class.) However, the competition among colleges for black students is so ferocious that only 29 of the 180 black applicants that Amherst accepted in 1995 enrolled there (*Journal of Blacks in Higher Education* (Spring 1996): 12; Sowell 1993: 123).

---

154. Since Amherst's president was using "test scores" to mean measurable academic performance, the last clause is historically false. In Section D of Chapter 3, I quoted from a letter that President Lowell of Harvard wrote in 1923 to the president of Amherst that Harvard was introducing non-academic criteria to deal with "the race [i. e., Jewish] question."

The president of Williams College said, "in applicants' academic potential . . . Williams students of color closely resemble the student body as a whole." Two years later, Williams was among the colleges in Bowen and Bok's database in *The Shape of the River* (1998: 40). I outlined the huge racial preferences that the colleges in that database confer and pointed out that Bowen and Bok never even suggested that the black students admitted now or in the past by any American college have ever had any qualifications that compensate for the huge racial differences in SAT scores and high school grades.

I will return to Harvard for my last two examples of the lies that *The Shape of the River* exposed. In 1988, an acrimonious scandal engulfed Harvard for months after black students made a charge of "racial insensitivity" against Professor Stephan Thernstrom, who had won the Bancroft Prize, the most prestigious prize awarded to an American historian. Among his insensitivities was that he said that affirmative action involves "preferential treatment in hiring, promotion and college admissions." The dean of Harvard College issued a statement in which he said that although people like Thernstrom "may be partly or wholly unaware of the import of their words," such incidents "should elicit . . . warnings and clear messages about the inappropriateness and insensitivity of such behavior" (D'Souza 1991: 194-7).

The year after the Thernstrom scandal, in the fall of 1989, Harvard's *Affirmative Action Newsletter* published the following in a section called "Myth and Reality":

> Myth: Affirmative action means applying a double standard—one for White males and a somewhat lower standard for women and minorities.
> Reality: Double standards are inconsistent with the principle and spirit of affirmative action (D'Souza 1991: 220).

Not only is the "Reality" a patent lie, but even the one sentence of the "Myth" contains two obvious lies. First, it lumps women together with minorities, even though no one thinks that women receive significant affirmative action in undergraduate admissions or marking. Second, it claims that the argument of opponents of affirmative action is that it "means applying . . . a *somewhat* [italics added] lower standard for . . . minorities." In fact, most opponents of affirmative action would be satisfied if the degree of discrimination were reduced to a level that would still be greater than "somewhat." For example, in *The Bell Curve* (1996: 475), Herrnstein and Murray wrote, "We urge that affirmative action in the universities be radically modified . . . [so] that the average minority student is at the 30th percentile of the white

distribution [i.e., 70 percent of whites would have better qualifications]."
Even if universities adopted that radical change, the 30th percentile would
be much more discrimination than "somewhat."

(Harvard's motto is *veritas*, which means "truth.")

CB BO

CR SO

Chapter 15
The Shape of the River: The Liars Defend
Affirmative Action

False facts are highly injurious to the progress of science, for they
often long endure. But false views, if supported by some evidence,
do little harm.

(Charles Darwin, *The Descent of Man and Selection in Relation
to Sex*, 1871)[155]

Derek Bok was president of Harvard from 1971 to 1991, when it published this Myth and Reality lie, when the Thernstrom controversy
raged, and when its administration was telling the blatant lies that
I have described about the admissions policy of its law school. During the
scandal created by Professor Davis' disclosures about its medical school,
Bok made the public statement (Davis 1986: 181), "I find no basis for any
implication that minority students are less than fully qualified for the M.D.
degree in accordance with the normal standards of the Harvard Medical
School." William Bowen was the president of Princeton who wrote the
description of its admissions policy that Justice Powell quoted with approval in his *Bakke* decision (#317, note 51): "race is not in and of itself a
consideration."

After universities were forced to disclose their student records, Bowen
and Bok blithely admitted in *The Shape of the River* (1998) that selective
American universities have been practicing massive racial discrimination
for decades.

Newspapers and television programs throughout the United States show-
ered *The Shape of the River* with adulatory reviews (Thernstrom 1999B:
1586). The *New York Times* alone praised it extravagantly in its Sunday
Book Review section, its daily book review, its news reporting, its Week in
Review section, and in an editorial (McGowan 2001: 170). Since then, it

---

155. The beginning of the last chapter (21) of Part II; page 385 in the
reprint by the Princeton University Press, 1981.

has been the most cited defense of academic anti-white discrimination by the media and the courts; including the Supreme Court, in its 2003 decision *Grutter v. Bollinger* (#41).

In their Preface (xxv), Bowen and Bok made a claim that they knew reviewers would constantly repeat: "When we began the study, we were far from certain what the data would reveal." However, Bowen was provost of Princeton from 1967 to 1972 and then president until 1988; Bok was dean of Harvard Law School from 1968 until 1971 and then president of Harvard University until 1991. They observed in *The Shape of the River* (xxiv), "[B]oth of us . . . worked hard, over more than three decades, to enroll and educate more diverse student bodies." As Stephan and Abigail Thernstrom pointed out (1999B: 1588-89),

> [I]t must have occurred to them that it would have been acutely embarrassing if their evidence had revealed that racially preferential admissions policies had not achieved their objectives or had produced unanticipated negative consequences. Critics would have legitimately asked why they had never studied the matter before. At any time in the many years they spent in charge of two fabulously wealthy universities, either one could have commissioned a careful analysis . . . They did not do so, however, and were thus left with the strongest incentive for giving high marks to a vital part of their own legacy.

The Thernstroms also wrote of the database (1999B: 1589-90, footnote 28) that Bowen and Bok used in *The Shape of the River*, which consisted of detailed information supplied by 28 colleges and universities:

> The authors had unique advantages that other scholars are unlikely to have in the future . . . their access to student records that schools have never made available to investigators before. Why did these institutions cooperate with Bowen and Bok in the project? It is reasonable to surmise that university administrators agreed to contribute to the foundation's "restricted access database" because they knew preferential policies had come under serious attack and were confident that the authors could be trusted to view the evidence in the most favorable possible light.
>
> In doing research for our book, *America in Black and White* [which is critical of affirmative action], we had quite a different experience. We knew that SAT scores broken down by race at many of the nation's leading colleges and universities were in the possession of the Consortium on Financing Higher Education. In theory, the Consortium's data are available for research by faculty members

at any member school. Although one of us is a professor at Harvard, a member institution, our request was flatly denied. . . .

[I]t is common for scholars . . . to make the data [they use] available for reanalysis by other scholars. . . . *The Shape of the River*, with its "restricted access database," cannot be subjected to searching critical scrutiny of this kind. As a result, critics of the work are limited to the information the authors have chosen to put forward, and must work in the categories that they employ. . . . If those who stand at the helm of our elite institutions of higher education today are as proud as they claim to be of the preferential policies they pursue, why are they so obsessed with preserving confidentiality?

However, even the data that Bowen and Bok chose to report do not support the conclusions that they drew from them.

The first question to ask about any defense of affirmative action is: What lies does it tell? I will begin with a crucially important lie, perhaps the most important of all the lies in *The Shape of the River*. On the first page (15) of Bowen and Bok's discussion of "the admissions process," they make an assertion that they knew would be constantly repeated by the media and in subsequent discussions of academic affirmative action:

One of the most common misunderstandings concerns the number of institutions that actually take account of race in making admissions decisions. . . . Nationally, the vast majority of undergraduate institutions accept all qualified candidates and thus do not award special status to any group of applicants.

In a footnote, Bowen and Bok support this statement observing, "*Peterson's Guide* [*to Four-Year Colleges*] classif[ies] colleges and universities by their degree of selectivity . . . . The 1998 edition of *Peterson's Guide* placed only 212 four-year colleges and universities, or about 12 percent of the institutions they classified, in one of the top two categories." I could not find the 1998 edition, but I did find the 1997 edition of *Peterson's Guide*, which could not be significantly different. On pages 51-8, it lists all the four-year colleges and universities in the North America and a few in Europe in five categories, in accordance with the stringency of their admissions requirements: Most Difficult, Very Difficult, Moderately Difficult, Minimally Difficult, and Noncompetitive.

I, like Bowen and Bok, considered only four-year colleges and universities in the United States. There were 1,819 in total. Among them, 219 were in the first two categories, that was 12 percent of all American four-year colleges and universities, the same percent as Bowen and Bok record. However, 1,105 were in the third category (Moderately Difficult). That is 60.7 percent of all American four-year colleges and universities. *Peterson's* defined this category as: more than 75 percent of the freshmen were in the top half of their high school class and scored over 1010 on the Verbal+Math SAT and over 18 on the ACT. In 1996-97, the average Verbal+Math SAT score of blacks was 854 and of Mexican Americans, 909.[156] At every college that rejects any high school graduates and whose racial statistics have been published, black and Hispanic students have much lower high school grades and SAT or ACT scores than white and Asian students (Lerner and Nagai 2002). Moreover, the colleges in the second category (Very Difficult) are defined as: more than half of their freshmen scored over 1150 on Verbal+Math SAT. That means that they must have taken nearly every black and Mexican college applicant in the United States with Verbal+Math SAT scores over 1000, and many with SAT scores between 850 and 1000. Since over 75 percent of the freshmen at the colleges in the third category had combined SAT scores over 1010, these colleges (60.7 percent of all American colleges) must have practiced (and still practice) massive racial discrimination in admissions. So, at least 72.7 percent (the top three categories) of American colleges practice massive affirmative action in admissions. But even the fourth category (Minimally Difficult) is defined as: most freshmen scored somewhat below 1010 on Verbal+Math SAT and below 19 on the ACT. That category includes 293 colleges (16.1 percent of the total), and they must also practice affirmative action in admissions. So, only the colleges in the lowest category, which accept all applicants and consist of 202 colleges (11.1 percent of the total), do not practice racial discrimination in admissions. Even these statistics are misleading because the colleges in the lowest two categories are small, with few students.

Not only did Bowen and Bok lie about the proportion of American colleges that practice racial discrimination, they also lied about the extent of its impact on its victims. That was pointed out by Andrew Hacker, an impassioned advocate of affirmative action, in a review of *The Shape of the River* in the Autumn 1998 issue (pages 129-31) of the *Journal of Blacks in Higher Education*, whose purpose is to advance academic affirmative action:

> If places are given on affirmative action grounds, some with more traditional credentials will necessarily be turned down. In response, Bowen and Bok suggest that the number is small. . . . The book refers to Proposition 209, which ended race-based admissions in California's public universities. But it does not mention that . . . the numbers of Whites and Asians [who were more qualified than the Blacks and Hispanics who were admitted but were] turned down by Berkeley and UCLA were far from small . . . 21 percent of academi-

---

156. http://nces.ed.gov/FastFacts/display.asp?id=171

cally qualified Asians and 39 percent of qualified Whites . . . did not
make UCLA's 1994 freshman class.

A. Diversity

Before discussing Bowen and Bok's defence of diversity, I will point
out that neither they nor any other diversity proponent has argued that diversity improves the academic performance of university students, which,
commonsensically, should be the main criterion. However, Charles, et al.,
(2009) did investigate this question in the 28 colleges that formed Bowen
and Bok's database. They found (pages 143-5) two effects: the presence of
more Hispanic students in a course improved white students' grades; but
the presence of more blacks depressed Asian students' grades. "Ironically,
in no case does the presence of a minority's own in-group members in large
numbers improve the grade performance of that minority itself."

I quote above Stephan and Abigail Thernstrom's observation that Bowen
and Bok had a great deal at stake in defending academic racial discrimination.
But the Thernstroms understated Bowen and Bok's personal involvement.
At the end of the chapter on diversity in *The Shape of the River* (253-4),
Bowen and Bok wrote,

> [A] solid empirical basis for assessing the impact of diversity on the
> development of students . . . is overdue. A sense of the educational
> value of diversity led Justice Powell in the *Bakke* case to affirm the
> continued use of race in admissions decisions. . . . [H]e was will-
> ing to rely on the statements of university officials . . . . [T]he time
> has come, after twenty years, to test them against the views and
> impressions of those who actually experienced racial diversity first
> hand. The findings in this chapter have been presented in an effort
> to provide such an accounting.

However, as Peter Wood pointed out (2003: 124), Bowen and Bok were
too modest. Who were the university officials who made the statements on
which Justice Powell relied? They were none other than Bowen and Bok, in
the *Amici* brief that the elite universities submitted in the *Bakke* case. Bok
was the president of Harvard when it submitted the description of its admissions program to which Justice Powell assigned primary importance; and
the *only* evidence that Powell cited (*Bakke* #312, note 48) for the value of
diversity was Bowen's statement, "a great deal of learning occurs informally
. . . through interactions among students . . . who have a wide variety of
interests, talents, and perspectives." Bowen did not provide any evidence for
this assertion. It was simply an attempted justification of Princeton's policy
of racial discrimination that Bowen, as Princeton's president, wrote in the

Princeton Alumni Weekly ("Admissions and the Relevance of Race" (September 26, 1977)). In the same article, Bowen told the lie about Princeton's admissions policy that Powell also quoted (*Bakke* #317, note 51): "race is not in and of itself a consideration."

During the following two decades, Bowen remained silent, as Powell's ruling, based solely on his unsubstantiated assertion about the value of diversity, shaped the admissions policies of America's undergraduate, graduate, and professional schools and the employment practices of America's businesses and municipal, state, and federal governments. Did he and Bok make up for that silence in *The Shape of the River* and fulfill their claim that they were supplying the "overdue" "solid empirical basis for assessing the impact of diversity on the development of students"?

Bowen and Bok put great emphasis (pages 229-40) on the fact that 56 percent of the white 1989 matriculants in their database reported that they "knew well" two or more black fellow students while at college and that of those whites who said that they knew well two or more blacks in college, "72 percent reported that they had also gotten to know well two or more blacks after leaving college." However, as Andrew Hacker pointed out in his review of *The Shape of the River* from which I quote above,

> Bowen has been quoted as saying "we found there has been an enormous amount of interaction between black and white students" . . . Yet at no point in *The Shape of the River* does he or his co-author detail instances of interracial socializing in dining halls or elsewhere. All we find is that 56 percent of the white respondents claimed they "knew well" two or more black students. It hardly needs saying that most whites like to declare they have black friends. . . . How far affirmative action has fostered social relationships is an important question and deserves more inquiry than citing survey responses.

Hacker's objection to survey data is well founded. Steinhorn and Diggs-Brown (1999) showed the absurdity of the responses that white Americans give in surveys about the extent of their contact with blacks. For example (pages 13-14),

> [M]any surveys show . . . that 60 to almost 90 percent of whites claim to have a close, personal friend who is black. . . . In fact, nearly half of all counties in the United States have fewer than 250 blacks, and in areas where large numbers of blacks live, very rarely are the neighborhoods genuinely mixed. . . . If three quarters of whites have close black friends, then every black person in America—including the isolated underclass locked in inner cities and the substantial number of blacks who say they don't have any meaningful contact

. . . with whites—will on average be close friends with five or six white people. Or put it another way: there would have to be about 160 million blacks in America, not the 30 million who live here today, if every Black were to have one close white friend. A 1992 *Boston Globe* survey of Massachusetts youth found that if whites and blacks were telling the truth about interracial dating habits, "then each black person would have had to date an average of nine white people."

A survey by the National Research Center of the University of Chicago found that a lower proportion of whites—42 percent—than in the surveys that Steinhorn and Diggs-Brown cite said that they "had a good friend who was black." But it also found that when whites were asked to list the names of their good friends and then were asked their race, only six percent were black (*Journal of Blacks in Higher Education* (Spring 2000): 69).

Steinhorn and Diggs-Brown also provided the explanation for the glaring omission that Hacker observed ("at no point in *The Shape of the River* does he or his co-author detail instances of interracial socializing in dining halls or elsewhere"). Why did the 28 universities in Bowen and Bok's database not make such a simple and obvious study, or, more probably, why did they make such a study and its results were not reported? Steinhorn and Diggs-Brown outlined the results of one such study (49):

> One university administrator decided to track how many times black and white students sat down together at the dining center. Not until the eleventh day did an interracial pair finally eat together. Look almost everywhere else on campus—fraternities, sororities, parties, dances, social gatherings, student clubs—and the same separation is evident day after day.

The University of Wisconsin (UW) had to resort to a fraud to show diversity in action. The cover of its 2001 application form had a picture of students at a UW football match, one of whom was black. But a reporter for the student newspaper discovered that the picture of the black student had been digitally inserted. The dean of admissions explained that "his office spent the summer searching for cover photos that would illustrate greater diversity at UW, where minorities are 10 percent of the 40,000 students . . . [but] could not find one." (UW has a program for minority high school students that guarantees them a five-year full scholarship at UW if they complete it (Claiborne 2000).)

Bowen and Bok pretended to compensate for not investigating interracial socializing by citing the work of Linda Sax and Alexander Astin, which Bowen and Bok say (1998: 228), "conclude[d] that racially diverse college environments and involvement by students in activities that cut across racial lines contribute to what they term greater 'cultural awareness' and stronger commitments to improving racial understanding." Since 1966, Astin has been the director of the Higher Educational Research Institute, which has amassed the world's largest database of academic inputs and outputs. It has analyzed 83 cognitive and non-cognitive outcome variables, including student self-reports about their racial sensitivity and understanding, for nearly eight million students at 1,300 institutions. Although Astin has asserted that his data shows that academic racial diversity has benefits, the data itself does not support that conclusion (Wood and Sherman 2001). Finally, in 2001, Astin conceded that the question of whether "more-diverse campuses better educate their students" "is yet to be demonstrated. The research still needs to be done that would demonstrate the link."[157]

Bowen and Bok also reported the results of all sorts of other surveys of student and ex-student opinion (pages 220-24, 241-52). However, there is a glaring omission amidst all the surveys that they cited. They recorded no survey that asked students about the advisability of racial discrimination in admissions; that is, no question about whether the practice that they wrote their book to defend should exist. The reason for this omission is obvious from the surveys that have asked this question.

The *Journal of Black in Higher Education* of Autumn 2000 (pages 22-4) reported a survey of student opinion, in which "the highly regarded polling firm Zogby International . . . survey[ed] 1004 college students . . . The sample was national in scope and mirrored the proportion of the nation's college student population by gender, region, family income, public vs. private institution, age, and political ideology." When asked, "Should schools give minority students preferences in the admissions process?" 77.3 percent said no. Even more striking was that more than 75 percent of college students agreed with the statement, "Fairness and academic standards are more important in admissions policies than ethnic diversity." The same article reported that a poll conducted by the *New York Times* and CBS News found that only 21 percent of whites agreed that in some circumstances "preferential treatment should be given to racial minorities."

---

157. Schmidt 2001. Bowen and Bok did report (page 441) their own survey, which found that white students at colleges with higher proportions of blacks had more favorably attitudes to racial diversity than white students at colleges with lower proportions of black students. But their survey made no attempt to control for any potentially confounding variables; for instance, whether the colleges with a higher proportion of blacks may be disproportionately small, private colleges and that is what accounts for the differences in responses. Astin's data, which Bowen and Bok must have known, did control for these variables and showed the importance of doing so.

The most extensive survey of this question was conducted in 1999 (Rothman, Lipset and Nevitte 2002). The sample consisted of 1,643 students, 1,632 faculty members and 808 administrators at 140 American colleges and universities, which were representative of all American universities in region, quality, and size. They were asked whether they "strongly agree," "moderately agree/agree with reservations," "moderately disagree/disagree with reservations," or "strongly disagree" with statements about racial discrimination. I have rounded off the percent choosing each response to the nearest whole number. Consequently, the percents do not always equal 100.

In response to the statement, "No one should be given special preference in jobs or college admissions on the basis of gender or race," 67 percent of the students strongly agreed, 19 percent moderately agreed, 10 percent moderately disagreed, and 5 percent strongly disagreed.[158]

In response to the statement, "More minority group undergraduates should be admitted here even if it means relaxing standards," 7 percent of the students strongly agreed, 18 percent agreed with reservations, 32 percent disagreed with reservations, and 43 percent strongly disagreed.[159]

In response to the statement, "The normal academic requirements should be relaxed in appointing members of minority groups to the faculty here," 7 percent of the students strongly agreed, 17 percent agreed with reservations, 30 percent disagreed with reservations, and 46 percent strongly disagreed.[160]

Every survey of student and faculty opinion on this subject has found the same result. These surveys include one conducted by Alexander Astin, whose work Bowen and Bok cite to support the benefits of academic racial

---

158. Of the faculty members, 34 percent strongly agreed, 21 percent moderately agreed, 33 percent moderately disagreed, and 11 percent strongly disagreed. Of the administrators, 26 percent strongly agreed, 22 percent moderately agreed, 41 percent moderately disagreed, and 10 percent strongly disagreed.

159. Of the faculty members, 9 percent strongly agreed, 32 percent agreed with reservations, 31 percent disagreed with reservations, and 26 percent strongly disagreed. Of the administrators, 8 percent strongly agreed, 36 percent agreed with reservations, 34 percent disagreed with reservations, and 21 percent strongly disagreed.

160. Of the faculty members, 3 percent strongly agreed, 16 percent agreed with reservations, 32 percent disagreed with reservations, and 49 percent strongly disagreed. Of the administrators, 1 percent strongly agreed, 16 percent agreed with reservations, 35 percent disagreed with reservations, and 48 percent strongly disagreed.

discrimination. Astin asked the faculty of UCLA whether they agreed with the statement, "The normal academic requirements should be relaxed in appointing members of minority groups to the faculty." Only 2 percent strongly agreed, 6 percent agreed with reservations, 7 percent were neutral, 22 percent disagreed with reservations, and 63 percent strongly disagreed (Wood 2001: 35-6).

In addition to scrupulously omitting any information on student and faculty opinion on racial discrimination, Bowen and Bok, like all defenders of discrimination, exploited an ambiguity in the term "diversity." In the *Bakke* decision (#314), Justice Powell said that diversity is essential because a "law school . . . cannot be effective . . . [without] the interplay of ideas and the exchange of views with which the law is concerned;" and a "medical student with a particular background . . . may bring to a professional school of medicine experiences, outlooks, and ideas that enrich the training of its student body."

However, the argument that diversity justifies racial discrimination ignores the obvious fact that the only type of diversity that racial discrimination achieves is racial, which has meant, from the beginning of affirmative action, that race and ancestry obliterate all other considerations. The daughter of a black lawyer (who himself may have only one black grandparent) and an Anglo-Saxon mother who grew up in an upper-class suburb is given preference over the better qualified daughter of an Albanian immigrant who works as a car-park attendant. The son of a white corporate executive is given preference in admissions, financial aid, and graduation over the son of a white laborer because the last name of the corporate executive's son is Perez and the last name of the laborer's son is Pirelli; even though Perez's ancestors may have owned black slaves, but Pirelli's ancestors certainly did not.

To their credit, Bowen and Bok were more honest than their predecessors. They did not use the "slum-child vs. suburban-child" lie. Instead, they illustrated the advantages of diversity with the example (page 280), "The black student with high grades from Andover [an elite private school] may challenge the stereotypes of classmates just as much as the black student from the South Bronx." This is closer to the actual practice of affirmative action than their predecessors' lies, but it is still a lie. "High grades" suggest a student who does not need affirmative action. But in that case, his admission would not need justification. If Bowen and Bok's hypothetical black Andover graduate was admitted through affirmative action, he had a worse academic record than my hypothetical daughter of an Albanian immigrant car-park attendant and son of a laborer who were rejected.

Bowen and Bok were also more honest than most defenders of affirmative action in that they quoted with approval (220, note 4) the observation, "Racial identity is regarded as important by many middle-class African Americans . . . in part because there are so few true cultural differences between them and comparable white Americans." However, Bowen and Bok ignored the result that must follow inevitably from this fact. That result was pointed out by Terrance Sandalow, who was a professor at the University of Michigan Law School and was its dean from 1978 to 1987. In a review of *The Shape of the River* (1999: 1906), he recorded:

> My own experience and that of colleagues with whom I have discussed the question . . . is that racial diversity is not responsible for generating ideas unfamiliar to some members of the class . . . . [E]ven though the subjects I teach deal extensively with racial issues, I cannot recall an instance in which, for example, ideas were expressed by a black student that have not also been expressed by white students.

If diversity of opinion and outlook is desirable, the obvious way to achieve it is directly, not circuitously by proxies such as skin color, hair texture, ancestry, and surname; and if it is desirable anywhere, surely that is in the views of professors in the social science and humanities. In 2002, a study was conducted of the political parties with which professors at representative universities and colleges throughout the United States were registered.[161] Below are the results for those in social studies and humanities departments for whom political registration could be ascertained with certainty. The first number is those who were registered with parties of the Left: Democrats, Greens, and Working Families Party. The second number is those who were registered with parties of the Right: Republicans and Libertarians. Next to some, I added in parenthesis the number of those affiliated with Right-wing parties who were in Economics Departments. Many economists favor free markets, but economics is a specialized subject that is taken by few students who major in other subjects.

Brown	47 and 1 (in the Economics Department)
Cornell	166 and 6 (3 of the 6 in Economics)
Davidson	10 and 1
Denver College	35 and 1

---

161. "The Shame of America's One-Party Campuses." *American Enterprise* (September 2002): 18-25.

Harvard	50 and 2 (1 of the 2 in Economics)
Pennsylvania State	59 and 10 (4 of the 10 in Economics)
Pomona College	18 and 2 (both in Economics)
San Diego State	80 and 11
State University of New York at Binghamton	35 and 1
Syracuse University	50 and 1 (in Economics)
University of California at Los Angeles	141 and 9
University of California at San Diego	99 and 6
University of California at Santa Barbara	72 and 1
University of Colorado at Boulder	116 and 5
University of Houston	45 and 14
University of Maryland	59 and 10
University of Texas at Austin	94 and 15

In 2004, Daniel Klein and Andrew Western did a carefully study of the political registration of the faculties of Berkeley and Stanford. Following are their findings for those professors in the humanities, social sciences, and law about whose political registration they could be certain.

Berkeley: humanities	103 Democrats and 6 Republicans
Berkeley: social sciences	105 Democrats and 5 Republicans
Berkeley: law school	36 Democrats and 6 Republicans
Stanford: humanities	72 Democrats and 2 Republicans
Stanford: social sciences	72 Democrats and 8 Republicans (6 of the 8 in Economics)
Stanford: law school	19 Democrats and 2 Republicans

Klein and Charlotta Stern studied this subject from a different approach. In 2002, they mailed questionnaires to members of six academic associations. Among the questions was, "To which political party have the candidates you've voted for in the past ten years mostly belonged?" Klein and Stern excluded from their analysis the members of these associations who were not professional academics and those who were older than seventy (and, consequently, probably retired from teaching). Among the rest, the ratios of Democrats to Republicans were:[162]

American Anthropological Association	30 to 1
American Economics Association	3 to 1
American Historical Association	10 to 1
American Political Science Association	7 to 1
American Society of Political and Legal Philosophy	14 to 1
American Sociological Association	28 to 14

Klein and Western pointed out that this bizarre imbalance in political opinion creates a nearly insurmountable barrier to the entry of diverse viewpoints into the classroom because, "University governance [concerning which courses to offer, the content of those courses, whom to hire, etc.] consists primarily of departmental autonomy, and departments operate on the basis of majoritarianism (and to a small extent on chair prerogative). A ratio of even 2 to 1 is deadly to a minority."

The religious uniformity of the faculties of American universities is as unrepresentative of the diversity of views in American society as is their political uniformity. Professor Eugene Volokh of UCLA Law School observed (1996: 2070-73) that if universities should use a proxy to attain diversity of opinions on controversial issues, religion would manifestly be a much better proxy than physical appearance, ancestry, or surname, especially since there are so few fundamentalist Protestants and devout Catholics among the students, and, even more, among the professors at elite American universities. Volokh cited a study that found that among the professors at American law schools, the proportion who identified themselves as Christians of all denominations, was half the proportion of all employed Americans; the proportion who identified themselves as Jews was over 13 times the proportion of employed Americans; and three times more answered "No Religion" than did all employed Americans. Volokh also observed that even these statistics greatly understated the irreligiosity of faculty members since most of those who classify themselves as Christians or Jews are only nominally so. He estimated that the rate of attendance at religious services among the faculty

---

162   Klein and Western and Klein and Stern reported the results of their studies on pages 40-52 and 53-65 of the Winter 2004-05 (18, 1) issue of *Academic Questions*. There, Klein and Western and Klein and Stern also discuss other studies of the political allegiances of American professors, all of which came to the *same conclusion*.

of UCLA Law School is about one-quarter that of the general population. The result is, "I very rarely hear any distinctively Christian inputs from either my colleagues or my students."

Because of this lack of diversity, some of the most controversial issues in American life—abortion, homosexual marriage, sex education, prayer in the public schools—are not debated, on the assumption that only one point of view is reasonable.

Of course, neither Professor Volokh nor I advocate giving preference in university admissions or in faculty hiring to conservative Republicans, libertarians, or born-again Christians. We, like most people, think that everyone is entitled to be judged on his own merits without regard to any group to which he may belong. We are simply pointing out that if diversity of opinion and outlook is important enough to justify discrimination, there are incomparably more sensible criteria on which to base discrimination than physical appearance or ancestry.

Even if racial diversity among students does not have the benefits that universities claim for it, it has been applied to all occupations; although for most—accountants, anaesthesiologists, tax lawyers, carpenters, welders, fire-fighters—the most ingenious diversity-advocate would not be able to find any benefit. Derek Bok himself pointed out (1982: 112) that "even the most avid proponent of diversity would be hard put to argue that the special perspective of a minority scholar will contribute much to teaching and research in the natural sciences or in classics, English literature, logic, or in many other important fields of study."

But the ultimate irony is that American universities have consistently supported policies that curtail interracial contact and have consistently tried to impose uniformity of opinion. I will quote again the only evidence that Justice Powell quoted (*Bakke* #312, note 48) for the benefits of diversity, from William Bowen:

> [A] great deal of learning occurs informally . . . through interactions among students . . . who have a wide variety of interests, talents, and perspectives; and who . . . stimulate one another to reexamine even their most deeply held assumptions . . . People do not learn very much when they are surrounded by the likes of themselves.

In *The Shape of the River*, Bowen and Bok constantly reiterated this argument. Therefore, they must agree with Akhil Amar and Neal Katyal (1996: 1778), who observed in their defense of *Bakke*'s diversity argument for racial discrimination, "schools that permit de facto residential segregation may be estopped [*sic*] from pleading *Bakke* as defense for affirmative action in admissions. Schools are not required to adopt affirmative action policies . . . but if they do . . . they should live up to the goal of encouraging people to learn from each other." So, it is highly significant that Bowen and Bok did not mention an incident that occurred while they were working on their book at one of the universities in their database. Wesleyan provides its students with residences called "Malcolm X," "Women of Color," "Asian/ Asian American," and "La Casa." In 1996, an unexpectedly large freshman class arrived, so the university assigned nine whites to empty spaces at Malcolm X House. But when black students objected to living with whites, Wesleyan consigned the nine students to the basement of the Philosophy building (Thernstrom 1999B: 1607).

Racial dormitories are ubiquitous. Stanford provides an "Ujamaa" residence for blacks, "Casa Zapata" for Hispanics, "Muhwekma-tah-ruk" for Native Americans, and "Okada" for Asian Americans. Since Stanford, like many American universities, also provides separate freshman orientation programs and graduation ceremonies for blacks, Hispanics, Native Americans, and Asian Americans, "a minority student, if so inclined, could spend all four years at Stanford without ever eating, living, speaking, or graduating with someone from a different race."[163] I have discussed Stanford because it is typical, except for the fact that *52 percent of the students it admitted in 2001 were minorities.*

University courses further segregate minority students and re-enforce the uniformity of opinion among them. A word-check of the Brown College catalogue of 1999-2000 found 42 courses with the words "black" or "African" in the course description. No course description mentioned Washington or Lincoln (Iannone 2003/2004: 58). The course catalogue of the University of California at Santa Barbara in 2001-02 included 62 courses in "Chicano Studies," including Methodology of the Oppressed, Racism in American History, and Dance and the Chicano. Thirteen other courses on Hispanic and Chicano Studies were listed in the History Department, in addition to broader studies of race and oppression. By contrast, no department at Santa Barbara offered a single course on the American Revolution or World War II. Arthur Levine, president of Columbia University's Teachers College, reported a typical incident: "[T]here was a Puerto Rican studies program. The Dominican students wanted a Dominican studies program. The president proposed a Caribbean studies program. It was flatly rejected

163. Sacks and Thiel 1995: 131-2. Separate graduation ceremonies for different racial groups are common (Shapiro 2004: 175-6). In 2006, ten of the 30 highest ranked American colleges held racially segregated graduation ceremonies ("Separate Black Graduation Ceremonies at the Nation's Highest-Ranked Universities." *Journal of Blacks in Higher Education* (Summer 2006): 36).

by all quarters" (Levine 2000).

(I cannot resist pointing out that the main accusation against research into genetically determined ethnic and racial differences is that it allegedly involves, or will cause, "reifying" of races; that is, treating races as fixed, objective categories.)

However, even if all undergraduates constantly mixed with each other, the diversity that would be achieved would be solely racial and ethnic. It would involve black, white, Hispanic, and Asian students from the same middle- and upper-class backgrounds. Delia Ibarra, one of the very few Stanford Hispanic students from a poor background, pointed out in *The Stanford Daily*,

> The thing I found most startling when I came here was how few people were like me. . . . My problem with Stanford diversity is that there really isn't much diversity at all. We have a wide assortment of students of color . . . But there are almost no students of color from the inner city (Sacks and Thiel 1995: 133-4).

Universities try to prevent students questioning their racial and ethnic practices by imposing compulsory courses and programs to justify affirmative action and "to enlighten students with regard to . . . ways in which the dominant society manifests and perpetuates racism;" so that they "learn to compare groups in the context of the history of structured inequalities and prejudicial exclusion in the United States" (Finn 1989: 19; Iannone 2003: 13). A survey conducted by the American Association of Colleges and Universities in 1998 found that 54 percent of the 543 responding colleges, universities, and community colleges (and 60 percent of the 434 responding four-year colleges) had a diversity requirement for graduation and another eight percent were developing one (Iannone 2003: 12).

This indoctrination is often indirect and, consequently, more sinister. Stanford University's job description for a Multicultural Educator explained that he must be circumspect because "if students believe that the institution is trying to remake them, inculcate ideas, and push an agenda it will be easier for them to resist" (Sacks and Thiel 1995: 40). However, sometimes direct confrontation has proved to be necessary. When an undergraduate on the University of Pennsylvania's planning committee for "diversity education" wrote a memo to her colleagues about "my deep regard for the individual and my desire to protect the freedoms of all members of society," an administrator sent her memo back with the word "individual" circled and the comment (capitals in the original), "This is a 'RED FLAG' phrase today, which is considered by many to be RACIST. Arguments that champion the individual over the group ultimately privileges [*sic*] the 'individuals' who belong to the largest or dominant group" (Kors 1989). It is no wonder that even a university with as stringent admissions requirements as the University of Pennsylvania requires its students to study racism, since they must learn that racism consists of regarding people as individuals, without taking their race into consideration.

Universities guard the orthodoxy they inculcate by voluntarily following the practice that the Japanese army imposed on Japanese educators during the 1930s: "protect students from dangerous ideas." A study of the political orientation of graduation speakers over a 10-year period at 32 colleges, including all the Ivy League colleges, found that liberals outnumbered conservatives by 226 to 15. At 22 of these colleges, 171 liberals were invited to speak but not one conservative (Shapiro 2004: 20). Universities also prescribe text books with strong left-wing biases (Schweikart 2002) and prevent their few conservative faculty members from exposing students to arguments and facts that conflict with their orthodoxy. For example, in 1999, in response to complaints by students at Bowling Green State University that they had to express the "correct" views on social issues in order to pass courses, Professor Richard Zeller of the Sociology Department proposed a course in which students would read books by politically incorrect authors such as Dinesh D'Souza, Charles Murray, and Thomas Sowell. No department would allow him to teach it under its auspices. The head of the Sociology Department said, "Unfortunately . . . Rich[ard] Zeller has tenure, so he cannot be fired." The Director of Women's Studies said, oxymoronically, "We forbid any course that says we restrict free speech" (Elder 2000). Even controversy outside of the classroom is dangerous. Thomas Klocek was an adjunct member of the faculty of DePaul University for fifteen years. In 2004, DePaul fired him because he engaged in a dispute on a campus thoroughfare with pro-Palestinian students who argued that Israel's treatment of Palestinians was the same as the Nazis' treatment of the Jews (Miller 2005).

Universities also try to suppress student publications that conflict with their orthodoxies (D'Souza 1991: 10, 144-7; Finn 1989: 21). The best known example is the conservative *Dartmouth Review*. The Dartmouth administration tried to prevent alumni from donating money to it; when an administrator physically assaulted a student distributing it, the faculty voted 113 to 5 to censure the student, not the administrator, even though it was the latter who was fined by a court of law; an editor was fined for publishing information marked "cleared for release;" one of its reporters was suspended from college on a charge of plagiarism by a left-wing professor, who adduced no evidence. (When the episode received national media coverage, the university dropped the charge of plagiarism on the condition that the student promise not to sue.) In 1988, the university suspended its senior editors for a year and a half; but the New Hampshire Superior Court ordered their reinstatement. Dartmouth's president, James Freedman, explained that the *Dartmouth Review* was guilty of "racism, sexism" and, above all, of threatening diversity. Amazingly, Freedman accused it of opposing "pluralism of persons and points of view . . . unconventional approaches and unfashionable stances" and said that it was "virtually designed to have the effect of discouraging women and members of minority groups from joining our faculty and enrolling as students." When Freedman made these accusations, three members of the *Review*'s staff were black, its editor was a Sikh woman, and she was its second Asian editor and its third woman editor since its inception seven years earlier. *Rolling Stone* magazine, hardly a right-wing publication, described its multi-racial staff as "co-existing in the kind of casual harmony liberals yearn for."[164]

After these examples of how thoroughly American universities enforce liberal orthodoxy, the reader will not be surprised to learn that the reason for the paucity of conservative professors is not that conservatives lack academic ability or ambition. Discrimination against conservatives in faculty hiring and promotion is pervasive.[165] As Professor Mark Bauerlein of the English Department of Emory University noted (Bauerlein 2004), "I've met several conservative intellectuals in the last year who would love an academic post but have given up after years of trying." However, he also observed that the war that universities wage against diversity of opinion involves much more than overt discrimination and rests on a deep and insidious foundation:

> [I]n the humanities and social sciences . . . academics shun conservative values and traditions, so their curricula and hiring practices discourage non-leftists from pursuing academic careers. What allows them to do that, while at the same time they deny it, is that the bias takes a subtle form . . . an indirect filtering process that runs from

164. Sowell 1993: 190-1, 194; Kors and Silverglate 1998: 239-43. It often happens that when I think I am inured to the left-wing idiocy of academia, and I think that I can no longer be startled by any nonsense that universities pull, I find that I am mistaken. I urge all readers to go to Katherine Kersten's blog (http://kerstenblog.startribune.com/kerstenblog). Scroll down to "Battle Lines Drawn against U Initiative (December 12, 2009) and "At U, Future Teachers May Be Reeducated," (November 21, 2009).

165. Rothman, et al., 2005; Horowitz 1999: 143-5; Lee 2002: 26. For a typical example, see www.campus-watch.org/article/id/3646 ("Colleges Score Perfect Grade in Liberal Bias," June 29, 2007), where Timothy Furnish describes his denial of an academic position at a state university because a professor found evidence that he "appeared to be more conservative than others in my field." (The field was the history of Islam.)

graduate school to tenure and beyond. Some fields' very constitu-
tions rest on progressive politics and make it clear from the start
that conservative outlooks will not do. Schools of education, for
instance, take constructivist theories of learning as definitive . . . .
Other fields allow the possibility of studying conservative authors and
ideas, but narrow the areas of advancement. Mentors are disinclined
to support your topic, conference announcements rarely appeal to
your work, and few job descriptions match your profile. A fledgling
literary scholar who studies anti-communist writing and concludes
that its worth surpasses that of countercultural discourse in terms of
the cogency of its ideas and morality of its implications won't go
far in the application process. No active or noisy elimination need
occur, and no explicit queries about political orientation need be
posed. Political orientation has been embedded into the disciplines
. . . As an Americanist said in a committee meeting that I attended,
"We can't hire anyone who doesn't do race." . . .

Conservatives and liberals square off in public, but on campuses,
conservative opinion does not qualify as respectable inquiry. . . .
One can see that phenomenon in how insiders, reacting to [David]
Horowitz's polls [on academic liberal bias], displayed little evidence
that they had ever read conservative texts or met a conservative
thinker. Weblogs had entries conjecturing why conservatives avoid
academe—while never bothering to find one and ask—as if they
were some exotic breed . . . . Such parochialism . . . [is] the outcome
of a course of socialization that aligns liberalism with disciplin-
ary standards and collegial mores. . . . The ordinary evolution of
opinion—expounding your beliefs in conversation, testing them in
debate, reading books that confirm or refute them—is lacking, and
what should remain arguable settles into surety. . . . The assumption
is that all strangers in the room at professional gatherings are liberals.
Liberalism at humanities meetings serves the same purpose that the
scientific method does at science assemblies. It provides a base of
accord. . . . [M]embers may speak their minds without worrying about
justifying basic beliefs . . . . An assertion of the genocidal motives of
early English settlers [in America] is put forward not for discussion
but for approval. . . . [T]he Modern Language Association's Delegate
Assembly . . . last year, charging that governments use language to
"misrepresent policies" and "stigmatize dissent" . . . urged faculty
members to conduct "critical analysis of war talk . . . in classrooms."
. . . [This resolution] passed 122 [votes] to 8 without discussion.

Ricardo Duchesne (2009: 174-5) outlined how this self-perpetuating
process operates in history departments:

H-NET Job Guide . . . posts openings for academic positions in history, the humanities, and the social sciences. . . . I have looked at it regularly for two years . . . . Rarely are any job announcements listed under the heading "Western Civilization." The few openings I have observed have typically been for single courses on a part-time or temporary basis. By contrast, numerous tenure-track openings in world history are posted. . . . [C]lose to *100 percent* of the descriptions I have seen for world history positions *exclude* expertise in European and North American history [Duchesne's italics]. . . . When the words "European" or "North American" appear, they do so in relation to such themes as "imperial or colonial studies," "British imperial history," or the "Atlantic slave trade." . . . [T]here are numerous openings listed in such "Area Studies" as African, African-American, Islamic, Asian, Hispanic, and Aboriginal studies . . . . [T]here are no graduate programs in Western civilization.[166]

B. Merit

In *The Shape of the River*, Bowen and Bok never put quotation marks around the phrase "race sensitive/sensitivity," which is the ludicrous euphemism they used for racial discrimination. But they invariably put quotation marks around the word "merit." On pages 25 and 276-9, they explain that merit at universities is an ambiguous and amorphous concept and does not mean what most people think it means. However, the merit of a university student is easier to define and measure unequivocally than merit in nearly any other activity. No one had the slightest doubt about what the merit of a university student was until the need arose to practice racial discrimination circuitously. In fact, Bowen and Bok themselves knew full well what academic merit is. They also knew that they had to show that it is not compromised by affirmative action. In their Preface (page xxiv), they stated, "Until now, the debate [over affirmative action] has proceeded without much empirical evidence . . . . The chapters that follow seek to remedy this deficiency . . . . We are concerned primarily with the performance, in college

---

166. Since the publication, in September 2008, of Bruce Smith, Jeremy Mayer, and A. Lee Fritschler's *Closed Minds: Politics and Ideology in American Universities*, it has been frequently cited and quoted to prove that there is no basis for the accusation that American universities attempt to indoctrinate students with liberalism (e.g., *New York Times*, November 3, 2008: "Professors' Liberalism Contagious? Maybe Not," by Patricia Cohen). The fraudulence of this book's methods and conclusions is analyzed on pages 240-45 of the Spring 2009 (22, 2) issue of the journal *Academic Questions*. See also my reader's review in Amazon.com.

and after college, of black and white students."

As for performance in college, on pages 74-5, they demonstrated that "based on the student's cumulative four-year GPA [grade-point-average]":

> [C]lass rank varies directly with SAT scores. Among both black and white students, those in the highest SAT interval had an appreciably higher average rank in class than did those who entered with lower SAT scores. . . . Moreover, the positive relationship between students' SAT scores and their rank in class . . . remains after we control for gender, high school grades, socioeconomic status, school selectivity, and major, as well as for race.

However, Bowen and Bok also pointed out (pages 77-8; their italics) "The average rank in class for black students is appreciably lower than the average rank for white students *within each SAT interval*" and, "Hispanic students also have a lower average rank in class than one would predict on the basis of their SAT scores (after controlling for other variables)." They also noted that the SAT's overprediction of minority college performance (i.e., the SAT is biased in favor of minorities) "is consistent with the results of a considerable amount of other research." Oddly, Bowen and Bok were not aware of (or did not admit that they were aware of) the universal phenom-enon, which I discuss in Section D of Appendix III, for intelligence tests to overpredict the performance of members of lower performing groups for all activities (universities, business, civil service, armed forces, etc.). So, they overpredict the performance of Gentiles relative to Jews, of the children of laborers relative to the children of professionals, and of women relative to men in mathematics-based subjects.[167]

Bowen and Bok observed (page 72) that the result of the combination of huge racial differences in average SAT scores and the SAT's overprediction of minority performance was that racial differences in college performance in their database were "very large . . . . The average rank of black matriculants was at the 23rd percentile of the class [i.e., 77 percent of other student had a higher average] the average Hispanic student ranked in the 36th percentile, and the average white student ranked in the 53rd percentile."

---

167. Bowen and Bok offered (78-85) several explanations for this overprediction: the need to work during the school year, low self-esteem, anti-academic peer pressure, etc. Not one of these can be correct. A higher proportion of white than black college students have jobs, blacks have higher self-esteem than whites, and even John Ogbu, who proposed the explanation that blacks are pressured by their peers not to succeed academically, has repudiated that explanation. (Ogbu is the only source that Bowen and Bok cite for this explanation.)

However, Terrance Sandalow, ex-dean of the University of Michigan Law School, explained (1999: 1886-87) why even this "very large" racial difference in college performance "offers too rosy an estimate" of the college performance of the blacks in Bowen and Bok's database. He pointed out, "[b]ecause of the very low mean [average], it is likely that well over half the African-American students . . . scored below, many well below, the average." He provided the example of nine black students whose percentile rankings are 70, 40, 28, 23, 20, 16, 7, 5, and 1. Their average is 23, but five are below the average and three above it. Sandalow also pointed out that this type of distribution was probable because, although Bowen and Bok were trying to justify racial discrimination, their calculation of average class rank was for all black students, including those who would have been admitted without racial discrimination. The latter comprised a small fraction of all black students, but they undoubtedly had much higher class ranks. So, they must have significantly raised the average black class rank. Thus, the median black class rank, which Bowen and Bok chose not to report, would have been more informative than the average black class rank. Sandalow concludes, "[I]t is difficult to perceive the basis of Bowen and Bok's conclusion [page 88] that '[t]hese students certainly do not appear to have been "over-matched" academically by their colleges.'" And Sandalow, like Bowen and Bok, did not consider affirmative marking.

More seriously, Bowen and Bok completely disregarded what they described as the "very large" difference in college performance between blacks, Hispanics, and whites when they summarized their data. In the chapter they entitled "Informing the Debate," the first section (page 256) is "Assessing the Performance of Minority Students." It begins with a statement that they knew they could count on the media to repeat: "The data assembled in this volume should dispel any impression that the abilities and performance of the minority students admitted to selective colleges and universities have been disappointing. On the contrary . . . ."

Bowen and Bok's main proof that racial discrimination in admission does not compromise academic merit is that a higher proportion of blacks than whites who graduated from their sample of colleges obtained advanced degrees. First (101-3), they considered only the top tier of medical, law, and business schools, which consisted of schools that grant less than ten percent of all American medical, law, and business degrees. The proportion of blacks in their database who graduated from these top schools was 25 percent in medicine, 26 percent in law, and 37 percent in business. The proportion of whites who graduated from these top schools was 21 percent in medicine, 18 percent in law, and 22 percent in business.

They then considered the proportion of blacks and whites who obtained advanced degrees from all professional, graduate, and business schools. They observed (106-107), "Among both white and black graduates . . . the percentage earning advanced degrees increases as SAT scores rise;" "the academic skills measured by SAT scores continue to play a substantial role in predicting which undergraduates go on to attain higher degrees even after we take account of . . . high school grades, socioeconomic status, and [undergraduate] school selectivity."

However, their chart on page 107 shows that although SAT scores correlated closely with rate of obtaining advanced degrees for both blacks and whites, the actual SAT scores of blacks and whites were radically different. Of blacks with SAT scores below 1000, 32 percent gained a professional or doctoral degree; of whites, 17 percent. Of blacks with SAT scores between 1000 and 1099, 46 percent gained a professional or doctoral degree; of whites, 27 percent, etc. This is despite the universal tendency of the SAT and similar tests to overpredict the performance of blacks relative to whites.

Bowen and Bok also recorded (112-13) that among all students, college grades also correlated closely with obtaining advanced degrees, but again actual grades were radically different for blacks and whites. Among those who were in the lowest third of their college class, 28 percent of blacks and 12 percent of whites obtained degrees from professional schools; of those in the middle third, 45 percent of blacks and 17 percent of whites obtained professional degrees; of those in the top third, the percents were 57 and 38.

Bowen and Bok's statistics are for graduation from professional and graduate schools, not for admission to them. They argued (109-10) that this proves that affirmative action does not compromise academic merit. Nowhere in a long and detailed book that purports to consider all the issues involved in the affirmative-action debate did Bok and Bowen mention affirmative marking and graduation, even though their existence is widely known in the academic world; and the most publicized scandal involving them erupted at Harvard Medical School when Bok was Harvard's President. If Bok and Bowen had any evidence to disprove the existence of massive affirmative grading and graduation, they would have offered it.

Indeed, the *Journal of Blacks in Higher Education* (*JBHE*) (Autumn 2001: 20) substantiated the title of an article, "How the LSAT [Law School Admission Test] Damages Blacks' Chances for Admission to Highly Ranked Law Schools" by outlining a study by William Kidder, which found that among black and white applicants to Berkeley's law school with the same undergraduate grade-point-average [UGPA] from leading colleges, the blacks had much lower LSAT scores. However, the *JBHE* pointed out a serious flaw in the study. "But, regrettably, Professor Kidder does not address the issue of whether the African Americans who had grade point averages similar to whites might have been the beneficiaries of preferential grad[ing]."[168]

Another stunning omission is that Bowen and Bok promised in their Preface (xxiv) that they would "remedy" the "deficiency" in "empirical evidence" in the debate over affirmative action "primarily with the performance, in college and after college, of black and white students." However, they said not one word about the huge racial disparities on the medical qualifying examinations taken during and after medical school and on the bar examination taken to qualify for the legal profession, even though these exams are at the center of the debate. (In Chapter 16, I discuss the crucial role that racial differences in passing the bar examination has in the affirmative-action debate.)

If a single study had ever found that black university students even remotely approximated white university students in any measure of academic achievement, Bowen and Bok would known about it and would have used it.

The reader may have noticed that most of the information I have discussed in this book on racial discrimination in granting advanced degrees is from law and medical schools. The main reason is that when a law or medical degree is obtained, standardized tests must also be passed for certification. The same is true for teachers in most states, and I have discussed the huge gap between white and minority teachers on these tests. Considering the desperation of American universities to give degrees to minority students, the lack of certifying exams for possessors of other post-graduate degrees—PhDs, MBAs, etc.—nearly certainly means that racial discrimination is greater in granting them than in granting degrees in law, medicine, and teaching.

Bowen and Bok's statistics support this conjecture. They reported (page 102) that among the students in their database, the difference between the proportion of blacks and whites who graduated from a top-tier business school (37 percent and 22 percent) was much greater than the difference between blacks and whites who graduated from a top-tier medical school (25 percent and 21 percent) or law school (26 percent and 18 percent). Elsewhere (85, footnote 39), they recorded that 26 percent of black applicants to law schools in 1990-91 were accepted, 39 percent of minority (not just black)

---

168. An even more important consideration is that, as Linda Wightman observed (1997: 32, 29, footnote 63, 34) in her defense of affirmative action at law schools (which I discuss in Chapter 16), "the LSAT is a substantially better predictor of . . . performance in law school than is the UGPA;" and LSAT scores "are as valid or more valid predictors" of law school performance for blacks and Hispanics as for whites. Wightman (1998: 37) also observed that LSAT scores are much better predictors than UGPA of passing the bar examination.

applicants to medical schools in 1996 were accepted, but "the acceptance rate of black applicants to their first or second choice business schools was much higher (70 percent)."

C8 80

CR SO

Chapter 16
The Ultimate Lie

In Chapter 4, I document the disastrous consequences of banning open, honest racial discrimination.

In *Grutter v. Bollinger*, one of the reasons the majority of the Supreme Court ruled that racial discrimination was legal was to protect universities from having to de-emphasize or abandon standardized tests and grades as admission criteria. The majority pointed out (#16, 24) that the U.S. District Court of the Eastern District of Michigan, which was the first court that considered this case, ruled against the University of Michigan Law School on the grounds that consideration of race was illegal. The majority then observed (#58):

> The District Court took the Law School to task for failing to consider race-neutral alternatives such as "using a lottery system" or "decreasing the emphasis for all applicants on undergraduate GPA and LSAT scores." But these alternatives would require a dramatic sacrifice of . . . the academic quality of all admitted students.

One of Bowen and Bok's reasons for writing *The Shape of the River*, maybe their main reason, was also to defend universities from having to de-emphasize or abandon standardized tests and grades as admission criteria. They discussed (1998: 269-74, 287-9) other means that have been proposed to get non-negligible numbers of minorities into leading universities, besides the present practice of using grades and standardized tests and admitting minority applicants with radically lower scores. They pointed out that some, like using socioeconomic background, would not increase the number of minorities, and others, like admitting all those in the top four or ten percent of their high school class, would be academically calamitous. They also quoted (page 288) a professor at Berkeley Law School who had supported Proposition 209, the California referendum that prohibited racial discrimination:

> I didn't realize until Proposition 209 went into effect that affirma-

tive action . . . allowed you to have some racial diversity and at the same time to maintain intellectual standards for the majority of your institution. It was a form of limiting damage. Now that you have to have race-neutral methods, if you want to get African-Americans and Hispanics in, you have to . . . lower standards for everyone.

A suspicion must now suggest itself: Was this the purpose of Bowen and Bok's blatant lies and mumbo-jumbo, which not even they could have believed? Was their purpose to allow universities to go on "limiting damage"? However, I will leave that suspicion aside and continue with the subject of this chapter.

For decades, American universities kept selecting students on the basis of standardized tests and grades, while they lied that their minority students did as well on them as their other students, or only marginally worse. When this lie was exposed, they fell back on the lie that mysterious, never disclosed, un-measurable qualifications compensated for the huge differences in all known qualifications.

Universities could have protected themselves from the constant danger of being caught in these horribly embarrassing lies by discarding or de-emphasizing standardized tests and grades. Obviously, they knew that they are so superior to any other criteria that they had to keep using them, even though their use incurred the constant danger of exposure.

It was only after all other affirmative action lies had been exposed, that studies began to be produced to support the only lie left—by far the most lethal lie of all—that contrary to every one of the innumerable studies that have ever been done, standardized tests and grades do not have significant predictive accuracy for academic performance.

I will now outline the two studies that have been the most frequently cited evidence against academic qualifications.

One is an article by Robert Davidson and Ernest Lewis in the *Journal of the American Medical Association* (*JAMA*) of October 8, 1997[169] about the subsequent careers of students "admitted by a special consideration admissions program" between 1968 and 1987 to the medical school of the University of California at Davis, which was the medical school involved in the *Bakke* case. Davidson and Lewis began by pointing out, "The regents of the University of California recently . . . prohibit[ed] the use of race as a factor in admission decisions at all the University of California campuses." Therefore, the only means left to retain significant numbers of minority students in medical schools was to argue that although minority students are admitted with much lower Medical College Admission Test [MCAT] scores

169. "Affirmative Action and Other Special Consideration Admissions at the University of California, Davis, School of Medicine:" 1153-58.

and undergraduate grade-point-averages (UGPAs), they are not beneficiaries of discrimination because they become as good doctors as students with much higher MCAT scores and UGPAs.

Davidson and Lewis claimed that that is what they found. They began their article with a summary of it, which concluded, "An admissions process that allows for ethnicity . . . to be used heavily in admission decisions . . . shows no evidence of diluting the quality of the graduates." In an editorial in the same issue of *JAMA* ("Medical School Admission Criteria:" 1196-7), the editors stated, "Davidson and Lewis demonstrate that . . . MCAT scores and GPAs . . . are not . . . meaningful admission factors."

The newspapers, magazines, and television programs of the world reported these statements to their readers and viewers. If they were true, they would contradict every other study that has ever been conducted on this subject, including many published in *JAMA*, several of which I cite in my discussion of Professor Davis' exposé of Harvard Medical School (e.g., Dawson, et al., 1994). I will add here a study by the Rand Corporation (Keith, Bell, Williams 1987: 8, 36, table 27), which found that the rate at which students become board certified is closely correlated with their MCAT score and their UGPA; and that among medical school graduates, 49 percent of minorities (80 percent of whom were black) eventually became board certified, compared with 80 percent of whites and Asians.

In fact, Davidson and Lewis' study did not contradict the other studies. Davidson and Lewis reported that three times as high a proportion (six percent) of Davis' "special consideration admissions" students failed to graduate from medical school as normally admitted students (two percent); that "all course scores [grades] were significantly higher for the regular admission" students; and that on Parts I and II of the NBME exam, the average scores of the specially admitted students were 86 and 90 points lower than the average scores of the normally admitted students. Davidson and Lewis described this as "significantly lower." It was a significant difference indeed; 100 points was a full standard deviation. Moreover, 50 specially admitted students failed Part I, but only eight regularly admitted students, and "special consideration students were more likely to repeat the examination to receive a passing grade." (They supplied no information on failure rates on Part II.)

Davidson and Lewis provided only one piece of evidence to substantiate their claim that using race in admissions decisions "shows no evidence of diluting the quality of the graduates:" evaluations by directors of residency programs "showed no difference between the two populations." These evaluations were responses to surveys that Davidson and Lewis mailed to residency directors more than 15 years after many of these students had been residents. Davidson and Lewis do not tell us what questions were asked or how they were answered (a scale of 1 to 10, yes/no, etc.) The reader should also remember the strong tendency, which I discuss in Section B of Chapter 9, of white markers to give much higher grades and make much more favorable comments on essays they think were written by blacks than on essays that they think were written by whites (Harber 1998).

Moreover, Davidson and Lewis' data on "special consideration admissions" students grossly overstated the performance of Davis' affirmative-action students. Davidson and Lewis stated in their closing comment (1157), "This study was prompted in large part by a controversial decision of the Board of Regents of the University of California to bar ethnicity as a criterion for admission." They intended for the media to report that their study concerned only affirmative-action students, which the media obligingly did. However, their data was for all "special consideration admissions" students, only 42.7 percent of whom were black, Hispanic, or Native American. There could be enormous variation in the rest. Among them may have been an MIT physics graduate with a perfect MCAT score but poor college grades because of the extraordinary competition at MIT (Heriot 1997A).

Davidson and Lewis provided no separate information on the affirmative-action students in their sample, but we can deduce from other sources that they had much lower UGPAs and MCAT scores than the entire sample of specially admitted students. Davidson and Lewis reported that the "special consideration admissions" students at Davis Medical School between 1968 and 1987 had an average UGPA of 3.06 and an average MCAT score of 544 (on the old MCAT scale of marking, which was used until 1982). The transcript of the *Bakke* case (#277) reported that the affirmative-action students who entered the same medical school that Davidson and Lewis studied (Davis Medical School) in 1974 had an average UGPA of 2.62 and an average UGPA in their science courses of 2.42. In 1975-76, blacks admitted to all medical schools in the United States had an average MCAT score of 490; and Mexican Americans, 524. These averages included blacks and Mexican Americans who were admitted to medical schools without affirmative action (Klitgaard 1985: 244, note 4).

The stated purpose of Davidson and Lewis' article was to defend affirmative action for minorities. The only possible reason that they could have had for not providing any specific information on the performance of affirmative-action minorities in medical school or on the NBME was that they did much worse on them than the total sample of "special consideration admissions" students. They also undoubtedly had much worse records as residents. In a study published in *JAMA* (Yao and Wright 2000), 298 residency directors answered an 89-item questionnaire about the characteristics of "problem residents," which meant "a trainee who demonstrates a significant enough

problem that requires intervention by someone in authority." Despite the
strong tendency of whites to evaluate blacks more highly than whites, 28
percent replied that members of an "underrepresented minority" were more
likely to be problem residents than other residents.

None of these facts had the slightest influence on the media's reporting
of Davidson and Lewis' article. The media merely repeated the claim that
Davidson and Lewis made in their opening summary. For example, a front-
page article in the *New York Times* (Bronner 1997) reported that Davidson
and Lewis "found that those with lower scores and grades . . . went on to
careers indistinguishable from those admitted on academic merit alone."

The other study, besides Davidson and Lewis', that has been the most fre-
quently cited evidence against academic qualifications is Linda Wightman's
"The Threat to Diversity in Legal Education," which was published in the
New York University Law Review of April 1997.[170] Wightman conducted her
research while she was the head of Testing, Operations and Research of the
Law School Admission Council, whose resources enabled her to compile two
databases. The first was of over 90,000 applicants to law schools in 1990-91.
The second was of over 27,000 students who enrolled in law schools in the
fall of 1991, comprising 70 percent of those who enrolled that year in law
schools that were accredited by the American Bar Association.

Just as Davidson and Lewis began their article by pointing out that racial
discrimination had been banned at the University of California, so the editors of the *New York University Law Review* prefaced Wightman's article
with an outline that began by observing that the *Hopwood* decision made
it "unclear" whether "affirmative action policies" "will . . . be possible."
In 1996, when the *Hopwood* decision was announced, John Sexton, the
dean of New York University Law School, responded to it by saying, "[C]
olleges must make clear that affirmative-action programs in admissions do
not admit unqualified minority applicants over more-qualified white ones"
(Lederman 1996). The next year the *New York University Law Review*
published Wightman's article.

Wightman could show that law schools do not admit unqualified minority applicants over more-qualified white ones, and thus ward off the threat
to diversity in legal education, only by attacking the predictive accuracy of
UGPA and the LSAT.

One means she used was to provide no information on law-school grades,
even though her database had this information. This is a truly remarkable
omission. I pointed out in Chapter 13 that the grades that students obtain

---

170. Stephan Thernstrom (1997A, 1998A) and Gail Heriot (1997) wrote
excellent criticisms of Wightman's article. Some of my observations are
drawn from them.

in law school predict their income as practicing lawyers. No other factor—
undergraduate major, work in the private or public sector, race, sex—is
anywhere nearly as closely correlated with income as law school grades
(Sander 2006: 1764, 1793-5).

Wightman conceded (1997: 29, footnote 63) that with regard to law
school grades, "[O]verwhelming evidence [has found] that LSAT and UGPA
have [a] useful degree of predictive validity" and that (32) "the LSAT is a
substantially better predictor of first-year performance in law school than is
the UGPA." Moreover (33-34), "Research . . . have [sic] repeatedly demonstrated that LSAT scores used either alone or in combination with UGPA are
as valid or more valid predictors of first-year grades in law school for black,
Hispanic, and Mexican American students as they are for white students. . .
. [W]hen UGPA is used alone as a predictor, it is less correlated [than LSAT
scores] with first-year grades for black than for white students." However,
Wightman pointed out (29-31, footnote 64) that LSAT scores and UGPAs
have one defect: "LSAT and UGPA tend to overpredict minority group performance." In other words, if a white and a minority student have the same
UGPA and LSAT score, the minority student tends to do worse in law school.
This overprediction for minority students is large. For example, if a black
and white have the same UGPA and LSAT score, the white's grade average
at one of the top ten law schools will probably be one-half of a standard
deviation higher than the black's, an extremely large difference (Klitgaard
1985: 162-3); and that is despite affirmative grading at law schools, which
I discuss below. This is a manifestation of a universal tendency, which I
discuss in Section D of Appendix III, for academic qualifications to overpredict the performance of lower scoring groups. In other words, academic
qualifications are biased in favor of lower scoring groups.

Wightman observed (page 36), "The black students in this sample
came to law school with UGPAs that are, on average, nearly one standard
deviation below those of the white students and LSAT scores that average
more than one-and-a-half standard deviations below." That means that the
UGPAs of the black students in Wightman's database were in the bottom
16 percent of white students and their average LSAT scores in the bottom
6 percent; and that includes blacks who were admitted without affirmative
action. (The reader should remember that blacks' UGPA is raised by affirmative grading.)

Since the LSAT is a substantially better predictor than UGPA of law
school grades for all students, and especially for minority students, and
since it massively overpredicts the grades of minority students, the reader
will understand why Wightman gave no information about the law-school
grades of the minority students in her survey.

Instead, she used only one criterion for law school performance: whether students graduated from law school (34-7). Graduating from law school is tenuous evidence of legal ability and knowledge. In Wightman's sample, 89.1 percent of all students who entered a law school graduated. Clearly, American law schools have adopted a policy of graduating everyone whom they admit except the egregiously incompetent. They have thus abandoned one of the most important social functions that law schools should obviously perform: certifying that their graduates are capable of practicing law. They were forced into this flagrant disregard of a crucially important social obligation because if they did not graduate nearly all of the students they admit, few of their affirmative-action students would graduate. In an article in the *Stanford Law Review* (Sander 2004), Professor Richard Sander of UCLA Law School outlined (380) a study that was published in 1975:

> When the nation's law schools initiated [affirmative action], while readily admitting that the admissions standards to be used for minority applicants were "different" or even lower, the schools also assured the bar that the same rigorous standards that applied to white students would be applied to minority students. . . . [But] the schools changed grading systems, altered retention rules, readmitted students dismissed for scholarship, and in some cases graduated students who clearly did not meet the past standards of the school.

Thus, American law schools have been forced to pursue the same socially disastrous policy as American medical schools: graduating nearly all the students they admit. I describe this policy in Section D of Chapter 9; and I will remind the reader that in Davidson and Lewis' study of Davis Medical School, only six percent of the specially admitted students and two percent of the regularly admitted students failed to graduate.

So, Wightman used graduation rates instead of obviously much more informative law school grades because graduation rates yielded results that were closer to those she wanted. Nevertheless, even this evidence revealed stunning racial differences. In her database (page 36), 19.5 percent *of Black students who would have been admitted if the sole admission criterion were LSAT scores and UGPAs* failed to graduate, twice the dropout rate of whites (9.7 percent); and that includes whites who would not have been admitted if the sole admission criteria were LSAT scores and UGPAs. This is a manifestation of the universal tendency of academic criteria to greatly overpredict the performance of lower scoring groups.

Wightman used one other attack (pages 37-9) on UGPA and the LSAT: rates of passing the bar examination. She concluded her study of bar examination passage rates with the statement (39), "Thus, the data suggest little or no difference in the likelihood of passing the bar examination between students predicted to be admitted to law school [if the sole criteria were UGPAs and LSAT scores] and those predicted not to be admitted . . . only on LSAT score and UGPA."

If that were true, it would contradict the unanimous conclusion of thousands of studies that LSAT scores accurately predict performance on the bar exam, some of which I outline in Chapter 13. In fact, the correlation between the average LSAT score of a law school and the percentage of its graduates who pass the bar exam on the first try is over 90 percent (Klein 2001-2002: 37). Among the studies that found a close correlation between LSAT scores and bar exam pass rates was one by Wightman herself, which used the same database as her "The Threat to Diversity in Legal Education" article. As Wightman reported (1998: viii, cf. 30, 34, 37, 39), "Both law school grade-point-average (LGPA) and the Law School Admission Test (LSAT) score were the strongest predictors of bar examination passage rates for all groups studied." Socioeconomic background—as determined by parents' income, level of education, and occupation—had a small correlation with bar exam pass rates among Asians and Hispanics, but none among blacks and whites (Wightman 1998: 35-6, 41, 58). Wightman (1998: 30-31, 34) also found that LSAT scores accurately predict bar exam pass rates for all races; nevertheless, in accordance with the universal tendency for academic qualifications to overpredict the performance of lower scoring groups, blacks, Hispanics, Native Americans, and Asian Americans have considerably lower pass rates than whites with the same LSAT scores. Consequently, of the law school graduates in Wightman's database, 38.6 percent of blacks who took the bar exam failed on their first attempt, but only 8.1 percent of whites did.[171]

Then, how did Wightman come to the conclusion that UGPA and LSAT scores make "little or no difference in the likelihood of passing the bar examination"?

All other studies of bar exam pass rates, including Wightman's 1998 article, use the criterion of passing on the first try. However, in her "The Threat to Diversity in Legal Education" article, Wightman used a different criterion. There, her criterion was whether a student passed a bar exam at any time within three years of graduating from law school. Therefore, she reported (page 39) that 94 percent of all the law school graduates in her

171. Wightman 1988: 27. First time failure rates for other ethnic groups were: Native Americans, 33.6 percent; Puerto Ricans, 30.5 percent; "Hispanic," 25.2 percent; Mexican Americans, 24.1 percent; and Asians, 19.3 percent. Wightman pointed out (page 14) that these failure rates were slightly lower than in most years because "the fall 1991 entering class was among the academically most able ever to enter."

database passed the bar exam.

Most states offer the bar exam twice a year, so some of those whom Wightman classified as "passed" in her "The Threat to Diversity in Legal Education" article passed on the sixth attempt. It is reasonable to assume that most law-school graduates who need several retakes to pass the bar exam are not as capable of understanding the complex structure and sophisticated nuances of the law as those who pass it on their first attempt. Moreover, although the National Commission of Bar Examiners sets the multiple choice questions that are part of the bar exam in every state, each state adds its own questions, usually essay questions and sometimes simulations of real-life legal problems. More importantly, each state sets the passing grade that must be attained to qualify to practice law in that state. These differ widely. For example, until 2002, the passing grade in New York (660 out of 1,000) was considerably lower than the passing grade in neighboring Connecticut and New Jersey (www.nybarexam.org). A law school graduate who fails the bar exam in one state can then take it in another state that has an easier exam or a lower passing grade. Since many more minorities than whites fail on the first try, this considerably diminishes the overall racial differences in pass rates.

However, even the idiosyncratic data that Wightman chose showed the predictive accuracy of LSAT scores and UGPAs. She recorded (page 38) that of blacks who graduated from law school, 9.8 percent of those who would have been admitted if the sole admission criterion were LSAT scores and UGPAs failed to pass the bar exam on all tries; but the failure rate on all attempts was 27.1 percent for blacks who would not have been admitted on the basis of their LSAT scores and UGPAs. Among whites, the proportions were 3.4 percent and 6.7 percent, respectively.[177] And a much higher proportion of blacks than whites who enter law school do not graduate and so do not make it to the bar exam.

What proportion of the blacks and whites in Wightman's study who entered law school eventually achieved the absurdly low criteria she chose: graduating from law school and then passing the bar examination within three years of graduation? Of whites who would have been admitted if the only admission criteria were LSAT scores and UGPAs, 87 percent eventually went on to pass the bar exam. Of whites who would not have been admitted on the basis of LSAT scores and UGPAs, 83 percent eventually passed the bar exam. Of blacks who would not have been admitted if the only admission criteria were LSAT scores and UGPAs, only 57 percent eventually

172. In Whitman's 1998 article, she provided the statistics (page 56) of those who failed on the first attempt but eventually passed: 75 percent of whites and Asians and 69 percent of blacks passed on the second attempt.

passed the bar exam.

These statistics also illustrate how insignificant non-academic criteria are for whites in law school admission. Eighty-one percent of whites were admitted purely on the basis of their UGPAs and LSAT scores (Wightman 1997: 36); and for the other 19 percent, non-quantifiable criteria (letters of recommendation, geographical origin, disadvantaged family background, being the child of an alumnus, etc.) were clearly of minor importance.

Even these statistics understate racial differences on the bar exam, since they do not include the law school graduates about whose bar exam performance Wightman had no information, presumably because they did not fill in a questionnaire. Undoubtedly, an extremely high proportion of them did not pass the bar exam. They were not randomly distributed. Bar examination results were not available for 8.0 percent of white graduates, 9.8 percent of black graduates, and 10.1 percent of black graduates who were admitted through preferences (Thernstrom 1998A: 38, footnote 59).

The media reported Wightman's article as if it vindicated affirmative action. A front-page article in the *New York Times* (Bronner 1997) stated, "Professor Wightman's study of law school admissions found that 73 percent of the black law students who would not have been admitted under a pure scores-plus-grades formula went on to graduate and pass their bar exams." In fact, Wightman found that 73 percent of these students who *graduated from law school* passed the bar exam. Only 57 percent of these students *both* graduated from law school *and* passed the bar exam.

Some newspapers, newsmagazines and television programs echoed the assertion in the outline of Wightman's article that preceded it: "Professor Wightman found no significant differences in the graduation rates and bar passage rates between those minority students who would have been accepted to law schools [on the basis of their LSAT scores and UGPAs] and those who would not." For example, *Newsweek* ("The Color Bind" (May 12, 1997): 32) told its readers, "Wightman's study . . . found no real difference either in graduation or bar-passage rates between those minorities who would have been admitted without affirmative action and those admitted because of it." Courts have also cited this assertion to justify anti-white discrimination in admission to law school.[173] In fact, Wightman reported (page 38) that the bar exam failure rate, on all attempts, of black law school graduates who would have been admitted on the basis of their LSAT scores and UGPAs was 9.8 percent, but the failure rate was 27.1 percent for black law school graduates who would not have been admitted if the only admission criteria were LSAT scores and UGPAs.

---

173. For example, the majority decision of the U.S. Court of Appeals for the Sixth Circuit in *Grutter v. Bollinger*, II. B (May 14, 2002).

Some newspapers, magazines, and television commentators told their readers that Wightman proved what not even the outline of her article claimed. For example, *Time* (Gwynne 1997) told its readers that Wightman found that the minority law students who would not have been admitted on the basis of LSAT scores and UGPAs "had graduation and bar-exam pass rates similar to *whites* [italics added]." The *Los Angeles Times* (Weiss 1997) reported that Wightman found "that black students showed no significant differences from other students in graduating from law school and passing the bar." The *Chicago Sun-Times* (Cose 1997) reported that among *all* law students, those "without high grades or test scores . . . perform almost precisely as well as those with the high numbers." The *Denver Post* (Delgado 1997) told its readers, "A massive study by researcher Linda Wightman . . . showed that minorities, after a short period of adjustment, did as well as anyone." Tim Russet stated on *Meet the Press* that Wightman's study "concluded that blacks who were admitted under affirmative action performed just as well as *whites in law school* [italics added] and on passing the bar exam" (Heriot 1997). In fact, Wightman reported (page 38) that only 4.2 percent of whites failed the bar exam, and she scrupulously avoided any mention of the relative performance of different races in law school, for reasons I have discussed.

Some of these summaries of Wightman's study may have derived from misleading statements that Wightman inserted in her article for the media to repeat; for instance, (page 39) "Thus, the data suggest little or no difference in the likelihood of passing the bar examination between students predicted to be admitted to law school [on the basis of their UGPAs and LSAT scores] and those predicted not to be admitted . . . only on LSAT score and UGPA;" and (52), "[L]aw school graduation is statistically independent of admission predicted from LSAT and UGPA." In fact, on May 19, 1997 Wightman said on National Public Radio ("All Things Considered") that although minority students were "admitted with lower credentials, they were passing and graduating from law school at the same rates as whites."

Time (Gwynne 1997) went even further. It told its tens of millions of readers that Wightman proved what she had not even investigated: minority law students who would not have been admitted on the basis of their LSAT scores and UGPAs "had an incalculable value to the black community, as both professionals and role models."[174]

---

174. I do not have the space in this book to discuss all the arguments for affirmative action. I will observe here that the argument for the desirability of role models of the same race or sex has never had the slightest empirical support. To their credit, Bowen and Bok did not mention it in *The Shape of the River*. During an earlier defense of affirmative action, Bok quoted

As Law Professor Gail Heriot (1997) observed, "Wightman apparently relied on the media not to look too closely at the details of the study. She got her wish."

The title of *Time*'s article is significant: "Back to the Future: Forced to Scuttle Affirmative Action, Law Schools See Minority Enrollment Plummet to 1963 Levels." Incredibly, its author did not notice the implications of this fact. A black in his early twenties in 1995 was more than twice as likely to have parents who attended *college* than a black in 1963 was to have parents who graduated from *high school*. Nevertheless, blacks' academic performance did not improve at all in those thirty-two years.[175]

(1982: 113) the results of "a careful review of the research" on the question of whether "gender matching or race matching between young people and their elders has a significant influence on career choice. We might like to think that there is such an effect; it may have intuitive appeal; but the facts that are assumed to exist simply don't." A later survey of empirical studies concluded, "[T]here is no systematic evidence that same-gender or same-race [role] models have significant influence on a range of dependent variables that they are assumed to influence, including occupational choice, learning, and career success" (Cole and Barber 2003: 169).

175. Thernstrom (1997: 190, 389, 391) provides tables on the proportion of blacks attending and graduating from high school and college over the past several decades.

In fact, for a long time before 1963, most of the black students in elite colleges and professional schools would not have been admitted if they were white (Synnott 1979: 207-8; Karabel 2005: 213; Oren 2000: 197-8; Wechsler 1977: 208, note 21). By 1963, blacks were also recipients of affirmative graduation (Jencks and Phillips 1998: 7, footnote 16). Nevertheless, 1963 was the beginning of the modern academic affirmative-action era. Robert Zelnick (1996: 160-61) provides a brief history of this process at Cornell, a process that was going on at nearly every selective American university at that time (I have italicized two key lies that were already basic affirmative-action jargon):

In 1963, President James E. Perkins organized the Committee on Special Education Projects . . . to "recommend and initiate programs through which Cornell could make a larger contribution to the education of *qualified* students who have been *disadvantaged* by their cultural, economic, and educational environments." . . . [P]rofessors were taken aback when suddenly substantial numbers of students appeared in their courses who were neither prepared for class nor able to keep up with the work. Informally, however, the word spread that it would be unwise to flunk these students.

One more point should be made. Racial differences in bar exam pass rates would be much greater if passing it were more difficult. In recent years, boards of bar examiners in many states have recommended raising the passing grade on their state's bar exam because the current passing grade is too low to ensure even minimum competence to practice law. Several states have rejected these recommendations for the explicit reason that a higher passing grade would increase racial differences in pass rates (Mangan 2004). The result, as I have noted, is that in Wightman's sample, 93.3 percent of whites *who would not have been admitted to law school on the basis of LSAT scores and UGPAs* but who took the bar exam passed it in three years. In 2004, 92 percent of all white American law school graduates passed the bar exam on their first try, and 97 percent eventually passed. (The percents for blacks passing the bar exam were 61 on the first try and 78 percent eventually).[176]

As with national qualifying examinations for doctors, which I discuss in Section D of Chapter 9, the desire to have most minority students pass the bar exam has created a situation in which nearly all whites pass it. Again, as always, explicit quotas would be incomparably better. The legal profession should announce in advance how many of each racial and ethnic group will pass the bar examination and set the passing marks for each group accordingly. Then, the public could know that at least the whites and Asians who pass it are qualified to practice law.

CB €

---

176. "How Putting an End of Race-Sensitive Admissions at the Nations' Top Law Schools Would Affect the Legal Profession." *Journal of Blacks in Higher Education* (Spring 2005): 14-15.

CR SO

Chapter 17
Closing the Racial Gap in Education

U ntil the early 20th century, in order to graduate from the *eighth grade* or *enter high school*, students had to pass tests that most of today's college graduates would fail. For instance, at the beginning of the 20th century, in order to graduate from the *eighth grade* in Kansas, students had to pass an examination which included defining words like "zenith" and "panegyric" and solving mathematical problems such as finding the interest on a $900 note, at 8 percent, after 2 years, 2 months, and 6 days. Questions of similar difficulty were asked in geography and history (Sowell 1993: 7). Following are typical questions on an examination required for *admission* to Jersey City *High School* in 1885:[177]

> Define Algebra, an algebraic expression, a polynomial.
> Write a homogeneous quadrinomial of the third degree.
> Divide 6a4+4a3x-9a2x2-3ax3+2x4 by 2a2+2ax-x2.
> Write a sentence containing a noun used as an attribute, a verb in the perfect tense potential mood, and a proper adjective.
> Name three events of 1777. Which was the most important and why?
> Name the four principal ranges of mountains in Asia, three in Europe, and three in Africa.
> What are the principal exports of France? Of the West Indies?
> Name the capitals of the following countries: Portugal, Greece, Egypt, Persia, Japan, China, Canada, Tibet, and Cuba. [It is interesting that these questions are not at all American-European-centric.]

As for the courses that were taken in high school, Thornton Wilder assumed in *Our Town* (beginning of Act II) that in 1904 every senior in a high school in a small town in New Hampshire, nearly none of whom would attend college, studied solid geometry, and Cicero's orations in Latin.

Between 1900 and 1940, the proportion of American adolescents who

---

177. The complete test is in "Sharpen Your Pencil, and Begin Now." *Wall Street Journal* (June 9, 1992): A16.

graduated from high school rose from six to 50 percent (Herrnstein and Murray 1996: 144). But still in 1940, high school graduation required a level of academic knowledge that most of today's college graduates do not possess. For example, two of the questions in history on the 1940 New York State Regents Examination, which must be passed in order to obtain a New York State academic high school diploma, were to discuss "Factors that helped to unite the Roman Empire" and "The meaning of Cardinal Wolsey's belief in the necessity of maintaining the balance of power" (Kramer 1996: 62-3).

In the 1950s and 1960s, the American educational establishment and federal, state, and municipal governments decided that the primary goal of American high schools should be to graduate all students and, thus, close the racial gap in graduation. That goal has nearly been achieved. In 1995, 86.5 percent of blacks and 87.4 percent of whites between the ages of 25 and 29 were high school graduates (Thernstrom 1997: 191). That has been accomplished in the only way possible:

> In 1990, the Boston School Committee voted to require that high school seniors demonstrate eighth-grade reading competence in order to graduate. The committee beat a hasty retreat from this pathetically modest demand, however, when the school superintendent said that . . . 84 percent of white students, but only 53 percent of those who were black . . . were expected to make the grade. . . . [I]n 1996 . . . the Chicago public school system decided to stop giving its students the Iowa Tests of Basic Skills, which it had been doing for thirty years. The reason? Chicago public school pupils—nearly nine out of ten of them black or Hispanic—were so far behind educationally that the Iowa tests had ceased to be a useful yardstick (Thernstrom 1997: 360-1).

The standardized tests now required for high school graduation do not present any barrier to these students. In the 1992-93 academic year, the passing rate for New York State's minimum competency test for a high school diploma was 98 percent. Nor is it much harder to obtain a NY State Regents (Academic) diploma. NY Regents Exams in every subject have been made much easier, and every exam now has enough easy questions for a student to pass without answering any difficult questions (Kramer 1996: 63-6).

Grade inflation is making university graduation as meaningless as high school graduation. Jerome Murphy, Dean of Harvard's School of Education, observed, "If you have a high school diploma—and can walk and talk—you can graduate from college" (Rubenstein 1998). As a result, between 1985 and 2004, the proportion of American bachelor's degrees given to blacks rose from 5.9 percent to 9.4 percent; the proportion of American master's degrees given to blacks rose from 5.0 percent to 9.1 percent; and the proportion of professional degrees given to blacks rose from 4.3 percent to 7.1 percent.[178] Between 1987 and 2007, the proportion of doctorates awarded to American citizens that went to blacks increased from 3.6 percent to 6.6 percent.[179]

This closing of the racial gap in attainment of degrees has occurred while the gap between whites and blacks has widened on all measures of academic ability and achievement (SAT, SAT-II (achievement test), ACT, school grades). (I discuss this phenomenon in Section F of Appendix III.)

However, I will also repeat an important point I made at the end of Section A of Chapter 9. The academic ability and achievement of *all* Americans at each level of completed higher education keeps declining. The reason is that in the 25 years from 1983 to 2008, the number of Americans enrolled in higher education increased by more than a third (McCluskey and Schaeffer 2009), but the average intelligence of Americans did not increase. I pointed out that in 1992 and 2003, the U.S. Department of Education conducted surveys of the proficiency of a representative sample of American adults in Prose Literacy, Document Literacy, and Quantitative Literacy. The average scores of all Americans did not change significantly. In fact, the Department of Education divided the scores into Below Basic, Basic, Intermediate, and Proficient; and the proportion of American adults in the highest category (Proficient) declined in both Prose and Document Literacy from 15 percent in 1992 to 13 percent in 2003. The proportion of American adults who were proficient in Quantitative Literacy remained the same at 13 percent.[180] Consequently, the average scores of all American adults at all levels of completed higher education was considerably lower in 2003 than in 1992. In 1992, the average scores of all Americans with four-year college degrees and no more in Prose Literacy, Document Literacy, and Quantitative Literacy were 325, 317, and 324, respectively. In 2003 the average scores the average scores of all Americans with only four-year college degrees were 314, 303, and 323. In 1992, the average scores of all Americans with post-graduate degrees in the three types of literacy were 340, 328, and 336; in 2003, the average scores of all American with post-graduate degrees were 327, 311, and 332. The reader should notice that the decline was greater among those who received a post-graduate degree than among those who received only a four-year college degree. The reason is that the number of the former increased more

---

178. "The Solid Progress of African Americans in Degree Attainment." *Journal of Blacks in Higher Education* (Summer 2006): 54-9.

179. "Number of Blacks Earning Doctorates in 2007 Increases by 10 Percent." *Journal of Blacks in Higher Education* (Winter 2008/2009): 36.

180. http://nces.ed.gov/naal/kf_demographics.asp

than the number of the latter.[181]

In Sections C and D of Chapter 6, I described the enormous amounts of the American people's money that has been thrown down the drain of education. I have also pointed out that a state's economic growth is negatively correlated with the amount of money it spends on its public universities (Vedder and Denhardt 2007). The reason is that the proportion of the American people who are intelligent enough to benefit from a high-school, college, or graduate education was surpassed decades ago.

Cß ßC

---

181. http://nces.ed.gov/fastFacts/display.asp?id=69

CR ED

Chapter 18
After University: The Lie Continues

A. Diversity in the Workplace

By the middle 1990s, 44 of the 50 largest American corporations had or were planning diversity programs, and 56 percent of businesses with a hundred or more employees provided diversity training. Most government agencies also have diversity programs (Lynch 1997: 7, 104-5, 179-80, 184-6). In return for fees that range from $2,000 to $10,000 *a day*, diversity consultants give the following advice:

> "Qualifications" is a code word ... with very negative connotations.
>
> The weight placed on math, science and engineering credentials may be considered biased.
>
> [E]xpendable requirements [include] the two-page memo or a certain [i.e., clear and coherent] writing style.
>
> Bringing minorities into companies and training them to fit into the value system of WASPs puts them at a disadvantage and sets them up to fail (MacDonald 1993).

An example of the proper implementation of diversity in the legal profession is the law firm of Weil, Gotshal & Manges, where it is a violation of diversity policy, punished by severe sanctions, to say that "persons of color are less qualified or only in the firm because of affirmative action" (MacDonald 1993: 25).

However, despite huge expenditures of time, effort and money, "diversity adherents acknowledge that they are unable to document the advantages of diversity training" (MacDonald 1993: 25).

It would be extremely odd if they could. The abilities that comprise the "value system of WASPs"—in which American Jews, Armenians, Greeks, North-East Asians, and Asian Indians function much more successfully than Americans of English origin (Thernstrom 1997: 542)—are not simply one type of abilities among many types of equally useful abilities. They are the abilities that provide what nearly everyone wants.

Stephan and Abigail Thernstrom (1997: 645, note 84) quote a criticism in the *American Sociological Review* of a study that found (as nearly all studies do) that blacks earn considerably more than whites who have the same scores on tests of reading comprehension, vocabulary, and arithmetic reasoning. The criticism was that these tests measure only "exposure to the values and experience of the white middle class." The Thernstroms commented, "Employers are apparently guilty of class and racial bias if they want employees to be able to read a training manual or to calculate how many bags of grass seed and fertilizer a customer will need to make a lawn that is 60 feet long and 40 feet wide."

Similarly, in 1987, the New York Board of Regents, which controls pre-university public education in New York State, distributed to 15,000 educators a booklet entitled *Increasing High School Completion Rates*, which stated,

> Children's racial, ethnic and emotional backgrounds and cultures influence the manner in which they learn concepts and process information. For example, qualities noted in African-Americans include . . . preference for inferential reasoning rather than deductive and inductive reasoning . . . [and a] tendency to approximate space, number and time instead of aiming for complete accuracy (Uhlig 1987).

It is obvious from school performance and academic tests that most blacks are much less able than most whites and Asians to reason deductively and inductively and to attain complete accuracy in computing number, space, and time. *Increasing High School Completion Rates* claimed that this is not a defect and that blacks' education should be adjusted accordingly. But would any member of the New York Board of Regents want to cross a bridge that was built by people who did not aim at complete spatial accuracy, or fly in a plane whose pilot only approximates time at landings, or buy insurance from a company whose employees do not aim at complete numerical accuracy, or entrust his health to a doctor who merely infers what medication to prescribe, instead of inducing or deducing it?

Some diversity proponents define "white" values more broadly, as constituting a "white" culture. In 1996, a leading diversity expert, Pam Fomalont, who says she is "tired of hearing white males whine," provided a typical definition of "white-male culture:" "very goal-oriented, future-oriented, very competitive, intensely individualistic, work-centered, oriented to objective goals and measurements" (Lynch 1997: 127, 327).

Again, cultural values must be assessed by their results. For a person who is intent on suicide, cyanide is preferable to champagne. No other culture has proved to be even remotely as successful as "white-male culture" at providing food; clothing; medicines; travel; homes with plumbing, heating, and electrical appliances; and other products and services. If rejecting this culture is as valid as accepting it, then the people who reject it cannot complain if they do not have these things. And why would people whose culture is not competitive, work-centered, and goal-oriented be bothered if few of their members are corporate executives or professionals?

There are people, like the Amish, who reject much of "white-male culture" and what it provides; and no one holds that against them. But they are extremely rare. Nearly every country in the world is trying to reshape its economic and political system into the type that white males (in fact, primarily Anglo-Saxon, Protestant males) created; and over 99 percent of migration between cultural zones is from non-Western to Western countries. That was even true of South Africa while it was ruled by a universally execrated white government. In the 1980s, 1.5 million black migrants from black-ruled African countries, most of them illegal immigrants, lived in white-ruled South Africa (Williams 1989: 147).

B. The War on Qualifications: *Griggs* and Following

Nineteenth century British Liberals introduced qualifying examinations to break the aristocracy's monopoly on attendance at Oxford and Cambridge and in the higher positions of the civil service. Reformers like Lord Macaulay and Charles Trevelyan pointed out that the most democratic tests are those that do not depend on candidates' educational background; in other words, those that evaluate "the candidate's powers of mind," not "ascertain the extent of his metaphysical reading." For the same reason, 20th century British socialists, like Sydney and Beatrice Webb, championed IQ tests to determine which children should attend academic schools; and "R. H. Tawney, the doyen of socialist educationalists, welcomed IQ tests for pointing to the huge number of talented working-class children who were overlooked in the existing system" (Wooldridge 1995). Tawney's prediction proved to be correct. IQ tests have been found to send a higher proportion of children of working-class families and a lower proportion of the children of professional families to academic junior and senior high schools than any other criterion (recommendations from elementary school teachers, headmasters' interviews, achievement tests) (Mackintosh 1998: 23-4).

The British army made the same discovery about intelligence tests. Between the beginning of World War II, in September 1939, and the summer of 1942, it selected officers by a twenty-minute interview conducted by a board of officers. Nearly all British officers were from upper- and upper-middle-class backgrounds, and they selected men to whom they could relate. The result was that many of the selected officers were incompetent. In the summer of 1942, War Officer Selection Boards (WOSBs) were established, which relied on a variety of "real life" situations, interviews, and paper-and-pencil intelligence tests. For a time WOSBs functioned side by side with the old procedure. During that time, 35 percent of the officers recommended by the WOSBs were found to be above average and 25 percent below average. Of those recommended by the old method, 22 percent were above average and 37 percent below average. A later investigation found that *for all occupations—drivers, clerks, mechanics, etc.—the WOSBs' intelligence test predicted success better than the whole procedure combined.* (The least accurate predictors were psychiatrists' evaluations.) (Eysenck 1998: 82-4, 87-8, 205).

In the United States, one of the central reforming crusades of the late nineteenth and early twentieth century was to base civil service hiring and promotion on qualifying tests. Congress passed the first Civil Service Act in 1881. Soon, ten percent of federal jobs were filled through examinations. That rose to 60 percent in 1908; "and the practice was emulated by many of the larger and more progressive states and cities," because it greatly increased the efficiency of the civil service (Zelnick 1996: 79).

Businesses discovered empirically that intelligence tests were extremely valuable tools. In 1940, 26 percent of American businesses used intelligence tests as a criterion for hiring and promotion. That increased to 63 percent in 1957 and 90 percent in 1963 (Snyderman and Rothman 1988: 22; Zelnick 1996: 73).

As I explain in Appendix IV, subsequent research has confirmed beyond possibility of doubt that forward-looking businessmen and political reformers were correct. Intelligence tests are by far the most accurate predictors of success in nearly all types of occupations, much more accurate than recommendations, level and type of education, amount of job experience, interests, and other criteria that are used to assess job applicants.

However, in 1971, the Supreme Court issued one of its two most important rulings, along with *Bakke*, with regard to racial discrimination: *Griggs v. Duke Power Company*. In *Bakke*, the Supreme Court ruled that universities *could* practice racial discrimination. In Griggs it ruled (in effect, although not in theory) that all employers, both private and public, *must* practice racial discrimination. However, the *Griggs* decision was identical to *Bakke* in one crucial respect. In order to maintain a pretense of non-discrimination, *Griggs*, and subsequent Supreme Court rulings and congressional acts pursuant to it, mandated that racial discrimination be practiced in the most inefficient and unfair manner possible: without explicit quotas.

Title VII of the Civil Rights Act of 1964 stated (703a), "It shall be an un-lawful employment practice for an employer to . . . discriminate against any individual . . . because of such person's race, color, religion, sex or national origin." In *Griggs*, the U.S. Supreme Court ruled (#430), "Under the [Civil Rights] Act, practices, procedures, or tests [that are] neutral on their face, and even neutral in terms of intent, cannot be maintained if they operate to 'freeze' the status quo of prior discriminatory employment practices." The only justification for a qualification that has a disparate impact on different groups is that it has "a demonstrable relationship to successful performance of the jobs for which it was used" (#431). "More than that, Congress has placed on the employer the burden of showing that any given requirement must have a manifest relationship to the employment in question" (#432).

A critically important aspect of the *Griggs* decision was (#433), "The facts of this case demonstrate the inadequacy of broad and general test-ing devices [i.e., intelligence tests] as well as the infirmity of diplomas or degrees." This was a bizarre interpretation of "the facts of this case." The Court explained (#427-8) that the requirement it outlawed was that in order to qualify for employment in Duke Power Company's operations, maintenance, or laboratory departments, an employee had to have a high school diploma or attain a score that approximated the national median of high school graduates on a widely used test of general intelligence and a test of mechanical comprehension. Since employees in these departments had to understand manuals about boilers, turbines, and other complicated mechanical and electrical equipment, it should have been obvious that this requirement did have a "manifest relationship to the employment in ques-tion" (Wolters 1996: 154-6; Epstein 1992: 192-4). The Court acknowledged (#432) that this requirement did not have "discriminatory intent" since the Duke Power Company paid two-thirds of the cost of education for lower-level employees, most of whom were black, to attain a high school diploma. But what mattered was "the consequences of employment practices, not simply the motivation."

Thus, the Supreme Court, not one of whose members had ever engaged in any activity that remotely resembled those involved in a power plant, ruled that the managers of a company whose existence depended on run-ning power plants efficiently and safely were mistaken. Their obviously commonsense requirement did not have "a demonstrable relationship to successful performance of the jobs for which it was used." The *Griggs* de-cision established the right and duty of courts and government bureaucrats to determine whether any criterion for hiring or promotion used by any employer, whether a stock brokerage firm or a municipal fire department, is related to the work it performs.

As I point out in Section B of Appendix II, Congress affirmed the *Griggs* decision with the Equal Employment Opportunity Act of 1972.

In 1975, in *Albemarle Paper Company v. Moody*, the Supreme Court ruled that even if an employer can prove a close and direct connection between job performance and qualifications that have a disparate racial impact for hiring and promotion, he is still guilty of illegal discrimination if the plaintiff can show that different qualifications have less disparate racial impact.

In 1982, in *Connecticut v. Teal*, the Supreme Court ruled that an employer is guilty of violating Title VII of the Civil Rights Act of 1964 if its qualifications do not satisfy the requirements of *Griggs* and *Albemarle*; *even if the employer hires and promotes the "correct" proportion of minorities.* As the Supreme Court explained in its *Teal* decision, the case involved the state of Connecticut's use of a written test as a first step in selecting permanent supervisors among candidates who had been promoted provisionally to supervisory status. Connecticut granted permanent status to 22.9 percent of the black candidates but only 13.5 percent of the white candidates, even though 80 percent of the whites but only 54 percent of the blacks passed the test. The Court ruled that the test was illegal because (#451) it "ignores the fact that Title VII guarantees these individual respondents [the blacks who failed the test] the *opportunity* to compete equally with white workers on the basis of job-related criteria." *Opportunity* is italicized in the Court's decision. It used *opportunity* and *opportunities* ten times in a thirteen-page decision. The Court never considered the possibility that this procedure had in any way violated whites' equality of opportunity. Mark Kelman explained in the *Harvard Law Review* (1991: 1169) that *Connecticut v. Teal* "frees each successful black applicant from the stigmatizing insult that she was hired 'politically' rather than 'meritocratically'."

The Equal Employment Opportunity Commission (EEOC) is the federal agency that monitors violations of Title VII. More than 85 percent of American private sector employees work for businesses whose hiring and promotion practices must comply with the EEOC's regulations. The EEOC's most fundamental rule is that if the proportion of minorities employed by any business does not equal at least four-fifths of their proportion in the population, then that business is presumptively guilty of racial discrimination and must prove its innocence. In order to do that, the business must prove not only that the qualifications it uses are absolutely necessary for job performance but also that there are no other job-related criteria that would qualify more minorities. The EEOC's regulations on validating qualifications with disparate racial impact are purposefully designed to make validation immensely difficult, time-consuming, and expensive. For example, if supervisors' ratings of employees correlate with their performance on a test, then the supervisors' ratings have to be examined for bias. Moreover, if a company manages to prove that a qualification for (e.g.) machinists is valid for one factory, it still has to prove that the same qualification is valid for machinists in other factories.[182] Mark Kelman and Elizabeth Bartholet, in articles whose purpose was to urge the extension and intensification of affirmative action, pointed out, "Validating tests locally can certainly be expensive, with costs running into hundreds of thousands of dollars" (Kelman 1991:1169, footnote 31); and employers who do not hire and promote the correct racial proportions face "trials lasting for weeks, following years of discovery, and involving a multitude of statistical and other experts and seemingly endless testimony about the credentials of a single candidate" (Bartholet 1982: 1002).

Following are three examples of the impossibility of finding a legitimate job-related qualification with disparate racial impact. The EEOC filed a lawsuit against a post office for refusing to hire a black mail-delivery man because his driver's license had been suspended four times (D'Souza 1995: 320). The Detroit Symphony Orchestra hired musicians on the basis of auditions during which applicants performed behind a screen, so the judges could not see them. However, because it had not hired a black musician for fourteen years, the Michigan State legislature withheld more than half of its subsidy until it hired a black musician *without an audition* (Wilkerson 1989). The United States may be the only country that hires Foreign Service officers without taking into consideration their ability to learn foreign languages or their knowledge of world history, geography, politics, and culture. In the 1960s, the State Department voluntarily dropped its requirement that applicants for the Foreign Service take a foreign language aptitude test because minority applicants did much worse on it than white applicants. In 1987, it was ordered by a judge to eliminate its test on world history, geography, politics, and culture because women did worse on it than men. Since then, the only test that applicants for the Foreign Service must pass is in English usage.[183]

182. D'Souza 1995: 222-3, 298, 318-20; Epstein 1992: 214-17; Wolters 1996: 177; Zelnick 1996: 89.

183. Even on the English usage test, minorities are passed with much lower scores than whites, and women with somewhat lower scores than men (Workman 1991).

As always, the best way to practice discrimination would be by means of an explicit quota. Then, the State Department could have kept the tests it had and set different passing scores for minorities and women. That would

Robert Zelnick (1996: 109-17), Jared Taylor (1992: 129-36), and Richard Epstein (1992: 218-22) outline many desperate, unsuccessful attempts by American cities to find civil service tests that would pass sufficient numbers of minorities. For example, the New York City Police Department devoted a huge amount of the taxpayers' money and more than ten years of effort to devise a qualifying test for sergeant that would gain court approval. Finally, minority representatives helped it to draw up a test, which had a video-based portion since any pencil-and-paper test was presumed to be biased against minorities. However, it also was disallowed when only five percent of the applicants who passed it were minorities; and only 1.7 percent of the blacks who took it passed, although many were college graduates (Pitt 1989: Snyderman and Rothman 1988: 8-9). The Houston Fire Department tried a different way to concoct a test without "biased" results. It gave a 100-question test for promotion. After the test was taken, the 28 questions on which minority candidates did worst were discarded. As a result, 32 candidates who had originally passed failed and 13 who had originally failed passed. But only one more minority candidate passed the revised test than had passed the original (Taylor 1992: 133-4).

Employers are not even safe if they hire a higher proportion of minorities than the proportion in their community. In 1989, thanks to an intensive recruiting campaign, 16 percent of the bank tellers and clerical workers that Liberty National Bank & Trust of Louisville, Kentucky hired were black, a higher proportion than in the American population and in the Louisville work force at the time. However, in 1991, the Office of Contract Compliance Programs of President Bush's Labor Department accused Liberty of racial discrimination because 32 percent of the applicants for these positions were black. In order to avoid a lawsuit, Liberty had to hire 18 blacks it had rejected and pay them the income they had lost by not being employed by the bank during the previous two years (Filiatreau 1991).

Most businesses follow the same course that Liberty followed and do not challenge the directives of government agencies in court; because the time, effort, and money required would bankrupt a small business and cause considerable financial loss to a large one. Nevertheless, *each year* in the 1980s about 6,000 affirmative-action lawsuits were brought at a cost of $300 million; and the number and expense has undoubtedly risen since then (Epstein 1992: 259).

An example is Sears, Roebuck & Co, which, since 1968, has had a policy

---

have ensured that at least white and Asian male Foreign Service officials have an aptitude for learning languages and a knowledge of world history, geography, politics, and culture, which obviously should be the two most important requirements for the Foreign Service.

of filling one out of every two job openings with a minority or a woman. Sears fought an EEOC accusation of nationwide discrimination against women in hiring, promotion, and compensation. To prove its case, the EEOC spent six years compiling evidence, at the taxpayers' expense. That was followed by seven years of litigation and a trial, the transcript of which is 15 feet (4.6 meters) high. At one point, Sears employed 250 people full-time to compile information to meet the EEOC's investigatory demands. That is in addition to the statisticians, sociologists, and other expert witnesses it had to employ, along with a team of lawyers. A federal district court ruled in favor of Sears Roebuck, finding it incredible that *during this whole process the EEOC was unable to present a single woman who claimed that she was a victim of discrimination* (Bolick 1996: 56; Lynch 1989: 145). This case was by no means atypical (Bovard 1995).

Once a minority member has been hired, it is nearly impossible to fire him. Dinesh D'Souza gives the following examples (1995: 320):

> One complainant had been late for work or absent for 70 out of 249 consecutive workdays. "When we fired him, I had to provide reams of data comparing lateness and absenteeism by observed skin color for all apprentices within his particular trade for a 52-week period." ... The EEOC has [used the taxpayers' money to] ... participate in discrimination lawsuits against a life insurance company which fired a black employee who committed expense account fraud; against an oil company that fired a minority employee who stole company property and falsified expense reports; against a company that fired a secretary for refusing to answer the telephone.

One attempt to circumvent the barriers to qualifications nearly succeeded. In the late 1940s, the U.S. Employment Service (USES) of the federal Department of Labor developed the General Aptitude Test Battery (GATB), an assemblage of examinations to test suitability for employment.[184] Until 1980, it was used primarily for vocational counselling at state job services. However, the development of powerful computers and sophisticated statistical software in the late 1970s enabled researchers to combine the results of hundreds of disparate studies of the predictive accuracy of employment qualifications and to analyze (i.e., meta-analyze) the cumulative result. These meta-analyses showed that tests of cognitive ability (i.e., intelligence tests), like the GATB, have a much higher predictive accuracy for nearly all types of jobs than anyone had previously thought. In 1980, the USES published

---

184. The GATB and the history of its race-norming are discussed by Baydoun and Neuman 1992; Herrnstein and Murray 1996: 70-3; Seligman 1992: 142-4, 198-99; Eastland 1996: 106-7; and Zelnick 1996: 99.

the results of a meta-analysis of 425 disparate studies of the predictive accuracy of the GATB. They are below. The first number after each level of job
complexity is the GATB's correlation with proficiency ratings; the second
number is its correlation with training success; the third number is the percent
of all American workers employed in a job with that complexity.

Job Complexity General Jobs			
High (synthesizing/coordinating)	.58	.50	14.7
Medium (compiling/computing)	.51	.57	62.7
Low (comparing/copying)	.40	.54	17.7
Industrial Jobs			
High (setup work)	.56	.65	2.5
Low (feeding/offloading)	.23	NA	2.4

As I explain in Section A of Appendix III, a correlation of .50 is extremely
significant, much more significant than a person unfamiliar with statistics
would think.

On the basis of these facts, the USES told state employment agencies
to recommend to public and private employers that they use of the GATB
to choose among job applicants. In order to avoid the GATB having illegal
"disparate impact" on different racial groups, the USES told state employment services to "race-norm" the results by reporting to employers not the
actual score that a job applicant got, but the percentile in which that score put
him in his racial group. To use an actual example, if a white/Asian, Hispanic,
and black applied for a job as a toolmaker and each had a raw score of 300 on
the GATB, that would place the white/Asian in the 39th percentile of white/
Asian test-takers (i.e., 61 percent scored higher), the Hispanic in the 62nd
percentile of Hispanics, and the black in the 79th percentile of blacks (i.e., 21
percent scored higher). It was these scores—39, 62, and 79—that were sent
to employers, without telling them that they had been race-normed. So, the
test had no disparate racial impact. By 1986, forty state governments were
secretly race-norming the results of the GATB. Many employers guessed or
knew that the scores they were getting had been race-normed, but they did
not object. They knew that they had to practice racial discrimination, and
race-norming enabled them to do it on the basis of a measure of ability that
was both accurate and easy to use. In fact, many businesses started secretly
race-norming the results of their own qualifying tests.

In 1986, the USES asked the National Academy of Sciences to study the GATB. Working through the National Research Council, it appointed a committee of experts to investigate the GATB. The committee reported that the GATB accurately predicted the job performance of members of all ethnic and racial groups for all types of jobs and recommended that race-norming be continued in order to ensure "equality of opportunity."[185]

However, in 1990 a government official mailed the racial conversion tables of the GATB to a newspaper, which published them.

Before that, in 1989, the Supreme Court, in *Wards Cove Packing Co., Inc. v. Atonio*, observed (#659) that proving that a qualification with "disparate impact" on different groups is "essential or indispensable for the employer's business . . . would be almost impossible for most employers." Consequently, the Court (#659) changed the justification for a qualification with disparate racial impact to the more flexible requirement that it "serves, in a significant way, the legitimate employment goals of the employer." It also shifted some of the burden of proving the validity of a hiring practice onto the plaintiff.

The Civil Rights Restoration Act, which Congress passed in 1991 and President Bush signed in 1992, reinstated the pre-*Wards Cove* requirements that qualifications with disparate impact had to meet, put the burden of proof completely back onto employers, and increased the compensatory payments that employers must pay if they cannot prove they are innocent. The law not only ensured that employers had to practice massive racial discrimination, it also tried to maintain a pretence of non-discrimination by prohibiting adjusting scores or altering test results based on race, color, or sex (Cathcart and Snyderman 1992). It thus outlawed the fairest and most efficient means of practicing discrimination. After the law passed, the USES announced that it would try to replace the GATB. It still has not come up with a replacement.

On July 19, 1995, President Clinton delivered the longest defense of affirmative action ever made by an American president. Like all defenders of affirmative action, Clinton constantly insisted that its purpose is to ensure equality of opportunity for qualified people, and he vehemently condemned quotas. Clinton attributed quotas largely to the fact that "some employers don't use it [affirmative action] in the right way. They may cut corners." On the same day, in the "Press Briefing on the President's Affirmative Action

---

185. In Section D of Appendix III, I point out that the GATB, like all intelligence-based tests, has one defect. It overpredicts the performance of lower scoring groups. The National Academy of Sciences committee found that of blacks and whites who pass the test with the same raw score, 13 percent of the whites but 38 percent of the blacks do poorly on the job (Hartigan and Wigdor 1989; Gottfredson 1994: 960; Jencks 1998: 75-6).

Position," Clinton's Senior Policy Advisor George Stephanopoulos and Chris Edley defended affirmative action but acknowledged that "it's certainly easier [for an employer] to use a quota than it is to really follow the [government's] guidelines set out under an affirmative action program."[186]

Two years earlier, in 1993, the Task Force on Reinventing Government, appointed by President Clinton and chaired by Vice President Gore, estimated that the "cost to the private sector of complying with regulations is at least $430 billion annually—9 percent of our gross domestic product."[187] The cost incurred by being prevented from hiring and promoting the best employees is many times greater.

So far, I have been documenting the disastrous consequences for employers of having to practice racial discrimination while being prohibited from using explicit quotas. It has also inflicted catastrophic collateral damage on American society. Many observers have bemoaned the fact that American high school students who do not intend to go on to tertiary education have little or no concern for their academic performance. Peter Applebome explained why (1995):

> Researchers studying the hiring practices of American businesses have been alarmed at . . . the way in which employers pay no attention to the grades and performance of high school students. The concern is that if employers do not care, why should students? . . . [E]mployers nearly never look at students' grades . . . [because] they are afraid they might get sued if they do. . . . A survey of American employers by the Census Bureau . . . found that in assessing job applicants, employers looked at nearly every other attribute . . . before they looked at the school [record]. Almost everyone agrees that this sends the wrong signal . . . that it's important to graduate, but not that it's better to graduate with B's than D's . . . If students aren't achieving, one reason for that is that they don't have an incentive to achieve. . . .
>
> [S]tudies of employers like the Lockheed Corporation have shown that *high school records are excellent predictors of success in the workplace.* [italics added] . . .
>
> In the landmark Griggs v. Duke Power decision, the Supreme Court ruled that employers were prohibited . . . from practices that "are fair in form but discriminatory in operation." . . . Many companies view the case as an indicator that they could be slapped with a

186. www.ibiblio.org/pub/archives/whitehouse-papers/1995/Jul/1995-07-19-Stephanopoulos-and-Edley-Affirmative-Action-Briefing

187. A. Gore (editor), *Creating a Government That Works Better and Costs Less*: 32.

lawsuit if they demand educational credentials.

To this day, the *Griggs* decision, with subsequent court decisions and laws based on it, governs public and private hiring and promotion. I urge all readers of this book to read Jared Taylor's analysis of the most recent Supreme Court modification, in *Ricci v. DeStefano*.[188]

Before leaving this subject, I will discuss two other important aspects of the *Griggs* decision. First, *Griggs* antedated *Bakke* by seven years. Diversity had not yet been invented as a justification for anti-white discrimination. In *Griggs*, the Supreme Court still used the older justification: redressing the effects of past discrimination. It ruled (#430) that "no practices, procedures, or tests" can be used "if they operate to 'freeze' the status quo of prior discriminatory employment practices." If the reader will look back at Section A of Chapter 2, she will see that Justice Powell demonstrated the absurdity of this argument in his ruling in *Bakke*. In *Griggs*, the Supreme Court, typically, spoke of Negroes and "minority groups" interchangeably (#432); and the *Griggs* decision was immediately applied to non-European immigrants and their descendants, none of whom had suffered from "prior discriminatory employment practices" in the United States. The principle established by *Griggs* still governs all private and public employment in the United States; although now the large majority of its beneficiaries are immigrants or descendants of immigrants who arrived after 1965 and have always received preferential treatment in the United States. That includes many, maybe most, black recipients of affirmative action, as I demonstrate in Section B of Chapter 19.

Second, I pointed out immediately before Chapter 2 that diversity is the most insidious and pernicious of all defenses of discrimination. However, the principle that *Griggs* established was even worse: employers have to pretend that they were not practicing discrimination; and that can be done only by, in effect, banning all qualifications. Justice Powell's diversity rul-

---

188. "Supreme Court Throws Whites a Bone." *American Renaissance* (August 2009): 5-8. It can be accessed online by going to www.amren.com, then pressing "Archives," and then "AR Back Issues." Each back issue has the title of its first article. So the title next to August 2009 is "What We Call Ourselves."

Taylor predicts that Barack Obama's Supreme Court nominees will overturn that decision. I hope they do. As I point out repeatedly, the banning of anti-white discrimination has invariably been catastrophic. Even in the *Ricci* case, which involved promotion to captain and lieutenant in the New Haven Fire Department, the tests were set at a tenth grade level to lessen disparate racial impact, although all firemen must be high school graduates.

ing allowed universities to continue using admissions tests and high school grades and discriminate on the basis of them. Was it to protect themselves from a decision like *Griggs* that universities presented the nonsensical arguments that they advanced in *Bakke*?

C. The Success of the War on Qualifications

Eliminating qualifications is closing the racial gap in occupation and income, just as it is closing the racial gap in education.

A frequently cited proof of the racism of American society is that blacks and Hispanics earn less than whites with the same level of education. The main reason is the tremendous racial differences in cognitive ability at every level of education, which I document in Section A of Chapter 9. In Appendix IV, I will discuss the accuracy with which intelligence tests predict income and occupational success, independent of level of education. For example, the average income of Jewish families that are headed by a man between 35 and 45 years old with four or more years of university education is 75 percent higher than the national average for families headed by a man of the same age with the same level of education (Silbiger 2000: 9). The reason is that the average Jewish IQ is nearly as much higher than the average white Gentile IQ as the average white Gentile IQ is higher than the average black American IQ (Herrnstein and Murray 1996: 275; Storfer 1990: 314-23).

From the first systematic study of the relationship between racial income and cognitive skills (e.g., reading and math), which was based on the 1970 census, American blacks have been found to have higher average incomes and job status than American whites with the same level of skills (Thernstrom 1997: 446, 646, note 85; Nyborg and Jensen 2001).

Three other factors also affect racial differences in income at the same level of education. The first is that, according to the 2000 census, 54 percent of blacks but only a quarter of whites live in the South, where the cost of living is lower than in the rest of the United States. The second is that Americans aged between 45 and 54 earn 47 percent more than Americans between 25 and 34 (Sowell 1995: 49). In 2004, the median age of non-Hispanic white Americans was 40.1 years, and the median age of black Americans was 31.4 years. In 2008, the median age of Hispanic Americans was 27.7 years.[189]

The third factor is that blacks and whites take radically different university courses. The Autumn 1998 issue (pages 33, 53) of the *Journal of Blacks in Higher Education* (*JBHE*) reported that in 1996 American blacks received 1.2 percent of all the doctorates awarded in engineering. The Au-

---

189. www.infoplease.com/spot/hhmcensus1.html; *Journal of Blacks in Higher Education* (Spring 2007): 55.

tumn 1999 issue of the *JBHE* (page 81) reported that in 1997, 5.3 percent of whites who had graduated from college in 1992-93 were employed as engineers and 1.7 percent of blacks. The *JBHE* (Autumn 1998: 33) also pointed out, "The unemployment rate for people with engineering degrees is 1.5 percent," and "students with bachelor's degrees in engineering are offered starting salaries of $40,000 or more [in 1998], usually accompanied by a signing bonus."

In what, then, do blacks get doctorates? The *JBHE* of Winter 2005/2006 reported (page 7) that in 2004, 41 percent of blacks' doctorates were in education; compared with 19 percent of whites' doctorates. It also pointed out that the president of Columbia's Teachers College (the pre-eminent American teachers college) made the sensible proposal that the Doctor of Education degree be eliminated and be replaced with a master's degree in educational administration. I will add that on the Graduate Record Examination, which is taken for admission to graduate school, the average score of engineering students is a full standard deviation higher than the average score of education students. However, the *JBHE* (Autumn 1999: 81) also pointed out that 16.4 percent of white college graduates were engaged in pre-university education, compared with 15.9 percent of the blacks. Moreover, "[B]lacks are more likely [than whites] to hold stable jobs with established large companies." On the other hand, a higher proportion of white college graduates (5.9 percent) are mechanical or manual workers than black college graduates (4.5 percent). The *JBHE* drew the obvious conclusion (Autumn 1999: 81) that these otherwise inexplicable facts reflect "a high demand for black college graduates for white-collar employment due to strong affirmative action programs."[190]

The *JBHE* of Spring 2007 reported that in 2004, the median income of blacks with doctorates was $74,207 and of whites with doctorates, $73,993. This is truly astonishing considering the differences in the fields in which blacks and whites obtain doctorates. The *JBHE* attributed it to "[t]he high demand for black academics at American colleges and universities."[191] Let

---

190. The percentage of all public elementary school teachers in the United States who are black declined from 12.3 percent in 1982 to 8.7 percent in 2004 (*Journal of Blacks in Higher Education* (Winter 2005/2006): 63).

191. "Higher Education Is the Main Force in Closing the black-white Income Gap:" 6-8.

The media often report studies that claim to have found racial discrimination in mortgage lending and in employment between equally qualified blacks and whites. Not one of these studies has held up under subsequent analysis (D'Souza 1995: 276-82; Thernstrom 1997: 447-9, 503-5; Zelnick 1996: 321-33; Taylor 1992: 55-6, 59-61).

us now see how high that demand is.

D. University Faculty

Because university professors have more clearly defined criteria of achievement than most other occupations, racial discrimination in hiring and promotion is more visible among them than elsewhere.

Before documenting the extent of that discrimination, I will repeat here a point I made in Section A of Chapter 15. The arguments in defense of diversity that Justice Powell used in the *Bakke* decision, and which the Supreme Court re-affirmed in 2003, applied specifically to university students. Even if racial diversity among students did have the benefits that universities claim for it, it was immediately and mindlessly applied to all occupations; although for most—accountants, anaesthesiologists, tax lawyers, carpenters, welders, fire-fighters—the most ingenious diversity-advocate would not be able to find any benefit. Derek Bok, the co-author of *The Shape of the River*, pointed out (1982: 112), "Even the most avid proponent of diversity would be hard put to argue that the special perspective of a minority scholar will contribute much to teaching and research in the natural sciences or in classics, English literature, logic, or in many other important fields of study."

Government enforced anti-white discrimination in university faculties began with an executive order that President Nixon issued in 1970, which stipulated that to be eligible for federal contracts, without which few universities could function, universities had to draw up proposals for racial hiring. If these proposals were rejected, the university had 30 days to rectify them. No accusation of discrimination had to be made, and no standards were divulged by which universities could measure their compliance. In the early 1970s, the Nixon administration withheld grants from 20 universities and threatened others until they filed satisfactory plans to hire more minority faculty members.[192]

Government enforced academic affirmative action is administered in the same way that all government enforced affirmative action is administered. The institutions involved are presumed guilty unless they prove their innocence to un-elected bureaucrats, who are prosecutors, judges, and juries, regard their job as remedying the problem of unequal racial success, and neither know nor care about the functioning of the institutions involved. For example, representatives of President Nixon's Department of Health,

192. Seabury 1972; Thernstrom 1997: 394, 636, note 17. This was the nefarious Order Number 4, which I discuss in Sections B and C of Appendix II. In 1971, Nixon issued Revised Order Number 4, which extended hiring requirements for contract compliance to women.

Education and Welfare (HEW)

> at one Ivy League university . . . demanded an explanation of why there were no women or minority students in the Graduate Department of Religious Studies. They were told that a reading knowledge of Hebrew and Greek [to read the Old and New Testaments] was presupposed. Whereupon the representatives of HEW advised: "Then end those old fashioned programs that require irrelevant languages and start up programs on relevant things which minority group students can study without learning languages" (Glazer 1975: 61).

However, the Nixon administration merely intensified and systematized the racial discrimination in faculty hiring that universities had already been practicing voluntarily. In 1969, of faculty members at American universities, 40 percent of white men and 17 percent of white women had a PhD; but only 23 and 7 percent of black men and women. In 1973, when government compulsion was just beginning to have an effect, 38 percent of white male faculty members and 11 percent of white female faculty members had written five or more published articles; the percentages for blacks were 16 and 3.[193]

That was the situation at the beginning of the affirmative action era. I could not find later statistics. However, racial discrimination must have intensified considerably since then, as is illustrated by the following examples. One of the best known black American academics is Angela Davis. In 1995 she was appointed to the Presidential Chair at the University of California at Santa Cruz, which is the highest honor that Santa Cruz can bestow. Professor Davis joined the Women of Color Research Cluster in the History of Consciousness Department. (These really are their titles.)[194] Professor Davis once began a PhD program, but never completed it. Besides an autobiography and a collection of speeches (*Women, Race and Class* (1998)), she has written one book of social analysis, *Women, Culture and Politics* (1982), in which she extolled Communist countries for having ended poverty. Historian Ronald Radosh, a longtime student of the American Left,

---

193. These statistics are from surveys conducted by the American Council of Education of more than 300 tertiary institutions of learning. Freeman (1977: 164) summarized them, along with other findings of these surveys. Freeman pointed out (162, footnote 4) that the number of published articles is the most important determinant of faculty salary. He also observed (169, footnote 15) that all other studies came to the same conclusions.

194. Titles like these of departments and courses are not uncommon. Sacks and Thiel (1995: 51-76, 80-82) provide examples at Stanford, such as an upper level history seminar, "Black Hair as Culture and History."

said about her, "Even left-wing scholars don't bother to cite her. Nobody takes her seriously" (Collier 1997; Horowitz 1999: 142). (Nobody except the taxpayers of California and the students at Santa Cruz and their parents, who pay her salary.)

At least Davis has published something. Black journalist Roger Wilkins was appointed University Professor of History at George Mason University, even though he had no qualifications at all. In fact, Wilkins was offered his choice of joining any department he wanted. He explained that he decided on history "because I was totally ignorant of history and figured that by teaching it I would learn it" (Horowitz 1999: 75).

Professor Carolivia Herron of Harvard, who is black, complained that the Harvard administration refuses to understand that the reason that so few minority members write books is that they find writing books "boring" (Thernstrom 1990: 24). But Harvard's administration obviously does understand that. In 1999, 8.5 percent of the professors at Harvard Law School were black; and that is a lower proportion than at many other leading law schools, like Georgetown (8.7 percent), Stanford and Columbia (10 percent), and Duke (12.5 percent).[195] In fact, whites seeking a position on a law school faculty are less than half as likely to be hired as minority applicants (Farber and Sherry 1997: 77).

The zeal with which American universities seek black faculty members is illustrated by Ali Mazrui. In 1989, the State University of New York at Binghamton was in such a severe financial crisis that it was considering selling its dining rooms' cutlery. Nevertheless, it offered Ali Mazrui a package worth over half a million dollars *a year* to join its faculty; and New York State Governor Mario Cuomo personally asked him to accept. At the time Mazrui was simultaneously holding positions at the University of Michigan, Cornell, and a university in Nigeria (Hollander 1992: 207) His views are encapsulated in the statement (Mazrui 1980: 86-7): "The decline of Western civilization might well be at hand. It is in the interest of humanity that such a decline should take place."

The *Journal of Blacks in Higher Education* (Cross 2000: 74-5) acknowledged, "It is well known that Harvard University and others may pay salaries of $250,000 a year or more to a highly coveted black professor, a sum far exceeding that paid to white professors with equal or greater academic credentials."

However, even that statement vastly understates the preference given to blacks in university hiring and promotion. The most accurate measure of

195. "The Progress of Black Students and Faculty at the Nation's Highest-Ranked Law Schools." *Journal of Blacks in Higher Education* (Winter 1999/2000): 48-50).

a scholar's work is not the number of his published articles but how often other scholars cite his articles. The *Journal of Blacks in Higher Education* of Spring 2005, had an article (pages 25-6) entitled "No Blacks among the 5,000 Most Cited Scholars in the Natural and Social Sciences." It reported,

> The Institute for Scientific Information (ISI) . . . has compiled a list of highly cited scholars at www.isihighlycited.com. Through an analysis of more than 19 million scholarly articles in the period 1981 to 1999, ISI determined which scholars were among the 250 most often cited authors in 21 different academic categories. In all, 4,800 scholars were identified . . . . The list . . . was recently expanded to include 1,000 names of scholars who were highly cited in the 1983 to 2002 period. . . . It appears that not one of these scholars is an African American.

The article also pointed out that four scholars on the list are on the faculties of predominantly black universities, but all of them are white.

The next time you see the proportions of blacks on the faculties of leading American universities, remember this fact.

Cß ßつ

ॐ ॐ

Chapter 19
Who Are The Victims?

A. The Recipients

Opponents of affirmative action argue that its recipients are its victims for two reasons. One is that it creates a mismatch between its
recipients and the colleges they attend. The most selective colleges
accept black and Hispanic students who are vastly inferior to their white and
Asian students. These students would have been better suited to second-tier
colleges, but since they attend top-tier colleges, second-tier colleges must
accept minority students who would be suited to third-tier colleges, etc. As
a result, the recipients of affirmative action drop out of outstanding colleges
instead of graduating from the mediocre colleges that they would have attended without affirmative action. However, in the 28 colleges in Bowen
and Bok's database, although individuals' SAT scores were closely correlated with the rate at which they graduate from college, blacks' graduation
rates rose sharply with the average SAT score of the college they attended
(Bowen and Bok 1998: 59-68). Sigal Alon and Marta Tienda (2005) used
two nationally representative studies—High School and Beyond and the
National Longitudinal Study—to asses the "mismatch" hypotheses. They
also found that the graduation rates of both blacks and Hispanics increased
linearly with the selectivity of the college they attended. To be specific, of
the students who entered American four-year colleges in 1995, 41 percent
of the blacks and 59 percent of the whites had graduated by 2001.[196] But of
the black students who entered Harvard, Amherst, and Princeton in 1999,
95 percent, 94 percent, and 93 percent, respectively, had graduated by 2005;
and the black graduation rate was above 85 percent at nearly other highly
selective college.[197]

---

196. "Searching for Some Good News on African-American College
Graduation Rates." *Journal of Blacks in Higher Education* (*JBHE*) (Summer 2003): 56-7.

197. At the following colleges, the percent of blacks who graduated is

Berkeley used to be an exception and, consequently, was constantly cited to illustrate the harm that preferential admission causes blacks. But the black graduation rate at Berkeley rose from 38 percent of those admitted in 1976 to 71 percent of those admitted in 1994.[198]

Berkeley is part of a national trend. Of the blacks who entered an American college in 1984, 34 percent of women and 28 percent of men graduated from the college they entered within six years; of those who entered in 1990, the proportions were 42 percent and 33 percent, respectively.; 41 percent of all blacks who entered in 1995 graduated by 2001[199] The black college graduation rate has increased while the proportion of blacks entering college has increased and while the gap between whites and blacks has widened on all measures of academic ability and achievement (SAT, SAT-II (achievement tests), ACT, school grades). (I discuss this phenomenon in Section F of Appendix III.)

The same is true of professional and graduate schools. In 1990-91, 17.5 times more blacks were admitted to the most selective American law schools than would have been admitted on the basis of their undergraduate grades and scores on the Law School Admission Test (Wightman 1997: 30). But 91 percent of the blacks who entered these law schools graduated, compared with the 78 percent the blacks who entered all American law schools in that year (Bowen and Bok 1998: 57). Ten years later, grade inflation had raised the black graduation rate at nearly every highly selective law school to above 95 percent. I point out in Section B of Chapter 15 that blacks receive even more preference in admission to graduate business schools than to law schools. But 100 percent of the blacks who enter most highly selective business schools graduate.[200]

---

in parenthesis: Wellesley (92), Brown (91), Northwestern (91), Wesleyan (90), Williams (90), Stanford (89), Yale (89), Dartmouth (88), Columbia (87), Duke (87), Georgetown (87), Smith (87), Swarthmore (86) ("Black Student College Graduation Rates Remain Low, but Modest Progress Begins to Show." *JBHE* (Winter 2005/2006): 88-96).

198. "New College Completion Rates at Berkeley Refute the Position that Affirmative Action Causes High Black Student College Dropout Rates." *JBHE* (Summer 1999): 24.

Thomas Sowell, who is one of the most influential proponents of the "mismatch" hypothesis, argued (2004: 146-7,154-8) that Bowen and Bok's data is inconclusive. However, he did not consider the much broader data that I cite from Sigal and Tienda and the *JBHE*.

199. Searching for Some Good News on African-American College Graduation Rates."*JBHE* (Summer 2003): 56-7.

200. Page 5 of the *Journal of Blacks in Higher Education* of Winter

The second argument that opponents of affirmative action constantly use is that it stigmatizes its recipients and robs them of the possibility of pride in their accomplishments.[201]

However, as I point out in Section B of Chapter 6, blacks at all levels of education have much higher self-esteem than whites; and that includes blacks attending colleges with whites and Asians who have vastly superior academic qualifications. Michael Levin (1997: 287, note 21) recorded that when he has asked black students how they felt about being selected over better qualified whites, "Their reactions have ranged from, 'It's a job and I'm happy to have it' to anger at the suggestion that they do not merit special treatment. I have found no sense of stigmatization." Other reactions are more light-hearted. Richard Blow, a graduate student at Harvard, recounted (1991), "A black student told a friend of mine that he had to reapply for a scholarship. 'Oh, do you have to maintain a certain GPA?' my friend asked. 'No,' the student laughed, 'I have to prove I'm still black'." Towards the end of Chapter 8, I quote descriptions of colleges' furious bidding war for black students from a *New York Times* article, "Colleges Lure Black Students with Incentives," and from a *Boston Globe* article. The author of the *Times* article recorded how some of these students felt about being offered huge scholarships to attend colleges that reject white applicants who are much better qualified and are from more deprived social backgrounds. Not one expressed any qualm or embarrassment or any worry that anyone would think

---

2004/2005 provided the graduation rates of blacks who entered the most highly regarded law and business schools.

Among the leading law schools, 100 percent of the blacks who entered graduated from the following: Columbia, Cornell, Georgetown, Northwestern, University of Michigan, University of Minnesota, University of Texas, University of Virginia, and Washington University. The black graduation rates at other leading law schools were: Duke, 97 percent; University of Pennsylvania, 97 percent; Harvard, 95 percent; Stanford, 91 percent; University of Chicago, 91 percent; Yale, 90 percent.

At leading business schools, 100 percent of the blacks who entered graduated from the following: Dartmouth, MIT, Northwestern, University of Minnesota, University of North Carolina, Stanford, Berkeley, UCLA, University of Texas, Georgetown, University of Washington, and USC.

201. Courts often use this argument in anti-affirmative action decisions (e.g., *City of Richmond v. J. A. Croson*, #493-94; quoted in *Cheryl J. Hopwood, et al. v. State of Texas, et al.*, A.2, footnotes 34 and 45), as does nearly every opponent of affirmative action. Examples among the sources I use frequently are Foster 1976: 20; Herrnstein and Murray 1996: 470; and Maguire 1992: 51.

less of him. The *Boston Globe* article began with Fred Abernathy, whom the University of Illinois' College of Engineering accepted even though his ACT score was in the lowest 40 percent of all test-takers while most of the whites it accepts have ACT scores in the upper 3 percent. Abernathy's reaction to his acceptance was, "I was really proud of myself. My mother was really proud of me."

Perhaps the most illuminating statistic is from the University of Michigan, whose massive racial discrimination I described in Section B of Chapter 2 and in Chapter 14. In a study that the university conducted to defend its affirmative action policies, fourth-year undergraduates were asked whether they thought, "students of color are given advantages that discriminate against other students at colleges and universities." Nearly two-thirds of whites but only six percent of blacks agreed (Schmidt 1998: 5-6). This response goes a long way toward explaining the fact, which that opponents of affirmative action love to quote, that in some surveys, most blacks say they are against pro-black discrimination. Even most black adolescents who grow up in wealthy suburbs think that affirmative action is a means to offset the anti-black discrimination that pervades American society (Ogbu 2003: 149-54).

Blacks, Hispanics, and Native Americans are no more the victims of anti-white discrimination than private-school-educated Anglo-Saxons were the victims of anti-Jewish discrimination.

B. The Showpiece of Affirmative Action and a Remarkable Immigrant Story

During President Clinton's much publicized national dialogue on race, he confronted affirmative-action critic Abigail Thernstrom with the question: "Do you favor the United States Army abolishing the program that produced Colin Powell? Yes or No" (Lane 1997).

Ex-Secretary of State Colin Powell, whom President Clinton singled out as the showpiece of affirmative action, provides a striking illustration of how it is reported and how it works.

As I discussed in Chapter 11, when affirmative action is not explicitly under discussion, a tacit agreement pervades American media and social sciences to pretend that it does not exist. An example is Judith Rich Harris' highly praised *The Nurture Assumption* (1998). Harris did the public a great service by making accessible the unanimous conclusion of studies of adopted children who were raised from infancy by adoptive parents. Harris pointed out that every adoption study, no matter who conducted it or under what conditions, came to the same conclusion (e.g., pages 37, 344, 385,

411, note 261):

> For IQ as for personality, the correlation between adult adoptees reared in the same home hovers around zero.
>
> The reason why parents who read to their children have smarter children is that these are smarter parents. . . . If there were an environmental reason why parents who read to children have smarter children, then we wouldn't find a zero correlation in IQ between two adoptive siblings reared by the same parents.
>
> [T]wo biologically unrelated children reared in the same home are not alike at all by the time they are in high school.
>
> IQ correlation between adopted children and their adoptive parents also declines to zero in adolescence.

Nevertheless, Harris argued (1998: 251) that racial differences in intelligence are not completely genetic. Cultural background is also important. Her evidence is (page 251) that among blacks in the United States, "Jamaicans are academic achievers and they do very well indeed; their success stories are reminiscent of those of Jewish immigrants a generation earlier." She cited only one source for Jamaican success, an article by Steven Roberts, "An American Tale: Colin Powell Is Only One Chapter in a Remarkable Immigrant Story," in *U.S. News and World Report* of August 21, 1995 (pages 27-30). Roberts began by informing his readers that "the experience of West Indian blacks in America" is "no less remarkable" than that of "Chinese or Jews." His proof was "Colin Powell's vast extended family." His niece "has a master's degree from Yale . . . Powell's son has a law degree from Georgetown. Other cousins attended MIT, Brown, Berkeley, Howard and Columbia." Roberts completely ignored the fact that in admission, graduation, and throughout their subsequent lives, Powell's relatives received and will continue to receive massive preferences over the children of white single mothers who supported them as waitresses.

Nor did Roberts mention that Colin Powell himself owed his rise to Chief of Staff of the United States Army (and from there to Secretary of State) to his race. Like every other American institution, the armed forces assume that all races must be equal in ability; so any racial disparities in promotion must indicate discrimination.

> If fewer Blacks are recommended for promotion than their percentage in the candidate pool, the [promotion] board must justify that. Nor does it end there. . . . Every officer evaluation report has an equal-opportunity checkbox. That single mark can make or break an officer's career. Commanders have been removed over it (Steinhorn and Diggs-Brown 1999: 230).

Obviously, an officer would destroy his career if he tried to justify not recommending as high a proportion of blacks and Hispanics for promotion as are in the candidate pool with the argument that they are not as qualified as the whites in the candidate pool.

As in other areas of American life, racial discrimination in the military is transparent and often quantifiable. A 1982 memorandum at the U.S. Air Force Academy, with the notation "for your eyes only," listed the lowest scores on the combined Verbal+Math SAT that would be considered for applicants of different races of applicants. A score as low as *520*, which is in the lowest one percent of all test-takers, was acceptable for blacks. For Hispanics and Native Americans, the cut-off score was somewhat higher. The average combined Verbal+Math SAT score of all students admitted was 1240, in the upper 20 percent of all test-takers; for whites and Asians it must have been considerably higher.[202]

Graduates then form part of the pool of candidates for promotion from which as high a proportion of minorities as whites must be promoted.

Colin Powell was a beneficiary of this process. He was promoted to general in 1977 because the Secretary of the Army refused to sign the list of promotions of colonels to general unless blacks were added to them. In 1981, Powell's commanding officer rated his performance as "average" but privately said that if the division ever had to go to war, he would request that Powell be replaced. Charles Lane, who recorded (1997) these facts, noted, "Such a rating would ordinarily [i.e., if he were white] have meant an early end to Powell's career."

Powell, like black multimillionaires Bill Cosby, O.J. Simpson, "Mr. T," Patrick Ewing, Julius Erving, and Donald McHenry (the owner of the Philadelphia Coca-Cola bottling company), also helped himself to huge profits from a Federal Communications Commission program that allowed tax deferrals on the sale of broadcasting properties to "minority-led investor groups" (Thernstrom 1997: 443; Eastland 1996: 177-80).

(I will remind the reader that I am not the one who chose Colin Powell to exemplify the way blacks achieve success in the United States or the virtues of affirmative action.)

The "remarkable immigrant story" of black immigrants in the United States illustrates another crucial aspect of affirmative action.

West Indian blacks' reputed success is supposed to be especially manifested in business ownership. But they are successful in business only relative to native blacks. The 2000 census reported that of every thousand employed

---

202. Sowell 1993: 145. A detailed record of the huge extent of racial discrimination in admission to the U.S. Military Academy at West Point and the Naval Academy can be found at www.ceousa.org.

Americans over the age of sixteen, 93 of the native-born were self-employed and 97 of the foreign-born. The highest rate of self-employment among immigrant nationalities (per 1,000) was among Greeks (253), Koreans, (205), and Iranians (203).[203] The highest rate of self-employment among black Caribbean immigrants (per thousand) was among Trinidadians (72), followed by Jamaicans (66), and Haitians (48). Of the 33 nationalities of immigrants whose rate of self-employment the census listed, Trinidadians were 25th, Jamaicans, 28th, and Haitians, 33rd (i.e., the lowest). Rate of self-employment is an important indicator of a group's economic success. In every immigrant group, the self-employed earn considerably more than paid employees who have the same level of education and length of residency in the United States (Portes and Rumbaut 2006: 81-4).

However, because of the strong tendency of the most intelligent blacks from the West Indies to immigrate to the United States, West Indian blacks are more successful than native American blacks. Consequently, until recently, they and their descendants have been the main black recipients of affirmative action in those regions, like New York City, in which they are concentrated. In 1970, "the highest ranking blacks in New York's Police Department were all West Indians, as were all black federal judges in the city" (Sowell 1981: 220). Recently, West Indians immigrants have been joined by increasing numbers of black immigrants from Africa, who, because of the nature of American immigration requirements, are even more successful than West Indians. In 2003 1.5 million Caribbean blacks lived in the United States, comprising about 70 percent of all black immigrants; most of the other black immigrants were from Africa. Blacks from Africa had an average of 14 years of education, considerably more than American whites (12.9) or Asians (13.1). In 2003, the median income of African blacks was $45,000; of Caribbean blacks, $41,000; and of native blacks, $36,000 (Massey, et al., 2007: 246).

So, it should not have been surprising that in 2003, a survey of black undergraduates at Harvard found that only about a third had four grandparents who were descendants of slaves in the United States. The rest were children of black immigrants or from mixed-race families. This survey was conducted by a black Harvard undergraduate from the United States, who said that when she would tell her black classmates that her family was from the United States, they would say incredulously, "No, where are you

203. The rate of self-employment among Iranian immigrants could be misleading. Iranian immigrants are disproportionately from Iranian ethnic minorities. Over a third of all Iranians in the United States live in Los Angeles County. Among them, by far the highest rate of self-employment (83 percent of men) is among Jewish Iranians (Min and Bozorgmehr 2000: 722).

really from?" Harvard officials tried to discourage the collection of this data (Rimer and Arenson 2004).

More recently, Massey, et al., (2007) analyzed the differences between native and immigrant blacks who entered in 1999 the 28 colleges that formed the data on which Bowen and Bok based their *The Shape of the River*. These colleges differ widely in selectivity, but all were at least moderately selective, and they include some of the most selective colleges in the United States. Their average Verbal+Math SAT ranged from 1105 at Howard to 1450 at Princeton (page 248). Massey, et al., (page 248) defined "immigrant blacks" as those at least one of whose parents were born abroad; all the others were "native blacks." Massey, et al., pointed out that this definition undoubtedly understates the number of blacks at these colleges who are descendants of immigrants, because it ignores those who are the grandchildren of immigrants.

In 1999, 13 percent of all American blacks aged 18-19 were first- or second-generation immigrants, but 27 percent of the blacks who entered in the 28 colleges in Massey, et al.'s survey were "immigrant blacks" (page 245). Moreover, the proportion of blacks at these 28 colleges rose steadily with their selectivity. At the Ivy League colleges in the survey (Columbia, Princeton, University of Pennsylvania, and Yale), 41 percent of the blacks were immigrants (page 248). This distribution partially (I explain below why only partially) reflected the fact that at all 28 of these colleges, the average Verbal+Math SAT score of the immigrant blacks was 1250, compared with 1193 for native blacks and 1361 for whites (pages 260-61).

That is not the average difference between blacks and whites at the same college, which is much greater, as I point out in my discussion of *The Shape of the River* at the beginning of Chapter 14. I ask the reader to go back and look again at the differences I record there in acceptance rates between black and white applicants with the same SAT scores at five highly selective colleges among these 28 colleges. Those racial differences would have been even greater if highly selective colleges were not able to fill up on immigrant blacks and had to rely solely on native blacks to have an acceptable proportion of black students. Not only do immigrant blacks have higher average SAT scores than native blacks, but by admitting large numbers of immigrant blacks, selective colleges decrease the number of native blacks they have to admit. Consequently, the native blacks they admit have higher average SAT scores than the native blacks they would have had to admit if they had no immigrant blacks.

I can supplement Massey, et al.'s study with information from the *Journal of Blacks in Higher Education* (*JBHE*) of Winter 2005/2006.[204] In 2003, 13.6

204. "A Solid Percentage of Black Students at U.S. Collages and Uni-

percent of the black students in kindergarten through twelfth grade in the United States had at least one parent who was born abroad, almost double the percentage of whites. Three and a half percent of blacks in pre-university education were themselves born abroad, more than double the percentage of whites. At all colleges in the United States in 2003, 22 percent of the blacks had at least one parent who was born abroad. That is less than the 27 percent at the colleges in Massey et al.'s study, which were more selective than the average American college. The *JBHE* also reported that in 2003, more than 15 percent of black undergraduates in the United States were themselves born abroad, compared to four percent of white undergraduates. Of the blacks at American graduate schools, 23 percent had one or both foreign-born parents, and 17 percent were themselves born abroad, compared with eight percent of whites. Undoubtedly, the percent of blacks graduate students who were children of immigrants or immigrants themselves was much higher at the most selective graduate schools.

In Chapter 13, I point out that after expending huge amounts of time and effort for nearly half a century to increase the number of black American scientists, in 2004, blacks received only 13 of the more than 1,200 American PhDs in physics and less than one percent of the PhDs in mathematics. It would be interesting to know how many of the "American" blacks who got PhDs in physics and mathematics were immigrants or the children of immigrants.

I observed above that the average SAT score of immigrant blacks only partially explains their appeal to American universities. Massey, et al., (2007: 252) provided another reason:

> Researchers . . . have universally mentioned the greater comfort level experienced by whites who interact with black immigrants compared with native blacks. To white observers, black immigrants seem more polite, less hostile, more solicitous, and "easier to get along with.". . . Such subjective evaluations are likely to reflect unconscious stereotyping as well as actual differences in behavior.

I know from personal experience that unconscious stereotyping has nothing to do with this perception. I am an American who has lived in South Africa since 1974. White American visitors to South Africa invariable comment on how pleasant and eager to please South African blacks are. The reason is that, in fact, they are. I have spoken to whites who have lived and worked elsewhere in black Africa. Their experience is the same.

Massey, et al., (2007: 245) also mentioned another important fact. During the past decade, the number of black immigrants has more than

versities are Foreign Born:" 11.

doubled. Their college statistics were for blacks entering college in 1999, and they included as immigrant blacks only those with at least one immigrant parent, not blacks with immigrant grandparents. By now, most blacks at highly selective colleges are nearly certainly immigrants or the children or grandchildren of immigrants. Among them must be nearly all of the children and grandchildren of the highest ranking blacks in New York's Police Department and black federal judges in New York in 1970; all of whom, as I point out above, were West Indian. This process must have decreased the difference in qualifications between their black and white students. The same is nearly certainly true of the blacks at the most selective professional and graduate schools. In the future, most of the black partners at the most prestigious law firms will be immigrants or the descendants of immigrants; as will be most of the top black executives at American corporations, etc. Thus, black immigration is a godsend to the most prominent American institutions. They can admit, hire, and promote significant numbers of blacks with much less sacrifice of competence and agreeability than if they had to rely on native blacks.

Two objections immediately impose themselves. The first is the blatant absurdity of this process. According to the 2000 census, 58 percent of Nigerian immigrants were college graduates, but only eight percent of Portuguese immigrants were college graduates (and 24 percent of all native-born Americans) (Portes and Rumbaut 2006: 69). Yet, Nigerian immigrants and their descendants will go through their lives receiving massive preferences over Portuguese immigrants and their descendants. However, that is no more absurd than white Latin American multimillionaires and their descendants receiving massive preferences over the same Portuguese immigrants and their descendants. Of course, a Portuguese immigrant can gain the same level of preferences for his/her descendants by marrying a Nigerian, or, if she is a woman, marrying a white Cuban (and thereby obtaining his Spanish surname for her descendants).

The second objection is that although immigrant blacks are more intelligent than native blacks, they are much less intelligent than whites and Asians. In fact, immigrant blacks in the colleges in Massey, et al.'s study did not earn higher college grade averages than native blacks (Massey, et al., 2007: 263, 268-9). Moreover, as I document in Section F of Appendix III, despite their presence, the difference in average performance between all American blacks and whites on all measures of academic ability and achievement has constantly increased.

Let us now return to Colin Powell, whom President Clinton chose to exemplify the virtues of affirmative action and whose family has been used to illustrate a "remarkable immigrant story." The reader will now realize that he and his remarkably successful family typify the workings of affirmative action in another fundamental way: not one of their ancestors ever suffered discrimination in the United States.[205]

Colin Powell has also been used as an example by opponents of affirmative action, to show that affirmative action degrades successful blacks. *Commentary* of March 1998 ("Is Affirmative Action on the Way Out? Should It Be?": 18-57) asked 20 widely known participants in the affirmative-action debate for their opinions. One opponent of affirmative action, Midge Decter, dwelled (page 24) on President Clinton's use of Colin Powell as the show-piece of affirmative action:

> How Colin Powell felt about being used as an example . . . I can guess . . . Deeply insulted and furious would be my bet, as any high-achieving Black must be at the possibility that his standing in the world is being chalked up to his having been given special consideration for the mere color of his skin.

But she guessed wrong. Powell supports affirmative action. Ethan Bronner, in a typically laudatory review of *The Shape of the River* in the *New York Times*,[206] quoted Powell's amusing comment about the supposed harm that affirmative action does to its recipients' self-esteem: "Asked about the stigma that opponents say affirmative action imposes on blacks who attend these elite colleges, General Powell was dismissive. 'I would tell black youngsters to . . . get one of those well-paying jobs [they will get through affirmative action] to pay for all the therapy they'll need to remove that stigma.'"

Before leaving this topic, I will point out that Massey, et al., reported (2007: 254) that in the 28 colleges they studied, 16 percent of the native blacks described themselves as mixed race, and 19 percent of the immigrant blacks described themselves as mixed race. It would be extremely interesting to know their average SAT scores and what proportion of both immigrant and native blacks at the Ivy League colleges in Massey, et al.'s database were mixed race. Since Massey, et al., had this information, the only reason that I can think of for their not reporting it was that they found it embarrassing.

C. Asians Should Be the Main Victims of Affirmative Action

---

205. A study of the origin and ancestry of Hispanic recipients of affirmative action would be extremely illuminating, but I could not find any.

206. "Study Strongly Supports Affirmative Action in Admissions to Elite Colleges" (September 9, 1998): B10.

When opponents of affirmative action are not criticizing the (non-existent) damage it does to its most obvious beneficiaries, blacks and Hispanics, they single out Asians as its victims. For example, Richard Nixon, who, as will be discussed in Section B of Appendix II, did more to entrench savage anti-white discrimination than any other American political leader, later attacked affirmative action (Nixon 1994: 188) with this example: "In the California college system, Asian applicants with superior qualifications are often discriminated against on the grounds that Asians are overrepresented."

Asians would be the main victims of affirmative action if its basic premise—that disproportional success is a problem that should be solved—were implemented consistently.

In 1999, the *New York Times* marked Martin Luther King Day (January 18) with a predictable editorial ("Martin Luther King's America": A16): "[For] the abyss between whites and blacks in income and wealth, one does not have to look far to find the damage done by intolerance and discrimination." However, according to the statistics published by the Census Bureau in 2006, the median household income of American racial groups in 2005 was: Asians, $57,518; Non-Hispanic whites, $48,977; Hispanics, $34,241; blacks, $30,134. Therefore, Asian Americans must be doing more damage to black Americans by intolerance and discrimination than are white Americans. In fact, Asian Americans must be damaging white Americans by intolerance and discrimination.

Every statistic that proves that whites are discriminating against blacks and Hispanics also proves that Asians are discriminating against whites. For example, banks are frequently accused of discriminating against blacks in granting mortgages. But banks grant a higher proportion of the mortgage requests of Asian than of white applicants (Thomas 1992). Similarly, a much publicized study claimed the location of toxic waste landfills was racist because 57 percent of blacks and Hispanics live near one, but only 54 percent of non-Hispanic whites. However, the same study found that only 46 percent of Asians live near a toxic waste landfill (Taylor 1992: 61).

Even these statistics understate the difference between whites and North-East Asians (Chinese, Japanese, Koreans) since, with the typical imprecision of American racial classifications, *Asian* usually includes everyone whose ancestors are from Asia east of Iran. North-East Asians are much more successful than many other ethnic groups of Asians. For example, the average income of Japanese Americans is nearly double the average income of Samoan Americans (Sowell 2004: 175).

My last example is from the computer industry:

In the early '70s corporate America first noticed the shortfall of Black engineers . . . No effort was spared in the ensuing campaign . . . Big firms like Exxon, G. E. and IBM offer huge signing bonuses both for new minority recruits and for existing minority employees who help bring them in. Then, when the newcomers arrive at the company, the human resources department typically spends a small fortune trying to raise the odds that they'll stay (Jacoby 1999: 24-5).

In 1991, the *Wall Street Journal* reported (Wynter 1991) that even though "[t]he recession is crimping job offers for college seniors, competition . . . remain[s] stiff for minority graduates . . . About 225 companies . . . are vying for . . . this spring's 125 engineering graduates at [mostly black] Howard University." Indeed, Howard's placement director told companies to contribute money to Howard to improve their chances of hiring its graduates.

Nevertheless, in the 1990s, in the San Francisco Bay area of California alone, the U.S. Labor Department accused more than a dozen high-tech companies of "affirmative action violations." This fact was reported in a front-page article in the *San Francisco Chronicle* of May 4, 1998, entitled "The Digital Divide: High Tech Boom a Bust for Blacks, Latinos." It began:

> Blacks and Latinos are largely missing out on the Silicon Valley technology boom . . . . Employment records for 33 of the leading Silicon Valley firms show that their Bay Area staffs, on average, are 4 percent black and 7 percent Latino—even though blacks and Latinos make up 8 percent and 14 percent of the Bay Area labor force, respectively. . . . It's pretty clear that there's an ethnic and occupational segregation going on in Silicon Valley. . . . [T]he community of color is being left behind.

However, later the article mentioned, "[T]he workforce at the 33 Silicon Valley firms is about 28 percent Asian, while the Bay Area workforce as a whole is 21 percent Asian." The article did not provide any statistics on whites. But if a reader was willing to do some simple arithmetic, he would have realized that whites were only slightly overrepresented: 57 percent of the population of the Bay Area and 61 percent of the employees of these companies.

Newspapers and magazines (e.g., Jacoby 1999: 22) then repeated the *Chronicle*'s statistics for blacks and Hispanics, but not those for Asians, thus depriving their readers of any means of questioning the *Chronicle*'s conclusion that "the community of color is being left behind."

An exception was *The Economist*, which provided fuller statistics than the *Chronicle* for the Asian presence in Silicon Valley's high-tech industry and thereby showed that the *Chronicle*'s statistics greatly understated Asian overrepresentation since its data were from large companies, like Intel and Oracle. But Asians are especially overrepresented among the owners, managers, and engineers of smaller companies (Graham 2002: 163-4). The *Economist*'s article, entitled "Latinos in Silicon Valley" ((April 17, 1999): 63-4), began, "Some in Silicon Valley claim to have invented a new society . . . one that has abolished class and race prejudice, and judges people purely on the basis of merit. . . . Almost a third of the region's scientists and engineers are Asian-born." Since almost a third of Silicon Valley's scientists and engineers were Asian-born, only a minority are probably white, since many are also American-born North-East Asians and Asian Indians.

The *Economist* then reported, "Latinos make up 23 percent of the region's population; but when the *San Francisco Chronicle* investigated 33 high-tech firms last year, it found that only 7 percent of the workforce were Latinos." The *Economist* pointed out, "Only 56 percent of Latino students graduate from high school . . . only 19 percent complete the basic courses you need to get into college; and only 11 percent are enrolled in an advanced maths class. One Latina in eight has a baby before her eighteenth birthday." Nevertheless, even as ardent champion of the free market as the *Economist* ignored these facts and statistics in the final sentence of the article: "The cyber-elite may yet have cause to regret that they did not take their talk of a colour-blind meritocracy a little more seriously."

D. Asians Are Beneficiaries of Affirmative Action

Thus, Asians should logically be the main victims of affirmative action. In fact, they are not. In *The Bell Curve*, Herrnstein and Murray (1996: 451-3) listed the average Verbal+Math SAT scores of whites, Asians, and blacks at 26 highly selective colleges. In most of the colleges on their list, Asians had higher average Verbal+Math SAT scores than whites. But the differences between whites and Asians are neither great nor universal. More importantly, the combined Verbal+Math SAT score is misleading since Verbal-SAT is more important than Math for most fields of study. In 2004, the average Asian and white SAT Verbal (now called Critical Reading) scores were 507 and 528; the average SAT Math scores of Asians and whites were 578 and 531. In the same year, on the ACT, which has sections on English, Mathematics, Reading Comprehension, and Science Reasoning, the average white score (on a 1-36 scale) was 21.8; the average Asian score was 21.9.[207]

Lerner and Nagai (2002) provided the median Verbal+Math SAT scores of whites and Asians at 27 American colleges. At 24, the median white Verbal score was higher than the median Asian Verbal score. At 14 of these colleges,

207. I will discuss more recent racial scores on the SAT and ACT in Section F of Appendix III.

the gap was 30 points or more. The Asian median Verbal score exceeded the white median at only three colleges, all by a small margin (10, 10, and 25 points). The median white Math score was higher at two of these 27 colleges; at six, they were the same; at 19, the median Asian Math score was higher. But at only six of these, was the gap 30 points or more. Lerner and Nagai 2002 also provided the median white and Asian ACT scores at 22 colleges. At 14, the median white score was higher. At four of these colleges, it was higher by three or more points (on a 36-point scale). At five colleges, the median white and Asian ACT scores were the same. At only three was the median Asian ACT score is higher, all by less than three points.

In Section A of Chapter 9, I provided statistics on the rate at which teachers pass teacher competence tests in various states. In all, whites' pass rates are much higher than Asians.'

The most frequently cited evidence of anti-Asian discrimination in undergraduate admission has been from its supposed existence at the University of California at Berkeley, UCLA, and Davis. In fact, in the late 1980s, when this accusation was constantly being made, of the California high school graduates who were academically eligible for Berkeley (on the basis of high school grades and SAT scores), 67.7 percent were white and 19.9 percent were Asian. But only 32.6 percent of the 1989 Berkeley freshman class was white and 21.2 percent was Asian. (Of California high school graduates, 61.1 percent were white, and 8.6 percent were Asian.) (Sarich 1990-91: 73-4, 76) As for UCLA, I will repeat a statistic that I mention in Chapter 4. In 2001, the average combined Verbal+Math SAT score of Hispanics who were *admitted* to UCLA was 1168; the average of Asians and whites who were *rejected* was 1174 and 1209, respectively. The average of Asians and whites who were accepted was 1344 and 1355 (Golden 2002).

In 2005, Thomas J. Espenshade and Chang Y. Chung (Espenshade and Chung 2005; also, Espenshade, et al., 2004) argued that in their study of a sample of highly selective colleges, being black gained an applicant 230 Verbal+Math SAT points, being Hispanic gained an applicant 185 Verbal+Math SAT points, and being Asian lost an applicant 50 Verbal+Math SAT points. If admissions decisions were based completely on Verbal+Math SAT scores, Asian applicants would gain four-fifths of the places that would be lost by black and Hispanic applicants, and white applicants would gain the other one-fifth. This conclusion has been widely repeated as a fact. However, William Kidder (Kidder 2006) showed that Espenshade and Chung's methodology is fundamentally flawed. During the course of his article, Kidder provided (footnote 36, on pages 612-13) the average Verbal+Math SAT scores of different "Asian-Pacific-American" national-origin groups who entered the undergraduate division of his own university, the University of California at Davis, in 1998. This is extremely valuable information, since, as I have pointed out several times, the category "Asian" is misleading, because it lumps together widely different ethnic/racial groups. The average Verbal+Math SAT score of white undergraduates at Davis was 1200. The average Verbal+Math SAT score of every national-origin Asian group was substantially lower. They were (the number of students in each group is in parenthesis): Japanese (75), 1187; Korean (100), 1177; East Indian and Pakistani (79), 1165; Pacific Islander (74), 1158; Chinese (567), 1137; Filipino (151), 1099; Vietnamese (194), 1060; "Other Asian" (78), 1045. (Many (maybe most) of the Vietnamese were ethnically Chinese; and "Pacific Islander" included students who trace their origin to Taiwan, as well as to Hawaii, Guam, and Samoa.) Again I will point out that the combined Verbal+Math SAT score is misleading, because Verbal-SAT is more important than Math for most fields of study, and the white-Asian difference at Davis was undoubtedly much greater in Verbal than in combined Verbal+Math.

Kidder also documented the constant accusation of critics of affirmative action, that its main victims are Asians, and showed that every such accusation is unfounded. For example, the Center for Individual Rights (CIR), which represented the plaintiffs in the University of Michigan *Grutter* and *Gratz* cases, argued to the Supreme Court that affirmative action harms "especially Asian Americans." However, the statistical analysis that CIR's expert witness presented did not show that Asians suffered greater discrimination than whites; even though "CIR would have been highly motivated to present evidence of unfairness towards APAs [Asian-Pacific-Americans] either in court or to the media, given that it would have yielded a large political payoff in terms of triangulating APAs as the principal victims of affirmative action" (Kidder 2006: 608, 622-3). Kidder also showed (2006: 620, footnote 55) that the often repeated assertion that Asians were the main beneficiaries of the ban on affirmative action at the University of Texas is untrue.

One more fact needs to be mentioned about the allegation of anti-Asian discrimination in undergraduate admissions. Anthony Carnevale and Stephen Rose (2003) studied the admissions qualification of students who attended a broad array of American four-year colleges in the late 1990s. They divided them into four "tiers." The top tier contained 146 colleges. Their students averaged approximately 1240 on Verbal+Math SAT and/or above 27 on the ACT. Of the students at these colleges, 12 percent were Asian, six percent blacks, and six percent Hispanic. If admission had been determined purely on the basis of high school record and entrance exams, then 1.6 percent of all 18-year old blacks would have been eligible to attend them, 2.4 percent of 18-year old Hispanics, and only seven percent of 18-year old Asians.

This does not indicate pro-Asian discrimination. It does mean that a much higher proportion of Asians than whites who are academically qualified to attend highly selective colleges apply to them (Carnevale and Rose 2003: 47). I have pointed out that Asians work harder than whites in high school and college and have higher expectations than whites of future academic attainment (Thernstrom 2003: 143; Charles, et al., 2009: 43, 78, 81). Also, a much higher proportion of Asians than any other group takes SAT coaching courses (Appendix III. B)

Let us now look at professional schools. In 1992, the average score on the Law School Admission Test (LSAT) of first-year Asians at American law schools was .32 of a standard deviation lower than the average LSAT score of white first-year students (Herrnstein and Murray 1996: 455-6). In 1990-91, 1.6 times more Asians were admitted to American law schools than would have been admitted on the basis of undergraduate grade-point-average (UGPA) and LSAT scores alone, and only .85 times as many whites (Wightman 1997: 16). The most recent data I could find on Asian and white law-school admissions was Linda Wightman's analysis (2003) of applicants to and acceptances by every law school accredited by the American Bar Association in 2000-01. Wightman divided law schools into six tiers, based on the average UGPA and LSAT score of their students. Below are the numbers of Asians and whites who would be predicted to be admitted to each tier on the basis of their UGPA and LSAT and the number who were actually admitted (Wightman 2003: 247):

	Asians		Whites	
	Predicted	Admitted	Predicted	Admitted
Tier 1:	731	834	6,198	6,074
Tier 2:	1,580	1,693	12,125	11,615
Tier 3:	983	1,135	15,099	14,952
Tier 4:	1,639	1,768	20,758	20,731
Tier 5:	220	244	5,928	5,878
Tier 6:	142	135	992	758

At every tier, fewer whites were admitted than should have been admitted on the basis of academic qualifications; and at every tier except the lowest (in which the numbers were small), more Asians were admitted than should have been admitted on the basis of academic qualifications.

Moreover, LSAT scores overpredict Asians' performance on the bar examination relative to whites.' Among students who entered American law schools in 1991, 89.85 of the Asians and 95.36 percent of the whites who had LSAT scores at or above the average LSAT score of all students passed the bar exam on the first try. Of those whose LSAT scores were below the average, 71.98 percent of the Asians and 86.97 percent of the whites passed the bar exam on the first try (Wightman 1998: 30). The most recent statistics I could find for the passing rates of whites and Asians on a bar exam was for the New York in 2006: 78.3 percent of the whites and 71.6 percent of the Asians passed the New York bar exam on the first try (www.nybarexam.org).

As with all affirmative action programs, the socioeconomic background of the recipients is not considered. For instance, Ron Chen got into Rutgers Law School through its Minority Student Program even though both his parents had PhDs and he attended one of the most elite private schools in the United States (Exeter) and Dartmouth. He told the *Washington Post* that he needed affirmative action to get into law school because "I goofed off in college" (Russakoff 1995).

In all my research, I could find only one indication of greater discrimination against Asians than whites in any area of university admissions. Since 1991, the Medical College Admission Test (MCAT) has consisted of four parts: Verbal Reasoning, Physical Science, Biological Science and a Writing Sample. Steven Sailer (2009) provides a comparison of the average college grade-point-average (GPA) and the average scores on three sections of the MCAT of whites, Asian Americans, Mexican Americans, and blacks who enrolled in American medical schools in 2007. (He does not provide information on the Writing Sample.) He makes this comparison by presenting the average performance of each non-white group in terms of what percentile it is of white performance. So, for example, the average college GPA of Asian matriculants is at the 48th percentile of the average white college GPA, which means that the average college GPA of 52 percent of white matriculants was higher than the average Asian GPA:

	Blacks	Mexican Americans	Asian Americans	Whites
Percent of total matriculants	6.4%	2.5%	19.9%	59.9%
		Percentile of White score		
College GPA	15	24	48	50
MCAT Verbal Reasoning	12	23	43	50
MCAT Physical Science	15	25	67	50
MCAT Biological Science	14	27	61	50

This seems to indicate a little more discrimination against Asians than against whites. Even if it does, it certainly does not justify the decades-long uproar about Asians being the main victims of affirmative action.

However, before 1991, the MCAT had five sections: Biology, Physics, Science Problems, Reading, and Quantitative. Extensive studies were done of how well each section predicted performance on the three parts of the National Board of Medical Examiners examinations (NBME). Here I will remind the reader that the courses in the first two years of medical school are devoted to the sciences relevant to medicine (anatomy, biochemistry, etc.). The courses in the third and fourth years involve specifically medical subjects (surgery, obstetrics/gynecology, pediatrics, etc.) Then, after a medical student has an MD degree, he works in a hospital as an intern. Part I of the NBME was taken at the end of the second year of medical school; Part II at the end of the fourth year; and Part III at the end of internship.

The Quantitative section of the MCAT was found to have little predictive value for all three parts of the NBME. The science sections had the highest predictive accuracy for Part I, as could be expected. The Reading section had slightly better predictive accuracy than the science sections for Part II. On part III, which is clearly the most important, the Reading section had by far the highest predictive accuracy. (One point on the combined science sections added 9.70 points to the score on Part III; one point on Reading added 14.45 points on Part III.) Karen Glaser, et al., (1992) who summarized these studies, concluded "verbal ability reflected in the reading skills scores of an applicant to medical school are a more important indicator of later physician competence . . . than the applicant's ability to solve science problems." It was for this reason that the Association of American Medical Colleges radically changed the contents of the MCAT in 1991. It eliminated the Quantitative section, reduced the science sections from three to two and added the Writing Sample, giving verbal ability equal weighting with science ability (Glaser, et al., 1992). Sailer does not provide a racial comparison for Writing, but it must be closely correlated with Verbal Reasoning.

Even more important is that the qualifications for admission to medical schools greatly overpredict the performance of Asians relative to whites. In 1992, a year after the new MCAT was introduced, the three parts of the NBME was replaced by Steps I, II, and III of United States Medical Licensing Examination (USMLE). At that time, extensive studies were done of the predictive accuracy of the new MCAT for grades in medical schools and on the USMLE. They found that a combination of undergraduate science grades with the new MCAT overpredicts grades in the first two years of medical school of Asians by .12 of a standard deviation (SD) and underpredicts the grades of whites by .08 SD (Koenig 1998: 1102). With regard to grades in the third and fourth years of medical school, the new MCAT overpredicts the grades of Asians by .23 of a SD and underpredicts the grades of whites by .10 SD. In other words, if an Asian and white have the same MCAT score, the white will, on average, have grades that are .33 SD higher than the Asian. To look at this fact from another perspective, the MCAT is graded on a 15 point scale, and 1 SD is between 2 and 2.3 points, depending on the year. So, a white with an MCAT score .7 points lower than an Asian will probably get the same grades in the third and fourth years of medical school (Huff, et al., 1999). The students who were the subjects of these studies entered medical schools in 1992. Among them, the average MCAT score of the Asians was 9.91 and of whites, 9.67, a difference of only .24.

As I have repeatedly shown, scores on standardized tests are the best measures of knowledge and aptitude. Of the students who entered medical schools in 1992, 93.4 of the whites and 86.8 percent of Asians passed Step I of the USMLE on the first try; and 96.3 percent of whites and 87.6 percent of Asians passed Step II on the first try (Case, et al., 1996: S91).

What is especially striking is that although the Asian superiority to whites is on the science sections of the MCAT, whites do better than Asians on even Step I of the USMLE, which has the same content as the science sections of the MCAT. Several explanations have been offered for this paradox. What is importance is that it exists and is known to the admissions boards of all medical schools. Since whites get higher grades than Asians in medical school and do better on the national medical qualifying examinations, it is absurd to accuse medical schools of greater discrimination against Asians than against whites in admissions.

In all spheres of American life besides university admission, Asians are among the greatest beneficiaries of affirmative action. Many university faculties and corporations recruit Asians to increase their proportion of minorities. For instance, in 1995, when New Hampshire's population was 97.4 percent white, the University of New Hampshire announced that it intended to increase its minority undergraduate enrollment to 7.5 percent by 2005 and the proportion of its minority tenure-track professors to 7.5 percent by 2000. Two-thirds of its minority professors are Asian. In 1995, only 0.84 percent of New Hampshire's population was Asian (Gorov 1995). Similarly, heroic efforts by the University of Michigan raised the proportion of its faculty who are minorities to 14.1 percent in 1995, more than half of whom (7.3 percent) were Asian (4.9 percent were black and 1.9 percent Hispanic). Blacks comprised 13.9 percent of Michigan's population, Hispanics 2.2 percent, and Asians 1.1 percent (Lynch 1997: 277-8, 312).

Asians are also by far the greatest beneficiaries of government set-aside contracts for minority business enterprises (MBEs). In 1996, Asians were twelve percent of the minority population of the United States, but they received 28 percent of MBE contracts (Graham 2002: 164).

Consequently, 61 percent of Asians in California voted against the 1996 referendum banning the California government from practicing racial discrimination (Beinart 1998).

This is undoubtedly surprising to people who have not studied affirmative action carefully because they constantly hear and read about its adverse effect on Asians. The reason is that opponents of affirmative action try any trick they can use to avoid defending its real victims: whites.

CR EO

Appendix I
The Inclusion of More Successful Groups in Affirmative Action

I have pointed out that affirmative action is based on the belief that inequality of success must indicate discrimination. Then why are Asian Americans among its beneficiaries even though they are more successful than white Americans?

Crucial to their inclusion was the manner in which eligibility for affirmative action was determined. Hugh Graham observed (2002: 140-41):

> The democratic model of policymaking features elected officials who hold public hearings, debate policy goals, argue the strengths and weaknesses of alternative means, cast their votes on the record, and are held accountable by the voters. ... [However, the choice of affirmative-action beneficiaries] was a closed process of bureaucratic policymaking. It was largely devoid not only of public testimony but even of public awareness that policy was being made. . . . [For] the agencies shaping the new definition of official minorities . . . affirmative action . . . paid rich dividends. . . . [T]he agencies provided no rationale to justify their racial and ethnic categories.

By increasing the number of beneficiaries of affirmative action, the agencies that enforced it enjoyed an explosion in their size, influence, and funding (nearly all derived from white taxpayers) (e.g., Graham 1990: 448, 458). So, they were receptive to pressure from politicians and ethnic organizations to include more and more groups.

Between 1956 and 1961, the U.S. Contract Compliance Committee required all businesses that applied for federal contracts to fill in forms that indicated how many Negroes they employed. Lobbying by Hispanic and Oriental organizations, supported by Hispanic and Oriental Congressmen (in the latter case, the Japanese American Citizens League, Chinese-American Senator Hiram Fong, and Japanese-American House member Daniel Inouye) persuaded David Mann, who was in charge of these forms, to revise them in

1962 to require all federal contractors to indicate how many Negroes, "Spanish Americans," "Orientals," and American Indians they employed. Then, the Civil Rights Act of 1964 created the Equal Employment Opportunity Commission (EEOC) to monitor racial discrimination in employment. From 1965, when it started to function, the EEOC interpreted its goal as forcing businesses to hire and promote more minorities. It based its employment surveys on Mann's forms, with their four official minorities. Other federal agencies and state and municipal governments followed its policies.[208]

In 1967, a member of the EEOC, Herbert Hammerman, proposed removing Orientals from the beneficiaries of affirmative action because "the statistics for Asians did not show any discrimination" (i.e., they were not less successful than whites). (The designations "Oriental" and "Asian" were used interchangeably.) Hammerman (1988: 131) later recalled, "No one disagreed, not even the chairman, who explained, however, that he could not take the political heat that removal would generate." At that time, Japanese had the second highest median income of any American ethnic group—after Jews—and Chinese were fourth. (Anglo-Saxons were seventh) (Graham 2002: 144).

Not only was the Oriental/Asian category retained, but it was greatly expanded by the federal Small Business Administration (SBA), which controls billions of dollars every year in contracts and loans. Other federal agencies, along with state and municipal governments, then used the SBA's definition of minorities in their innumerable programs to set aside contracts for and lend money to minority-owned businesses.

When Republican President Nixon took office, in 1969, he had the SBA direct nearly all its assistance to "minority" owned businesses. The SBA took over the EEOC's four official minorities, which came originally from Mann's 1962 forms. In these forms, "Orientals" included only Chinese, Japanese, and Filipinos, who were the only Eastern Asians of whom large numbers lived in the United States in the early 1960s. In 1979, the SBA added Vietnamese, Koreans, Samoans, Laotians, Cambodians, and Taiwanese, all of whom had begun to immigrate in considerably numbers in the 1970s (Graham 2002: 145).

Significant immigration from the Indian subcontinent also began in the 1970s. In 1981, the SBA rejected a petition by National Association of Americans of Asian Indian Descent (NAAAID) to include Asian Indians among recipients of affirmative action because they were not underrepresented among business owners. However, the next year the SBA accepted a petition by the NAAAID, which stressed their dark skin color. At that time,

---

208. Graham 2002: 136-7; Roberts and Stratton 1995: 88-95; Graham 1990: 241-2; Skrentny 1996: 127-30.

the Asian-Indian rate of business ownership was three and a half times the rate of all Americans. When the SBA published the inclusion of Asian Americans in the *Federal Register*, it also included Pakistanis and Bangladeshis. In 1989, the SBA added Indonesians and created the affirmative-action category "Subcontinental Asian Americans," which added Sri Lankans and Nepalese to Asian Indians, Pakistanis, and Bangladeshis (LaNoue and Sullivan 1994: 450-52, 459-60). That completed the process of defining recipients of affirmative action.[209]

209. Since the SBA played such an important role in defining affirmative action recipients, it is worthwhile outlining Jonathan Bean's history of it (Bean 2001). (I put Bean's page numbers in parentheses.)

The SBA was founded in 1953. Typically of government agencies, it was supposed to be temporary. It was scheduled to expire in two years. In 1955, it was extended for two more years; in 1957, it was made permanent. Between 1954 and 1960, its budget and the number of its personnel quadrupled, as it expanded both its functions and its definition of "small" businesses (9, 14-19).

When Richard Nixon became president, in 1969, he made the SBA into an affirmative action agency. Even though the delinquency rate for the SBA's Economic Opportunity Loans (EOLs) was 70 percent, by 1970 minority-owned businesses received 80 percent of the SBA's EOLs and 90 percent of its direct loan dollars (68, 168, note 28). More significantly, during the Nixon administration, the SBA greatly expanded the number and value of federal contracts that were set aside for minority-owned businesses. In 1968, only eight minority set-aside contracts were awarded (66). But between 1971 and 1974, the value of set-aside contracts for minority businesses increased from $68 million to $272 million, even though in 1973 two-thirds of these companies were delinquent in fulfilling these contracts (90, 92). In the late 1970s, a report by the government's General Accounting Office disclosed that only 15 percent of EOL borrowers were still in business; and a congressional investigation found that of the 15,000 firms that received set-aside contracts, only 70 were able to function independently of these contracts (100-101). Nevertheless, by 1980 new loan guarantees had increased to $3.6 *billion*, and set-aside contracts to $1.3 *billion*; 99 percent of which went to minorities (103, 108).

In 1984, at President Reagan's urging, more minority-owned companies were added to the set-aside program than in any year since 1969, and the value of contracts set aside for minority businesses increased by 30 percent. The liberal *New Republic* described Reagan as "an enthusiastic promoter" of the "spectacularly corrupt" SBA set-aside program (114-15). (Scandalous misuses of taxpayers' money in SBA programs were repeatedly exposed

At that time, the median household income of Asian Indians in the United States (most of whom were immigrants) was $48,320; the median household income of European immigrants, who are not eligible for affirmative action, was $30,892 (Graham 2002: 148). In the 2000, census, the median household income of Indian immigrants was $70,000; the median household income of immigrants from Europe, Canada, and Australia was $51,000. In the 2000 census, 24 percent of native-born Americans were college graduates. Among immigrants, the percentages of college graduates were 69 of Indians, 67 of Taiwanese, 58 of Nigerians, 51 of Pakistanis, 50 from Hong Kong, 46 of Filipinos, 43 of Koreans and Japanese, and 42 of Chinese (Portes and Rumbaut 2006: 69, 89). All these immigrants and their descendants are eligible for affirmative action.[210]

I pointed out that this absurd situation came about because the public had no idea that it was happening. The public's lack of awareness has been maintained both by the resolute ignorance of the media and by the equally resolute determination of most opponents of affirmative action to avoid defending its real victims—whites— and, consequently, to dwell on the harm it supposedly causes to blacks, Hispanics, and Asians.

ᘓ ᘔ

since the beginning of Nixon's presidency (86- 89, 111, 115-17).)

The SBA continued to grow during the Bush and Clinton administrations. In President Clinton's 2000 budget its loan budget was $14 billion (125). No white man, no matter how disadvantaged his background, has a chance of inclusion. In 1996, eight white women were in the SBA set-aside program (126). Moreover, the SBA's definition of "small' encompasses 99 percent of American businesses (129). I will add to Bean's account that in 2009, the SBA held more than $45 billion of loans, making it the largest single backer of businesses in the United States.

210. Asian Indians in the United States are more successful than white Americans because immigrants from India are much more intelligent than most Indians. American North-East Asians (Chinese, Japanese, and Koreans) are more intelligent than white Americans both because more intelligent North-East Asians immigrate to the United States and because North-East Asians in general are more intelligent than whites. The difference in average IQ between North-East Asians and whites is only approximately three points (Herrnstein and Murray 1996: 272-6). However, as I discuss in Section E of Appendix III, when attributes are distributed along a bell curve, small differences in averages produce great differences at the curve's extremes. Consequently, if one group of people has an average IQ three points higher than another group, then 31 percent more of the former have IQs over 120 than the latter and 42 percent more over 135 (Herrnstein and Murray 1996: 364-8).

CR SO

Appendix II
Constitutionality, Legality, and Democracy

A. Constitutionality

> No state shall make or enforce any law which shall abridge the
> privileges or immunities of citizens of the United States; nor shall
> any state deprive any person of life, liberty, or property, without due
> process of law; nor deny to any person within its jurisdiction the
> equal protection of the laws.
>   (Section One of the Fourteenth Amendment)

Since the Supreme Court's decision in 1954 in *Brown v. Board of Education of Topeka, Shawnee County, Kansas*, this prohibition has been the basis of the argument that racial discrimination—first anti-black, later anti-white—is unconstitutional. In the *Brown* decision, in which the Supreme Court ruled that this prohibition made racially segregated public schools illegal, it stated (#489) that what the "Congress and the state legislatures [that enacted and ratified the Fourteenth Amendment] had in mind cannot be determined with any degree of certainty." That is not true, and the Court knew it was not true. During the congressional debate over the Fourteenth Amendment, its supporters constantly guaranteed that it did not prohibit segregated schools. In fact, the same Congress that passed the Fourteenth Amendment, in 1866, funded a *de jure* racially segregated school system in Washington, DC; and that fact was pointed out in the segregation cases that the Supreme Court considered before *Brown* and in the debate over *Brown* itself (Tushnet 1994: 140, 170-71, 184, 191, 196-9, 212). Moreover, most of the state legislatures that ratified the Fourteenth Amendment permitted or required racially segregated school systems.[211]

Nor did the congressmen who voted for the Fourteenth Amendment

---

211. Klarman 1995: 1885-88. Klarman begins his informative study by observing, "[T]he overwhelming consensus among legal academics has been that *Brown* cannot be defended" as "consonant with the original understanding of the Fourteenth Amendment."

think they were banning government programs that targeted specific races. Nearly all the congressional supporters of the Fourteenth Amendment voted for federal programs that provided Negroes with food, education, land, legal aid, and other assistance, much of which was unavailable to poor whites. (Most Southern states did not provide free public education at the time.) These programs did not require their beneficiaries to be ex-slaves, poor, or victims of prior discrimination. The congressmen who supported these programs, nearly all of whom also voted for the Fourteenth Amendment, supported them over the objection that directing government assistance to a specified race was un-American, immoral and irrational, since some of the tax money came from poor whites and went to rich blacks (Schnapper 1985; Rubenfeld 1997: 427, 430-31).

In fact, "equal protection of the law" did not even bar states from denying American citizens the right to vote. Section Two of the Fourteenth Amendment states that if a state denies the right to vote to any of its male citizens over the age of 21, its representation in the House of Representatives will be reduced by the proportion of its citizens who are denied the vote.

The Fourteenth Amendment was a conservative alternative to an amendment proposed by Thaddeus Stevens, the leader in the radical Republicans in the House: "All national and state laws shall be equally applicable to every citizen, and no discrimination shall be made on account of race and color" (Kull 1992: 67). However, that was too radical for Congress, which passed instead the Fourteenth Amendment. Stevens said about the Fourteenth Amendment, "It falls far short of my wishes, but . . . I believe it is all that can be obtained in the present state of public opinion." He paraphrased Section One as:

Whatever law punishes a white man for a crime shall punish the black man precisely in the same way and to the same degree. Whatever law protects the white man shall afford equal protection to the black man. Whatever means of redress is afforded to one shall be afforded to all (*Congressional Globe*, Thirty-ninth Congress, May 8, 1866: 2459).

B. Legality

Opponents of affirmative action repeatedly point out that in *Griggs* and subsequent decisions, which I discuss in Section B of Chapter 18, the Supreme Court purported to enforce Title VII of the Civil Rights Act of 1964, but it actually subverted its manifest meaning. They quote especially three Sections of Title VII:

703(a)(1): It shall be an unlawful employment practice for an employer to . . . discriminate against any individual . . , because of such individual's race, color, sex or national origin.

703(h): [N]or shall it be an unlawful employment practice for an employer to give and act upon the results of any professionally developed ability test provided that such test, its use or action upon the results is not designed, intended, or used to discriminate because of race, color, religion, sex or national origin.

703(j): Nothing contained in this title shall be interpreted to require any employer . . . to grant preferential treatment to any individual or to any group on account of any imbalance which may exist with respect to the total number or percentages of persons of any race, color, religion or sex, or national origin employed by any employer.

Opponents of affirmative action also frequently quote the emphatic guarantees that the supporters of Title VII kept giving during the congressional debate over its passage. For example, its floor managers in the Senate, Joseph Clark and Clifford Case, stated,

There is no requirement in Title VII that employers abandon bona fide qualification tests where, because of differences in background and education, members of some groups are able to perform better on these tests than members of other groups.

[A]ny deliberate attempt to maintain a racial balance . . . would involve a violation of Title VII.

[N]o court could read Title VII as requiring an employer to lower or change the occupational qualifications he sets for his employees simply because proportionally fewer Negroes than whites meet them.[212]

During the debate, Senator Tower brought up a ruling by the Illinois Fair Employment Practices Commission that a general ability test used by Motorola as a criterion for hiring violated the Illinois Fair Practices Code because it was "unfair to culturally deprived and disadvantaged groups." Senator Case guaranteed, "the Attorney General and his office . . . have all worked diligently to avoid any possibility of such abuse;" and the Senate added Section 703h (quoted above) to Title VII to ensure that (Epstein 1992: 190-91: Graham 1990: 149-50).

Nevertheless, seven years later, in 1971, in its *Griggs* decision, the Supreme Court ruled that the Duke Power Company violated Title VII

---

212. 110 *Congressional Record* (1964) 7213, 7246-47. Epstein (1992: 160-65, 186-90) and Graham (1990: 150-51, 192-3, 198, 387-8) quote many similar guarantees by Title VII's supporters.

of the Civil Rights Act by using standard ability tests because they had a disparate impact on blacks and whites, even though the purpose of the tests was clearly not discriminatory.

However, in *Griggs* the Supreme Court observed accurately (#433) that it was following the guidelines of the Equal Employment Opportunity Commission (EEOC), which Title VII created to monitor employment discrimination and which assumed from its inception that statistical racial inequality meant discrimination.[213] The Labor Department and its Office of Federal Contract Compliance Programs (OFCC) also interpreted Title VI of the Civil Rights Act, which banned racial discrimination by federal contractors, as banning statistical inequality.[214]

Moreover, by the time of the *Griggs* decision, Congress had defeated the one attempt ever made to thwart the federal bureaucracy's interpretation of Title VI and Title VII. In 1967, Philadelphia's Federal Executive Board searched for racial discrimination in unions in the Philadelphia area. It managed to find it, but only among six craft unions to which four percent of Philadelphia's union members belonged. On that basis, bidders for federal construction contracts in Philadelphia were ordered to submit to the OFCC detailed lists of the number of minorities they would employ in all trade categories, and the OFCC would determine if they were "adequate." However, Elmer Staats, the controller general of the United States, ruled that this "Philadelphia Plan" violated Title VII of the Civil Rights Act. President Johnson's Labor Department rescinded it in November 1968. But in early 1969, the Labor Department of newly elected Republican President Nixon resurrected it. Nixon's Labor Department claimed that it did not violate the Civil Rights Act because it set a range of the percentages of minorities that must be hired, not a specific percentage, and it was sufficient for an employer to show that he had made "every good faith effort" to meet that range. However, Staats ruled again that it was illegal, and Senator Byrd added a rider to a hurricane relief bill that stated that no congressional appropriation could be used to finance any contract or agreement that the controller general found to violate a federal statute. The Senate passed the Byrd rider by 52 to 37. President Nixon then threatened to veto the Byrd rider if the House of Representatives also passed it, and he got Gerald Ford, the Republican

---

213. Roberts and Stratton 1995: 88-95; Graham 1990: 241-2; Skrentny 1996: 127-30.

214. Title VI stated, "No person in the United States shall, on the ground of race, color, or national origin . . . be subjected to discrimination under any program or activity receiving Federal financial assistance." (The tax-exempt status of non-commercial institutions, like universities, was interpreted as federal financial assistance.)

leader in the House and his successor as president, to make opposition to it a test of party loyalty. In the House vote, on December 22, 1969, Democrats supported the Byrd rider 115-84, but Republicans opposed it 124-41, which was enough to defeat it. Thus, it was House Republicans, a Republican president, and a future Republican president who defeated the one congressional attempt to preserve the clear meaning of the Civil Rights Act (Graham 1990: 284-97, 326-40; 2002: 32-3, 67-74, 138, 216, note 14).

After the defeat of the Byrd rider, the head of the AFL-CIO disclosed that the evidence of discrimination by the six Philadelphia unions that was used to justify the Philadelphia Plan "consisted of a memorandum by one government employee quoting the 'conservative estimate' of another government employee." On January 15, 1970, Senator Ervin announced that he had discovered that while President Nixon's Labor Department was assuring Congress that the Philadelphia Plan applied only to the practices by which construction workers were hired in Philadelphia and required only a "good faith effort" by contractors, it had secretly prepared a totally different order (Order Number 4), which it issued in early 1970. Order Number 4 applied to all federal contractors, which meant it covered between a third and half of American workers; and it required that for all contracts over $50,000, "The rate of minority applicants recruited should approximate or equal the ratio of minorities to [sic] the applicant population in each location" (Graham 1990: 341-3).

In 1971, Nixon's Labor Department issued Revised Order Number 4, which added women to the provisions of Order Number 4 and stipulated that government contractors and subcontractors must have the correct demographic proportions at all levels of employment (Graham 1990: 412-13).

By 1972, government-enforced statistical equality had generated such momentum and become so ingrained that Congress passed the Equal Employment Opportunity Act, which amended Title VII of the Civil Rights Act in such a way as to confirm *Griggs*. It strengthened the enforcement power of the EEOC and increased the discretion that federal judges had in applying affirmative action. At the same time, the Senate rejected, by a 44 to 22 margin, an amendment that stipulated that courts and government agencies could not require an employer "to practice discrimination in reverse by employing persons of a particular race . . . in either fixed or variable numbers, proportions, percentages, quotas, goals, or ranges." In the congressional discussion that preceded its passage, the fact was noted as a problem to be solved that the median income of black American families was $6,280, and of whites, $10,235, and that blacks held only three percent of American professional, managerial, and technical jobs (Wolters 1996: 158-9; Epstein 1992: 201-2). The Senate Report that accompanied the Act stated,

In 1964, employment discrimination tended to be viewed as a series of isolated . . . events, for the most part due to ill-will on the part of some identifiable individual or organization. . . . Experience has shown this view to be false. Employment discrimination as viewed today is a . . . pervasive phenomenon. Experts . . . now generally describe the problem in terms of "systems" and "effects" rather than simply intentional wrongs, and the literature on the subject is replete with discussion of . . . perpetuation of the pre-[1964] Act discriminatory practices through . . . testing and validation requirements (Epstein 1992: 202).

In 1977, Congress passed an amendment to the Public Works Employment Act that required at least ten percent of the $4 billion appropriation for public works projects go to businesses that were at least fifty percent owned by "Negroes, Spanish-speaking [*sic*], Orientals, [American] Indians, Eskimos, and Aleuts." The supporters of this amendment presented no evidence that any of these groups had ever suffered discrimination in government contracting, not even anecdotal evidence. The only fact they cited was that only one percent of federal contract dollars went to them. It was the first time in over a century that Congress explicitly identified the beneficiaries of a law by race or ethnicity. Yet, the House and Senate passed it by votes of 335-77 and 71-14 (Graham 2002: 88-91; Epstein 1992: 429-30).

Subsequently, both Republican and Democratic Congresses and presidents constantly expanded the scope of contracts that had to be "set aside" for minority contractors. In 1998, Congress, with substantial Republican majorities in both houses, required that ten percent of the entire federal procurement budget be set aside for minority contractors. That meant that whites were barred by their race from bidding on $117 *billion* in federal spending, nearly all of which was paid by their taxes; and that amount has constantly risen as federal spending rises (Graham 2002: 7). Mandatory set-asides for minority owned businesses have been constantly expanded in spite of repeated exposures of pervasive, blatant fraud.[215]

215. Yates 1994: 6-20. Three articles in the liberal *New Republic* in the middle 1980s examined and illustrated the absurdities inherent in minority set-aside programs.

An editorial on May 5, 1986, page 10 ("Set Set-Asides Aside") cited studies that uncovered omnipresent fraud and observed:

More study is the last thing this subject needs. After a trial period of nearly 20 years, it's clear that minority set asides are an abysmal failure. They've consistently been susceptible to widespread corruption. . . . The ten percent [of government contracts set aside for

minorities] provision applies just as much to Vermont, which has a
minority population of less than one percent, as [to states with large
minority populations] . . . To comply with its quota, Vermont has to
hire already successful black contracting firms in Massachusetts . .
. State and local set-aside laws have also included provisions with
quotas as high as 35 percent. Most recently, in 1983 President Reagan
issued an executive order requiring all federal agencies to . . . establish
minority contracting "objectives." These programs breed two kinds
of corruption. . . . In the first, firms that are actually owned by whites
employ black owners as fronts. The second involves actual minority
contracting firms that may not own a single shovel, winning contracts
in protected markets, and "brokering" subcontracts to white-owned
firms. . . . The Federal Highway Administration estimates that its
set-aside program added $180 million to its contracting costs in 1984
alone. . . . There's no evidence to support the assertion that set-asides
help black firms get started and gradually wean them from government handouts. . . . [I]n 1980, 12 years after 8(a) [set-asides] began,
exactly one firm graduated [from government assistance].

An article in the *New Republic* of December 24, 1984 (page 17) ("The
Set-Aside Scam") also cited numerous exposures of fraud in municipal,
state, and federal minority set-aside programs and observed that they are
ubiquitous: "billions [of dollars] in contracts for [building and maintaining]
subways, hospitals, schools, waterworks." The article quoted Herbert Hill,
"who as national director of the N.A.A.C.P. in the 1960s played a central
role in developing the set-aside program and getting it written into federal
law." Hill said, "What had a tremendous potential has been largely negated
as a result of corruption."

An article in the *New Republic* of October 21, 1985 (page 4) ("Com-
passion Reagan-Style") also cited many cases of fraud. For example, "[A]
national newsstand chain had given a one-fifth interest in their franchise at
O'Hare airport, worth millions of dollars, to a politically well-connected
black lawyer with no experience in the business, all for an investment of
$100." The article also observed that even if there were no corruption,
"Obviously it costs money every time government business goes to someone other than the lowest bidder." The owners of even legitimate minority
businesses are much richer than the average American, whose taxes pay for
these programs: "What's the point? I suppose there is some sense in which
black millionaires are more 'disadvantaged' than white millionaires. But is
this really a disadvantage we need to build social policy around?"

Since these articles appeared, the amount of money involved in minority
set-aside programs has increased exponentially. Typically, the *New Repub-*

How did categorical condemnation of racial discrimination become mandatory racial discrimination so quickly? The answer can be found in the Supreme Court's decision in *International Brotherhood of Teamsters v. United States* (1973). The Court observed (#335), "Undoubtedly disparate treatment [not impact] was the most obvious evil Congress had in mind when it enacted Title VII," and quoted Senator Humphrey, one of Title VII's most ardent champions, "the bill . . . provides that men and women shall be employed on the basis of their qualifications." But the Court did not quote this in order to repudiate *Griggs*. It stated (#340; italics added):

> [A]n erroneous theory [is] that Title VII requires an employer's work force to be racially balanced. Statistics showing racial or ethnic imbalance are probative . . . only because . . . *it is ordinarily to be expected that nondiscriminatory hiring practices will in time result in a work force more or less representative of the racial and ethnic composition of the population from which the employees are hired.*

If Title VII's advocates, who unequivocally guaranteed that it forbade considerations of race, had been presented with this statement, I doubt whether any would have disagreed with it. In fact, the reports of the supporters of the Civil Rights Act of 1964, in both the Senate and House of Representatives, contained long lists that compared white and non-white unemployment rates, income, and occupational status throughout the United States as proof of discrimination and denial of equal opportunity and the consequent need for banning employment discrimination. The report of the House supporters of the Civil Rights Act began, "Testimony supporting the fact of discrimination in employment is overwhelming. . . . In 1962, nonwhites made up 11 percent of the civilian labor force, but 22 percent of the unemployed. . . . Moreover, among Negroes who are employed, their jobs are largely concentrated among semiskilled and unskilled occupations" (Blumrosen 1971: 272-8).

I pointed out in Chapter 1 that President Kennedy and Martin Luther King also assumed that statistical inequality must mean discrimination when they said, "race has no place in American life or law" and "I have a dream that my four little children will one day live in a nation where they will not be judged by the color of their skin, but by the content of their character."

C. Democracy

lic equated "minority" with "black." However, when these articles were published, every millionaire with an ancestor from Spanish-speaking Latin America or from anywhere in Asia east of Iran was eligible for minority set-aside contracts.

John Skrentny (1996: 3) observed that in the 1960s, "advocacy of racial preference was one of those 'third rails' of American politics: Touch it and you die." Hugh Graham (2002: 88) pointed out that advocacy of racial preference has remained "the third rail of American politics" ever since. The reason is obvious from the many opinion surveys about affirmative action. Peter Schuck observed that every one has found that "opposition to, and anger over, affirmative action is pervasive among the white public and is just as strong among whites on the political left as among those on the political right." "No researcher in this field doubts . . . that the public's opinion remains decidedly and intensely negative."[216] Schuck also pointed out (2003: 171), "[I]f the public knew how large affirmative action preferences . . . actually are, opposition would probably be even more intense than it is." The public's hostility would also be much more intense if it fully realized that nearly all the beneficiaries of affirmative action are descendants of people who have received preferential treatment from the time they or their ancestors entered the United States.

Schuck observed (172) that affirmative action

> has been sustained by strong support by ethnic organizations, national media, leading educational institutions, large corporations, government bureaucracies, mainstream foundations and other opinion leaders. . . . Large corporations' strong support for affirmative action might seem counterintuitive . . . [but affirmative action] tend[s] to advantage large companies by imposing onerous reporting, staffing, and other compliance costs on smaller competitors who cannot bear them easily.

Government policy makers are aware of the public's hostility. In Appendix I, I illustrated the accuracy of Hugh Graham's observation (2002: 140) that un-elected government agencies constantly increased the number of ethnic groups that were eligible for affirmative action in "a closed process of bureaucratic policymaking largely devoid not only of public testimony but even of public awareness that policy was being made." Elected officials have also constantly expanded affirmative action by stealth: Congress by attaching affirmative action amendments to other bills in order to avoid committee hearings and floor debates, and presidents by issuing orders to the federal bureaucracy without any announcement to the public. Examples of the congressional amendment strategy are the minority set-asides that I discussed in Section B of Appendix II: the Public Works Employment Act of 1977 and the requirement voted by a Republican-controlled Congress in

---

216. 2003: 170-71; cf. Swain 2002: 190-97; Kuran 1995: 139-43, 372, note 13.

1998 that ten percent of the entire federal procurement budget be set aside for minority contractors. Neither the Senate nor the House held hearings on the former, and they passed it "after only a perfunctory floor discussion" (Graham 2002: 88). The latter was "quietly attached to an appropriation bill" and "passed largely unnoticed in the American media" (Graham 2002: 7).

> Similar preferences appear in appropriation or authorization acts governing . . . a wide variety of areas—agriculture, communications, defense, education, public works, transportation, foreign relations, energy and water development, banking, scientific research, and space exploration, among others. For instance, the Omnibus Diplomatic Security and Antiterrorism Act contains a minority set-aside in the allocation of funds appropriated for diplomatic security. . . . Other programs channel federal funds into minority neighborhoods, minority-owned banks . . . Thus, 10 percent of the Eisenhower Exchange Fellowship Program funds are "available only for participation by individuals who are representative of the United States minority populations." . . . These are all programs of which the American public is barely aware. Indeed they are often adopted surreptitiously (Thernstrom 1997: 441).

Examples of presidential orders are Order Number 4 and Revised Order Number 4, which I discussed in Section B of Appendix II. Order Number 4 required that for all federal contractors, who employ between a third and a half of the American work force, "the rate of minority applicants recruited should approximate or equal the ratio of minorities to [*sic*] the applicant population in each location" (Graham 1990: 341-3). Revised Order Number 4 added women to the provisions of Order Number 4 and stipulated that government contractors and subcontractors must have the correct demographic proportions at all levels of employment. High Graham (1990: 412-13) observed that it was published

> in the *Federal Register* on the last day of August, when the Labor Day holiday left Washington virtually depopulated. Then on a *Saturday* [the italics are Graham's] in early December, Revised Order No. 4 was officially promulgated to a non-observant nation. The *Wall Street Journal*, normally ever-vigilant for intrusions on entrepreneurial freedom by federal bureaucrats, registered it with a yawn on the fourth column of page 30.

In addition to issuing Order Number 4 and Revised Order Number 4, President Nixon's administration also increased the staff of the EEOC from 359 in 1968 to 1,640 in 1972 (Graham 1990: 448); and, over the objections of congressional Democrats, increased the value of set-aside contracts for minority businesses from $68 million in 1971 to $272 million in 1974, even though in 1973 two-thirds of these companies were delinquent in fulfilling these contracts. (In 1968, the year before Nixon became president, only eight minority set-aside contracts had been granted.) (Bean 2001: 66, 90-92).

However, in March 1972, with the next presidential election only eight months away, Nixon made a televised address to the nation demanding immediate congressional action to stop school busing for racial balance; in August, in his acceptance speech at the Republican convention, he said, "the way to end discrimination against some is not to begin discrimination against others;" in a Labor Day radio address, he said, "quotas are a danger-ous detour away from the traditional value of measuring a person on the basis of ability." Nixon knew that a large majority of Americans was opposed to race being considered in social, economic and political policies. The public could not be kept ignorant about school busing. However, with the help of the media, Nixon kept Order Number 4 and Revised Order Number 4 secret; and his radical expansion of the budget for affirmative-action enforcement agencies was "almost unnoticed" (Graham 1990: 445-8).

Very different was the pervasive publicity that accompanied the passage of the Civil Rights Act of 1964 and the Voting Rights Act of 1965, since they expressed the wish of a large majority of Americans for a non-racial society. The Immigration and Naturalization Act of 1965 had the same goal, but it received little media coverage since it was intended as a symbolic affirmation of non-racialism that would not affect American society. The law's sponsors in Congress and President Johnson's administration repeatedly guaranteed that it would not increase immigration or change the ethnic make-up of the United States. That guarantee was necessary since public opinion polls found that two-thirds of Americans opposed increasing the number of immigrants (Graham 2002: 60-64). As Hugh Graham observed (2002: 8):

> [I]n immigration policy, the reforms of 1965, intended to purge na-
> tional origin quotas but not to expand immigration or to change its
> character, produced instead a flood of new arrivals . . . [T]he ancestry
> of most immigrants . . . entitled them to . . . priority over . . . native-
> born Americans under affirmative action regulations. Congress in the
> 1960s never intended to create such a system. And it is doubtful that
> any Congress (or White House) today, in the twenty-first century,
> would build such a system anew and defend it before voters.

Even more incredibly, priority over native-born Americans is granted even to the offspring of non-European illegal immigrants, who have also been allowed to pour into the United States. Graham pointed out (2002: 11), in the form of questions, other fundamental aspects of post-1965 American immigration policy that no government would try to defend before voters:

> Why does American policy permit such a massive inflow of illegal entries? Why does policy for legal entry admit such huge numbers of poorly educated immigrants, ill suited for the knowledge-based economy of the future and requiring heavy social service expenditures? Why does U.S. policy allow immigrant flows to be determined externally . . . by kinship ties rather than internally by national needs? Why does the United States lack a modern, computer-based worker identification system, common to most other developed countries [which would detect the employment of illegal immigrants]?

Public opinion surveys have continued to find that a large majority of Americans—white, black, and Hispanic—want legal immigration reduced or ended, illegal immigrants barred from welfare benefits, and employers punished for employing illegal immigrants (Graham 2002: 112-13; Swain 2002: 100). Yet, the number of immigrants continues to increase, and no serious attempt has been made to penalize employers of illegal immigrants (Graham 2002: 122-28, 179).

CR SO

Appendix III: The SAT and Similar Tests

A. What SAT Correlations Mean

In Chapter 13, I point out that all studies of the SAT have found that it is an extremely accurate predictor of performance in college, graduate and professional schools, and "real world" activities. I also point out that a meta-analysis (Hezlett, et al., 2001) of 3,000 studies involving cumulatively more than a million students found that the SAT accurately predicts grades through all four years of college; and the correlation between SAT scores and freshman grade-point-average (FGPA) ranged from .44 to .62, when adjusted for restriction of range. A study (Kobrin, et al., 2008) of the effectiveness of the revised, post-2004 SAT involving 151,316 freshmen at 110 colleges and universities found that it correlates .53 with FGPA. Furthermore, the cor-relation of SAT with FGPA is higher for non-whites, especially blacks, than for whites. I also point out in Chapter 13 that a correlation between college grades and SAT scores of much above .60 would be impossible because of the unreliability of grading and the fact that students with high SAT scores take more difficult courses than student with low SAT scores. However, if the correlation is adjusted for difficulty of courses taken and stringency of grading, the correlation is .75 (Ramsit, et al., 1994: 3).

A correlation of even .50 is much more significant than a person who is ignorant of statistics would suspect. Here, I will consider it from the perspective of the admissions process, which is the way admissions tests are used. Let us consider as an example a hypothetical college that admits 10 percent of its applicants, and 20 percent of its applicants would fail to graduate if they were admitted. If this college admits applicants at random, then 20 percent of its students will drop out. If it admits on the basis of a test with a .50 correlation with college GPA, then only 3 percent of its students will drop out. If 5 percent of its applicants would perform in a manner that it regards as superb and it admits at random, then 5 percent of its students will have superb college performances. If it uses a test with a .50 correlation with college GPA, then 19 percent of the students it admits will perform superbly.

A common argument against using the SAT is that high school GPA (HSGPA) correlates with SAT scores, so HSGPA alone provides most of the predictive information that the SAT provides. The people who use this argument concede that using the SAT in combination with HSGPA adds to the predictive accuracy of HSGPA, but they argue that the increase is not significant. This argument relies on the public's ignorance of statistics. Suppose that HSGPA correlates .40 with college performance, and a combination of HSGPA with an admissions test raises that by only .20 (to .60). Then, if the hypothetical college we have been considering admitted at random, 20 percent of its students would drop out and 5 percent would perform superbly; if it admitted on the basis of only HSGPA, 5 percent would drop out and 16 percent would perform superbly; but if it used a combination of HSGPA and the test, 1 percent of its students would drop out and 24 percent would perform superbly.

Of course, these same correlations apply equally for an employer using a qualifying test to determine which job applicants will be satisfactory and which will be outstanding.[217]

B. Preparation/Coaching[218]

In 1981, Samuel Messick and Ann Jungeblut meta-analyzed the studies that had been done of the effectiveness of all types of preparation for the SAT,

---

217. Taylor and Russell (1939) provide charts that show the effect of using qualifications of different predictive correlations at all degrees of selectivity.

218. The five articles that I outline in this section were all published in world-renowned psychological, educational, and statistical journals. They are:

Messick and Jungeblut, "Time and Method in Coaching for the SAT." *Psychological Bulletin* 89.2 (1981): 191-216.

DerSimonian and Laird, "Evaluating the Effect of Coaching on SAT Scores: A Meta-Analysis." *Harvard Educational Review* 53.1 (1983): 1-15.

Becker, "Coaching for the Scholastic Aptitude Test: Further Synthesis and Appraisal." *Review of Educational Research* 60 (1990): 373-417.

Powers and Rock, "Effects of Coaching on SAT I: Reasoning Score." *Journal of Educational Measurement* 36 (1999): 93-118.

Briggs, "The Effect of Admissions Test Preparation: Evidence from NELS: 88." *Chance* 14.1 (2001): 10-18. (*Chance* is the journal of the American Statistical Association.)

No contradictory evidence or arguments have ever been published in a peer-reviewed, scholarly journal.

from commercial courses to students practicing sample questions on their own. They found that the effectiveness of preparation declines constantly with the amount of time expended. A hundred hours of preparation raises the Verbal score, which is more important than the Math score, by an average of 24 points; 260 hours is required to raise it by 30 points, and 1,185 hours to raise it by 40 points. Obviously, students would increase their chance of college admission much more by devoting that time to school courses, in which grades are more influenced by learning than are SAT scores.

Messick and Jungeblut's analysis is still widely cited. For example, Herrnstein and Murray in *The Bell Curve* (1996: 401) called it the best analysis of the effect on SAT coaching. However, in 1983, Rebecca DerSimonian and Nan Laird reanalyzed Messick and Jungeblut's data and corrected a serious methodological oversight. Messick and Jungeblut did not consider the sampling variability or design of the studies they used. DerSimonian and Laird found that in "a breakdown of the studies by controlled, uncontrolled, and matched and randomized groups . . . the difference in the estimated mean gains is . . . remarkably consistent for both verbal and math studies." They concluded that on each SAT test, "the real gains are likely to be small—around 10 points and almost certainly less than 15."

In 1990, Betsy Becker conducted the most comprehensive meta-analysis ever done of studies on how preparation affects SAT performance. She found that in the 48 studies she analyzed, the average gain from preparation was 9 points in Verbal and 19 in Math, but the more carefully conducted a study was, the less gain it found.

In 1999, Donald Powers and Donald Rock published a report of an investigation that concentrated on commercial SAT coaching programs. They analyzed the performance of 4,200 students who took the SAT in 1995-96, of whom 507 had attended a commercial SAT preparation program outside their school. Of these, 220 had taken a program offered by one of the two major preparation firms: Kaplan Educational Centers, which claimed to increase Verbal+Math SAT scores by an average of 120 points; and Princeton Review, which claimed to increase Verbal+Math SAT scores by an average of 140 points. Powers and Rock found that "medians for all analyses and over all programs were 8 points for verbal scores and 18 for math." They pointed out that "the estimates computed here for the two major commercial test preparation companies [Kaplan and Princeton] are generally consistent with the results of [other] studies that have provided estimates for these companies."

In 2001, Derek Briggs studied the performance of 4,730 students who had taken the Preliminary SAT (PSAT) and the SAT or ACT. He found that commercial SAT preparation courses improved performance by 13 points on the Verbal section and 17 on the Math; a private tutor by 7 and 19 points; an SAT preparation book by 4 and 7 points; a high school preparation course by 2 and 3 points; computer programs and videos had no effect at all. However, students who took commercial preparation courses were more likely than other students to be Asian, to do more homework, have higher PSAT scores, and have private tutors who helped them with their schoolwork. When Briggs equalized students who took a commercial preparation course with those who did not for these and other variables, the effect of a commercial preparation course was 6-8 points on SAT Verbal and 14-15 on Math. On ACT tests, which are graded on a 36-point scale, the effect was 0-0.4 on Math, 0.3-0.6 on English, and *minus* 0.6-0.7 on Reading Comprehension.

Even if coaching did have a significant impact, it would not explain the racial gap. The nearly universal assumption that whites get more preparation than minorities is not true. In Powers and Rock's database of students who took a formal SAT preparation program outside their school, 11 percent were black, and 58 percent were white. Both blacks and whites were slightly underrepresented compared with their proportion of the American student population in the 1990s. But blacks were less underrepresented than whites. That means that a higher proportion of blacks than whites took these courses. (The reason that both blacks and whites were underrepresented in these courses is that Asians were vastly overrepresented. Twenty-one percent of the students in these courses were Asians.)

A study by the Law School Admission Council found that in 1996-97, 28 percent of the blacks, 31 percent of the whites, and 38 percent of the Hispanics who took the Law School Admission Test had taken a preparatory course.[219]

C. Cultural Bias

For the subject of cultural bias, I will quote the *Journal of Blacks in Higher Education* (*JBHE*). An article in the Spring 1997 issue of *JBHE* (pages 28-9), entitled "After Many Years of Repair, the Test Content of the SAT Now Appears Fair," pointed out:

> [C]ulturally biased questions were removed from the SAT more than two decades ago. Since that time exhaustive efforts have been made by the Educational Testing Service to purge such cultural biases from the SAT. Before the test is given to students, it is picked over with a fine-tooth comb by experts in American language and culture.

219. "Theory of Unequal Access for Minorities to Test-Preparation Courses Is Challenged." *Chronicle of Higher Education* (May 22, 1998): A45.

Any question that might have even a possible or remote element of cultural bias is removed. Now consider the mathematics portion of the test. It would be extremely difficult to find cultural bias lurking in an algebraic equation or in the proof of a geometric theorem.

An article in the Summer 1998 issue of *JBHE* ("Does Black English Hamper African-American Students in the Study of Mathematics?:" 55) stated:

> As much as this journal deplores the exclusionary powers of standardized tests to deny admission to college and graduate school, it long has been our opinion that cultural and racial bias, although once a significant problem, has little or nothing to do with the black-white scoring gap on the Scholastic Assessment Test [SAT] and other standardized tests used for admission to college and graduate schools.[220]

D. The SAT and Other Measures of Mental Ability Overpredict the Performance of Lower Scoring Groups

Although the content of the SAT is not culturally biased, its results do have a serious bias. A member of a higher scoring group will, on average, do much better in college than a member of a lower scoring group who has the same SAT score. This is part of a universal tendency for measures of mental ability to overpredict the performance of members of lower scoring groups. In other words, they are biased in favor of lower scoring groups.

James Coleman, et al., (1966: Supplemental Appendix 9.10) conducted by far the most extensive study of pre-university testing ever undertaken. They gave verbal and nonverbal IQ tests and tests of reading comprehension and mathematics achievement to 645,000 students in grades 3, 6, 9, and 12 in 4,000 American public schools. They also gave a test of general informa-

---

220. In an article on pages 1-43 of the Spring 2003 issue of the *Harvard Educational Review* ("Correcting the SAT's Ethnic and Social-Class Bias: A Method for Reestimating SAT Scores"), Roy Freedle said that he found that blacks tend to do better on hard verbal questions and worse on easy verbal questions than whites with the same SAT-Verbal score. He argued that the reason is that easy verbal questions measure cultural background. Of course, the media gave a great deal of publicity to Freedle's article (e.g., *The Atlantic Monthly*, November 2003, "The Bias Question"). However, Freedle's revised scores have not been validated as predictors of college performance. Even if they are found to be better predictors, they close the black-white gap by only five percent for test-takers at the median black score or higher. I will also point out that in this article, Freedle acknowledged that the SAT is an extremely valuable instrument for predicting college performance.

tion to students in grades 9 and 12 in those schools. Whites did considerably better on the tests of reading comprehension, mathematics achievement, and general information than blacks, Mexican Americans, and Native Americans with *the same IQ*. In other words, IQ tests overpredicted the performance of minorities relative to whites. Arthur Jensen (1980: 478-81) provides a chart that shows the degree of this overprediction and observed, "Blacks evince the largest degree of overprediction . . . [But] overestimation of [all] minority achievement test means [i.e., averages] is considerable, amounting to as much as half a standard deviation or more in some instances."

As for college performance, in *The Shape of the River* Bowen and Bok (1998: 77) observed:

> [I]f the black students in the C&B schools [their database] had been equivalent to all C&B students in their SAT scores, high school grades, socioeconomic status, and . . . gender, selectivity of school attended, field of study, being an athlete or not, they would still have had an average class rank that was, on average, roughly 16 percentile points lower than the class rank of apparently comparable classmates.

They pointed out that 16 percentiles is "both highly significant and large." In fact, in their database (page 75) the average black with a combined Verbal+Math SAT score of over 1300 had a college GPA in the 36th percentile; the average white with a combined SAT score of less than 1000 had a college GPA in the 40th percentile. They also pointed out (page 78) that the fact that SAT scores greatly overpredict the college performance of blacks (i.e., the SAT is massively biased in favor of blacks) "is consistent with the results of a considerable amount of other research."[221] The reader should remember that this enormous overprediction occurs even though blacks get preferences in college grading and, as I discuss in Chapter 12, take easier college courses than whites.

Bowen and Bok also observed (77, footnote 28) that in their database,

---

221. Bowen and Bok (78, footnote 29) cite three sources. In one, "Miller (1995)," I could find no information on this subject. I quote from their second source, Ramist, et al., 1994, below. Their third citation is "Jencks and Philips (forthcoming)," in which Vars and Bowen (1998) provided a thorough study of the huge overprediction of the SAT for blacks relative to whites, adjusting for all possible factors (parental education, occupation, and income; extra-curricular activities; etc.).

Previous studies are listed by Manning and Jackson (1984: 203-4) and Herrnstein and Murray (1996: 783, note 33 (note 33 is on page 759 of the 1994 edition)).

"Hispanic students also have a lower rank in class than one would predict on the basis of their SAT scores (after controlling for other variables), but the Hispanic-white gap is . . . roughly 9 percentile points, as compared with 16 points for black matriculants."

High school grade-point-average (HSGPA) overpredicts the college grades of blacks, Hispanics, and Native Americans by an even greater margin than the SAT does. Relative to the whole college population, the SAT overpredicts the freshman college grades of Native Americans by .29 of a grade-point (GP), blacks by .23 of a GP, and Hispanics by .13 of a GP. HSGPA overpredicts the freshman college grades of Native Americans by .32 of a GP, of blacks by .35 of a GP, and of Hispanics by .24 of a GP (Ramist, et al., 1994: 15).

The reader can appreciate the significance of these overpredictions from Bowen and Bok's description of the effect that the overprediction of the SAT for blacks has on their class rank.

By contrast, the SAT and HSGPA *under*predict the freshman college grades of whites by .01 and .03 of a GP, and of Asian Americans by .08 and .02 of a GP, relative to the whole college population. As could be expected by the fact that the average Asian's SAT score is higher than the average white's in Math but lower in Verbal, the SAT *under*predicts Asians' college grades in mathematics-based courses but *over*predicts them in courses in English (literature and writing) and in education (Ramist, et al., 1994: 15, 32).

The SAT also overpredicts the college grades of women relative to men in mathematics-based subjects[222] and of white Gentiles relative to Jews (Klitgaard (1985: 247, note 35). In Israel, admissions tests for colleges overpredict the performance of Israeli Arabs relative to Jews (Shavit 1990: 120, note 3).

The same is true in professional schools. The difference between the average score of minorities and whites on the NBME (National Board of Medical Examiners), which measures what students learn in medical school, is much greater than the average racial difference in scores on the Medical College Admission Test (MCAT), which is taken for admission to medical school. Significantly, the racial difference increases as students progress through medical school. On Part I of the NBME, which is taken at the end of the second year of medical school, the average difference between minorities and whites is a quarter of a standard deviation (SD) greater than the average racial difference on the MCAT. On Part II of the NBME, which is

222. The SAT's overprediction of women's performance in mathematics-based subjects occurs in courses intended for math, physical science, engineering, and economics majors, not in mathematics-based courses intended for non-majors (Steele 1997: 615-16).

taken at the end of the fourth year of medical school, the racial difference is two-fifths of a SD greater than the racial difference on the MCAT (Klitgaard 1985: 163, 246, notes 25-7). The same is true of grades in medical school. MCAT scores overpredict the grades of blacks and Hispanics in the third and fourth years by .37 and .26 of a SD, respectively, and *under*predict the grades of whites by .10. In other words, in the last two years of medical school, the average grades of blacks and Hispanics are .47 and .36 SD worse, respectively, than the average grades of whites with the same MCAT score (Huff, et al., 1999: S43). (I could not find information on racial under and overprediction for grades in the first two years of medical school.)

In Chapter 16, I discuss Linda Wightman's defense of affirmative action. Wightman pointed out (1997: 29-31, footnote 64) that in her database, which included 70 percent of all students who enrolled in American law schools in the fall of 1991, the Law School Admission Test (LSAT) and undergraduate grade-point-average (UGPA) had only one predictive defect: "LSAT and UGPA tend to overpredict minority group performance." This overprediction is large. For example, if a black and white have the same UGPA and LSAT score, the white's grade average at one of the top ten law schools will probably be one-half of a standard deviation higher than the black's. That is a huge difference, and it is despite affirmative grading (Klitgaard 1985: 162-3). Even more significant is the overprediction of minorities perfor- mance on the bar exam, which tests what students learn in law school. In Wightman's database, among law-school graduates, *of the Black students who would have been admitted if the sole admission criterion were the LSAT scores and UGPA*, 9.8 percent failed the bar exam on all attempts. Only 3.4 percent of whites who were admitted on the same basis failed to pass the bar exam on all attempts (Wightman 1997: 38). Richard Sander (2004: 446) provides a chart that shows the first-try failure rates on the bar exam of the whites and blacks in Wightman's database compared with their scores on the 1,000-point index on which law schools base admissions decisions. This index is a combination of LSAT score and UGPA. Because the LSAT is a better predictor of performance in law school and on the bar exam, it contributes 600 points to the index; UGPA contributes 400 points. There is a strong, consistent, negative correlation between scores on 1,000-point index and first-try failure rates on the bar exam. However, black failure rates are much higher than whites with the same index points. For example, of the students who entered law school with index points between 760 and 820, which is the highest point level that Sander provides, 12 percent of blacks and 5 percent of whites failed the bar exam on their first try. Blacks in the 580-640 range had the same failure rate (34 percent) as whites in the 460-520 range.

The Affirmative Action Hoax

Tests and other qualifications overpredict the performance of lower-scoring groups in job performance by as much as they do in universities. The panel appointed by the American Academy of Sciences to study the predictive accuracy of the General Aptitude Test Battery, found, based on a review of approximately 700 studies, that of blacks and whites who pass the test with the same score, 13 percent of the whites but 38 percent of the blacks do poorly on the job (Hartigan and Wigdor 1989; Gottfredson 1994: 960; Jencks 1998: 75-6).

A six-year study by the Civil Service Commission found that test scores overpredict the performance of blacks and Hispanics on work samples and tests of job knowledge, even though "there is no substantial difference in background or experience variables for different ethnic groups." Studies by private companies have come to the same conclusion. A review by the National Research Council concluded that in "studies in business and industrial settings," the overprediction of the performance of "minority group employees" is "similar [in magnitude] to results in academic settings." "And careful studies of 24 job areas in the U.S. Air Force found overprediction of the grades of black trainees compared to white trainees . . . averaged a little less than half of one standard deviation" (Klitgaard 1985: 164). Even Mark Kelman (1991: 1218-19), in an article that advocates the extension and intensification of affirmative action, conceded that qualifying tests overpredict the performance of black workers.

Moreover, the tendency of tests to overpredict the performance of lower scoring groups is greatest at the highest test scores (Vars and Bowen 1998: 470). For example, at colleges whose students' average SAT score is one standard deviation above the average of all colleges, the overprediction of blacks' academic performance corresponds to 240 Verbal+Math SAT points, when high school grades are held constant. "In other words, to have unbiased prediction for blacks compared to whites, you would have to subtract about 240 points from the blacks' [Verbal+Math SAT] test scores" (Klitgaard 1985: 164; cf. 162-3 for law schools). And that does not take into consideration the facts that blacks take easier college courses than whites and get preferential grading.

Before leaving this discussion, I must discuss the growing demand that universities supplement racial affirmative action with social-class affirmative action. I think that the main reason for this demand is that the American public has become increasingly aware that the children of wealthy, educated black and Hispanic parents receive preferences in university admission over the children of poor, uneducated whites and Asians. However, the universal tendency of qualifications to overpredict the performance of lower-scoring groups applies to social class as well as race and ethnicity. On average, high-school grades and college-entrance examinations overpredict by a large amount the college performance of students from poor families relative to students from rich families of the same race (Klitgaard 1986: 76-86, 147; Snyderman and Rothman 1988: 117). Whatever social advantages class-based affirmative action may confer, they must be balanced against the harm that it will do to every institution in which it is applied.

E. Re-Centering and Bell Curve Distributions

Beginning in April 1995, the curve on which SAT raw scores (number of answers right or wrong) are converted into reported scores was changed to make what had been the average raw score on the Verbal and Math sections in 1990 yield a reported score of 500, in the center of the 200-800 range. Since the average Verbal score had been in the 420s, the result was that a raw score on the Verbal section that previously yielded a reported score of 420 now yields a reported score of 500; and a raw score that previously yielded a reported score of 730 now yields a reported score of 800. As a result, the median Verbal+Math SAT score of freshmen who entered Yale in 1995 (and took the SAT in 1994) was 1375; the median of freshmen who entered Yale in 1997 was 1485 (Cross and Slater 1997: 8). As will be explained, most of this increase was caused by the rise in scores on the Verbal section.

Re-centering thus deprived the Verbal section of the ability to distinguish among test-takers who used to score between 730 and 800. This mutilation of the SAT occurred at the same time as grade inflation made high grades meaningless. In 2004, 41 percent of students who took the SAT had high school averages of A- and above (90-100 percent); 6 percent had high school averages of A+ (97-100 percent).

What was the purpose of ending the ability of the Verbal section to differentiate at the high end of the scale, where differentiation is most needed?

The distribution of nearly all biologically determined mental and physical traits forms a bell curve, and if the averages of two groups differ on a trait whose distribution forms a bell curve, then the difference between them becomes more and more pronounced at the extremes. For instance, 30 times more American men than women are five feet, ten inches tall (1.78 meters); but 2,000 times more American men than women are six feet tall (1.83 meters) (Pinker 2002: 344). For the same reason, in 2005, when the average Math SAT score of men was 538 and of women 504, the proportion of men and women with scores in each of the higher SAT-Math ranges were:

	Percent of men	Percent of women	Ratio
600-649	13	10	1.3 to 1
650-699	10	7	1.4 to 1
700-749	6	3	2 to 1
750-800	3	1	3 to 1

I will now provide examples of how this tendency affects whites and blacks.

The ACT is graded on a 1-36 scale. In 2005, nearly twelve percent of the students who took the ACT were black. The average white score was 21.9; the average black score was 17. Of the whites who took the ACT, 12.1 percent scored 28 or above (in the upper eight percent of test-takers) and 1.1 percent of the blacks. In absolute numbers, 94,955 whites and 1,473 blacks scored 28 or above, a ratio of 64 to 1; 1,116 whites and 5 blacks scored 35, a ratio of 223 to 1; 124 whites but no blacks scored 36.[223]

In 2002, one percent of the applicants to American law schools who got 165 and above on the LSAT were black, 0.7 percent of those who got 170 and above, and 0.025 percent of those who got 175 and above.[224]

When undergraduate grade-point-average (UGPA) is combined with scores on these tests, bell curve distributions are even more extreme. In 2002, of the 4,500 applicants to law school with UGPAs of at least 3.5 and LSAT scores of at least 165, 29 (0.65 percent) were black. Of applicants with UGPAs of at least 3.75 and at least a 170 LSAT score, 636 were white, 83 were Asians, and only one was black. (Over half of the students at Yale Law School were in this category.) (Kay 2003: 44).

The reader will now understand what the re-centering of 1995 accomplished. By truncating the Verbal scale at the high end, where racial differences are greatest, it lessened the average white-black difference and greatly reduced it at the top. Thus, the greatest reduction in racial differences was at highly selective universities, where the debate over academic affirmative action is most publicized.

Re-centering affected the upper end of Math scores less than Verbal scores because Math scores had been higher. (In 1994, the average Verbal

223. "The Harsh Truth on the Racial Scoring Gap on the ACT Standardized College Admissions Test." *Journal of Blacks in Higher Education* (*JBHE*) (Summer 2005): 10-11. Average racial ACT scores for every year from 1998 through 2007 are at http://nces.ed.gov/programs/digest/d07/tables/dt07_138.asp

224. "What If *Grutter* Had Gone the Other Way?" *JBHE* (Autumn 2003): 32-3.

score was 424; the average Math score was 479.) After re-centering, a reported score of 800 indicates a raw score that yielded 780 or above before re-centering. Because re-centering could not raise reported Math scores by as much as Verbal scores, bizarre changes were introduced throughout the scale. Raw scores that previously yielded scores of 750 and 760 were raised by only 10 points. Raw scores that previously yielded scores of between 720 and 740 were not raised at all. Raw scores that previously yielded reported scores between 660 and 710 now yield scores that are 10 points *lower*. Raw scores that yielded reported scores between 600 and 650 now yield the same scores. Below 600, reported scores were raised by a constantly increasing amount: by 10 points for pre-re-centered scores between 550 and 590, by 20 points for pre-re-centered scores between 500 and 540, by 30 points between 450 and 490, by 40 points between 390 and 440, and by 50 points between 320 and 380. The increase gradually declined for scores that were 320 and below before re-centering: to 40 points added to scores that were between 310 and 290, 30 points added to scores that were 270 and 260, etc.[225]

Surely, it is not a coincidence that in 1990, the year that provided the data on which re-centering was based, the average black score on the Math SAT was 352, right in the middle of the range in which Math scores were raised the most (Levin 1997: 233). It is also extremely unlikely that it is a coincidence that these changes in both reported Math and Verbal scores were instituted when universities were being forced to divulge the full extent of the racial discrepancies of their students' SAT scores.

I will point out here that most of the SAT scores I cite in this book are from after the re-centering, which significantly reduced reported racial differences.

F. The Racial Divergence of SAT Scores and Other Academic Measures

In 2003, in their decision in *Barbara Grutter v. Lee Bollinger, et al.*, in which a majority of the Supreme Court reaffirmed Justice Powell's ruling in *Bakke* that universities could practice racial discrimination, they stated (*Grutter* #63-4):

It would be a sad day indeed, were America to become a quota rid-

225. My source for the effect of the re-centering is page D3 of *USA Today*, May 31, 1995 ("How the Old and New SAT Scores Stack Up"), which provides a chart that shows pre-1995 Verbal and Math SAT scores and the corresponding recentered score. This chart is arranged in ten-point intervals (200, 210, etc.). That is why there is a ten-point interval between the ranges of old and new Math scores I report.

den society, with each identifiable minority assigned proportional representation in every desirable walk of life. But that is not the rationale for programs of preferential treatment; the acid test of their justification will be their efficacy in eliminating the need for any racial or ethnic preferences at all. . . . It has been 25 years since Justice Powell first approved the use of race . . . . Since that time, the number of minority applicants with high grades and test scores has indeed increased. We expect that in 25 years from now, the use of racial preferences will no longer be necessary to further the interest approved today.

Twenty-five years earlier, the *amicus curiae* brief that the American Association of Law Schools submitted in the *Bakke* case stated (#27), "the premise of these special admissions programs is that, in time, they will disappear. They are essentially a transitional device to correct a time lag."

Much publicity was accorded to the convergence of black and white SAT scores from 1976 to 1988. However, this convergence was caused nearly completely by rising black scores at the lowest end of the range. Fifty-one percent of the rise in blacks' average scores on the Verbal section of the SAT, which is more important than the Math section, was caused by the decline of the proportion scoring in the 200s, which was in the lowest two percent of all test-takers (Herrnstein and Murray 1996: 294). Such gains are nearly invariably one-time. The white-black gap in SAT scores stopped decreasing in 1988 and then began increasing. In 1988, the average white-black difference in Verbal+Math SAT was 189 points. In 2009, it was 209 points, the largest difference in the past twenty years. As will be shown, the increase in the white-black gap would have been greater had it not been for the 1995 re-centering of reported scores. In 2006, a Writing sample was added to the SAT. The difference between the average white and black scores on the Writing sample increased by five points between then and 2009.[226]

The *Journal of Blacks in Higher Education* of Autumn 1999 (pages 95-100) discussed the racial divergence in an article appropriately entitled "This Wasn't Supposed to Happen." It pointed out that it could not be caused by more blacks from poor families taking the SAT, since between 1997 and 1999, the number of blacks from families earning less than $20,000 a year who took the SAT decreased by two percent, while the number of blacks from families with incomes over $80,000 who took it increased by 27.6 percent.

The white-black difference has also increased from ACT, from 4.2 points

226. "The Persisting Racial Chasm in Scores on the SAT College Entrance Examination." *Journal of Blacks in Higher Education* (Autumn 2009): 84-9.

in 1998 (the earliest year for which I could find average racial scores) to 5.3 points in 2009 (on a 1-36 scale).

Even more astonishing has been the constant increase in the white-black gap on SAT-II tests, which examine knowledge and understanding of high-school subjects. The Spring 2009 issue of the *Journal of Blacks in Higher Education* (page 24) provided a table that showed the difference in average scores between whites and blacks on the eleven most-taken SAT-II tests in 1999 and 2008. The difference in average scores increased on ten of the eleven and stayed the same on the other. On eight of the eleven, the difference between the average black and white scores increased by 24 or more points between 1999 and 2008. On four of the tests, the black/white difference increased by 30 or most points.[227]

The only information I could find on changes in the white-black difference on post-graduate examinations is from the Spring 2006 issue of the *Journal of Blacks in Higher Education*.[228] It reported that the average white-black difference on the combined Verbal+Quantitative score on the Graduate Record Exam (taken for admission to graduate programs in the arts, sciences, and education) increased from 236 points in 1996 to 241 points in 2003 (on a 400-1600 scale). On the Graduate Management Admission Test (taken for admission to graduate business schools) the difference between the average scores of whites and blacks (on a 200-800 scale) increased from 101 points in 2003, to 104 points in 2004, to 107 points in 2005.

Racial differences in high school grade-point-average (HSGPA) have also increased. Among high school students who took the SAT between 1992 and 2005 (the last year for which I could find this information), the difference in HSGPA between whites and other racial categories increased

---

227. Following are the difference between the average white and black scores on these tests in 1999 and 2008. They are arranged from the least to the most increase in racial difference between 1999 and 2008: Physics, 80 points difference in 1999 and 80 points difference in 2008; World History 88 and 93 points; Literature, 84 and 103; American History, 77 and 101; Math I, 77 and 104; Chemistry, 58 and 86; French, 9 and 38; Math II, 69 and 99; Spanish, 47 and 77; Latin, 15 and 47; Biology, 67 and 101.

Average white and black scores differ less on SAT-II tests than on the SAT-I because in 2008, 8.7 percent of blacks who took the SAT-I took an SAT-II test, compared with 16.4 percent of whites. The reason why the smallest racial difference is in French is undoubtedly that many (probably most) of the blacks who take it are native French speakers from Haiti or West Africa.

228. "The Widening Racial Scoring Gap on Standardized Tests for Admission to Graduate School:" 8-11.

from .32 to .38 for blacks, from .19 to .26 for Puerto Ricans, from .11 to .23 for "Other Hispanics" and from .09 to .14 for Mexican Americans. (Asian Americans have higher average HSGPAs than whites, but the difference decreased from .14 in 1992 to .02 in 2005.)

The constant increase in the white-black difference on all measures of intelligence and of academic ability and achievement over the past twenty years has occurred despite two trends which should have decreased racial differences. One is the sharp rise in the number of children of white-black couples, all of whom are classified as black, but who are more intelligent than the children of two black parents. The other is the immigration of large numbers of blacks from the West Indies and Africa, who, as I discussion in Section B of Chapter 19, are more intelligent than native American blacks.

Moreover, the number of blacks taking advanced placement courses has exploded in the past 25 years. In 1985, blacks took only 1.4 percent of all advanced placement examinations; that increased to 2 percent in 1990, 3.8 percent in 1997, 4.6 percent in 2003, and 5.2 percent in 2005.[229] This increase corresponds to the fact that the present generation of black children, adolescents, and young adults were raised by black parents who have much more money and much more formal education than previous generations of black parents.

However, students of racial differences in intelligence have been predicting for a long time that the difference in intelligence between whites and blacks must increase because low-IQ blacks have more children than low-IQ whites, but intelligent blacks have fewer children than intelligent whites.[230]

---

229. "There Is Good and Bad News in Black Participation in Advanced Placement Programs." *Journal of Blacks in Higher Education* (Winter 2005/2006): 97-101.

230. Jensen (1969: 95-6) pointed out that the 1960 census showed that black women aged 35 to 44 who were married to unskilled laborers had an average of 4.7 children, and non-black women (who in 1960 were nearly all white) who were married to unskilled laborers had an average of 3.8 children. Black women aged 35 to 44 who were married to professional or technical workers averaged 1.9 children; Non-black women married to professional or technical workers averaged 2.4 children. Jensen (1998: 483-7) observed that in 1978, the average number of children born to both white and black women aged 25-34 was negatively correlated with their IQ. But the negative correlation was greater for black women (-.96) than for white women (-.86). Herrnstein and Murray (1996: 352-4) pointed out that in 1992, the only educational level at which black women had fewer children than white

Let us now look at trends on the SAT and ACT for all American racial and ethnic groups.

Below are the average Verbal+Math SAT scores in 1990/91 and 2008/2009 of all the racial categories for which the College Board provides average scores. The 1990/91 scores have been adjusted to yield the reported scores that they would have yielded if their raw scores had been converted to reported scores after the 1995 re-centering.[231]

	Verbal/Critical Reading		Math	
	1990/91	2008/09	1990/91	2008/09
All Test-Takers	499	502	500	515
Whites	518	528	513	537
Blacks	427	430	419	426
Mexican Americans	454	454	459	463
Puerto Rican	436	456	439	453
Other Hispanic	458	455	462	461
Asian	458	513	548	581
Indian/Alaska Native:	470	485	468	491

On the ACT, the average scores (on a 1-36 scale) in 1998 (I could not find earlier racial averages) and 2009 were:[232]

	1998	2009
Whites	22.7	22.2
Blacks	17.9	16.9
Asian	22.6	23.2
American Indian/Alaskan Native	20.4	18.9

In 1998, the ACT reported an average score of 19.6 for Mexican Ameri-

women was an MA or higher. Herrnstein and Murray also pointed out that even if white and black women at each IQ level have the same number of children, the white-black IQ difference would constantly increase because a much larger proportion of black women than white women have low IQs.

231. http://nces.ed.gov/FastFacts/display.asp?id=171

232. http://nces.ed.gov/programs/digest/d07/tables/dt07_138.asp provides average racial ACT scores for every year from 1998 through 2007; http://act.org/news/data/09/pdf/National2009.pdf provides 2009 scores.

cans and of 20.7 for "Hispanics." The 2009 ACT had only a "Hispanic" category, for which the average score was 18.7.

I pointed out above that the difference between the average white and black Verbal+Math SAT score increased by 20 points between 1988 and 2009. The table above shows that if the 1990 average is adjusted for the 1995 re-centering, the increase in the white-black difference between 1990 and 2009 is 24 points. However, since the purpose of the re-centering was to raise black scores, the increase in the white-black difference would have been considerably greater than 24 points if the re-centering had not occurred; that is, if both 1990 and 2009 raw scores would be been converted to reported scores on the basis of the pre-1995 conversion or raw scores to reported scores.

What is really amazing is that on both the SAT and ACT, the white-Asian and white-Hispanic differences increased more than the white-black difference, despite widespread intermarriage. In the 2000 census, 32 percent of second-generation Hispanics and 57 percent of third-generation Hispanics were married to non-Hispanics; 34 percent of second-generation Asians and 54 percent of third-generation Asians were married to non-Asians (Rodriguez 2003: 96). The large majority of the spouses of these intermarried couples are white.

The increase in the white-Asian difference could be caused by selective immigration and/or by more intelligent whites marrying Asians and their children being classified as Asians. (Jewish-Asian marriages seem to be especially common.) If the latter is happening, it would be decreasing the average intelligence of Americans classified as white.

However, many aspects of the Asian-white divergence are inexplicable by any hypothesis I can think of. For example, the average white ACT score was higher than the average Asian ACT score in every year from 1998 through 2002; in 2003 and 2004, the average Asian score was 0.1 higher then the average white score; in 2005, the Asian-white difference was 0.2; in 2006, 0.3; in 2007, 0.5; in 2009, 1.0. I cannot imagine what could be causing such a sudden change.[233] Moreover, students who take the SAT are asked

---

233. In 2005, the ACT was taken by 1,186,251 students; that rose to 1,480,469 in 2009. The proportion of these students who were white decreased from 66 to 64 percent; the black proportion increased from 12 to 13 percent; the proportion of Hispanics increased from 7 to 9 percent; of Asians from 3 to 4 percent; American Indians remained at 1 percent; "Other/No Response" decreased from 11 to 9 percent. The number of Asians increased from 39,284 in 2005 to 59,093 in 2009 (http://www.act.org/news/data/09/pdf/National2009.pdf; Table 1.5). Could there be some change in the way many of the "Asians" classify themselves racially?

to indicate whether the first language they learned was English, or "English and Another Language," or "Another Language." In 2002 the average Math SAT score of Asians whose first language was English was 551; the average Math SAT score of Asians whose first language was "English and Another Language," and "Another Language" was 574, for both linguistic categories. So, why did the average Asian Math SAT score increase by 33 points from 1990 to 2009? I have no explanation.

Let us now turn to the white-Hispanic divergence. There is one exception: average Puerto Rican SAT scores rose significantly between 1990/91 and 2008/09. Puerto Ricans are the only Hispanic group that has not had significant immigration into the United States for the past thirty years. Could the constant, large-scale immigration of other Hispanic groups be the explanation for the huge increase in the difference between Hispanics and whites? A study done in 1995 found that among children of school age in the United States, 55 percent of those who were born in Mexico and a little over 40 percent of those who were born elsewhere in Latin America did not speak English "very well." Over a third of second-generation Mexican Americans and a slightly lower proportion of other second-generation Hispanics did not speak English very well. Since these statistics are from questionnaires filled in by family members, they nearly certainly overstated the English proficiency of these children. (Only seven percent of second-generation Asian Americans did not speak English very well.) (Thernstrom 2003: 111-12)

Until 1992, the NAEP asked test-takers to indicate their place of birth. In 1992, the scores of Hispanic children who were born in the United States were higher by a grade level or more on every NAEP test than the scores of Hispanic children who were born in Latin America (Thernstrom 2003: 110).

On the SAT, in 2002, 24 percent of the "Hispanic/Latino" category indicated that their first language was English; their average scores were Verbal, 488; Math, 484. Thirty-seven percent indicated "English and Another Language;" their average Verbal and Math scores were 458 and 456. Thirty-nine percent indicated "Another Language;" their average Verbal and Math scores were 435 and 453.

In Section A of Chapter 9, I discuss the results of the 1992 National Adult Literacy Survey (NALS), which assessed the proficiency of a representative sample of Americans in Prose Literacy, Document Literacy, and Quantitative Literacy. It provided the average scores for different American racial and ethnic groups of those who were born in the USA (US) and those who were born overseas (OS).[234] On the three literacy tests the averages were:

234. http://nces.ed.gov/pubs93/93275.pdf Page 41 of *Adult Literacy in America: A First Look at the Findings of the National Adult Literacy Survey*

Whites (US)	287	281	288
Whites (OS)	258	255	260
Hispanic/Mexican (US)	247	245	244
Hispanic/Mexican (OS)	158	158	158 (*sic*)
Hispanic/Puerto Rican (US)	226	225	223
Hispanic/Puerto Rican (OS)	186	171	166
Hispanic/Central/South American (US)	281	277	275
Hispanic/Central/South American (OS)	187	188	185
Hispanic/Other (US)	283	277	271
Hispanic/Other (OS)	210	204	191

Clearly, if Latin American immigration ended now, the difference in academic performance between whites and Hispanics would narrow considerably.

However, even if Latin American immigration ended completely, a significant white-Hispanic gap would remain, as the NALS shows. I pointed out in Section A of Chapter 6, that in 2002, the average combined Verbal+Math SAT scores Mexican Americans, Puerto Ricans, and "Other Hispanics" at least one of whose parents had a bachelor's degree were 985, 944 and 981, respectively. The average Verbal+Math SAT scores of whites and Asians neither of whose parents had more than a high school diploma were 985 and 995.

Moreover, much (maybe most) of the differences I have recorded—between the SAT scores of Puerto Ricans in 1990/91 and 2008/09, between the SAT scores of Hispanics who learned English as a first language and those who did not, and between Hispanics who were born in the United States and those born overseas on the NAEP and NALS—must be because many of the latter groups of "Hispanics" are the offspring of Hispanic-white couples.

No matter what the causes of the white-Hispanic divergence, Latin American immigration is not decreasing, and affirmative action is based on the premise that unequal success between ethnic groups, no matter what its cause, is a problem that must be solved. I pointed out in Section B of Chapter 19 that the low intelligence of blacks whose ancestors lived in the United States creates huge preferences for black immigrants and their descendants. Similarly, the linguistic and genetic deficiencies of Hispanic immigrants greatly increase affirmative-action preferences for Hispanics whose parents and grandparents were born in the United States (many of whom have as many European as Latin American ancestors).

(Published in 1993 by the U.S. Department of Education).

So, the United States can look forward to a constant increase in the proportion of its population that is classified as Hispanic, along with a constant increase in the difference of achievement levels between whites/ Asians on the one hand and Hispanics/blacks on the other; hence a constant intensification of anti-white/Asian discrimination.

G. One More Attack on the SAT

Conveniently, one short article—"Where's the Merit in the S.A.T.?" in the *New York Times* of December 24, 1997—contains all the major accusations that are made against the SAT. Its author is one of the most influential opponents of the SAT, Professor Eugene Garcia, the Dean of Berkeley's School of Education. His main points are:

> I recently suggested to the University of California Regents that the Scholastic Assessment Test's [SAT] role in admissions be diminished. . . . Our modest proposal is not about lowering standards. It's about insuring that all high-achieving students get a fair chance. . . . Any measure of merit should consider the circumstances in which students are schooled. Isn't a migrant worker's child who has excelled in academics, shown leadership ability and performed community service as meritorious as a prep-school graduate with a similar G.P.A. but no evidence of leadership? Now, what if the migrant student's S.A.T. is 100 points below that of the prep-school student, whose parents probably sent him to an expensive S.A.T. course?
>
> . . . The S.A.T.'s ability to predict success in college is questionable. At best, the scores are 25 percent accurate when it comes to predicting the variation in first-year college grades, and have not been shown to predict whether someone will graduate from college. The test does correlate highly to parents' income and educational level.

Professor Garcia cited no evidence to support these assertions; and, as the Dean of Berkeley's School of Education, he must have known the following:

The prohibition of racial discrimination in admission to California's public universities, like every other prohibition of racial discrimination, explicitly allowed socioeconomic background and non-academic strengths to be considered. In 1995, a study by Berkeley's admissions office found that preferences for applicants from poor families would not significantly increase the proportion of its black, Hispanic, or Native American students (Lubman 1995). Interracial comparisons of SAT scores and parental income show irrefutably that there is no causal connection between them. Even more important is that the only criterion of test bias is whether a test accurately

predicts future performance. Far from giving an unfair advantage to the
rich, SAT scores underpredict the university performance of the children of
the rich compared with children of the poor and of whites compared with
Hispanics and blacks.

As I pointed out in Chapter 13, literally thousands of studies of the
predictive accuracy of the SAT have been conducted. The large majority
found that the correlation between SAT scores and freshman grades is over
.50. Not one study has ever found a correlation of less than .44. Moreover,
SAT scores predict graduation rates more accurately than they predict
freshman grades. Professor Garcia must have known that because when
the undergraduate division of his own university, Berkeley, was finally
forced to divulge the academic records of its students in 1995, they showed
that there was an extremely close correlation between the SAT scores and
graduation rates (Thernstrom 1997: 407). In fact, in 1990, Professor Garcia's own Berkeley School of Education published a monograph entitled
Consequences of Nonlinearity for Validity and Selection,[235] which presented
the results of a study of the relative predictive accuracy of the SAT and high
school GPA for undergraduates who entered Berkeley in 1983. It found that
for both sexes and all races, SAT scores at all levels predict college grades
accurately. High school GPAs over 3.0 (on a 1-4 scale) also predict grades
accurately, but GPAs of 3.0 and less have no correlation with college grades
at all (pages 15-17). So, the predictive accuracy of GPA is nonlinear, as
the title of the monograph indicates. Consequently, the Berkeley School of
Education monograph recommended increased emphasis on the SAT. The
students in this study attended high school in the early 1980s. The massive
grade inflation since then must have raised the minimum level at which
high school grades have predictive accuracy to at least 3.5, or obliterated
it completely.

It is significant that even Professor Garcia did not have the audacity
to claim that the difference in social background and schooling between a
prep-school graduate and a migrant worker's child can cause more than a
100-point SAT difference. However, in 2001, the difference between average Math+Verbal SAT scores of Hispanics and non-Hispanic whites who
were admitted to UCLA was 187 points (Golden 2002); and the difference
in average SAT scores between blacks and whites at UCLA was even larger
than between Hispanics and whites (Wood 2003A: 20-21). Yet, nearly all
of these Hispanic and black students were from middle- and upper-class
families. (These differences exist even though racial discrimination is illegal
at the University of California system.)

Typically of the ignorance and/or bias of the press, the *New York Times*

235. By M. Wilson, S. Moore, S. Gumpel, and B. Gifford.

printed Professor Garcia's attack on the SAT without warning its readers that it has no more validity than arguments by the Flat Earth Society. Instead, the *Times* supported his assertions with its own internal headline: "Scores reflect parents' wealth, not college success."

☜ ☞

Appendix IV: The Predictive Accuracy of Intelligence Tests

Before discussing intelligence tests, I will clarify a common source of misunderstanding by quoting Karl Popper, whom *Scientific American* described as "far and away the most influential philosopher of modern science."[236] Popper wrote (1962: 13-14, 18-19; the italics are Popper's),

> The scientific view of the definition "A puppy is a young dog" would be that it is an answer to the question "*What shall we call* a young dog?" rather than an answer to the question "*What is* a puppy?" (Questions like "*What is* life?" or "*What is* gravity?" do not play any role in science.) . . . In modern science . . . definitions . . . do not contain any knowledge whatever, not even any "opinion;" they do nothing but introduce . . . arbitrary shorthand labels.
>
>   In science, *all the terms that are really needed must be undefined.* . . . [P]hilosoph[ers] have told us for so long how important it is to get a precise knowledge of the meaning of our terms that we are all inclined to believe it. . . . Philosophy, which for twenty centuries has worried about the meaning of its terms, is . . . appallingly vague and ambiguous, while a science like physics, which worries hardly at all about terms and their meaning, but about facts instead, has achieved great precision.

Carl Hempel explained the nature of *definition* in the same way and gave the same warning against its misuse in his classic *Philosophy of Natural Science* (1966: 85-7).

I will provide two examples that are relevant to this book. The number of pushups a man can do correlates with and, consequently, predicts his ability at certain activities. But none of these activities are commonly called intelligent. Therefore, pushups do not measure intelligence. On the other hand, the tests I discuss in this appendix and throughout this book have been found empirically to have an extremely high correlation with the ability to

---

236. "The Intellectual Warrior" (November 1992): 20-21.

perform activities commonly called intelligent. Therefore, they measure intelligence.

Scores on intelligence tests, including the SAT and ACT, correlate closely with each other, whether they involve solving problems that are expressed verbally or non-verbally (Hauser 1998: 229; Jensen 1985: 203). These problems include arithmetic reasoning ("If a car uses X gallons of gas to go Y miles, how many gallons will it use to go Z miles?"), arranging different shaped blocks or geometric patterns in a sequence, verbal analogies (e.g., "*Cut* is to *sharp* as *burn* is to (a) *fire* (b) *flame* (c) *hot* (d) *hurt*"), and number series completion (e.g., 2, 4, 7, 11, 16, ?). The reason why the scores on all these tests correlate closely with each other is that they all require analyzing, synthesizing, and manipulating information; distinguishing relevant from irrelevant information; and other types of abilities that are commonly called intelligent. For the same reason, intelligence tests have a low correlation with scores on tests of spelling or simple arithmetic computation (e.g., 12x15; 220÷14) (Jensen 1981: 55-62; 1980: 218, 670-5). Albert Einstein had difficulty balancing his checkbook. Conversely, Mrs. Shakuntala Devi, who can multiply two 13-digit numbers in 28 seconds and compute the eighth root of a 14-digit number in ten seconds, has an above average but not exceptional IQ (Coren 1994: 80; Jensen 1990).

Scores on intelligence tests are extremely accurate predictors of job performance. They are better predictors than recommendations, level and type of education, amount of job experience, interests, and other criteria that are used to assess job applicants. Frank Schmidt and John Hunter (1998) summarized the evidence for the predictive accuracy of 19 criteria that are used to predict job performance and concluded (page 264),

> GMA [General Mental Ability, as measured by intelligence tests] occupies a special place for several reasons. First, of all procedures that can be used for all jobs, whether entry level or advanced, it has the highest validity and the lowest application cost. . . . Second, the research evidence for the validity of GMA measures [i.e., intelligence tests] for predicting job performance is stronger than that for any other method. Literally thousands of studies have been conducted over the last nine decades. . . . Third, GMA has been shown to be the best available predictor of job-related learning. It is the best predictor of acquisition of job knowledge on the job and of performance in job training programs.

The most accessible source of information about the predictive accuracy of intelligence tests for job performance is *The Bell Curve*, in which Herrnstein and Murray (1996: 72-85) summarized the findings of studies that included the performance of 472,539 military personnel and the two most extensive meta-analyses ever done of civilian job performance. One was of an enormous compilation of job performance studies, mostly from 1900-1950; the other was of 425 more recent studies of the predictive validity of the General Aptitude Test Battery for job proficiency.

Herrnstein and Murray also summarized the irrefutable evidence that scores on intelligence tests taken in childhood are excellent predictors of divorce, illegitimacy, criminality, good parenting, and other crucial social attributes, and that a person's family and social background have little or no correlation with these attributes, except through the intelligence that his parents transmit to him genetically.[237]

It is important to point out that Herrnstein and Murray's main purpose in writing *The Bell Curve* was to present the massive evidence for the predictive accuracy of intelligence tests. The issue of genetic determinism of intelligence, which drew most of the attention of the media and public, was secondary. The few serious reviewers who questioned Herrnstein and Murray's arguments about genetic determinism still acknowledged the manifest incontrovertibility of their demonstration of the predictive accuracy of intelligence tests. For example, because black social scientist Thomas Sowell questioned genetic determinism of intelligence in his review of *The Bell Curve*, Steven Fraser (1995: 70-79) reprinted it in his anthology of attacks on *The Bell Curve*. But Sowell also observed (pages 71-2 of Fraser's anti-*Bell Curve* anthology):

> Herrnstein and Murray establish their basic case that intelligence test scores are highly correlated with important social phenomena, ranging from academic success to infant mortality, which is far higher among babies whose mothers are in the bottom quarter of the IQ distribution. Empirical data from a wide variety of sources establish that even differing educational backgrounds or socioeconomic levels of the families in which individuals were raised are not as good predictors of future income, academic success, job performance ratings, or even divorce rates, as IQ scores are. . . . Even in non-intellectual occupations, pen-and-pencil tests of general mental ability produce higher correlations with future job performance than do "practical" tests of the particular skills involved in those jobs. . . . In terms of logic and evidence, the predictive validity of mental tests is the issue least open to debate. On this question, Murray and Herrnstein are most clearly and completely correct.

To take the example of criminality, studies in many countries that have

---

237. 1996: 171-90, 220-5, 245-50, 375-84, 723, note 6 (note 6 is on page 699 of the 1994 edition).

followed large numbers of people for decades, starting from early childhood, have all found a very strong negative correlation between childhood IQ and adult criminality for children who were raised in the same socioeconomic background.[238] In the standard textbook, *Handbook of Juvenile Delinquency*, Herbert Quay observed (1987: 107; italics added), "IQ is generally more predictive of offending than social class or cultural backgrounds. . . . *We know of no current research findings contrary to this conclusion.*"

Since then, two studies have strengthened that conclusion. One found that the average IQ of criminals is ten IQ points lower than their non-criminal full siblings with whom they were raised (Jensen 1998: 297).

The other is the most careful and comprehensive study ever conducted of a group of people over a period of time, the National Longitudinal Survey of Labor Market Experience of Youth (NLSY), which has studied 12,686 nationally representative participants since 1979, when they were between the ages of 14 and 22. Detailed records have been kept of the participants' childhood environment, parental socioeconomic status education, work history, family formation, and other factors. In 1980, 94 percent of the participants took the Armed Forces Qualification Test (AFQT), which is an intelligence test whose scores correlate closely with scores on standard IQ tests (Herrnstein and Murray 1996: 608-9; 1994: 584-5). In order to avoid controversy, the armed forces do not call the AFQT an IQ test. However, that is what it is, and I will follow the practice of researchers who study it and refer to its scores as IQ scores.

Herrnstein and Murray (1996) reported the results of the NLSY through 1990. Among the men and boys in the NLSY who were incarcerated in a correctional institution for juvenile delinquents or in a prison during any of the interviews that were conducted with them between 1979 and 1990, 45 percent had IQs in the lowest 10 percent of the American population and 62 percent in the lowest 20 percent (Herrnstein and Murray 1996: 375-6). Herrnstein and Murray (245-50) also considered only the white males in the NLSY, in order to allay any suspicion of racial bias. Among them, 12 percent of those with IQs in the lowest 5 percent, and 7 percent of those with IQs between the 5th and 25th percentiles (i.e., above the lowest 5 percent but below 75 percent) had been interviewed at least once while incarcerated, but only 1 percent of those in the top 25 percent. Independently of IQ, there was no correlation between incarceration rate and socioeconomic status (SES), as determined by parental educational level, income, and occupational status. Moreover, being raised in a "broken home" (i.e., not by the person's biological father and mother) had only a marginal effect independently of IQ. A man or boy

238. Herrnstein and Murray 1996: 243-4, 734-5, notes 19 and 29 (pages 710-11 of the 1994 edition).

from a broken home with an IQ in the normal range (between the 25th and 75th percentile) from an average SES background had a 4 percent chance of having been interviewed while incarcerated. A man or boy from a broken home and the same SES but with an IQ in the lowest 20 percent had a 22 percent chance of having been interviewed while incarcerated.[239]

Most criminals were raised in low SES backgrounds and/or broken homes, but clearly that was not the cause of their criminality. People who have low occupational status and income and who do not take care of their children tend to have low IQs and to transmit their low IQs genetically to their children. However, genetic determinism involves tendencies and averages, not certainties. Some parents with low IQs have children with high IQs and *vice versa*. In every study of criminality, the average IQ of criminals is low, whether they were raised in a high or low SES background or in a broken or intact family.

This finding is confirmed by every adoption study that has been conducted. The largest sample consisted of nearly everyone adopted in Denmark between 1927 and 1947, over 14,000 adoptees. At birth, all the adoptees were taken from their biological mothers. A little over a quarter were immediately placed in their adopting homes; the rest were put in orphanages. Of the latter, a little over half were placed in their adopting homes before they were one. The age at which they were adopted had no effect on their subsequent criminality. Because of the low rate of female criminality, only adopted men were considered. I will quote from the most accessible summary, in *Science* (Mednick, et al., 1984). (*Science* is the journal of The American Association for the Advancement of Science.):

> If neither the biological nor the adoptive parents are convicted [of a crime], 13.5 percent of the sons are convicted. If the adoptive parents are convicted and the biological parents are not, this figure rises to only 14.7 percent. However, if the adoptive parents are not convicted and the biological parents are, 20.0 percent of the sons are convicted.

But the force of genetics on criminality is even stronger than these statistics indicate because, "The mean number of convictions for the chronic[ally criminal] adoptee increases as a function of biological parent recidivism." This is extremely important because, although most criminals commit only one crime, most crimes are committed by chronic criminals. Only 4 percent of these adoptees were convicted three or more times, but they committed

---

239. For several reasons, the negative correlation between criminality and IQ cannot be because more dumb criminals are caught than smart criminals (Gordon 1997: 315-16).

69 percent of the crimes.

I will now return to the NLSY. Charles Murray (1998) divided its participants into five cognitive classes: *Very Bright* (whose childhood IQs were in the upper ten percent of the American population; i.e., IQs of approximately 120 and above), *Bright* (percentiles between 75 and 90; IQs between 110 and 120); *Normal* (percentiles between 25 and 75; IQs between 90 and 110); *Dull* (percentiles between 90 and 75; IQs between 80 and 90), and *Very Dull* (the lowest ten percent; IQs below 80).

Murray used these IQ classes to reconsider the question of the relative influence of social background and IQ, but he employed a more stringent criterion of social background than *The Bell Curve*'s criteria of parental education, occupation, and income. He examined only full biological siblings in the NLSY who lived in the same home with both their biological parents through at least the younger sibling's seventh year and among whom one sibling had an IQ in the Normal range and one in another range. This involved 1,074 sibling pairs (pages 12-13). Murray had NLSY data available through 1993.

In this group, in 1993, when they were between the ages of 28 through 36, fewer than 1 percent of the Normals were professionals (lawyers, doctors, professors, engineers, scientists, accountants). Of their siblings, who were raised in the same family, 12 percent of the Very Brights, 3 percent of the Brights, 0.3 percent of the Dulls, and none of the Very Dulls were professionals (pages 15-19).

In 1993, the median earned income (i.e., not derived from investments) of the Normals was $22,000 (in 1993 dollars). Of their siblings, who were raised in the same family, the Very Brights already earned $11,500 more in that year; the Very Dulls, $9,750 less. Each IQ point for siblings raised in the same family corresponded with a difference of $453 in earned income in 1993 (pages 21-5).

Murray also used another sample from the NLSY (pages 32-3). He examined all those who were raised by both their biological parents until the younger sibling was at least seven years old and whose parents were not in the lowest 25 percent of income in 1978-79. So, the lowest income of this sample in 1978-79 was $28,500 (in 1993 dollars). This left 3,908 people, whom Murray called a "utopian sample," since they were raised in conditions that "we ideally want to achieve through social policy;" i.e., unaffected by illegitimacy, desertion, early divorce, or poverty.

By 1993, when these people, all of whom were raised by their biological parents in non-poor homes, were 28-36 years old, 49 percent of the Very Dull women, 33 percent of the Dull women, 14 percent of the Normal women, 6 percent of the Bright women, and 3 percent of the Very Bright women had

had an illegitimate child (pages 39-40). Since the average IQ of the children of the Very Dull women will be considerably lower than the children of the Very Bright women, they will have a much higher crime rate. It is for this reason that illegitimate children have a much higher crime rate than children who were raised by both their biological parents.

In this utopian sample, nearly all of the parents must have wanted their children to go to college and could afford to pay for it. Eighty percent of the Very Brights were college graduates, 57 percent of the Brights, 19 percent of the Normals, 4 percent of the Dulls, and 1 percent of the Very Dulls. The median earned income of the Very Brights was $38,000; of the Brights, $27,000; of the Normals, $23,000; of the Dulls, $16,000; and of the Very Dulls, $11,000 (pages 34-7).

People have a strong tendency to marry people with a similar IQ. Consequently, the difference in family income between people of different intelligence levels is greater than the difference in individual income. Among the people in the NLSY who were raised by both their biological parents in non-poor families, the median income of the employed spouses of the Very Brights was $30,500; of the employed spouses of the Very Dulls, $15,500. This factor is magnified by the facts that the higher a person's IQ, the more likely he is to marry, the less likely to divorce and the more likely a married woman is to work. In the utopian sample, 58 percent of the Very Brights and 61 percent of the Brights had employed spouses, compared with 53 percent of the Normals, 38 percent of the Dulls, and 30 percent of the Very Dulls. The result is that in 1993 the median family income of the Very Brights was $53,000; of the Brights, $47,000; of the Normals, $37,750; of the Dulls, $25,000; of the Very Dulls, $17,000 (pages 37-9). I will remind the reader that this is a difference in a population all of whom were raised by both their biological parents, who had at least a lower-middle-class income.

However, even this income difference is merely the beginning of a gap that will widen greatly in the future, since the correlation between childhood IQ and adult income increases with age. Murray (1998: 7) provides a chart of the year-by-year median income of each of the five cognitive classes. It widened every year between 1984 and 1993. But in 1993, the people in the NLSY were still only between 28 and 36; and the correlation between IQ and income increases the fastest after the middle thirties (Mackintosh 1998: 51-2). The average income of lawyers, businessmen, engineers, and accountants increases much more rapidly than the average income of laborers, waiters, factory operatives, and clerks. Moreover, in any given occupation, more intelligent people rise to higher levels than their less intelligent co-workers. Between 1970 and 1973, a study was done in Britain of the occupational history of 6,022 men and 1,006 women who had taken an intelligence test in 1931, when they were eleven years old. It found,

> IQ's [i.e., scores on the test they took when they were eleven] influ-
> ence increases as men move through their careers. This receives
> some support from . . . the Warsaw studies, which found that people
> with high IQs tend eventually to become high earners irrespective of
> educational attainments and from the finding that higher IQ workers
> tend to move up in job complexity over their careers (Deary, et al.,
> 2005: 467).

So, in the years after 1993, the difference in individual income between
the members of the cognitive classes in Murray's sample must have increased
greatly; the difference in family income must have increased by more than
the difference in individual income; and the difference in net worth must
have increased by more than the difference in family income.

Even the projected difference in net worth understates the difference in
success between these cognitive classes, since, as Murray pointed out (1988:
2), many of the highest status occupations are not the most lucrative. The
public's rating of the status of occupations has been remarkably consistent
for generations, and scientists and professors are invariably among the five
occupations with the highest status. Consequently, the correlation between
IQ and occupational status is closer than between IQ and income (Jensen
1980: 339-41; 1998: 292-3; Mackintosh 1998: 51).

Socioeconomic background has as little effect on the status of a person's
occupation as it has on his income. By far the most extensive data for occupational mobility consists of every child born in the United Kingdom
between March 3 and March 9, 1958. They were studied six times since then,
most recently in 2000. At the age of eleven, they took the General Ability
Test (GA), which resembles a standard IQ test. The results were analyzed
by Daniel Nettle (2003), who divided occupations into five categories, the
highest being professional and the lowest unskilled. He found (pages 557-9)
that in 2000, the difference in GA scores between the men in the highest and
lowest occupational status was 24.1 points, or 1.55 of a standard deviation.
"[A]s other studies have also found, attained social class in adulthood is
more strongly related to GA score than parental social class is." Moreover,
"There is no tendency for men who have moved up into higher occupational
classes to have higher [GA] scores than those who have reached them by
staying put or moving down. . . . This finding accords with those of other
studies." This means that it is no more difficult for the son of a laborer to
become a professional than it is for the son of a professional with the same
IQ. In fact, "The relationship of parental social class to attained social class
was weak . . . only 3 percent of the variation . . . [can be] explained by direct

effects of parental class on occupational opportunities."

The reader will now appreciate that the studies I mentioned in Chapter 13 of the predictive accuracy of the SAT for future income and occupational success are merely drops in an ocean of studies that have unanimously found that tests of intelligence are extremely accurate indicators of future success.

Besides the sources I have cited for the superior predictive accuracy of intelligence tests over criteria for occupational success and job performance, I recommend Seligman (1992: 44-6, 136-48), Eysenck (1998: 82-4, 87-8, 205), and Jensen (1998: 111, 387-8). Brand (1996: 318) provides a bibliography for the predictive accuracy of intelligence tests for emotional maturity and social skills.

The absence of any counter-evidence is evident from the fact that the two most influential attacks on intelligence tests—Stephen Jay Gould's *The Mismeasure of Man* and Daniel Goleman's *Emotional Intelligence: Why it Can Matter More than IQ*—had to resort to blatant lies and misrepresentations. In fact, not one of the sources that Goleman cited to denigrate intelligence tests says what he claimed it says. Most say the opposite.[240]

CB EO

---

240. My analyses of Gould's and Goleman's books are available at www. affirmativeactionhoax.com.

CR SO

Bibliography

Adler, Jerry and Foote, Donna 1982: "The Marva Collins Story." *Newsweek* (March 8): 64.

Alon, Sigal and Tienda, Marta 2005: "Assessing the 'Mismatch' Hypothesis: Differences in College Graduation Rates by Institutional Selectivity." *Sociology of Education* 78: 294-315.

Amar, Akhil Reed and Katyal, Neal Kumar 1996: "*Bakke*'s Fate." *UCLA Law Review* 43, 6: 1745-80.

Applebome, Peter 1995: "Class Notes: Why Employers Aren't Interested in High School Grades of Prospective Workers." *New York Times* (May 17): B8.

Applebome, Peter 1996: "2 Decisions Reflect Bitter Conflict Surrounding University Affirmative Action Policies." *New York Times* (March 22): A12.

Bartholet, Elizabeth 1982: "Application of Title VII to Jobs in High Places." *Harvard Law Review* 95: 947-1027.

Basinger, Julianne 1999: "Higher Standards for Schoolteachers Will Hurt Diversity, Researchers Say." *Chronicle of Higher Education* (March 12): A31.

Basinger, Julianne 1999A: "Agreement Nears in Suit over Teacher Testing in Alabama." *Chronicle of Higher Education* (July 16): A32.

Bauerlein, Mark 2004: "Liberal Groupthink Is Anti-Intellectual." *Chronicle of Higher Education* 51, 2 (November 12): B6.

Baydoun, Ramzi and Neuman, George 1992: "The Future of the General Aptitude Test Battery (GATB) for Use in Public and Private Testing." *Journal of Business and Psychology* 7 (Fall): 81-91.

Baynes, Norman H. (translator and editor) 1942: *The Speeches of Adolf Hitler, April 1922- August 1939*, Volume I. New York: Oxford University Press.

Bean, Jonathan J. 2001: *Big Government and Affirmative Action: The Scandalous History of the Small Business Administration*. Lexington, Kentucky: University of Kentucky Press.

Beinart, Peter 1998: "How the GOP Lost Asian America." *New Republic* (January 5 &12): 10-12.

Belz, Herman 1991: *Equality Transformed.* New Brunswick, New Jersey: Transaction Publishers.

Benbow, Camilla 1988: "Sex Differences in Mathematical Reasoning Ability in Intellectually Talented Preadolescents." *The Behavioral and Brain Sciences* 11, 2 (June): 169-232.

Benbow, Camilla 1992: "Academic Achievement in Mathematics and Science of Students between Ages 13 and 23." *Journal of Educational Psychology* 84, 1: 51-61.

Berger, Joseph 1990: "Pessimism in the Air as Schools Try Affirmative Action." *New York Times* (February 27): B1.

Bloomgarden, Lawrence 1953: "Medical School Quotas and National Health." *Commentary* (January): 29-37.

Blow, Richard 1991: "Mea Culpa." *New Republic* (February 18): 32.

Blumrosen, Alfred W. 1971: *Black Employment and the Law.* New Brunswick, New Jersey: Rutgers University Press.

Bodner, Allen 1997: *When Boxing Was a Jewish Sport.* Westport, Connecticut: Praeger.

Bohannan, Paul and Curtin, Philip 1995: *Africa and Africans.* Prospect Heights: Waveland Press.

Bok, Derek 1982: Beyond the Ivory Tower: Social Responsibilities of the Modern University. Cambridge, Massachusetts: Harvard University Press.

Bolick, Clint 1996: *The Affirmative Action Fraud: Can We Restore the American Civil Rights Vision?* Washington, DC: Cato Institute.

Bovard, James 1995: "The Latest EEOC Quota Madness." *Wall Street Journal* (April 27): 14.

Bowen, William G. and Bok, Derek 1998: *The Shape of the River: Long-Term Consequences of Considering Race in College and University Admissions.* Princeton, New Jersey: Princeton University Press.

Bragg, Rick 2000: "Minority Enrollment Rises in Florida College System." *New York Times* (August 30): A18.

Brand, Chris 1996: "Doing Something about *g.*" *Intelligence* 22, 3: 311-26.

Bronner, Ethan 1997: "Colleges Look for Answers to Racial Gaps in Testing." *New York Times* (November 8): A1.

Bronner, Ethan 1999: "College Applicants of '99 Are Facing Stiffest Competition." *New York Times* (June 12): A1.

Broun, Heywood and Britt, George 1931: *Christians Only: A Study in Prejudice.* Reprinted 1974: New York: Da Capo Press.

Bunzel, John H, 1988: "Affirmative Action Admissions: How it 'Works' at Berkeley." *Public Interest* (Fall): 11-29.

Caldwell, Edward and Hartnett, Rodney 1967: "Sex Bias in College

Grading?" *Journal of Educational Measurement* 4, 3: 129-32.

Camara, Wayne, et al., 2003: "Whose Grades Are Inflated?" College Board Research Report No. 2003-4. www.collegeboard.com.

Carlson, Tucker 1993: "DC Blues." *Policy Review* 63: 26-34.

Carnevale, Anthony and Rose, Stephen 2003: Socioeconomic Status, Race/Ethnicity, and Selective College Admissions." New York: The Century Foundation. www.tcf.org/publications/education/carnevale_rose.pdf

Carter, Launor F. 1984: "The Sustained Effects Study of Compensatory and Elementary Education." *Educational Researcher* 13: 4-13.

Carter, Stephen L. 1991: *Reflections of an Affirmative Action Baby*. New York: Basic Books.

Case, Susan M. and Swanson, David B. 1993: "Validity of NBME Part I and Part II Scores for Selection of Residents in Orthopaedic Surgery, Dermatology and Preventive Medicine." *Academic Medicine* 68, 2 (Supplement): S51-S56.

Case, Susan M., et al., 1996: "Performance of the Class of 1994 on the New Era of USMLE." *Academic Medicine* 71, 10 (October, Supplement): S91-3.

Cathcart, David and Snyderman, Mark 1992: "The Civil Rights Act of 1991." *The Labor Lawyer* 8: 849-922.

Ceci, Stephen J., Rosenblum, Tina B., Kumpf, Matthew 1998: "The Shrinking Gap between High- and Low-Scoring Groups: Current Trends and Possible Causes." In *The Rising Curve: Long–Term Gains in IQ and Related Measures*, edited by Ulric Neisser, 287-302. Washington, DC: American Psychological Association.

Chabris, Christopher F. 1998: "IQ since 'The Bell Curve." *Commentary* (August): 33-40.

Chait, Jonathan 1997: "Numbers Racket." *New Republic* (December 22): 8.

Charles, Camille, et al., 2009: *Taming the River: Negotiating the Academic, Financial, and Social Currents in Selective Colleges and Universities*. Princeton, New Jersey: Princeton University Press.

Chauncey, George 1994: *Gay New York: Gender, Urban Culture, and the Making of the Gay Male World 1890-1940*. New York: Basic Books.

Chavez, Linda 1999: "Rein in Affirmative Action." www.ceousa.org.

Chavez, Linda 2002: *An Unlikely Conservative: The Transformation of an ex-Liberal*. New York: Basic Books.

CHE 1991: "Georgetown Law Student Disciplined, Will Graduate." *Chronicle of Higher Education* (May 29): A2.

Chevalier, Judith and Ellison, Glenn 1996: "Are Some Mutual Fund Managers Better Than Others?" Cambridge, Massachusetts: National Bureau of Economic Research (*Working Paper 5852*). It can be acquired by calling 617-868-3900.

Chou, April 1996: "Racial Classifications." In *Race versus Class: The New Affirmative Action Debate*, edited by Carol M. Swain, 45-71. Lanham, Maryland: University Press of America.

Chun, K. and Zalokar, N. 1992: *Civil Rights Issues Facing Asian Americans in the 1990s*. U.S. Commission on Civil Rights.

Cipolla, Carlo M. 1969: *Literacy and Development in the West*. London: Penguin Books.

Claiborne, William 2000: "Black-White Issue Leaves University Red-Faced; Brochure Photo Altered to Illustrate Diversity." *Washington Post* (September 21): A2.

Cloud, John 2001: "Should SATs Matter?" *Time* (March 12): 62.

Cohen, Richard 1993: "Snake Oil for DC Schools." *Washington Post* (September 10): A25.

Cohen, Carl 1996: "Race, Lies and 'Hopewell'." *Commentary* (June): 29-45.

Cole, Stephen and Barber, Elinor 2003: *Increasing Faculty Diversity: The Occupational Choices of High-Achieving Minority Students*. Cambridge, Massachusetts: Harvard University Press.

Coleman, James S., et al., 1966: *Equality and Educational Opportunity*. Washington, DC. U. S. Office of Education.

Collier, Peter 1997: "The Red and the Black." In *The Race Card*, edited by Peter Collier and David Horowitz, 169-77. Rocklin, California; Prima Publishing.

Comarow, Avery 1998: "Grades Are Up, Standards Are Down." *America's Best Colleges: 1999*. Published by *U.S. News and World Report*, 1998: 19-20.

Cook, Philip J. and Ludwig, Jens 1998: "The Burden of 'Acting White': Do Black Adolescents Disparage Academic Achievement?" In *The Black-White Test Score Gap*, edited by Christopher Jencks and Meredith Phillips, 375-400. Washington, DC: Brookings Institution Press.

Coren, Stanley 1994: *The Intelligence of Dogs*. New York: Bantam Books.

Cose, Ellis 1997: "NAACP Needs Help Getting out the Right Message." *Chicago Sun-Times* (July 19): E18.

Coulson, Andrew 2009: "Paul Krugman vs. *The Daily Show*."
http://www.cato-at-liberty.org/2009/10/12/paul-krugman-vs-the-daily-show/

Cronbach, Lee 1975: "Five Decades of Public Controversy over Mental Testing." *American Psychologist* 30: 1-14.

Cross, Theodore 1994: "Suppose There Was No Affirmative Action at the Most Prestigious Colleges and Graduate Schools?" *Journal of Blacks in Higher Education* (Spring): 44-51.

Cross, Theodore 1994A: "What if There Were No Affirmative Action in College Admissions?" *Journal of Blacks in Higher Education* (Autumn): 52-55.

Cross, Theodore 1996: "Why the *Hopwood* Ruling Would Remove Most African Americans from the Nation's Most Selective Universities." *Journal of Blacks in Higher Education* (Spring): 66-70.

Cross, Theodore 2000: "*Hopwood* in Doubt: The Folly of Setting a Grand Theory Requiring Race Neutrality in All Programs of Higher Education." *Journal of Blacks in Higher Education* (Autumn): 60-84.

Cross, Theodore and Slater, Robert Bruce 1997: "Why the End of Affirmative Action Would Exclude All But a Very Few Blacks from America's Leading Universities and Graduate Schools." *Journal of Blacks in Higher Education* (Autumn): 8-17.

Dale, Stacy Berg and Krueger, Alan B. 2002: "Estimating the Payoff to Attending a More Selective College; An Application of Selection on Observables and Unobservables." *Quarterly Journal of Economics* 117, 4: 1491-1527.

Davis, Bernard D. 1986: *Storm over Biology: Essays on Science, Sentiment, and Public Policy*. Buffalo, New York: Prometheus Books.

Dawson, Beth, et al., 1994: "Performance on the National Board of Medical Examiners Part I Examination by Men and Women of Different Race and Ethnicity." *Journal of the American Medical Association* 272,9 (September 7): 674-9.

Deary, Ian J., et al., 2005: "Intergenerational Social Mobility and Mid-Life Status Attainment; Influences of Childhood Intelligence, Childhood Social Factors, and Education." *Intelligence* 33, 5: 455-72.

Degler, Carl N. 1991: *In Search of Human Nature: The Decline and Revival of Darwinism in American Social Though*t. New York: Oxford University Press.

Delgado, Richard 1997: "Affirmative Action Critics Misfired." *Denver Post* (November 2): I.3.

Dillon, Sam and Schemo, Diana Jean 2004: "Charter Schools Fall Short in Public Schools Matchup." *New York Times* (November 23): A21.

Dinnerstein, Leonard 1994: *Antisemitism in America*. New York: Oxford University Press.

D'Souza, Dinesh 1991: *Illiberal Education: The Politics of Race and Sex on Campus*. New York: Free Press.

D'Souza, Dinesh 1995: *The End of Racism: Principles for a Multiracial*

Society. New York: Free Press.

Duchesne, Ricardo 2009: "The Word Without Us." *Academic Questions* 22, 2: 138-76.

Eastland, Terry 1996: *Ending Affirmative Action: The Case for Color-blind Justice*. New York: Basic Books.

Elder, Larry 2000: "The Politically Incorrect Professor." www.townhall. com/columnists/Larry Elder (September 28).

Elliot, Rogers 1988: "Tests, Abilities, Race, and Conflict." *Intelligence* 12: 333-50.

Epstein, Richard A. 1992: *Forbidden Grounds: The Case against Employment Discrimination Laws*. Cambridge, Massachusetts: Harvard University Press.

Erlandson, Julia 2007: "Score Gaps Stir Dispute over Holistic Approach." (UCLA) *Daily Bruin* (May 2) (www.dailybruin.com/articles/2007/5/2)

Espenshade, Thomas, et al., 2004: "Admissions Preferences for Minority Students, Athletes, and Legacies at Elite Universities." *Social Science Quarterly* 85, 5: 1422-46.

Espenshade, Thomas and Chung, Chang 2005: "The Opportunity Cost of Admission Preferences at Elite Universities." *Social Science Quarterly* 86, 2: 293-305.

Ewers, Justin 2004: "Scaling the Ivory Tower." *2005 Edition America's Best Colleges*. Published by *U.S. News and World Report*, 2004: 10-15.

Eysenck, Hans J. 1998: *A New Look at Intelligence*, New Brunswick, New Jersey: Transaction Publishers.

Fallows, James 2003: "The New College Chaos." *Atlantic Monthly* (November): 106-114.

Farber, Daniel A. and Sherry, Suzanna 1997: *Beyond all Reason: The Radical Assault on Truth in American Law*. New York: Oxford University Press.

Farmaian, Sattareh 1992: *Daughter of Persia: A Woman's Journey from Her Father's Harem through the Islamic Revolution*. New York: Crown Publishers.

Featherman, David, et al. 2009: *The Next Twenty-five Years; Affirmative Action in Higher Education in the United States and South Africa*. Ann Arbor: University of Michigan Press.

Ferguson, Ronald F. 1991: "Paying for Public Education: New Evidence on How and Why Money Matters." *Harvard Journal on Legislation* 28: 465-98.

Ferguson, Ronald F. 2001: *A Diagnostic Analysis of Black-White GPA Disparities in Shaker Heights, Ohio*. Brookings Institution Press: Washington, DC.

Feuer, Lewis F. 1982: "The Stages in the Social History of Jewish Professors in American Colleges and Universities." *American Jewish History*: 432-65.

Filiatreau, John 1991: *Business Week* (July 8): 56.

Finn, Charles Jr 1989: "The Campus: 'An Island of Repression in a Sea of Freedom'." *Commentary,* (September): 17-23.

Fogg, Piper 2002: "U. of California Admits More Minority Students." *Chronicle of Higher Education* (April 19): A26.

Foster, J. W. 1976: "Race and Truth at Harvard." *New Republic* (July 17): 16-20.

Fraser, Steven (editor) 1995: *The Bell Curve Wars: Race, Intelligence, and the Future of America*. New York: Basic Books.

Freeman, Richard B. 1977: "The New Job Market for Black Academicians." *Industrial and Labor Relations Review* 30, 2: 161-74.

Ganeshananthan, V. V. 2003: "The Late-Decision Program." *Atlantic Monthly* (November): 116-18.

Gewertz K. 1992: "Acceptance Rate Increases to 76 percent for the Class of 1996." *Harvard University Gazette* (May 15): 1.

Glascoe, Frances P. 2001: "Can Teachers' Global Ratings Identify Children with Academic Problems?" *Developmental and Behavioral Pediatrics* 22,3: 163-68.

Glaser, Karen, et al., 1992: "Science, Verbal, or Quantitative Skills: Which is the Most Important Predictor of Physician Competence?" *Educational and Psychological Measurement* 52: 395-406.

Glazer, Nathan 1975: *Affirmative Discrimination: Ethnic Inequality and Public Policy*. New York: Basic Books.

Glazer, Nathan 1999: "The End of Meritocracy: Should the SAT Account for Race." *New Republic* (November 27): 26-9.

Glazer, Nathan 2002: "Do We Need the Census Race Question?" *Public Interest* 149 (Fall): 21-31.

Golden, Daniel 2001: "Admission: Possible: Language Test Gives Hispanic Students a Leg up in California." *Wall Street Journal* (June 26): A1.

Golden, Daniel 2002: "To Get Into UCLA, It Helps to Face 'Life Challenges'." *Wall Street Journal* (July 12): A1.

Golden, Daniel 2003: "Case Study: Schools Find Ways to Achieve Diversity without Key Tool." *Wall Street Journal* (June 20): A1.

Goldman, Roy D. and Slaughter, Robert E. 1976: "Why College Grade Point Average Is Difficult to Predict." *Journal of Educational Psychology* 68: 9-14.

Gordon, Robert A. 1988: "Thunder from the Left." *Academic Questions* 1: 75-92.

Gordon, Robert A. 1997: "Everyday Life as an Intelligence Test." *Intelligence* 24, 1: 203-320.

Goren Arthur A. 1980: "Jews." In *Harvard Encyclopedia of American Ethnic Groups*, edited by Stephan Thernstrom, 571-98. Cambridge, Massachusetts: Harvard University Press.

Gorov, Lynda 1995: "Pursuing Diversity: In the Race for Multiculturalism UNH Lags despite Efforts." *Boston Globe* (February 1): A1.

Gose, Ben 1997: "Efforts to Curb Grade Inflation Get an F from Many Critics." *Chronicle of Higher Education* (July 25): A41.

Gose, Ben 1999: "U. of Pittsburgh Will Cut School Budget if Minority Graduation Rates Don't Rise." *Chronicle of Higher Education* (January 29).

Gottfredson, Linda 1986: "Societal Consequences of the *g* Factor in Employment." *Journal of Vocational Behavior* 29: 379-419.

Gottfredson, Linda 1994: "The Science and Politics of Race-Norming." *American Psychologist*: 955-63.

Graham, Hugh Davis 1990: *The Civil Rights Era: Origins and Development of National Policy 1960-1972*. New York: Oxford University Press. Republished by Baker & Taylor, Bridgewater, New Jersey.

Graham, Hugh Davis 2002: *Collision Course: The Strange Convergence of Affirmative Action and Immigration Policy in America*. New York: Oxford University Press.

Gray-Little, Bernadette and Hafdahl, Adam 2000: "Factors Influencing Racial Comparisons of Self-Esteem: A Quantitative Review." *Psychological Bulletin* 126, 1: 26-54.

Greene, Jay and Winters, Marcus 2005: "Five Myths Crying for Debunking." *National Review* (October 24): 49-51.

Guess, Andy 2008: "Diversity Meets Data at George Mason Law School." *Inside Higher Education* (June 26)

Gwynne, S. C. 1997: "Back to the Future." *Time* (June 2): 48.

Haigh, Anna 2004: "Tipping the Balance." *2005 Edition America's Best Colleges*. Published by *U.S. News and World Report*, 2004: 15.

Hammerman, Herbert 1988: "'Affirmative Action Stalemate': A Second Perspective." *Public Interest* (Fall): 130-34.

Hanushek, Eric A. 1991: "When School Finance 'Reform' May Not Be Good Policy." *Harvard Journal on Legislation* 28: 423-56.

Harber, Kent D. 1998: "Feedback to Minorities: Evidence of a Positive Bias." *Journal of Personality and Social Psychology* 74: 622-8.

Harris, Judith Rich 1998: *The Nurture Assumption: Why Children Turn out the Way They Do*. New York: Free Press.

Hartigan, John and Wigdor, Alexandra (editors) 1989: *Fairness in Em-*

ployment Testing: Validity Generalization, Minority Issues, and the General Aptitude Test Battery. Washington, DC: National Academy Press.

Hauser, Robert M. 1998: "Trends in Black-White Test-Score Differentials: I. Uses and Misuses of NAEP/SAT Data." In *The Rising Curve: Long –Term Gains in IQ and Related Measures*, edited by Ulric Neisser, 219-49. Washington, DC: American Psychological Association.

Hebel, Sara 2000: "States without Affirmative Action Focus on Community-College Transfers." *Chronicle of Higher Education* (May 26): A35.

Brookings Institution Press.

Hempel, Carl 1966: *Philosophy of Natural* Science. Englewood Cliffs, New Jersey: Prentice-Hall.

Heriot, Gail 1997: "The Truth about Preferences." *Weekly Standard* (July 21): 13.

Heriot, Gail 1997A: "Doctored Affirmative-Action Data." *Wall Street Journal* (October 15): A22.

Heriot, Gail 2008 "The ABA's 'Diversity' Diktat." *Wall Street Journal* (April 28, 2008).

Hernandez, Peggy 1988: "Many Chances to Dispute Malones Firefighters' Minority Status Unchallenged for 10 Years." *Boston Globe* (November 7): Metro, 1.

Hernandez, Peggy 1989: "Firemen Who Claimed to Be Black Lose Appeal." *Boston Globe* (July 26): Metro, 13.

Heron, W. T. 1935: "The Inheritance of Maze Learning in Rats." *Journal of Comparative Psychology* 19: 77-89.

Herrnstein, Richard 1982: "IQ Testing and the Media." *Atlantic Monthly* (August): 68-74.

Herrnstein, Richard and Murray, Charles 1996: *The Bell Curve: Intelligence and Class in American Life*. New York: Free Press. The addition of an Afterword on pages 553-75 of the 1996 edition makes its subsequent pagination different from the original, 1994, edition.

Hess, Frederick M. 2004: "The Limits of Money." *National Review* (October 11): 46-8.

Hezlett, et al., 2001: "The Effectiveness of the SAT in Predicting Success Early and Late in College: A Comprehensive Meta-Analysis." www.collegeboard.com

Hodgson, Godfrey 2000: "Ivy League Apart." *Manchester Guardian Weekly* (June 14): page 11 of the Comment and Analysis Section

Hollander, Paul 1992: *Anti-Americanism: Critiques at Home and Abroad, 1965-1990*. New York: Oxford University Press.

Hook, Sidney 1979: "Anti-Semitism in the Academy." *Midstream* 25: 49-54.

Hoover, Eric 2004: "Princeton Proposes Limit on Number of A's." *Chronicle of Higher Education* (April 23): A40.

Horowitz, David 1999: *Hating Whitey and Other Progressive Causes.* Dallas, Texas: Spence Publishing Company.

Huff, Kristen, et al., 1999: "Validity of MCAT Scores for Predicting Clerkship Performance of Medical Students Grouped by Sex and Ethnicity." *Academic Medicine*, 74, 10 (October Supplement): S41-S44.

Iannone, Carol 2003: "The Unhappy Difference Diversity Makes." *Academic Questions* (Spring): 9-20.

Iannone, Carol 2003/2004: "What Happened to Liberal Education?" *Academic Questions* (Winter); 54-66.

Issacharoff, Samuel 1998: "Can Affirmative Action Be Defended?" *Ohio State Law Review* 59: 669-95.

Jackson, Douglas and Rushton, J. Philippe 2006: "Males Have Greater *g* ..." *Intelligence* 34, 5: 479-86.

Jacoby, Jeff 1997: "Affirmative Action Can Sometimes Be Fatal." *Boston Globe* (August 14): A19.

Jacoby, Tamar 1998: *Someone Else's House: America's Unfinished Struggle for Integration.* New York: Free Press.

Jacoby, Tamar 1999: "Color Bind." *New Republic* (March 29): 23-7.

Jencks, Christopher 1998: "Racial Bias in Testing." In *The Black-White Test Score Gap*, edited by Christopher Jencks and Meredith Phillips, 55-85. Washington, DC: The Brookings Institution Press.

Jencks, Christopher and Phillips, Meredith 1998: *The Black-White Test Score Gap.* Washington, DC: The Brookings Institution Press.

Jensen, Arthur 1969: "How Much Can We Boost IQ and Scholastic Achievement?" *Harvard Educational Review* 39, 1: 1-123.

Jensen, Arthur 1980: *Bias in Mental Testing.* New York: Free Press.

Jensen, Arthur 1981: *Straight Talk about Mental Tests.* New York: Free Press.

Jensen, Arthur 1985: "The Nature of the Black-White Difference on Various Psychometric Tests: Spearman's Hypothesis." *The Behavioral and Brain Sciences* 8: 193-263.

Jensen, Arthur 1990: "Speed of Information Processing in a Calculating Prodigy." *Intelligence* 14: 259-74.

Jensen, Arthur 1993: "Psychometric *G* and Achievement." In *Policy Perspectives on Educational Testing*, edited by Bermard R. Gifford, 125-226. Boston: Kluwer Academic Publishers.

Jensen, Arthur 1998: *The g Factor: The Science of Mental Ability.* Westport, Connecticut : Praeger.

Kane, Thomas J. 1998: "Racial and Ethnic Preferences in College Admissions." In *The Black-White Test Score Gap*, edited by Christopher Jencks and Meredith Phillips, 431-56. Washington, DC: The Brookings Institution.

Karabel, Jerome 2005: *The Chosen: The Hidden History of Admission and Exclusion at Harvard, Yale, and Princeton*. Boston: Houghton Mifflin Company.

Kay, Jonathan 2003: "The Scandal of 'Diversity'." *Commentary* (June): 41-5.

Keith, Steven N., Bell, Robert M., Williams, Albert P. 1987: *Assessing the Outcome of Affirmative Action in Medical School: A Study of the Class of 1975*. Rand Corporation publication R-3481-CWF.

Keller, Morton and Phyllis 2001: *Making Harvard Modern: The Rise of America's University*. New York: Oxford University Press.

Kelman, Mark 1991: "Concepts of Discrimination in 'General Ability' Job Testing." *Harvard Law Review* 104: 1158-1247.

Kidder, William 2006: "Negative Action versus Affirmative Action: Asian Pacific Americans Are Still Caught in the Crossfire." *Michigan Journal of Race and Law* 11 (Spring): 605-24.

Kimball, Merdith 1989: "A New Perspective on Women's Math Achievement." *Psychological Bulletin* 105, 2: 198-214.

King, Martin Luther 1964: *Why We Can't Wait*. New York: The New American Library.

Klarman, Michael 1995: "*Brown*, Originalism, and Constitutional Theory: A Response to Professor McConnell." *Virginia Law Review* 81: 1881-1935.

Klein, Stephen P. 2001-2002: "Law School Admissions, LSATs and the Bar." *Academic Questions* 15, 1 (Winter): 33-8.

Kleiner, Carolyn 2001: "Diversity in Demand." *America's Best Colleges*. Published by *U.S. News and World Report*, 2001: 71.

Klitgaard, Robert 1985: *Choosing Elites: Selecting the "Best and Brightest" at Top Universities and Elsewhere*. New York: Basic Books.

Klitgaard, Robert 1986: *Elitism and Meritocracy in Developing Countries: Selection Policies for Higher Education*. Baltimore, Maryland: Johns Hopkins University Press.

Kobrin, et al., 2008: "Validity of the SAT for Predicting First-Year College Grade Point Average." College Board Research Report No. 2008-5. www.collegeboard.com.

Koenig, Judith, et al., 1998: "Evaluating the Predictive Validity of MCAT Scores across Diverse Applicant Groups." *Academic Medicine* 73, 10: 1095-1106.

Kors, Alan Charles 1989: "It's Speech, Not Sex, the Dean Bans Now." *Wall Street Journal* (October 12).

Kors, Alan Charles and Silverglate, Harvey A. 1998: *The Shadow University: The Betrayal of Liberty on America's Campuses*. New York: Free Press.

Kramer, Rita 1996: "New York's Regents Exam: The Assault on a Standard." *Academic Questions* (Spring): 61-70.

Krauss, Michael I. 2003: "The Underside of *Grutter*." *Academic Questions* (Summer): 30-35.

Kull, Andrew 1992: *The Color-Blind Constitution*. Cambridge, Massachusetts: Harvard University Press.

Kuran, Timur 1995: *Private Truths, Public Lies: The Social Consequences of Preference Falsification*. Cambridge, Massachusetts: Harvard University Press.

Lane, Charles 1997: "TRB from Washington: The Powell Puzzle." *New Republic* (December 29): 10, 45.

LaNoue, George and Sullivan, John 1994: "Presumptions for Preferences: The Small Business Administration's Decisions on Groups Entitled to Affirmative Action." *Journal of Policy History* 6: 439-67.

Lazarou, Jason, et al., 1998: "Incidence of Adverse Drug Reactions in Hospitalized Patients: A Meta-analysis of Prospective Studies." *Journal of the American Medical Association* 279, 5: 1200-1205.

Lederman, Douglas 1996: "Colleges Defend Affirmative Action." *Chronicle of Higher Education* (April 5): A29.

Leatherman, Courtney 1990: "2 of 6 Regional Accrediting Agencies Take Steps to Prod Colleges on Racial, Ethnic Diversity." *Chronicle of Higher Education* (August 15): A1.

Leatherman, Courtney 1990A: "Baruch College Wins Renewal of Its Accreditation after Planning to Renew Minority Programs." *Chronicle of Higher Education* (July 11).

Lee, Kenneth 2002: "Time to Fight Back." *The American Enterprise* (September): 26-8.

Leovy, Jill 1999: "Dropout, Failure Rates in Nursing Programs Soar." *Los Angeles Times* (November 23): A1.

Lerner Robert and Nagai, Althea K. 1998: "Racial Preferences in Michigan Higher Education." www.ceousa.org

Lerner, Robert and Nagai, Althea 2000: "Preferences at the University of Virginia: Racial and Ethnic Preferences in Undergraduate Admissions, 1996 and 1999." www.ceousa.org.

Lerner, Robert and Nagai, Althea 2002: "Pervasive Preferences: Racial and Ethnic Discrimination in Undergraduate Admissions across the Nation." www.ceousa.org.

Levin, Michael 1994: "Comment on the Minnesota Transracial Adoption

Study." *Intelligence* 19,1: 13-20.

Levin, Michael 1997: *Why Race Matters: Race Differences and What They Mean*. Westport, Connecticut: Praeger.

Levine, David O. 1986: *The American College and the Culture of Aspiration, 1915-1940*. Ithaca, New York: Cornell University Press.

Levine, Arthur 2000: "The Campus Divided, and Divided Again." *New York Times* (June 11): D17.

Lewis, David Levering 2000: *W. E. B. DuBois: The Fight for Equality and the American Century, 1919-1963*. New York: Henry Holt and Company.

Lipset, Seymour Martin and Riesman, David 1975: *Education and Politics at Harvard*. New York: McGraw-Hill.

Lott, John Jr. 2000: "Does a Helping Hand Put Others at Risk? Affirmative Action, Police Departments, and Crime." *Economic Inquiry* 38 (April): 239-77.

Lubman, Sarah 1995: "Campuses Mull Admissions without Affirmative Action." *Wall Street Journal* (May 16): B1.

Lynch, Frederick R. 1989: *Invisible Victims: White Males and the Crisis of Affirmative Action*. Westport, Connecticut: Praeger.

Lynch, Frederick R. 1997: *The Diversity Machine: The Drive to Change the "White Male Workplace."* New York: Free Press.

Lynn, Richard 1994: "Some Reinterpretations of the Minnesota Transracial Adoption Study." *Intelligence* 19, 1: 21-7.

MacDonald, Heather 1993: "The Diversity Industry." *New Republic* (July 5): 22-25.

MacDonald, Heather 2007: "Elites to Anti-Affirmative Action Voters: Drop Dead." *City Journal* 17, 1 (Winter 2007) (www.city-journal.org).

Mackintosh, N. J. 1998: *IQ and Human Intelligence*. New York: Oxford University Press.

Maguire, Timothy 1992: "My Bout with Affirmative Action." *Commentary* (April): 50-52.

Mangan, Katherine S. 1998: "Black Enrollment Jumps at Berkeley Law School." *Chronicle of Higher Education* (September 4) A53.

Mangan, Katherine S. 2004: "Raising the Bar." *Chronicle of Higher Education* (September 10): A35.

Manning, Winton H. and Jackson, Rex 1984: "College Entrance Examinations." In *Perspectives on Bias in Mental Testing*, edited by Cecil R. Reynolds and Robert T. Brown, 189-220. New York: Plenum Press.

Manno, Bruno V. 1996: "The Swamp of College Remedial Education." *Academic Questions* (Summer): 78-82.

Mazrui, Ali 1980: *The African Position*. London: Heinemann Education Books.

Massey, et al., 2007: "Black Immigrants and Black Natives Attending Selective Colleges and Universities in the United States." *American Journal of Education* (February): 243-71.

McCluskey, Neal and Schaeffer, Adam 2009: "Investing in What Doesn't Work." (February) online.

McGowan, William 2001: *Coloring the News: How Crusading for Diversity Has Corrupted American Journalism*. San Francisco: Encounter Books.

McGrory, Brian 1995: "Pathways to College." *Boston Globe* (May 23): A1.

Mednick, Sarnoff A., et al., 1984: "Genetic Influences on Criminal Convictions: Evidence from an Adoption Cohort." *Science* (May 25): 891-4.

Miller, John J. 2001: "DC Blue – Very Blue; The Force that Marion Barry Built (or Wrecked)." *National Review* (August 20): 34-6.

Miller, John 2005: "Pariahs, Martyrs – and Fighters Back." *National Review* (October 24): 40-5.

Min, Gap and Bozorgmehr, Mehdi 2000: "Immigrant Entrepreneurship and Business Patterns: A Comparison of Koreans and Iranians in Los Angeles." *International Migration Review* 34, 3: 707-38.

Mitchell, Lee Clark 1998: "Inflation Isn't the Only Thing Wrong with Grading." *Chronicle of Higher Education* (May 8) A72.

Murray, David W. 1996: "Racial and Sexual Politics in Testing." *Academic Question* (Summer): 10-17.

Murray, Charles 1998: *Income Inequality and IQ*. Washington, DC: American Enterprise Institute.

Nesiah, Devanesan 1997: *Discrimination with Reason?* Delhi, India: Oxford University Press.

Nettle, Daniel 2003: "Intelligence and Class Mobility in the British Population." *British Journal of Psychology* 94: 551-61.

Nissimov, Ron 2000: "Meet Russell Crake: He Graduated from Bellaire High School with a 3.94 GPA and an SAT Score of 1240. So Why Is He Holding a Rejection Letter from the University of Texas?" *Houston Chronicle* (June 4): A1.

Nixon, Richard 1994: *Beyond Peace*. New York: Random House.

Novick, Peter 1988: *The Noble Dream: The "Objective Question" and the American Historical Profession*. New York: Cambridge University Press.

NR 1998: "For the Record." *National Review* (July 20): 6.

Nuland, Sherwin B. 1997: "Hate in the Time of Cholera." *New Republic* (May 26): 32-7.

Nyborg, Helmuth and Jensen, Arthur 2001:"Occupation and Income

Related to Psychometric *g.*" *Intelligence* 29, 1: 45-55.

Ogbu, John U. 2003: *Black American Students in an Affluent Suburb: A Study in Academic Disengagement.* Mahwah, New Jersey: Lawrence Erlbaum Associates.

O'Neill, June 1990: "The Role of Human Capital in Earnings Differences between Black and White Men." *Journal of Economic Perspectives* 4, 4: 25-45.

Oren, Dan A. 2000: *Joining the Club: A History of Jews and Yale.* Second edition. New Haven, Connecticut: Yale University Press.

Page, Ellis B. 1986: "The Disturbing Case of the Milwaukee Project." In *The Raising of Intelligence*, by Herman H. Spitz, 115-40. Hillsdale, New Jersey: Lawrence Erlbaum Associates.

Peterson, William 1978: "Harvard's Admissions Formula: It's All in the Numbers." *Washington Post* (June 30): A4.

Phelps, Richard P. 2003: *Kill the Messenger: The War on Standardized Tests.* Transaction Publishers: New Brunswick, New Jersey.

Pinker, Steven 2002: *The Blank Slate: The Modern Denial of Human Nature.* New York: Viking.

Pitt, David 1989: "Despite Revisions, Few Blacks Passed Police Sergeant Test." *New York Times* (January 13): A1.

Pollak, Oliver B. 1983: "Anti-Semitism, the Harvard Plan, and the Roots of Reverse Discrimination." *Jewish Social Studies* 45: 113-120.

Popper, Karl 1962: *The Open Society and its Enemies*, Volume II. Second edition. London: Routledge and Kegan Paul.

Portes, Alejandro and Rumbaut, Rubén 2006: *Immigrant America: A Portrait.* Third edition. Berkeley: University of California Press.

Pressley, Sue Anne 1997: "Texas Campus Attracts Fewer Minorities: First School Ordered to End Admissions Preferences Opens with Less-Diverse Classes." *Washington Post* (August 28): A1.

PUPI 2002: *Profile of Undergraduates in U. S. Postsecondary Institutions: 1999-2000.* Washington, DC: National Center of Education Statistics, U.S. Department of Education.

Quay, Herbert C. 1987: "Intelligence." In *Handbook of Juvenile Delinquency*, edited by Herbert C. Quay, 106-111. New York: John Wiley & Sons.

Ramist, Leonard, et al., 1994: *Student Group Differences in Predicting College Grades: Sex, Language, and Ethnic Groups.* College Board Report No. 93-1. www.collegeboard.com.

Ramsay, Paul, et al., 1989: "Predictive Accuracy of Certification by the American Board of Internal Medicine." *Annals of Internal Medicine* 110: 719-26.

Raspberry William 1990: "Affirmative Action Reassessed." *Wilmington News Journal* (August 30): A6.

Rimer, Sara and Arenson, Karen W. 2004: "Top Colleges Take More Blacks, but Which Ones?" *New York Times* (June 24): A1.

Roberts, Paul Craig and Stratton, Lawrence M. 1995: *The New Color Line: How Quotas and Privilege Destroy Democracy*. Washington, DC: Regnery Publishing.

Rodriguez, Gregory 2003: "Mongrel America." *Atlantic Monthly* (January-February): 95-7.

Rosen, Jeffrey 1994: "Is Affirmative Action Doomed?" *New Republic* (October 17): 25-35.

Rosenstock, Morton 1971: "Are There Too Many Jews at Harvard?" In *Anti-Semitism in the United States*, edited by Leonard Dinnerstein, 102-108. New York: Holt, Rineheart and Winston.

Rothman, Stanley, Lipset, S. M., and Nevitte, Neil 2002: "Diversity and Affirmative Action: The State of Campus Opinion." *Academic Questions* (Fall): 52-66.

Rothman, Stanley, et al., 2005: "Politics and Professional Advancement among College Faculty." *Forum* 3.

Rowan Jr., Carl T. 1995: "Who's Policing DC Cops? Cronyism and Misconduct Endanger Our Lives." *Washington Post* (October 8): C1.

Rowan Jr., Carl T. 1998: "DC Confidential." *New Republic* (January 19): 20-23.

Roznowski, Mark, et al., 2000: "A Further Look at Youth Intellectual Giftedness and Its Correlates: Values, Interests, Performance, and Behavior." *Intelligence* 28, 2: 87-113.

Rubenfeld, Jed 1997: "Affirmative Action." *Yale Law Journal* 107: 427-72.

Rubenstein, Edwin S. 1998: "The College Payoff Illusion." *American Outlook* (Fall): 14-18.

Russakoff, Dale 1995: "Rutgers Proud of Law School's Set-Asides; Affirmative Action Program Has Been Changing the Face of New Jersey's Bar." *Washington Post* (April 10): A1

Sachar, Howard M. 1992: *A History of the Jews in America*. New York: Alfred A. Knopf.

Sacket, Paul, et al., 2004: "On Interpreting Stereotype Threat as Accounting for African American-White Differences on Cognitive Tests." *American Psychologist* 59: 7-13.

Sacks, David O. and Thiel, Peter A. 1995: *The Diversity Myth: "Multiculturalism" and the Politics of Intolerance at Stanford*. Oakland, California: The Independent Institute.

Sailer, Steven 2009: "Graduate School Admissions, Race, and the White Status Game," http://isteve.blogspot.com/2009/03/medical-school-test-scores-gpas-and_27.html

Salam, Reihan 2010: "To Educate, Innovate." National Review (June 21): 22-6.

Salholz, Eloise and Zeman, Ned 1998: "Going after Detroit's Rogue Cops." *Newsweek* (September 5): 37.

Sandalow, Terrance 1999: "Minority Preferences Reconsidered." *Michigan Law Review* 97 (May): 1874-1916.

Sander, Richard 2004: "A Systematic Analysis of Affirmative Action in American Law Schools." *Stanford Law Review* 57: 367-484.

Sander, Richard 2006: "The Racial Paradox of the Corporate Law Firm." *North Carolina Law Review* 84: 1755-1822

Sarich, Vincent 1990-91: "The Institutionalization of Racism at the University of California at Berkeley." *Academic Questions* 4: 72-81.

Satel, Sally 2000: *PC, M. D. How Political Correctness Is Corrupting Medicine*. New York: Basic Books.

Scarr, Sandra 1985: "Constructing Psychology: Making Facts and Fables for Our Times." *American Psychologist* 40: 499-512.

Scarr, Sandra 1987: "Three Cheers for Behavior Genetics: Winning the War and Losing Our Identity." *Behavior Genetics* 17: 219-28

Scarr, Sandra and McCartney, Kathleen 1983: "How People Make their Environments: A Theory of Genotype to Environment Effects." *Child Development* 54: 424-35.

Scarr, Sandra and Weinberg, Richard A. 1976: "IQ Test Performance of Black Children Adopted by White Families." *American Psychologist*: 726-39.

Scarr, Sandra and Weinberg, Richard A. 1983: "The Minnesota Adoption Studies: Genetic Differences and Malleability." *Child Development* 54: 260-67.

Schectman, Joel and Monahan, Rachel 2009: "CUNY's Got Math Problem" (*sic*). *New York Daily News* (November 12).

Schemo, Diana Jean 2004: "Charter Schools Trail in Results, U.S. Data Reveals." *New York Times* (August 17): A1.

Schlesinger Jr., Arthur 1965: *A Thousand Days: John F. Kennedy in the White House*. Boston: Houghton, Mifflin Company.

Schmidt, Peter 1998: "U. of Michigan Prepares to Defend Admissions Policy in Court." *Chronicle of Higher Education* (October 30): A32.

Schmidt, Peter 2001: "Debating the Benefits of Affirmative Action: Defenders Use Research to Bolster their Case." *Chronicle of Higher Education* (May 18): A25.

Schmidt, Peter 2003: "New Admissions System at U. of Michigan to Seek Diversity through Essays." *Chronicle of Higher Education* (September 5): A28.

Schmidt, Peter 2003A: "Affirmative Action Remains a Minefield, Mostly Unmapped." *Chronicle of Higher Education* (October 24): A22.

Schmidt, Frank L. and Hunter, John E. 1998: "The Validity and Utility of Selection Methods in Personal Psychology: Practical and Theoretical Implications of 85 Years of Research Findings." *Psychological Bulletin* 124, 2: 262-74.

Schnapper, Eric 1985: "Affirmative Action and the Legislative History of the Fourteenth Amendment." *Virginia Law Review* 71: 753-98.

Schneider, Alison 1998: "What Happened to Faculty Diversity in California?" *Chronicle of Higher Education* (November 20): A10.

Schrader, W. B. 1977: *Summary of Law School Validity Studies, 1948-1975*. Law School Admission Council Report Series (LSAC 76-8).

Schuck, Peter H. 2003: *Diversity in America: Keeping Government at a Safe Distance*. Cambridge, Massachusetts: Harvard University Press.

Schweikart, Larry 2002: "History to the Left of US." *The American Enterprise* (September): 30-31.

Scott, Ralph 1987: "'Push-Through' Educational Programs: Threat to Academic Integrity and to the Nation's Economic Productivity." *Journal of Social, Political and Economic Studies* 12: 203-26.

Seabury, Paul 1972: "HEW and the Universities." *Commentary* (February): 38-44.

Seligman, Daniel 1992: *A Question of Intelligence: The IQ Debate in America*. New York: Carol Publishing Group.

Selingo, Jeffrey 1999: "Florida's University System Plans to End Affirmative Action in Admissions." *Chronicle of Higher Education* (November 19): A36.

Selingo, Jeffrey 1999A: "Clinton Urges Law Schools to Strive for Racial and Ethnic Diversity." *Chronicle of Higher Education* (July 21): A29.

Selingo, Jeffrey 2000: "What States Aren't Saying about the 'X-Percent Solution'." *Chronicle of Higher Education* (June 2): A31.

Selingo, Jeffrey and Brainard, Jeffrey 2001: "Call to Eliminate SAT Requirement May Reshape Debate on Affirmative Action." *Chronicle of Higher Education* (March 2): A21.

Shapiro, Ben 2004: *Brainwashed: How Universities Indoctrinate America's Youth*. Nashville, Tennessee: WND Books.

Shavit, Yossi 1990: "Segregation, Tracking, and the Educational Attainment of Minorities: Arabs and Oriental Jews in Israel." *American Sociological Review* 55:115-2.

Shea, Christopher 1998: "Do Smaller Classes Mean Better Schools?

Economists Aren't So Sure." *Chronicle of Higher Education* (April 3): A17.

Shudson, Michael 1972: "Organizing the 'Meritocracy:' A History of the College Entrance Examination Board." *Harvard Educational Review* 42, 1: 34-69.

Siegel, Fred 1997: *The Future Once Happened Here*. San Francisco: Encounter Books.

Silberberg, Eugene 1985: "Race, Recent Entry, and Labor Market Participation." *American Economic Review* 75: 1168-77.

Silberman, Charles 1985: *A Certain People: American Jews and Their Lives Today*. New York: Summit Books.

Silbiger, Steven 2000: *The Jewish Phenomenon: Seven Keys to the Enduring Wealth of a People*. Atlanta, Georgia: Longstreet Press.

Skerry, Peter 1981: "Race Relations at Harvard." *Commentary* (January): 62-64.

Skousen, Mark 2001: *The Making of Modern Economics: The Lives and Ideas of the Great Thinkers*. Armonk, New York: M. E. Sharpe.

Skrentny, John David 1996: *The Ironies of Affirmative Action: Politics, Culture, and Justice in America*. University of Chicago Press.

Slater, Robert Bruce 1995: "Why Socioeconomic Affirmative Action in Admissions Works against African Americans." *Journal of Blacks in Higher Education* (Summer): 57-9

Snyderman, Mark and Rothman, Stanley 1988: *The IQ Controversy, the Media, and Public Policy*. New Brunswick, New Jersey: Transaction Books.

Sommer, Robert and Barbara A. 1983: "Mystery in Milwaukee." *American Psychologist* 38: 982-5.

Sorensen, Theodore 1965: *Kennedy*. New York: Harper & Row.

Sowell, Thomas 1981: *Ethnic America: A History*. New York: Basic Books.

Sowell, Thomas 1993: *Inside American Education: The Decline, the Deception, the Dogmas*. New York: Free Press.

Sowell, Thomas 1995: *The Vision of the Anointed: Self-Congratulation as a Basis for Social Policy*. New York: Basic Books.

Sowell, Thomas 1998: *Conquests and Cultures*. New York: Basic Books.

Sowell, Thomas 2004: *Affirmative Action around the World: An Empirical Study*. New Haven, Connecticut: Yale University Press.

Spitz, Herman H. 1986: *The Raising of Intelligence: A Selected History of Attempts to Raise Retarded Intelligence*. Hillsdale, New Jersey: Lawrence Erlbaum Associates.

Spitz, Herman H. 1999: "Beleaguered *Pygmalion*: A History of the Controversy over Claims that Teacher Expectancy Raises Intelligence." *Intelligence* 27, 3: 199-234.

Steele, Claude 1997: "A Threat in the Air: How Stereotypes Shape Intellectual Identity and Performance." *American Psychologist* 52,6: 613-29.

Steele, Claude and Aronson, J. 1995: "Stereotype Threat and the Intellectual Test Performance of African Americans." *Journal of Personality and Social Psychology* 69: 797-811.

Steele, Kenneth M. 1998: Letter to *Commentary* (November): 18.

Steinberg, Stephen 1974: *The Academic Melting Pot: Catholics and Jews in American Higher Education.* New York: McGraw-Hill.

Steinberg, Jacques 2002: *The Gatekeepers: Inside the Admissions Process of a Premier College.* Viking (Penguin Putnam Inc.): New York.

Steinhorn, Leonard and Diggs-Brown, Barbara 1999: *By the Color of our Skin: The Illusion of Integration and the Reality of Race.* New York: Dutton.

Stevenson, Harold W., Chen, Chuansheng, Uttal, David H. 1990: "Beliefs and Achievement: A Study of Black, White, and Hispanic Children." *Child Development* 61: 508-23.

Storfer, Miles D. 1990: *Intelligence and Giftedness: The Contributions of Heredity and Early Environment.* San Francisco: Jossey-Bass.

Swain, Carol M. 2002: *The New White Nationalism in America: Its Challenge to Integration.* New York: Cambridge University Press.

Swanson, David B., et al., 1992: "Impact of the USMLE Step I on Teaching and Learning of the Basic Biomedical Sciences." *Academic Medicine* 67, 9 (September): 553-56.

Sykes, Charles J. 1995: *Dumbing Down Our Kids: Why American Children Feel Good About Themselves but Can't Read, Write, or Add.* New York: St. Martin's Griffin.

Synnott, Marcia Graham 1979: *The Half-Opened Door: Discrimination and Admissions at Harvard, Yale, and Princeton, 1900-1970.* Westport, Connecticut: Greenwood Press.

Synnott, Marcia Graham 1986: "Anti-Semitism and American Universities: Did Quotas Follow the Jews?" In *Anti-Semitism in American History*, edited by David A. Gerber, 233-71. Urbana, Illinois: University of Illinois Press.

Tamblyn, Robyn, et al., 1998: "Association between Licensing Examination Scores and Resource Use and Quality of Care in Primary Care Practices." *Journal of the American Medical Association* 280, 11: 989-96.

Taylor, Jared 1992: *Paved with Good Intentions: The Failure of Race Relations in Contemporary America.* New York: Carroll & Graf.

Taylor, H. C. and Russell, J. T. 1939: "The Relationship of Validity Coefficients to the Practical Effectiveness of Tests in Selection: Discussion and Tables." *Journal of Applied Psychology* 23: 565-78.

Thernstrom, Abigail 1990: "The Scarcity of Black Professors." *Commentary* (July): 22-6

Thernstrom, Stephan and Abigail 1997: *America in Black and White: One Nation Indivisible*. Simon & Schuster: New York.

Thernstrom, Stephan 1997A: "The Scandal of the Law Schools." *Commentary* (December): 27-31.

Thernstrom, Stephan 1998: "Farewell to Preferences." *Public Interest* 130 (Winter): 34-49.

Thernstrom, Stephan 1998A: "Diversity and Meritocracy in Legal Education: A Critical Evaluation of Linda F. Wightman's 'The Threat to Diversity in Legal Education'." *Constitutional Commentary* 15, 1: 11-43.

Thernstrom, Abigail and Stephan 1999: "Racial Preferences: What We Now Know." *Commentary* (February): 44-50.

Thernstrom, Stephan 1999A: "Alamo in Ann Arbor." *National Review* (September 13): 38-42.

Thernstrom, Stephan and Abigail 1999B: "Reflections on *The Shape of the River*." *UCLA Law Review* 46: 1583-1631.

Thernstrom, Stephan 2002: "The Demography of Racial and Ethnic Groups." In *Beyond the Color Line: New Perspectives on Race and Ethnicity in America*, edited by Abigail and Stephan Thernstrom, 13-36. Stanford, California: Hoover Institution Press.

Thernstrom, Abigail 2002A: "The Racial Gap in Academic Achievement." In *Beyond the Color Line: New Perspectives on Race and Ethnicity in America*, edited by Abigail and Stephan Thernstrom, 259-76. Stanford, California: Hoover Institution Press.

Thernstrom, Stephan 2002B: "One Drop Still." *National Review* (April 17): 35-7.

Thernstrom, Abigail and Stephan 2003: *No Excuses: Closing the Racial Gap in Learning*. New York: Simon & Schuster.

Thomas, Paulette 1992: "Race and Mortgage Lending in America." *Wall Street Journal* (November 30): A1.

Thomas, Piri 1967/1997: *Down These Mean Streets*. New York: Random House.

Tortella, Garbriel 1994: "Patterns of Economic Retardation and Recovery in South-Western Europe in the Nineteenth and Twentieth Centuries." *Economic History Review* 47, 1: 1-21.

Townsend, Laird 1994-95: "Is Diversity Taking a Back Seat at Stanford?" *Journal of Blacks in Higher Education* (Winter): 109-12.

Turkheimer, Erik, et al., 2003: "Socio-economic Status Modifies Heritability in IQ of Young Children." *Psychological Science* 14, 6 (November 2003): 623-8.

Turner, Barbara J., et al., 1987: "Using Ratings of Resident Competence to Evaluate NBME Examination Passing Standards." *Journal of Medical Education* 62 (July): 572-81.

Tushnet, Mark V. 1994: *Making Civil Rights Law: Thurgood Marshall and the Supreme Court, 1936-1961.* New York: Oxford University Press.

Uhlig, Mark A. 1987: "Learning Styles of Minorities to Be Studied." *New York Times (*November 21): A29.

Vars, Fredrick E. and Bowen, William G. 1998: "Scholastic Aptitude Test Scores, Race, and Academic Performance in Selective Colleges and Universities." In *The Black-White Test Score Gap*, edited by Christopher Jencks and Meredith Phillips, 457-79. Washington, DC: The Brookings Institution.

Vedder, Richard and Denhardt, Matthew 2007: "Michigan Higher Education: Facts and Fiction." http://mackinac.org/article.aspx?ID=8647.

Veloski, J. Jon, et al., 2000: "Prediction of Students' Performance on Licensing Examinations Using Age, Race, Sex, Undergraduate GPAs and MCAT Scores." *Academic Medicine* 75, 10: S28-S30.

Volokh, Eugene 1996: "Diversity, Race as Proxy, and Religion as Proxy." *UCLA Law Review*: 2059-76.

Wade, Nicholas 2005: "Researchers Say Intelligence and Diseases May Be Linked in Ashkenazic Genes." *New York Times* (June 3): A21

Webb, Carmen, et al., 1997: "The Impact of Nonacademic Variables on Performance at Two Medical Schools." *Journal of the National Medical Association* 89, 3: 173-80.

Wechsler, Harold S. 1977: *The Qualified Student: A History of Selective College Admissions in America.* New York: John Wiley & Sons.

Weiner, Stephen S. 1990: "Accrediting Agencies Must Require a Commitment to Diversity When Measuring a College's Quality." *Chronicle of Higher Education* (October 10): B1.

Weiss, Kenneth 1997: "UC Law Schools' New Rules Cost Minorities Spots." *Los Angeles Times* (May 15): A1.

Welch, Susan and Gruhl, John 1998: *Affirmative Action and Minority Enrollments in Medical and Law Schools.* Ann Arbor, Michigan: University of Michigan Press.

Wightman, Linda 1997: "The Threat to Diversity in Legal Education: An Empirical Analysis of the Consequences of Abandoning Race as a Factor in Law School Admission Decisions." *New York University Law Review* 72, 1: 1-53.

Wightman, Linda 1998: "LSAC National Longitudinal Bar Passage Study." Law School Admission Council Research Report Series.

Wightman, Linda 2003: "The Consequences of Race-Blindness: Revisiting the Models with Current Law School Data." *Journal of Legal Education* 53, 2: 229-53.

Wilkerson, Isabel 1989: "Discordant Notes in Detroit: Music and Affirmative Action." *New York Times* (March 5): A1.

Williams, Walter E. 1989: *South Africa's War against Capitalism*. New York: Praeger.

Wilson, James and Herrnstein, Richard 1985: *Crime and Human Nature*. New York: Simon & Schuster.

Wilson, Robin 1991: "Article Critical of Black Students' Qualification Roils Georgetown U. Law Center." *Chronicle of Higher Education* (April 24): A 33.

Winerip, Michael 2003: "What Some Much-Noted Data Really Showed about Vouchers." *New York Times* (May 7): B12.

Wolters, Raymond 1996: *Right Turn*. New Brunswick, New Jersey: Transaction Publishers.

Wood, Thomas E. 2001: "Who Speaks for Higher Education on Group Preferences?" *Academic Questions* 14,2 (Spring): 31-45.

Wood, Peter 2003: *Diversity: The Invention of a Concept*. San Francisco, California: Encounter Books.

Wood, Thomas E. 2003A: "Race, Admissions, and Litigation after Michigan." *Academic Questions* (Summer): 18-22.

Wood, Thomas E. and Sherman, Malcolm J. 2001: "Is Campus Racial Diversity Correlated with Educational Benefits?" *Academic Questions* 14, 3 (Summer): 72-88.

Wooldridge, Adrian 1995: "Bell Curve Liberals." *New Republic* (February 27): 22.

Workman, James 1991: "Gender Norming." *New Republic* (July 1): 16.

Wright, Lawrence 1994: "One Drop of Blood." *New Yorker* (July 24): 46-55.

Wynter, Leon 1991: "Minority Grads Remain in Demand Despite Slump." *Wall Street Journal* (April 18): B1.

Yao, David C. and Wright, Scott M. 2000: "National Survey of Internal Medicine Residency Program Directors Regarding Problem Residents." *Journal of the American Medical Association* 284, 9 (September 6): 1099-1104.

Yates, Steven 1994: *Civil Wrongs*. San Francisco: California Institute for Contemporary Studies.

Young, Jeffrey R. 2002: "Homework? What Homework? Students Seem to Be Spending Less Time Studying Than They Used To." *Chronicle of Higher Education* (December 6): A35.

Zelnick, Robert 1996: *Backfire: A Reporter's Look at Affirmative Action.* Washington, DC: Regnery Publishing.

Zigler, Edward and Muenchow, Susan 1992: *Head Start.* New York: Basic Books.